第 3 辑
Volume 3

管理会计师协会教学案例
IMA Educational Cases

（汉英双语版）

瑞夫·劳森（Raef Lawson） 编

杨继良 译
胡金凤 校

经济科学出版社

图书在版编目（CIP）数据

管理会计师协会教学案例. 第3辑：汉英对照/（美）劳森编；杨继良译. —北京：经济科学出版社，2012.7
（2016.10重印）
ISBN 978-7-5141-1959-6

Ⅰ. ①管… Ⅱ. ①劳… ②杨… Ⅲ. ①管理会计-案例-汉、英 Ⅳ. ①F234.3

中国版本图书馆 CIP 数据核字（2012）第110103号

图字：01-2012-3856

管理会计师协会教学案例（第3辑）

IMA Educational Cases-Volume 3

© 2012 Institute of Management Accountants, All rights reserved
© 2012 中英文双语版专有出版权属经济科学出版社

No part of this book may be reproduced in any form without the written permission of Institute of Management Accountants and Economic Science Press

未经管理会计师协会（IMA）和经济科学出版社的书面许可，本书的任何部分均不可以任何形式翻印。

责任编辑：周国强
责任校对：杨晓莹
技术编辑：邱 天

管理会计师协会教学案例
（第3辑）

瑞夫·劳森（Raef Lawson） 编

经济科学出版社出版、发行　新华书店经销
社址：北京市海淀区阜成路甲28号　邮编：100142
编辑部电话：88191350　发行部电话：88191540
网址：www.esp.com.cn
电子邮件：esp@esp.com.cn
北京密兴印刷有限公司印装
787×1092　16开　21.75印张　560000字
2012年8月第1版　2016年11月第2次印刷
印数：3001—5000册
ISBN 978-7-5141-1959-6　定价：58.00元
（图书出现印装问题，本社负责调换）
（版权所有　翻印必究）

始于1919年的管理会计专业机构——美国管理会计师协会

美国管理会计师协会（The Institute of Management Accountants，简称IMA®）成立于1919年，是全球领先的国际管理会计师认证和服务机构，属非营利性组织，总部设在美国新泽西州，在全球120个国家、200个分会中拥有超过6.5万名会员，并通过设立在苏黎世、迪拜和北京的办事处为会员提供本土化服务。

在国际上，作为COSO委员会的创始成员和国际会计师联合会（IFAC）的主要成员，IMA在管理会计、公司内部规划与控制、风险管理等领域始终参与最前沿的实践。此外，IMA还在美国财务会计准则委员会（FASB）和美国证券交易委员会（SEC）等组织中发挥举足轻重的作用。

自2007年进入中国以来，IMA发展迅速，已经成为凝聚财务高管和企业决策制定者的高端平台。IMA会员遍布工商界、学术界、政府部门以及各类非营利机构内部，这些财务专业人士凭借其先进的财务理念、出色的战略思维、卓越的管理能力和严格的道德准则，不断推进企业和机构整体绩效的提升。

40 年的卓越铸就黄金证书——CMA 认证

IMA 旗下的美国注册管理会计师（Certified Management Accountant，简称 CMA®）认证是对会计和财务专业人士的权威鉴定。2012 年恰逢 CMA 认证推出 40 周年，在这 40 年的卓越历程中，CMA 一直秉承 IMA 的使命，即用最实用的知识体系培养管理会计精英，用最严格的测评标准保证认证的权威性，现已发展成为全球财务的黄金标准。

CMA 知识体系具有很强的实践性。其所侧重的预算预测、内部控制、决策分析、风险管理等内容非常符合企业对会计人才的需求。

CMA 认证提供英文和中文两种考试语言。作为唯一一个进行汉化的管理会计认证，CMA 认证专注测试知识体系和专业技能，让更多的中国财务专业人士全面、透彻地了解管理会计的精髓。2009 年 11 月，中国国家外国专家局培训中心与 IMA 签约，将 CMA 认证列为国家人才重点培养项目，在国资委和大型央企的支持下，培养高层次、国际化的管理会计人才。

CMA 认证是高薪"敲门砖"。IMA 2012 年中国区会员薪酬调研显示，持有 CMA 认证的会员平均年薪为 27.8 万元，比非持证者高 34%。

IMA 学习资源

- CMA 学习教材　CMA Learning System

- 《管理会计公告》Statement of Management Accounting

- 《管理会计季刊》　Management Accounting Quarterly

- 《IMA 教学案例期刊》IMA Educational Case Journal

- 《战略财务杂志》Strategic Finance Magazine

- 《管理会计在中国》Management Accounting In China

- 《财务报告内部控制与风险管理》Financial Report, Internal Control and Risk Management

译者的话

管理会计师协会（IMA）① 编辑出版的《管理会计师协会教学案例杂志》是一个丰富的资源。管理会计在中国传播已经 30 年了，以案例教学，已经逐渐普及，各大学都开始积累自己的文库。现在出版的这一套案例，是美国这方面杰作的集锦，其内容的丰富，披阅一下就明白了。这些案例最突出、为中国已出版的案例所不具备的特点是，对每一篇案例都为教师准备了十分详尽的教案。教案也编辑成集，教师们可向管理会计师协会驻中国办事处申请取得。

2003 年我"二度退休"后，总还想发挥些余热之余的余热，于是向 IMA 请缨，开始逐篇翻译这本期刊。改革开放之后，当我们开始有机会接触到西方（主要是美国）的管理会计资料时，我就开始从事译述。那是"编译"，也就是读了之后，按自己的理解写出来。在文字上比全译原著简练，容易被杂志的编者接受。同时，老实说，也是个偷懒、取巧的做法——可以不求甚解；难解之处，略去就是了。等到自己"真刀真枪"逐句翻译，才真正体会到翻译之难。复旦外语学院前院长陆谷孙同志有一次对我说，没有译过 100 万字，不可以议论翻译。诚哉斯言！现在逐字逐句译完了这本期刊三年的文章，够这个字数，勉强可以谈感想了；一字以概之，难。

幸亏我有老师可以请教。最初，有了疑难，就找该刊编辑瑞夫·劳森（Raef Lawson）请教；后来和一位退休的飞行员麦迈克（Mike Meiser）交了朋友，他热情帮助，对我每一个问题，必详细回答。我遇到的问题是多方面的。有的作者用词遣句不"传统"，还夹杂了不少新的成语，加以涉及许多行业、领域，他都不厌其烦地一一找到妥当的解释。没有他的帮助，我就做不下去。

周学园、林峰、胡金凤、赵澄、唐洋、周曙光、易颜新、慕勇、费峰和程秋芬都在校订文稿上，出了不可替代的大力。前后三次校订，每一次都使我惭愧不已。现在虽已出版，但真正的校订，还没有开始——更重要的校订意见，还等待读者来完成。读者在阅读、应用这些案例的过程中，必能找出更多被疏忽、遗漏的问题。写这篇"译者的话"，就是为了表达恳请读者不吝来函指正之意。我的电邮地址是 jiliang_y@163.com。我必逐一回答。

杨继良

2011 年 10 月 25 日

---

① IMA，原文中没有"美国"两字，在本案例各辑中也就没有译成"美国管理会计师协会"，但实际上这是一个美国组织，犹"美国注册会计师协会（AICPA）"。——译者

序　言

本书是《管理会计师协会教学案例杂志》(*IMA Educational Case Journal*) 的案例研究合辑。管理会计师协会（IMA）出版这些案例研究的翻译版本，其目的是在全球范围内提升管理会计课程的教学质量，从而促进管理会计职业的发展进程。

采用案例研究教学方法，学员需要分析和讨论现实生活中的实例，这些实例涉及有关组织所面临的决策、症结及问题等事项。案例研究教学方法与传统的教学方法完全不同，在传统课堂上，学员参与分析和讨论的机会少之又少，而案例研究教学方法则要求学员积极参与课堂讨论。

如果学员过去接受的是传统教学方法，现在就会认识到这种学习方法必须加以改变。一则案例研究不仅仅是一道问题。一道问题只有一个正确答案，而一则案例研究往往没有独一无二的正确答案。决策者在面临案例研究所描述的情形下，通常可以在多种备选做法中选取一种，而这些备选做法都有理有据。

案例研究会提供详细而有趣的信息，来对企业的实际情况展开说明，这会大大增加学员学习案例所涉及概念的兴趣。案例所述的实例都涵盖了某些管理上的理论概念，因而也能加深学员对管理理论的理解。

采用案例教学的好处还不止这些。通过学习案例的分析方法和在课堂上的演示方法，学员所掌握的技能就会得以提升，这些技能对于学员未来作为商界专业人士的生涯是极为重要的。案例研究方法能提高学员针对具体症结而提出恰当问题的能力，也能提升学员针对具体情形而识别和把握症结所在的能力（而不只是提出一些抽象的问题）。案例研究反映了现实生活中管理决策的实际情况，在现实生活中管理决策往往是建立在不充分的信息基础之上。案例研究将要告诉学员管理决策伴有模糊性和复杂性。案例研究还能使学员获得管理工作的整体视野，因为作出管理决策往往需要把各种理论和概念综合起来，而这些理论和概念又来源于营销和制造等不同的职能领域。

祝君成功。望大家喜欢这些案例。

瑞夫·劳森，PhD, CFA, CMA, CPA
IMA 常驻教授、研究副主席
IMA 教学案例期刊编辑
管理会计师协会

Preface

This book contains a selection of case studies published in the *IMA Educational Case Journal*. Through publication of the translations of these case studies, the Institute of Management Accountants (IMA) is pursuing its goal of enhancing the teaching of management accounting world-wide, thereby furthering the development of the global management accounting profession.

The case study method entails learning by analyzing and discussing a real-life situation involving a decision, problem, or issue faced by an organization. Unlike traditional lecture-based teaching where student participation in the classroom is minimal, the case study method requires students to be actively involved and to participate in the classroom discussion.

If you have been exposed only to traditional teaching methods, you will find that you need to change your approach to learning. A case study is not a problem. A problem has a unique, correct solution. On the other hand, there typically no unique, correct answer to a case study. A decision-maker faced with a situation described in a case study can usually choose between several alternative courses of action, each of which can be supported by logical argument.

By providing detailed, interesting information about real business situations, case studies can make learning about the concepts covered in a case more interesting. Cases will also enhance your grasp of management theory by providing real-life examples of the underlying theoretical concepts.

But the use of case studies does much more than that. By learning how to analyze and present a case study, you will be developing skills that are essential to your future career as a business professional. These include the development of analytic and decision-making skills and learning how to express your views. The case study method will improve your ability to ask the right questions in a given problem situation and to identify and understand the underlying problems in a given situation rather than the superficial issues. Case studies reflect the reality of managerial decision-making in the real world, where often decisions are based on insufficient information. Cases reflect the ambiguity and complexity that accompany most management decision-making. They can also provide an integrated view of management, as managerial decision-making frequently involves integration of theories and concepts learnt in different functional areas such as marketing and manufacturing.

I wish you success and hope you enjoy these cases!

Raef Lawson, PhD, CFA, CMA, CPA
Professor-in-Residence and Vice President of Research
Editor, IMA Educational Case Journal
Institute of Management Accountants

目 录

成本习性与成本管理

Argento 乳牛场 / 3
黄昏之星有机农场 / 24
Bridgestone 行为医疗保健中心：为编制计划和控制所作的
　成本—数量—利润（CVP）分析 / 38
阿帕鲁萨县日托中心 / 59

成本计算方法

另类成本计算法：精密涂漆工厂的两难处境 / 79

平衡记分卡

Tri-Cities 社区银行——一则平衡记分卡的案例 / 99
爱荷华州滑铁卢市：设置财务总监职位 / 116

编制计划与预算

浦东咖啡馆 / 133

业绩考核与报酬

通过记分为变革创造激励 / 151
JEA：迈向成本透明的大道 / 166
Perelson Weiner 会计师事务所业绩管理 / 205

公司治理与职业道德

Ace 肥料公司：合乎道德规范的成本分配和定价方法 / 265
我的注册会计师为我省下了数百万美元……他为我省下了吗？/ 280

可持续发展

强生公司：一则关于编制可持续发展报告书的案例研究 / 297

Contents

▌ Cost Behavior & Cost Management ▌

Argento Dairy Farm / 13
Even' Star Organic Farm / 30
Bridgestone Behavioral Health Center: Cost – Volume – Profit (CVP) Analysis
  for Planning and Control / 48
Appaloosa County Day Care Center, Inc. / 67

▌ Costing Methodologies ▌

Alternative Costing Methods: Precision Paint Shop's Dilemma / 87

▌ Balanced Scorecard ▌

Tri-Cities Community Bank—A Balanced Scorecard Case / 107
City of Waterloo, Iowa: Organizing a Chief Financial Officer Function / 122

▌ Planning & Budgeting ▌

The Pudong Coffee Shop / 140

▌ Performance Measurement & Compensation ▌

Creating Incentives for Change by Keeping Score / 158
JEA: On the Road to Cost Transparency / 184
Performance Management at Perelson Weiner LLP / 233

Corporate Governance & Ethics

Ace Fertilizer Company: Ethical Cost Allocations and Price Determination / 272
MY CPA SAVED ME MILLIONS…OR DID HE? / 287

Sustainability

Johnson & Johnson: A Case Study on Sustainability Reporting / 316

成本习性与成本管理
Cost Behavior & Cost Management

Argento 乳牛场

Marcela Porporato
York University

Nelson Waweru
York University

"我的名字叫詹娜,今年 22 岁。我现在正计划注册拥有一家乳牛场①,生产可供食用的牛奶。我的乳牛场将独立于我父母的农场。"

简介

2008 年 3 月,当詹娜(Jenna)作上述声明时,她参加父母的农场,管理一家小的乳牛场,生产供动物耗用的牛奶。她未来的计划是要结婚、在加拿大安大略省中部的尚伯格(Schomberg)(从多伦多市沿 400 号高速公路驱车北行约 30 分钟)办一家乳牛场,生产供人食用的牛奶。附近有几家农场从事同一种经营,并取得成功;她有意于在未来取得类似的成功。詹娜相信,要在乳牛场取得成功,唯一的秘诀在于照料好牛群、以有效率的方式挤奶。其余的事就要由安大略奶农协会(Dairy Farmers of Ontario, DFO)② 来负责了。只要是在协会规定的额度内生产出牛奶,在分销上就没有任何问题,因而对畜牧业富有经验的农民,更有吸引力。(参见附录中对安大略省该行业所作的详细概括。)

历史

詹娜出生在农场,到 2008 年止,她与母亲、继父和弟弟一起在尚伯格生活和工作。詹娜家的农场面积不到 300 英亩,90% 的土地生产经证明为不施化肥的作物。他们还经营肉牛/小牛业务(购入初生牛犊③来养),但这是一项次要的营业(相当于 20% 的收入和成本)。另外一项副业是在夏天养育小鸡和火鸡,由她的母亲照管。

詹娜给短角牛(shorthorn)挤奶,很有经验,大家认为这是一种稀有的

---

① 一家领有执照的乳品设施,是向安大略奶农协会(Dairy Farmers of Ontario)取得执照的乳品生产企业。安大略奶农协会向奶农分配生产的配额、负责销售牛奶,并由经任命在现场的人员检查合格后定为 A 级奶。
② 这是一个合作社性质的组织,负责对奶农进行检查。如果够得上标准,协会就买他的牛奶,高温灭菌并均质(免得奶油分离)后,批发卖给杂货铺。协会也生产奶酪和其他奶制品。——译者
③ 饲养这些初生牛犊的目的是长大后卖作牛肉,而不是养成奶牛。这些初生牛犊购自其他农场,非她的牛群所产。——译者

奶牛品种。短角牛在全省的牛群中少于1%，其体型较小——比霍斯坦牛（Holstein）小，但比泽西牛（Jersey）大。从詹娜2000年获得这个品种的第一头奶牛以来，到2008年总共繁殖到17头（10头奶牛、7头小牛）之多，可见她对养育这种奶牛富有经验。在她的管理经营下，这群奶牛的牛奶产量逐年增加、消耗则逐年减少。对此，詹娜的解释是：

我在分隔的牛棚内给10头奶牛挤奶。我们不把挤出的奶直接供人食用，而是分一部分给小牛吃（这些牛养大了当作小牛肉④卖），另外一部分卖给邻近的农户。我和家人之间的一切交易（卖牛奶、买谷物和干草，和请人运输），都按市场价格结算。

我的牛群是从有了第一头纯种小奶牛开始的，然后不断繁殖增多。我现在总共拥有17头牛，从出生仅1个月的小牛到8岁的母牛。在这17头奶牛中，13头是短角牛（包括6头小牛）；此外的4头中，一头是根西牛（Guernsey）、一头是泽西牛、2头是霍斯坦牛（其中1头是小牛）。所有这些牛都向协会登记在册，以Argento作为登记号的前缀⑤。

短角奶牛是奶牛中的珍稀品种，也是肉牛最好的良种。这一种牛以性格平和闻名、容易养育。母牛人工饲养，所以可以由我从加拿大甚至世界各国挑拣配种的公牛。

我每天早上6：30和下午5：30用自动化挤奶装置⑥各取一次奶。在冬春两季（除非天气太冷），每天把奶牛驱到谷仓前的场地上。在夏秋两季，则驱到草地上。目前，我所用的各项设施都同时用于养育肉牛，面积10英亩；这块地的土质不良（沙地），不宜种植。如果要扩大经营，我有足够的土地建一个当今第一流的乳制品设施，足以养育200头；但我宁愿我的奶制品业务只出产大量优质的短角牛奶，我要让我的良种奶牛享誉全世界。

詹娜有一本记事小册，把去年的经营情况用一张表格作了概括，还加上若干说明。在2007年中，她从9头母牛取奶、另养育6头小牛；这使她的银行存款净增5 842美元，另外还出售了3头公牛，获得4 500美元。詹娜认为，各类母牛对其银行存款的增加有多大的贡献，她了如指掌。详情见图表1。

图表1 詹娜对各类母牛净毛利的估计——2007				
母牛种类	短角牛	霍斯坦牛	根西牛	泽西牛
每头母牛每年产奶公升数	7 180	9 300	6 420	5 950
估计收入 （如按每公升 $72.45 美元卖给 DFO）	$5 202	$6 738	$4 651	$4 311
每头母牛估计净利	$737	$600	$420	$400
每头母牛产奶数 （每年平均10个月）	6	1	1	1
估计净利总额 = $5 842	$4 422	$600	$420	$400

---

④ veal，小牛肉，指取自未断奶的小牛的肉，比较鲜嫩。——译者

⑤ 饲养的母牛应向某个组织（如奶农协会或农业部的某个机构）登记在案，并编了号，以便识别。如果发生疯牛病或其他遗传性疾病，便可以此追索根源。——译者

⑥ bucket milker，是一种自动把牛奶吸出入桶的装置，1922年发明后，沿用至今。——译者

牛奶生产的基本知识

牛奶生产围绕奶牛的生殖周期而呈周期性。和其他哺乳动物一样，母牛在生小牛以后，开始出奶。大约在两岁的时候进入繁殖的成熟期。母牛通常产奶10个月，随后奶汁"干枯"——停止出奶——两个月，准备下一次生育。在这个时期，不产奶的母牛通常都被集聚在空地、牧场或谷仓的一角。

母牛必须在有了小牛——生育了——之后，才能产奶。小母牛⑦需要饲养15个月，然后通常进行人工授精。大约9个月后，产出一头约40~50公斤的牛犊。母牛以初乳哺之，而当母牛开始分泌乳汁后，一部分用于养育小牛、一部分作为供人食用的牛奶，为期10个月。一头母牛可以生育和分泌乳汁多次，在加拿大，大概平均分泌乳汁4~5次。为了尽量降低成本和提高生产水平，农户通常选择留养他最好的小母牛，每年更换他/她的牛群中的1/4。生下来的小牛有一半是公的，小公牛中饲养长大的占少数，大部分奶牛场的小公牛都作小牛肉来卖。

对未来的计划

看到这些数字，詹娜真的担心将要做生意的可行性，而缺乏盈利让她在近年来未必能独立于父母。她期盼到2009年时她有3头短角牛小牛能够产奶了，另外有一头短角母牛会停止繁殖和产奶，还会出生三头短角牛小牛。由于生物资产的自然生命周期，随着自然繁殖带来的增长，她每年可以增加净利润20%达到12 798美元，此数还不能够使她独立，不过生意还得顺应自然规律。她关心的另外一个问题是，为了照看和管理19头母牛的牛群，她每年需要工作2 000小时以上。此外，拥有了一个独立于她父母的奶牛场，她又是一个单身女子、没有个合伙人，在她生病或者外出时，就有无人看管奶牛场的风险。

为了算出2007~2009年的数字，詹娜详细列出饲养每一头母牛在牛奶场和农场方面的收入和成本，和为维持生意而引起的固定成本。为了列出细目并遵照ODF的会计制度规定的2007年报表格式办事，她按这个行业通常的做法，编制了分项目的每头母牛的收入和成本报表（见图表2）。

詹娜还想到另外一个计划方案：作巨额投资，更快地建起一个乳牛场。除了设施和设备估计需要花费70 000美元以外，为了改变牛群的组合以提高出奶率，需要再买进5头霍斯坦母牛，每头估计成本2 300美元。霍斯坦

---

⑦ 这里有一些英语中奶牛业的专用语。Heifers是尚未孕育小牛的雌牛，此处简单译成"小母牛"；尚未交配的雌牛，称为Open Heifers（以下简单译为"尚未交配的母牛"）；已经交配但尚未孕育小牛的雌牛，称为Bred Heifers（以下简译为"已交配但尚未孕育小牛的母牛"）；母牛（cow）则指已经生育过小牛的雌牛。在翻译中避免用"雌牛"一词，从我们的习惯。——译者

母牛产奶较高,但短角母牛因品种闻名,所生育的公牛每公斤平均可以卖得3美元。

根据詹娜饲养母牛的经验,她估计她的牛群明年可能通过两个途径有所增长:1) 自然繁殖,即主要随着饲养短角的奶牛和牛犊繁殖而增长(繁殖短角奶牛的成功率为40%;2) 积极进取[8],如果采取这个途径,则促进这类增长的因素有二——在自然繁殖增长(即随着她饲养短角奶牛的增加而获得的增长)的同时,投资购入霍斯坦奶牛和饲养它们需要增加的设施能力,获得更多的增长。(她估计饲养并养大霍斯坦奶牛的成功率可达33%)。图表3列示了各该方案下增长的详细情况。

詹娜很明白,如果采用积极进取的途径,她就需要获得一笔银行贷款,以支付新设施的成本;但按银行的规定,购买母牛的费用,就得用她自己的银行存款来支付了。按银行和信用社的规定,如果用银行贷款来购买母牛,就得为母牛投保,结果就会减少詹娜的营业利润。她可以从储蓄中拿出12 000美元作投资,够买5头霍斯坦母牛,这是经"加拿大霍斯坦"[9]确认的最好的品种。为了购买设备,她可以从当地的一家合作银行取得70 000美元为期5年的贷款,年利率为7%。图表4列示了需购设备的明细项目(大部分明细项目得自 http://www.milk.org)。

詹娜对于2009年该怎么干,心中无数。她的母亲建议,两年后她的牛群增加到30头奶牛时再看着办。她的兄弟建议说,早一点把乳牛场办起来,会让她对这门生意有更多经验,在她满25岁之前在经济上取得独立。

图表2
牛奶收入和开支(2007年和2009年)

2007年收入明细:					2009年收入明细:				
牛种	公升	每头母牛收入	母牛数	收入合计	牛种	公升	每头母牛收入	母牛数	收入合计
短角牛	7 180	$5 201.91	6	$31 211	短角牛	7 180	$5 201.91	8	$41 615
霍斯坦牛	9 300	6 737.85	1	$6 738	霍斯坦牛	9 300	6 737.85	1	$6 738
泽西牛	5 950	4 310.78	1	$4 311	泽西牛	5 950	4 310.78	1	$4 311
根西牛	6 420	4 651.29	1	4 651	根西牛	6 420	4 651.29	1	4 651
				$46 911					$57 315

---

[8] 在本案例中反复提到詹娜可以选择采取两种把她的乳牛场办大的途径,一是采取自然繁殖(vegetative)的方式,二是在自然繁殖的同时,还在她力所能及的范围内向外购入母牛、扩大牛群,称为积极进取(aggressive)的方式。——译者

[9] Holstein Canada,这是一个专事霍斯坦牛牛种培育的机构,负责确定一头母牛是否纯种、是否出自出奶多(或少)的种系,类似一个母牛等级的评定机构。——译者

图表 2
按詹娜的发展计划经营的结果

	2007 年自然繁殖的实际结果，母牛头数：15		2009 年自然繁殖的预计结果，母牛头数：19	
	每头母牛	合计	每头母牛	合计
收入				
牛奶销售：	$3 127	$46 911	$3 017	$57 315
乳品家畜存量变化	100	1 500	100	1 900
公牛出售	300	4 500	300	5 700
净收入	$3 527	$52 911	$3 417	$64 915
乳品直接费用				
按奶牛给养搭配计算的饲料	$50	$750	$50	$950
蛋白质补充剂	350	5 250	350	6 650
盐与矿物质	100	1 500	100	1 900
代乳品与按给养搭配计算的小牛饲料	23	345	23	437
兽医与药物	150	2 250	150	2 850
分配来的间接费用	80	1 200	80	1 520
牛棚和挤奶房用的物料	110	1 650	110	2 090
牛奶运输与执照费用	320	4 800	320	6 080
其他与乳品有关的费用	190	2 850	190	3 610
直接费用合计	$1 373	$20 595	$1 373	$26 087
分配计入乳品的农作物费用				
外购大宗谷物和粮草	$50	$750	$50	$950
种子	90	1 350	90	1 710
肥料	100	1 500	100	1 900
除草剂和杀虫剂	40	600	40	760
临时雇工做的活	100	1 500	100	1 900
燃油和润滑油	150	2 250	150	2 850
田间作业机械修理	200	3 000	200	3 800
土地租金	50	750	50	950
其他农作物费用	50	750	50	950
农作物费用合计	$830	$12 450	830	$15 770
扣除直接和农作物费用后的收益	$1 324	$19 866	$1 214	$23 058
分配计入的间接费用				
谷仓设备与建筑修理	$250	$3 750	$200	$3 800
保险	90	1 350	90	1 710
电话与水费	120	1 800	100	1 900
税金	60	900	60	1 140
其他间接费用	115	1 725	90	1 710
间接费用合计	$635	$9 525	$540	$10 260
扣除一切费用后的收益	$689	$10 341	$674	$12 798
总共需要的劳动力（小时）	113	1 695	113	1 695

（1）按她把牛奶卖给 DFO 的运作量作出的估计
（2）全部都是经过认证的有机产品

注：初生牛犊的头三天用初乳饲养。其后，用母牛的奶或代乳品（均用奶粉冲制）混合饲养，并逐渐添加固体食物、逐渐断奶，直到它们能够完全吃固体食物。断奶以后，干草、青贮饲料和某些谷物将是它们的主饲料。

图表 3
两种不同增长模式下牛群头数进展情况

	自然繁殖的增长模式				积极进取的增长模式			
	出奶母牛	小牛	总头数		出奶母牛	小牛	总头数	
2007					**2007**			
短角牛	6	5	11		6	5	11	在第 2 年出生的出奶
霍斯坦牛	1	1	2	在第 2 年出生的出奶	1	1	2	母牛数：2
泽西牛	1		1	母牛数：2	1		1	不再出奶的母牛数：0
根西牛	1		1	不再出奶的母牛数：0	1		1	购买小牛数：0
总计	9	6	15		9	6	15	
2008					**2008**			
短角牛	7	6	13		7	6	13	在第 2 年出生的出奶
霍斯坦牛	1	1	2	在第 2 年出生的出奶	1	1	2	母牛数：2
泽西牛	1		1	母牛数：2	1		1	不再出奶的母牛数：0
根西牛	1		1	不再出奶的母牛数：0	1		1	购买小牛数：0
总计	10	7	17		10	7	17	
2009					**2009**			
短角牛	8	7	15		8	7	15	在第 2 年出生的出奶
霍斯坦牛	1	1	2	在第 2 年出生的出奶	6	1	7	母牛数：3
泽西牛	1		1	母牛数：3	1		1	不再出奶的母牛数：1
根西牛	1		1	不再出奶的母牛数：1	1		1	购买小牛数：5
总计	11	8	19		16	8	24	
2010					**2010**			
短角牛	10	8	18		10	8	18	在第 2 年出生的出奶
霍斯坦牛	2	1	3	在第 2 年出生的出奶	12	3	15	母牛数：6
泽西牛	1		1	母牛数：3	1		1	不再出奶的母牛数：1
根西牛	1		1	不再出奶的母牛数：1	1		1	购买小牛数：5
总计	14	9	23		24	11	35	
2011					**2011**			
短角牛	13	8	21		13	8	21	在第 2 年出生的出奶
霍斯坦牛	2	1	3	在第 2 年出生的出奶	19	7	26	母牛数：10
泽西牛	1		1	母牛数：4	1		1	不再出奶的母牛数：1
根西牛	1		1	不再出奶的母牛数：1	1		1	购买小牛数：5
总计	17	9	26		34	15	49	
2012					**2012**			
短角牛	17	8	25		17	8	25	在第 2 年出生的出奶
霍斯坦牛	3	1	4	在第 2 年出生的出奶	28	11	39	母牛数：13
泽西牛	1		1	母牛数：5	1		1	不再出奶的母牛数：1
根西牛	1		1	不再出奶的母牛数：1	1		1	购买小牛数：5
总计	22	9	31		47	19	66	
2013					**2013**			
短角牛	21	9	30		21	9	30	在第 2 年出生的出奶
霍斯坦牛	3	1	4	在第 2 年出生的出奶	39	16	55	母牛数：18
泽西牛	1		1	母牛数：7	1		1	不再出奶的母牛数：2
根西牛	1		1	不再出奶的母牛数：2	1		1	购买小牛数：5
总计	26	10	36		62	25	87	

图表 4
设施与设备投资

- 詹娜估计,她需要花 15 000 美元购买材料,把现在系养的畜棚改装成带有挤奶房、让牛群自由活动的畜棚。让牛群自由活动的畜棚可以容纳 100 头出奶的母牛和大约 15 头不出奶的母牛。
- 詹娜计划安装板条式的地台,使粪肥和废物得以落下去、易于打扫。这一改装要花 5 000 美元。
- 需要花费 5 000 美元,建造一个深 10 英尺、直径 50 英尺盛放牛粪的水槽,与牛棚相联结。
- 饲料青贮窖。Jenna 准备花费 5 000 美元建造一个水泥仓罐储置苞米青饲料。
- 詹娜计划投资 20 000 美元盖一个挤奶房,同时可以容纳给 10 头母牛挤奶(两边各 5 头)。
- 詹娜要在挤奶房里安装一个带有控制盘的高功率真空泵,估计需要 8 000 美元。
- 詹娜计划购入、安装一台容积为 2 000 公升的不锈钢冷藏水槽,牛奶可以放在里面两天不变质。有人向她报价 10 000 美元。
- 购入并安装一台温度序时记录器的总价为 2 000 美元。
- 按詹娜的看法,对装牛奶的卡车运走的牛奶作出记录,并不需要花钱。
- 詹娜估计,在照看她的牛群时同时运行各项设施,是不需要花费其他投资的。

附录——行业展望

安大略省的乳品行业有一些对农民很有吸引力的特点。乳品业是安大略省最大的农业部门,占该省农业产值的 20%。安大略省有 4 800 家乳牛场,每年生产牛奶 25 亿公升。

所有未经高温消毒的牛奶,必须由安大略奶农公司(Dairy Farmers of Ontario, DFO)独家经销。按《乳品法》的规定,DFO 是向奶农收购乳品的独家合法收购者,又是进行高温消毒后出售乳品的独家经销者。安大略的 716 法规(即所谓《乳品法》)概括了在安大略与生产和加工牛奶有关的各项要求。未经高温消毒的牛奶,只能由 DFO 卖给经安大略农业部食品与农村事务局发给执照的乳制品加工公司。

DFO 的业务,就像一个供销合作社。安大略乳品加工场的牛奶,都购自 DFO。DFO 规定安大略未经消毒的"生奶"价格。乳制品加工者按生产成本的价格支付。对安大略的零售价格并无控制管理。DFO 从加工者收到的价款,减去牛奶和奶制品的推销费、从乳牛场运牛奶到乳制品厂的运输费、DFO 的行政管理费,以及研究费用后,悉数支付给奶农。合计起来,这些抵减费用占到支付给奶农价格的 6%。在 2008 年中,奶农从 DFO 获得的净价为每公升原奶 0.7245 美元;当编写本案例时,已宣布称 2009 年的支持性价格[10]将增加 0.01 美元。

奶农的收入,按其产奶的总量和质量计算,随奶牛的品种而异(参见附录中的图表 1)。牛奶的销售收入与运输和推销成本,是把五个省(安大略、魁北克、新不伦瑞克、诺瓦斯科舍、爱德华王子岛)所产生的金额合

---

[10] support price,支持性价格;一般指政府为了促进农业发展而制订的某种农产品的最低销售价格。——译者

在一起计算的，形成一个地区性的联营，称为"五省联营"。这就意味着这五个省的奶农都在一个共同的大市场内，每百公升（1公升＝100升）牛奶都支付同一个价格的运费和推销费。

牛奶所含的固体成分——牛奶中的脂肪、蛋白质和其他固体（乳糖和矿物质）——和加工者如何利用这些固体物质，将决定牛奶的价值。付款的那一套办法，称为"多元定价制"。DFO按各类、各种产品的生奶利用程度给加工者开发票。安大略的奶农每月按上月的实际牛奶运输量支付一次运费。

附录图表1
不同品种比较表

	霍斯坦牛	泽西牛	艾尔夏牛	短角奶牛	瑞士褐牛	根西牛
说明（大小与颜色）	最大型的牛种，黑白色或红白色	最小型的牛种，稍带浅黄/褐色	大型牛种，红与白色	中型牛种，红与白色（往往是菊花青色的）	大型牛种，银褐色	中型，浅黄与白色
在安大略乳牛群中所占%	93%	4%	1%	<1%	<1%	<1%
起源地	荷兰	泽西岛	苏格兰	英格兰	瑞士	根西岛
平均每年出奶量	8 600公升	6 200公升	6 800公升	6 500公升	7 000公升	7 000公升
平均牛奶成分（脂肪、蛋白质）	3.8%脂肪 3.2%蛋白质	4.9%脂肪 3.8%蛋白质	3.9%脂肪 3.3%蛋白质	3.9%脂肪 3.7%蛋白质	3.9%脂肪 3.5%蛋白质	4.4%脂肪 3.5%蛋白质
2岁时的平均体重	575公斤或1 265磅	390公斤或858磅	500公斤或1 100磅	500公斤或1 100磅	575公斤或1 265磅	500公斤或1 100磅

按生产成本确定价格

参加"五省联营"的各省都支持采用全国通用的"生产成本（cost of production, COP）"计算式作为确定液体和工业用牛奶的定价方法。"工业用牛奶"指的是用于制造乳制品（诸如奶油、奶酪和酸奶）的牛奶。全国COP的计算，以从各省成本计算的调查中所收集到的数据为基础。把各省COP的数字按各自牛奶数量为权数，得出平均的全国COP。

在安大略省，"安大略乳牛场会计项目（Ontario Dairy Farm Accounting Project, ODFAP）"被用作数据的来源。ODFAP是DFO、安大略农业与食品部、加拿大乳品委员会和圭尔夫大学共同合作的一个项目，它从安大略乳牛场中取100户为样本，从这些样本的实际记录中取得数据。（有关的表格，请参阅附录中的图表2与图表3。）

附录图表 2：乳品企业收入和费用——2007（每头母牛）

收入	最低 15 户	中间 15 户	最高 15 户	全部 84 户
牛奶销售	$5 169.27	$6 161.05	$6 249.30	$5 999.71
牛奶质量与其他罚款	—	(21.97)	(5.76)	(15.15)
母牛与公牛出售	175.97	147.53	139.20	151.12
其他乳品家畜出售	118.06	95.57	54.72	92.29
乳品家畜存量变化	98.86	99.44	51.76	90.82
净收入	**$5 562.16**	**$6 481.62**	**$6 489.22**	**$6 318.79**
直接乳品费用				
按奶牛给养搭配计算的饲料	$86.82	$76.90	$92.27	$81.42
蛋白质补充剂	347.72	402.95	372.24	387.60
盐与矿物质	110.61	89.30	108.17	96.48
代乳品与按给养搭配计算的小牛饲料	48.24	51.91	57.01	52.16
其他外购饲料	3.42	22.72	33.79	21.25
兽医与药物	153.08	178.99	139.39	167.29
分配来的间接费用	82.47	75.80	56.02	73.46
牛棚与挤奶房用的物料	126.00	117.69	99.87	115.99
牛奶运输与执照费用	307.06	368.84	372.27	358.42
家畜推销费	12.52	14.59	14.42	14.19
乳品其他费用[1]	193.04	184.52	205.10	189.71
直接费用合计	**$1 470.98**	**$1 584.21**	**$1 550.55**	**$1 557.97**
分配计入乳品的农作物费用				
大宗谷物和粮草购买	$156.26	$147.28	$46.55	$130.89
种子	93.89	90.38	71.36	87.61
肥料	92.54	112.14	52.64	98.02
除草剂和杀虫剂	26.88	43.73	46.17	41.15
临时雇工做的活	129.06	136.42	150.38	137.60
燃油和润滑油	167.96	153.69	120.50	150.31
田间作业机械修理	195.94	183.11	115.69	173.36
土地租金	35.85	52.59	50.98	49.32
其他农作物费用[2]	49.96	41.18	39.62	42.47
农作物费用合计	**$948.34**	**$960.52**	**$693.89**	**$910.73**
扣除直接和农作物费用后的收益	**$3 142.84**	**$3 936.89**	**$4 244.78**	**$3 850.09**
分配计入的间接费用				
谷仓设备与建筑修理	$262.64	$233.54	$176.31	$228.52
外雇劳动力费用	754.86	455.30	295.17	480.20
利息费用	870.74	572.29	795.10	665.37
保险	105.42	76.85	89.74	84.25
电话与水费	159.81	131.09	99.41	130.56
税金	66.22	62.12	38.67	58.66
其他间接费用[3]	134.33	108.17	104.77	112.23
间接费用合计	**$2 354.02**	**$1 639.36**	**$1 599.17**	**$1 759.79**
扣除一切费用后的收益	**$788.82**	**$2 297.53**	**$2 645.61**	**$2 090.30**
乳品家畜购入				
母牛与公牛购入	$87.26	$86.45	$86.54	$86.61
其他乳品家畜购入	19.64	22.29	8.14	19.29
乳品家畜购入合计	**$106.90**	**$108.74**	**$94.68**	**$105.90**
净收益	**$681.92**	**$2 188.79**	**$2 550.93**	**$984.40**
总共需要的劳动力（小时）[4]	154.53	98.43	51.56	100.80

1. 乳品其他费用包括垫料、饲料加工费、家畜检验与登记费、家畜保险、家畜推销费和建筑物租金。
2. 其他农作物费用包括绳索、种子清洗、农作物保险和机械租金。
3. 其他间接费用包括五金器具、汽车费用和其他费用。
4. 对劳动力所作的估计，以每天计工单上所记小时数作出。

附录图表 3
农场生产基本参数——2007

农场数	最低 15 户	中间 15 户	最高 15 户	全部 84 户
奶牛（头数）	44.9	70.6	134.4	77.4
尚未交配的母牛（6个月以上）	17.7	23	36.3	24.4
已交配但尚未孕育小牛的母牛（头数）	12.8	21.2	38.4	22.8
出售牛奶/每个农场（公升）[1]	316 885	609 471	1 182 762	659 597
出售牛奶/每头母牛（公升）[1]	6 972	8 512	8 595	8 252
测得乳脂（公斤/百公升）	4.02	3.87	3.90	3.9
劳动力的约当人数	2.3	2.3	2.2	2.3
农场可使用土地（英亩）[2]	138	135	157	140
主要经营者的平均年龄	47.2	47.9	43.4	47.0

本行业具体数据的其他来源（自 2009 年 6 月起）：

行业规则和规定：

http://www.milk.org/Corporate/pdf/Publications-DFOPolicyBook.pdf

价格结构：

http://www.dairyinfo.gc.ca/pdf/dm90904.pdf

带有财务数据的研究项目（本附录中的图表 2 与图表 3 均可在此网址取得）：

http://www.milk.org/Corporate/pdf/Publications-ODFAPReport.pdf

安大略乳品公司的情况和数字（本附录中的图表 1，可在此网址取得）：

http://www.milk.org/Corporate/pdf/DairyEducation-FactsAndFiguresEN.pdf

Argento Dairy Farm

Marcela Porporato
York University

Nelson Waweru
York University

> "*My name is Jenna and I'm 22 years old. I am currently planning to launch my own licensed dairy farm to produce milk for human consumption[1] that will operate independently from my parents' crop farm.*"

INTRODUCTION

In March 2008, when making the above statement, Jenna participated in her family farm by running a small dairy farm that produced milk for animal consumption. Her future plans included getting married and setting up a dairy farm to produce milk for human consumption in Schomberg, central Ontario (30 minutes north of Toronto via Highway 400). There were several neighboring farms that were successful in this business and she was interested in having similar success in the future. Jenna believed that the only key success factor in the dairy farm business was to be able to take care of the herd and milk it in an efficient manner. The rest of the efforts are the responsibility of Dairy Farmers of Ontario (DFO). No sales effort or distribution planning has to be made for the milk produced within the quota, making it even more attractive for farmers versed in raising cattle. (See the appendix for a detailed summary of the industry outlook in Ontario.)

HISTORY

Jenna was born on a farm, and by 2008 she lived and worked with her mother, stepfather, and brother on their farm in Schomberg. Jenna's family had

---

[1] A licensed dairy facility is a milk production enterprise at which a producer has been licensed by Dairy Farmers of Ontario, has been allotted a quota to produce and market milk, and the milk has been designated as Grade A by an appointed field person.

a crop farm of just under 300 hectares, with 90% of the land certified organic. A minor line of business (up to 20% of revenues and costs) was a beef cow/calf operation, where they bought in stocker calves to raise. Another minor line of business (less than 3%), which was operated by her mother, comprised of raising laying chickens and turkeys in the summer.

Jenna had experience with milking shorthorns, which is considered a rare dairy breed. Shorthorns make up less than 1% of the total provincial herd. The shorthorn is a small cow—smaller than a Holstein but usually a bit bigger than a Jersey. Jenna's experience breeding milking shorthorns was reflected in the growth of her herd since she acquired her first cow in the year 2000: by 2008 she had a total of 17 heads (10 milking cows and 7 calves). Under Jenna's management and operation, the herd's average milk production for animal consumption improved from year to year. Jenna went on to explain:

I'm milking 10 cows in a tie-stall barn. Instead of shipping the milk for human consumption, it is divided up and fed to calves that we, my family, raise for veal, as well as sold to neighboring farmers. All transactions with my family (selling milk, buying grain and hay, and services such as transportation) are done at market prices.

My herd got started with my first purebred dairy calf and just kept growing from there! I own 17 animals in total, ranging from a 1-month-old calf to an 8-year-old cow. Of the 17 head, 13 are milking shorthorns (including 6 calves). I also had one Guernsey, one Jersey, and two Holsteins (one calf). All my cows are registered and my prefix is Argento.

Milking shorthorns are one of the rare dairy breeds, but are among the best for beef. The breed is known for its quiet temperament and ease of calving. Cows are bred artificially, which allows me to select bulls not only from Canada but from any other country in the world.

I use a bucket milker for milking my cows twice a day. They are milked at 6:30 a.m. and 5:30 p.m. The cows are turned outside into the barnyard every day in the winter and spring unless it is too cold. In the summer and fall they go out onto grass. Currently all the facilities I use are shared with the beef business, and are located in an area of 10 hectares that cannot be used for crops due to the poor quality of the soil (sand). If I want to expand, I have enough land to build a 'state of the art' dairy facility capable of holding a milking herd of up to 200 head; but I'd rather have a dairy operation that ships large volumes of quality shorthorn milk and develop the pedigrees and cow families renowned around the world.

Jenna had a small notebook with several annotations and a table that summarized the last year of operations. During 2007 she milked nine cows and raised six calves; this contributed a net increase of $5 842 in her bank account plus $4 500 from the sale of three bulls. Jenna believed that she had a fair idea of how much each type of cow contributed to the bottom line of her bank account, as detailed in Exhibit 1.

Exhibit 1
Jenna's Estimation of Net Profit Margin per Type of Cow – 2007

Type of cow	Shorthorn	Holstein	Guernsey	Jersey
Liters per cow per year	7 180	9 300	6 420	5 950
Estimated revenues (if sold to Dairy Farmers of Ontario at $72.45 hl)	$5 202	$6 738	$4 651	$4 311
Estimated net profit per cow	$737	$600	$420	$400
Head producing milk (average of 10 months per year)	6	1	1	1
Total estimated net profit = $5 842	$4 422	$600	$420	$400

MILK PRODUCTION BASICS

Milk production revolves around the reproductive cycle of the cow. As a mammal, a cow starts to produce milk after she gives birth to a calf. Breeding maturity is reached at about 2 years of age. Cows are usually milked for about 10 months and then "dried off" —milking is stopped—for 2 months as they prepare for the birth of their next calf. Dry cows are usually grouped together in yards, pastures, or a separate part of the barn during this time.

A cow must first calve—give birth—before she produces milk. A heifer (female calve) is bred at about 15 months of age, usually through artificial insemination. About nine months later, she has a calf weighing 40 to 50 kg. The calf is fed her colostrum, and when the cow's lactation begins, she becomes part of the milking herd and will produce milk for about 10 months. A cow can have several calves and lactations, the average in Canada being four to five lactations. To optimize costs and the level of production, the farmer keeps the best heifers to renew about one quarter of his/her herd every year. Half of all calves born are male (bull) calves, and a small percentage of these are raised for breeding purposes. Most dairy bull calves are raised for veal.

THE PROJECT

Looking at the numbers, Jenna was really concerned about the future viability of her planned business and the lack of profitability that would allow her to become independent from her parents in the near future. For 2009 she expected that three of her shorthorn calves would became productive, one shorthorn cow would stop breeding and milking, and three new shorthorn calves would arrive. This vegetative growth of her business, due to the natural cycle of life of living assets, would allow her to increase net profit by 20%, to $12 798 per year, but this would not be enough to make her independent. Another point of concern was that in order to attend and manage a herd of 19 cows she would need to work more than 2 000 hours per year. Also, having a dairy farm independent from her parents and being single or without a partner posed the risk of having nobody to tend her herd when she was ill or away.

To come up with the numbers for 2007 and 2009, she detailed the revenues and costs per cow breed related to the dairy and farming sides of the business as well as the fixed costs that have to be incurred to maintain her business. Going into more details and following the format of the Annual Report 2007 of the Ontario Dairy Farm Accounting Project, Jenna prepared the breakdown of revenues and costs per average cow and in total, as is normally reported in this industry (Exhibit 2).

As an alternative, Jenna had thought about investing heavily and building a milking farm faster. Besides the facilities and equipment that were estimated to cost $70 000, she would need to buy five Holstein cows in order to improve the milk yield by changing the mix of her herd, at an estimated cost of $2 300 per cow. Although Holstein cows have a higher yield, the breed prestige of her milking shorthorns allowed her to sell bulls for an average of $3 per kilogram.

Based on Jenna's experience with breeding cows, she estimated that in the next years her herd could grow in two ways: 1) vegetatively, where the main driver is her capacity to breed and raise calves of milking shorthorns (actual rate of success of breeding milking shorthorn cows is 40%); or 2) aggressively,

Exhibit 2

Breakdown of Dairy Revenues and Expenses for 2007 and 2009

Revenue details for 2007:					Revenue details for 2009:				
Breed	Liters	Revenue per Cow	Number of Cows	Total Revenue	Breed	Liters	Revenue per Cow	Number of Cows	Total Revenue
Shorthorn	7 180	$5 201.91	6	$31 211	Shorthorn	7 180	$5 201.91	8	$41 615
Holstein	9 300	6 737.85	1	$6 738	Holstein	9 300	6 737.85	1	$6 738
Jersey	5 950	4 310.78	1	$4 311	Jersey	5 950	4 310.78	1	$4 311
Guernsey	6 420	4 651.29	1	4 651	Guernsey	6 420	4 651.29	1	4 651
				$46 911					$57 315

Exhibit 2: Results of Jenna's explotation	Real For 2007 Vegetative growth # of cows: 15		Estimated for 2009 Vegetative growth # of cows: 19	
	Per cow	Total	Per cow	Total
REVENUE				
Milk Sales:	$3 127	$46 911	$3 017	$57 315
Dairy Livestock Inventory Change	100	1 500	100	1 900
Bulls Sold	300	4 500	300	5 700
Net Revenue	$3 527	$52 911	$3 417	$64 915
DIRECT DAIRY EXPENSES				
Dairy Ration	$50	$750	$50	$950
Protein Supplements	350	5 250	350	6 650
Salt & Minerals	100	1 500	100	1 900
Milk Replacer & Calf Ration	23	345	23	437
Vet & Drugs	150	2 250	150	2 850
A. I. Fees (1)	80	1 200	80	1 520
Stable & Milk House Supplies	110	1 650	110	2 090
Milk Transport & Licence Fees (1)	320	4 800	320	6 080
Other Dairy Expense	190	2 850	190	3 610
Total Direct Expense	$1 373	$20 595	$1 373	$26 087
DAIRY SHARE OF CROP EXPENSES				
Bulk Grain & Forage Purchases	$50	$750	$50	$950
Seed	90	1 350	90	1 710
Fertilizers (2)	100	1 500	100	1 900
Herbicides & Pesticides (2)	40	600	40	760
Custom Work	100	1 500	100	1 900
Fuel & Lubricants	150	2 250	150	2 850
Field Machinery Repairs	200	3 000	200	3 800
Land Rent	50	750	50	950
Other Crop Expense	50	750	50	950
Total Crop Expense	$830	$12 450	830	$15 770
Returns Over Direct & Crop Expenses	$1 324	$19 866	$1 214	$23 058
ALLOCATED INDIRECT & OVERHEAD EXPENSES				
Barn Equipment & Building Repairs	$250	$3 750	$200	$3 800
Insurance	90	1 350	90	1 710
Telephone & Hydro	120	1 800	100	1 900
Taxes	60	900	60	1 140
Other Overhead Expenses	115	1 725	90	1 710
Total Indirect & Overhead Expenses	$635	$9 525	$540	$10 260
Returns Over Expenses	$689	$10 341	$674	$12 798
TOTAL LABOUR REQUIRED (Hrs)	113	1 695	113	1 695

(1) Estimated for the volume of operation as if she sells to the DFO
(2) All are organic certified
Note: Calves receive colostrum for their first three days. After that, calves are fed a balanced diet of either cow's milk or milk replacer (made from milk powder) until they are old enough for solid food, which is slowly introduced as part of the diet to prepare the calves for weaning. After weaning, dry hay or silage and some grains will be the main feed.

where there are two drivers—continued vegetative growth (her capacity to breed milking shorthorns), and her financial capacity to buy Holsteins and the operating capacity to breed them. (She estimated the success rate of breeding and raising milking Holsteins would be 33%.) The details of each type of growth are detailed in Exhibit 3.

To proceed with the aggressive growth, Jenna knew that she could get a bank loan to cover the costs of the new facilities, but she had to use her own savings to buy the cows due to bank practices and regulations. Banks and credit unions required a special insurance on cows acquired with a bank loan, making Jenna's operation less profitable. She could invest up to $12 000 from her savings, which would allow her to buy five Holstein cows qualified as "excellent" by Holstein Canada. To buy the equipment she could obtain a five-year loan for $70 000 from the local branch of a cooperative bank at an annual rate of 7%. Exhibit 4 has a breakdown of the required equipment. (Most of the details were obtained from http://www.milk.org.).

Jenna is unsure of what to do for 2009. Her mother suggested that she needed to wait for a couple of years until her herd increased to 30 milking cows. Her brother, however, commented that launching a dairy farm early would allow her to better learn the business and be economically independent before she turns 25.

APPENDIX-INDUSTRY OUTLOOK

The dairy industry in Ontario has several particularities that make it quite attractive for farmers. Dairy is the largest agriculture sector in Ontario, making up close to 20% of the province's agricultural products. Ontario's 4 800 dairy farmers produce 2.5 billion liters of milk each year.

All unpasteurized milk in Ontario must be purchased from Dairy Farmers of Ontario (DFO). DFO is the sole legal purchaser from producers and sole legal seller to processors of unpasteurized milk, in accordance with the "Milk Act." Ontario Regulation 761, known as the "Milk Act," outlines a number of the requirements associated with the production and processing of cow's milk in Ontario. DFO may only sell unpasteurized cow's milk to a company or dairy processor that has been licensed by the Ontario Ministry of Agriculture, Food and Rural Affairs (OMAFRA).

Exhibit 3
Herd Size Progression Under Two Different Growth Models

	Vegetative Growth					Vegetative Growth			
	Miking cows	Calfs	Total Heads			Miking cows	Calfs	Total Heads	
2007					**2007**				
Shorthorn	6	5	11		Shorthorn	6	5	11	Future milking cows born in the year: 2
Holstein	1	1	2	Future milking cows born in the year: 2	Holstein	1	1	2	Retired: 0
Jersey	1		1	Retired: 0	Jersey	1		1	Purchases: 0
Guersey	1		1		Guersey	1		1	
Total	9	6	15		Total	9	6	15	
2008					**2008**				
Shorthorn	7	6	13		Shorthorn	7	6	13	Future milking cows born in the year: 2
Holstein	1	1	2	Future milking cows born in the year: 2	Holstein	1	1	2	Retired: 0
Jersey	1		1	Retired: 0	Jersey	1		1	Purchases: 0
Guersey	1		1		Guersey	1		1	
Total	10	7	17		Total	10	7	17	
2009					**2009**				
Shorthorn	8	7	15		Shorthorn	8	7	15	Future milking cows born in the year: 3
Holstein	1	1	2	Future milking cows born in the year: 3	Holstein	6	1	7	Retired: 1
Jersey	1		1	Retired: 1	Jersey	1		1	Purchases: 5
Guersey	1		1		Guersey	1		1	
Total	11	8	19		Total	16	8	24	
2010					**2010**				
Shorthorn	10	8	18		Shorthorn	10	8	18	Future milking cows born in the year: 6
Holstein	2	1	3	Future milking cows born in the year: 3	Holstein	12	3	15	Retired: 1
Jersey	1		1	Retired: 1	Jersey	1		1	Purchases: 5
Guersey	1		1		Guersey	1		1	
Total	14	9	23		Total	24	11	35	
2011					**2011**				
Shorthorn	13	8	21		Shorthorn	13	8	21	Future milking cows born in the year: 10
Holstein	2	1	3	Future milking cows born in the year: 4	Holstein	19	7	26	Retired: 1
Jersey	1		1	Retired: 1	Jersey	1		1	Purchases: 5
Guersey	1		1		Guersey	1		1	
Total	17	9	26		Total	34	15	49	
2012					**2012**				
Shorthorn	17	8	25		Shorthorn	17	8	25	Future milking cows born in the year: 13
Holstein	3	1	4	Future milking cows born in the year: 5	Holstein	28	11	39	Retired: 1
Jersey	1		1	Retired: 1	Jersey	1		1	Purchases: 5
Guersey	1		1		Guersey	1		1	
Total	22	9	31		Total	49	19	66	
2013					**2013**				
Shorthorn	21	9	30		Shorthorn	21	9	30	Future milking cows born in the year: 18
Holstein	3	1	4	Future milking cows born in the year: 7	Holstein	39	16	55	Retired: 2
Jersey	1		1	Retired: 2	Jersey	1		1	Purchases: 5
Guersey	1		1		Guersey	1		1	
Total	26	10	36		Total	62	25	87	

Exhibit 4

Facility and Equipment Investments

- Jenna estimated that she needed materials worth $15 000 to transform her current tie-stall barn into a free-stall barn with space for the milking parlor. A free-stall barn can house 100 milking cows and about 15 dry cows.
- Jenna planned to install slatted floors that allow manure and waste to fall through for easy clean up. This improvement would cost $5 000.
- A tank 10 feet deep by 50 feet in diameter to hold her cows' manure can be built and connected to the stall barn for $5 000.
- Feeding bunker silo. Jenna planned to install a corn silage to be stored in a cement bunker at a cost of $5 000.
- Jenna planned to install the milking parlor in a building adjacent to the barn that was not used by her family. She planned to invest $20 000 in a milking parlor where 10 cows can be milked at the same time (5 on either side).
- To install a powerful vacuum pump in the milk house and a control panel for it, Jenna estimated that $8 000 was required.
- Jenna was planning to buy and install a 2 000 – liter refrigerated stainless steel tank that would hold the milk for up to two days. She obtained a quote for $10 000.
- A time-temperature recorder can be bought and installed for a total of $2 000.
- Jenna estimated that the cost to install a milk truck recording system was nil.
- Jenna estimated that no new investments were needed in the facilities she already had to handle when caring for her animals.

DFO operates like a marketing cooperative. All milk bought by Ontario processors is purchased from DFO. DFO sets the price for raw milk in Ontario. Prices paid by processors are based on production costs. There is no control of Ontario's retail pricing. Every dollar collected from processors by DFO is returned to milk producers, less deductions for promotion of milk and dairy products, the costs to transport milk from their farms to the dairies, and administration of DFO, as well as deductions for research. In total these deductions amount to about 6% of the price paid to the farmer. The net price per liter of raw milk that the farmers received from DFO in 2008 was $0.7245; as of this writing, it has been announced that the support price will be increased by $0.01 in 2009.

Dairy farmers are paid both for the amount and the quality of milk they produce, which varies between breeds. (See Exhibit 1 of this appendix.) Revenue for milk sales and costs for transportation and promotion costs are pooled among five provinces—Ontario, Quebec, New Brunswick, Nova Scotia, and Prince Edward Island—which have formed a regional pool known as the P5. This means producers in each of these five provinces all share one large market and also pay the same amount per hectoliter (1 hectoliter = 100 liters) for transportation and promotion.

Appendix Exhibit 1
Comparative Table of the Different Breeds

	Holstein	Jersey	Ayrshire	Milking Shorthorn	Brown Swiss	Guernsey
Description (Size & Colour)	Largest breed Black & white or red & white	Smallest breed Shades of fawn/brown	Large size Red & white	Medium size Red & white often roan	Large breed Silvery brown	Medium size Fawn & white
% of Ontario Dairy Herd	93%	4%	1%	<1%	<1%	<1%
Origin	The Netherlands	Jersey Island	Scotland	England	Switzerland	Isle of Guernsey
Average Annual Milk Production	8 600 litres	6 200 litres	6 800 litres	6 500 litres	7 000 litres	7 000 litres
Average Milk Components (Fat, Protein)	3.8% fat 3.2% protein	4.9% fat 3.8% protein	3.9% fat 3.3% protein	3.9% fat 3.7% protein	3.9% fat 3.5% protein	4.4% fat 3.5% protein
Average Weight at 2 Years Old	575 kg or 1 265 pounds	390 kg or 858 pounds	500 kg or 1 100 pounds	500 kg or 1 100 pounds	575 kg or 1 265 pounds	500 kg or 1 100 pounds

The components or solids in milk—butterfat, protein, and other solids (lactose and minerals)—and how they are used by processors determine milk value. The system of payment is referred to as a multiple component pricing payment system. DFO invoices processors according to the utilization of the raw milk components in each class and in each product. Ontario milk producers are paid for their milk shipments on a monthly basis for the previous month's milk deliveries.

PRICING BASED ON PRODUCTION COSTS

All the P5 provinces support the national cost of production (COP) formula as the basic reference for establishing milk prices for both fluid and industrial milk. "Industrial milk" refers to milk used in the production of dairy products such as butter, cheese, and yogurt. The national COP formula is based on a uniform collection of data from provincial costing studies. The COP figures from each province are weighted according to all milk shares.

In Ontario, the Ontario Dairy Farm Accounting Project (ODFAP) is used as the source of data. ODFAP, which collects farm data from the actual farm records of a representative sample of about 100 Ontario dairy farms, is a joint project of DFO, the Ontario Ministry of Agriculture and Food, the Canadian Dairy Commission, and the University of Guelph. (See Exhibits 2 and 3 of this appendix for the relevant tables.)

Appendix Exhibit 2: Dairy Enterprise Revenue and Expenses – 2007 (per cow)

	Bottom 15	Middle 15	Top 15	All 84
REVENUE				
Milk Sales	$5 169.27	$6 161.05	$6 249.30	$5 999.71
Quality and penalties leavies	—	(21.97)	(5.76)	(15.15)
Cows & Bulls Sold	175.97	147.53	139.20	151.12
Other Dairy Livestock Sold	118.06	95.57	54.72	92.29
Dairy Livestock Inventory Change	98.86	99.44	51.76	90.82
Net Revenue	$5 562.16	$6 481.62	$6 489.22	$6 318.79
DIRECT DAIRY EXPENSES				
Dairy Ration	$86.82	$76.90	$92.27	$81.42
Protein Supplements	347.72	402.95	372.24	387.60
Salt & Minerals	110.61	89.30	108.17	96.48
Milk Replacer & Calf Ration	48.24	51.91	57.01	52.16
Other Purchased Feeds	3.42	22.72	33.79	21.25
Vet & Drugs	153.08	178.99	139.39	167.29
A. I. Fees	82.47	75.80	56.02	73.46
Stable & Milk House Supplies	126.00	117.69	99.87	115.99
Milk Transport & Licence Fees	307.06	368.84	372.27	358.42
Livestock Marketing	12.52	14.59	14.42	14.19
Other Dairy Expense[1]	193.04	184.52	205.10	189.71
Total Direct Expense	$1 470.98	$1 584.21	$1 550.55	$1 557.97
DAIRY SHARE OF CROP EXPENSES				
Bulk Grain & Forage Purchases	$156.26	$147.28	$46.55	$130.89
Seed	93.89	90.38	71.36	87.61
Fertilizers	92.54	112.14	52.64	98.02
Herbicides & Pesticides	26.88	43.73	46.17	41.15
Custom Work	129.06	136.42	150.38	137.60
Fuel & Lubricants	167.96	153.69	120.50	150.31
Field Machinery Repairs	195.94	183.11	115.69	173.36
Land Rent	35.85	52.59	50.98	49.32
Other Crop Expense[2]	49.96	41.18	39.62	42.47
Total Crop Expense	$948.34	$960.52	$693.89	$910.73
Returns Over Direct & Crop Expenses	$3 142.84	$3 936.89	$4 244.78	$3 850.09
ALLOCATED INDIRECT & OVERHEAD EXPENSES				
Barn Equipment & Building Repairs	$262.64	$233.54	$176.31	$228.52
Hired Labour Expenses	754.86	455.30	295.17	480.20
Interest Expense	870.74	572.29	795.10	665.37
Insurance	105.42	76.85	89.74	84.25
Telephone & Hydro	159.81	131.09	99.41	130.56
Taxes	66.22	62.12	38.67	58.66
Other Overhead Expenses[3]	134.33	108.17	104.77	112.23
Total Indirect & Overhead Expenses	$2 354.02	$1 639.36	$1 599.17	$1 759.79
Returns Over Expenses	$788.82	$2 297.53	$2 645.61	$2 090.30
DAIRY LIVESTOCK PURCHASES				
Cows & Bulls Purchased	$87.26	$86.45	$86.54	$86.61
Other Dairy Livestock Purchases	19.64	22.29	8.14	19.29
Total Dairy Livestock Purchases	$106.90	$108.74	$94.68	$105.90
Net Returns	$681.92	$2 188.79	$2 550.93	$984.40
TOTAL LABOUR REQUIRED (Hrs) [4]	154.53	98.43	51.56	100.80

  1. Other diary expense includes bedding materials, feed processing expense, livestock testing and registration, livestock insurance, livestock promotion expense and building rent.
  2. Other crop expense includes twine, seed cleaning, crop insurance and machine rentals.
  3. Other overhead expense includes hardware, car expenses and miscellaneous expense.
  4. Labour estimated based on the recorded hours from daily time sheets.

Appendix Exhibit 3
Basic Farm Production Parameters - 2007

Number of Farms	Bottom 15	Middle 15	Top 15	All 84
Dairy Cows (hd)	44.9	70.6	134.4	77.4
Open Dairy Heifers, 6 months & older (hd)	17.7	23	36.3	24.4
Bred Dairy Heifers (hd)	12.8	21.2	38.4	22.8
Milk Sold/Farm (liters)[1]	316 885	609 471	1 182 762	659 597
Milk Sold/Cow (liters)[1]	6 972	8 512	8 595	8 252
Butterfat test (kg/hl)	4.02	3.87	3.90	3.9
Person-Equivalents of Labour	2.3	2.3	2.2	2.3
Workable Land Farmed (hectares)[2]	138	135	157	140
Average Age of Principal Operator	47.2	47.9	43.4	47.0

ADDITIONAL SOURCES FOR INDUSTRY SPECIFIC DATA (AVAILABLE AS OF JUNE 2009):

Industry Rules and regulations:

http://www.milk.org/Corporate/pdf/Publications-DFOPolicyBook.pdf

Price structure:

http://www.dairyinfo.gc.ca/pdf/dm90904.pdf

Research project with financial data (Exhibits 2 and 3 of the appendix can be found here):

http://www.milk.org/Corporate/pdf/Publications-ODFAPReport.pdf

Ontario Dairy facts and figures (Exhibit 1 of the appendix can be found here):

http://www.milk.org/Corporate/pdf/DairyEducation-FactsAndFiguresEN.pdf

黄昏之星有机农场

Alfred J. Nanni, Jr.
Babson College

Dessislava Pachamanova
Babson College

Julia Shanks
Babson College

屋子里静悄悄的,布雷特开始煮他这天的第一杯咖啡。太阳正从田间升起,雄鸡高啼。这是2001年6月的第一个星期,但对于农场来讲,已经可以看出这很可能是个困难的季节。晚春异乎寻常地湿冷。大雨冲走了许多刚播下的种子。他的特产作物番茄已经因花蒂腐病遭到损失。结果是,产量显然会低于计划数。此时,阳光射入厨房,布雷特必须对如何销售即将收获的作物作出决定。

他的业务在过去几年中已经有了增长,并几乎达到他所认为的财务稳定。他在三个不同的市场渠道上有许多潜在的客户:餐馆、农贸市场和社区支持型农业(community-supported agriculture,CSA)① 订购户。今年的产量低于寻常,他不见得能满足这三个方面的所有需求。因此,他不知道应该供应哪个渠道、各个渠道又应供应多少客户。

公司历史

黄昏之星②有机农场创建于1997年。布雷特·格罗斯加尔(Brett Grohsgal)辞去了他在首都华盛顿的厨师职务,改为种植有机番茄,供应给首都地区高级餐馆。他和妻子克里斯蒂娜(Christine)一起在南马里兰州买下100英亩土地。夫妇俩留了1英亩供个人使用,在上面盖了一栋农舍。他们造了一些农业用建筑(一个谷仓和一个温室),并在四周围上栅栏。为此,他们花费了大笔储蓄,还欠下了不少债。

最初几年收成歉丰。在农场开始有点盈利之前,他们的生活依靠克里斯蒂娜在外面获得的有限的收入。布雷特希望在不久的将来农场会有足够的盈

---

① community-supported agriculture,CSA,根源于瑞士,是消费者为了寻找不受污染的食物,与生产有机作物的农民或农场达成供需协定,直接送货上门的一种供销形式。在中国也已经有了这样的做法。——译者引自《有道词典》

② Even' Star,Evening Star 的简写,我国通称昏星或蠓星,学名长庚星,与启明星(Morning Star)相对。这实际上是一颗行星,即金星(太白星)。本文直译作"黄昏之星"。——译者

利，使他们过上好日子。他感到对未来这个夏天的市场所将做的销售计划对于达成这个目标至关重要。

布雷特必须面对凡农民都要关心的问题，这其实也是任何企业家都要关心的问题：他的价值主张、市场需求与价格、生产的数量和质量（例如他种植什么作物和收成多少）、经营成本和现金流量。

通过三个渠道销售有机农作物

布雷特是个小农户，所以把产品直接卖给客户。最初，他只卖给高级餐馆，通常每个餐馆每星期购入的各类产品总共是8箱。随着农场的扩大，布雷特开始向农贸市场销售。去年他开始通过社区支持型农业（CSA）销售。这三个销售渠道各有其定价方式。另外，这三个渠道所需要的辅助作业和资源利用的水平也各有不同。

布雷特与销售有关的主要投资是一辆送货用的卡车。他购入时花了7 000美元，在报废之前预期能行驶100 000英里，每行驶1英里的保养和修理费约为0.13美元。他还密切注意送货途中的油耗；按这一年加油站的预期价格，即将到来的夏天中每行驶1英里的平均油费为0.21美元。

餐馆渠道

餐馆要求在星期四送货，以供周末大量用餐者之需。布雷特去年给10家餐馆送货，每次往返约220英里，需要整整8个小时。据他估算，在向第一家餐馆送货之后，从第二家开始，每增加一家需要多花费30分钟、5英里路程。

为了给餐馆供货，去年布雷特每周花费6个小时给10家餐馆打电话。他需要告诉厨师们，现在有哪些货，然后再取得他们的订单。厨师们不是非常容易联系到的，有时需要打几次电话才能接通一个。不过，布雷特仍然认为这是一个扩展市场的重要环节，并且打算今年继续这样做。去年，在给餐馆打电话上，布雷特大约每周要花费电话费4.10美元。为每一家餐馆把货物包装起来，大约只花费5分钟。去年有10个客户，每周花在包装并搬上车的劳动为50分钟。图表1列示了每周给这些餐馆送去货的平均箱数。

图表 1
向餐馆送货的每周平均数（10个客户的总量）

	箱数
番茄（大）	21.75
番茄（小）	35
西瓜	4
秋葵	1.5
罗勒	2
黄瓜	9
甘薯	3.33
冬南瓜	2.25

CSA 渠道

CSA 的成员，需在为期 15 个星期的销售季节初，向该组织缴付会员费 400 美元。每个会员每星期都会获得一盒新熟的农产品，按餐馆和农贸市场之间的价格计算，搭配的这一盒农产品约值 27 美元。每个星期的这一盒内装哪些农产品，由布雷特决定。选装的都是当时收获得的产品，但装入哪些品种和数量，则由布雷特定夺。此外，他知道作为特产的大番茄应该是给 CSA 会员送去的主要品种。他认为，如果客户们收到的大番茄少于当季产品的 1/8，他们明年很可能就不会再向他购买了。

跟餐馆一样，在 CSA 的订单方面，也需要每周与对方沟通。这一沟通在电话上所花费的时间要少得多。去年，他在 CSA 渠道方面所花费的长途电话费平均每周仅 0.27 美元。为了扩展对 CSA 会员的服务，他还通过电邮把本周准备配装入盒的农产品种类通知给他的顾客们。他的电邮信箱总是挤满了客户们发来的问题和意见，需要逐一作答。去年，布雷特花费在与 CSA 会员们通信的时间，每周约为 2.5 小时。

布雷特每星期五向 CSA 会员送货。发给所有会员的盒子，都运送到同一个地点。去年，每往返一次约有 70 英里，花费 2 小时。布雷特认为，不管 CSA 会员数有多少，这一里程数和花费的时间是不变的。

为 CSA 渠道所花费的主要劳力，只是把各种农产品装入要发放给会员的盒子而已。每位 CSA 订户每周收到一个纸板盒（根据收成情况不同而不同），装满了农场最近提供的农产品。客户对装入的内容没有选择的余地，因此，当收成好时可以将未销售完的产物装入盒中，这是一个处理剩余产物的绝好方法。图表 2 列示了在一个季节中一个 CSA 盒内各种农产品的比率情况。

图表 2
每个 CSA "盒" 平均装入量

	在一般的收成情况下装入的各项农产品价值所占的平均百分率	CSA 整盒的价格	CSA 整盒中各种农产品的价格
番茄（大）	12.50%	$36.00	$4.50
番茄（小）	8.25%	36.00	2.97
西瓜	10.00%	20.00	2.00
秋葵	5.00%	36.00	1.80
罗勒	5.00%	24.00	1.20
黄瓜	16.67%	24.00	4.00
甘薯	10.00%	36.00	3.60
冬南瓜	18.75%	36.00	6.75
按对 CSA 所用的价格算出每盒农产品的价值			$26.82

通过 CSA 销售的缺点是，花费在每一盒的包装和装车的时间要 8 分钟。去年，布雷特的 CSA 会员客户有 33 个，每周为这些客户包装盒子和装车需要劳力 4.5 小时。为了正确计算企业的利润数字，同时，他也认为需要为自己在这上面所花费的时间按每小时"付出" 10 美元。他支付劳力每小时 10 美元，因而去年每周在这方面的包装和装车"劳力"成本为 44 美元。

农贸市场渠道

夏天的农贸市场，属于高风险/高回报一类的经营。在阳光明媚的日子里，布雷特从农贸市场回来时，往往已把带去的农作物销售一空。他可以把他任何农作物都拿到农贸市场去销售，但因为卡车的容量有限，整个季节只能销售 600 箱。此外，由于买主选购的数量往往比较少、比较挑剔，布雷特在农贸市场上出售农产品的价格能够高于向餐馆或 CSA 会员销售的价格。缺点是如果天气恶劣，就有风险了。最糟的是雨天，顾客不来市场，布雷特卖不掉带回家的，会有半数之多。有些卖不掉的农产品，最终腐烂、只好丢掉，没有任何销售价值。大、小番茄、罗勒和秋葵的情况，尤其如此。根据过去的经验，即下雨的可能性对销售水平和农产品腐坏率的影响，布雷特估计在农贸市场上销售的以上四类农产品的平均损失达 15%。其他几类农产品（西瓜、黄瓜、甘薯和冬南瓜）比较"硬朗"，有一些可以到下个星期再拿到农贸市场上去卖。去年农贸市场销售这些品种的总的损失率为 10%。

去年，布雷特在两个集市日推销。在季节开始时，他就向政府组织者登记要在这两个集市日上推销。每一个集市都要求他在为期 15 个星期的整个季节内，承担占用一个摊位的责任。除了在集市日与组织者见面外，不需要和那些组织者作任何联系。星期六的农贸市场，设在马里兰州的查维切斯（Chevy Chase），往返一次大约 180 英里。为了在上午 9 点开场时就能应对蜂拥而入的顾客，布雷特必须在早上 6 点离家。通常他要到下午 6 点以后才回自己的农场。星期日的农贸市场，设在维吉尼亚州的阿灵顿（Arlington），距离比较近（往返一次约 110 英里），途中和销售所花费的时间要少一个小时。

在农贸市场上销售，占用布雷特很多时间，但这还不是这项业务之所以属于"劳动力密集型"的唯一因素。准备装车，也很花费时间。为每个集市日做准备，要花费他两个小时的时间。因为他需要带去的，是整个一个"便携式零售店"。他必须把标志、横幅、装饰品、能够摺叠的桌子和一个遮阳帐篷包装起来。装车一事至关重要，因为一到达集市，所有这些要向顾客展示的东西，都需要迅速有序地各就各位、安置妥当。

农产品

在夏天的时候，布雷特种植 25 种番茄，广义来说可分为两大类：樱桃（小）番茄和主要作物的（大）番茄。他也种植黄瓜、秋葵、西瓜、西葫芦、甘薯和罗勒。春天的时候,布雷特种植一种播前覆盖作物,亦称苜蓿。在种植夏季作物之前,要把苜蓿翻到土里,为新秧苗提供养料。不同的作物采用不同的苜蓿。番茄用的那一种苜蓿,每英亩种植和翻入土里之下的成本为 50 美元。甘薯不需要有覆盖作物。其余的农作物采用一种含磷较高的苜蓿,每英亩成本为 60 美元。

番茄要先在温室里培育秧苗,需要仔细照料,每天温柔地浇水。然后,逐渐地从小盆移植到中盆、再到比较大的盆,直到它们能承受外界的环境因素为止。布雷特估计,每棵秧苗从种子到植入土里的成本约为 1 美元。他每英亩种植 7000 棵番茄(不论番茄大小,都是如此)。其他作物种植到土里的费用要低一些。例如西葫芦是直接播种的,种子直接撒在土里。

种子和秧苗种在土里后,要用黑色的塑料护盖物遮上,并在护盖物上为植物通一个孔。每覆盖一英亩土地的成本为 133 美元。塑料遮盖物能防止野草在作物周围丛生,避免作物必不可少的水分被蒸发,也可用来遮隔阳光。遇到干旱,要使作物有充分的水分,用它来护盖非常重要。

在干旱期,老天不浇地,就得靠灌溉系统了。在一个季节之中,通常每英亩地在灌溉上要花费 50 美元。当各种作物成熟时,工人采集作物,放进适用于该作物的木条箱(盒)内。把作物运到餐馆去时,用的也是这种容器。一周卖剩下的农产品,也用它作为容器送往农贸市场;当然,农产品必须从箱中取出,向顾客展示。而在向 CSA 订户发货时,农产品必须从箱中取出、挑选分类,然后重新装入纸板箱。

布雷特的决定

作物的产量与气候密切相关。这一个作物成长的季节中,并不风调雨顺。于是布雷特预计,在这个夏天他的 8 种作物中,有 5 种的收成会低于常年。小番茄和秋葵的产量可能比常年低 10%;大番茄可能要低 12.5%;西瓜也可能减产 16.7%,黄瓜减产 25%。

不需要作详细的计算,布雷特也知道他不可能满足潜在客户的全部需求。除了去年供应的 10 家餐馆之外,还有另外 10 家餐馆有意从他这里购货,他相信他能够把产品卖给任何一家。此外他还相信:他的 CSA 订户总数可以从去年的 33 家增加到 90 家,而他向 CSA 付出的会费则仍然是 400 美元不变。

布雷特收集了过去几个季节的一些其他数据。图表 3 列示了与本季作物有关的一些其他数据。图表 4 则列示了当前的各项销售价格。

不管他选择从什么渠道销售,所有的作物都必须收割。另外,对于每一个餐馆客户和他所接受的 CSA 订户,都必须在整个 15 个星期的这一季节中充分供应。如果他在季节中对任何一个客户中断了供应,他的声誉就会受到重大损害,来年有可能不会再获得这整个客户群体了。同样的,他相信一旦决定在农贸市场上销售,在整个的季节中都必须持续参与,不可中断。

布雷特知道,他所做出的每一个决定,对他的成功都至关重要。他必须立即确定整个季节中、他应该在三个客户渠道之间，如何安排他的销售活动。他应该在哪些渠道中经营、每个渠道中又该接受多少客户？他显然需要考虑他所作出的抉择对这个季节的收入的影响。因而他需要对每一种渠道/客户人数的组合的变化所引起的利润增减额作一考量。同时，他还必须时刻记住：他在销售方面作出的抉择，会对未来若干年产生长远的影响。

图表 3
各项生产数据

	每英亩地的种子或秧苗成本	每英亩地的肥料成本	种植的英亩数	每英亩地的收成按标准装入量计算的箱数	每英亩地的人工小时数（种植、照料和收获）
番茄（大）	$7 000.00	$36.00	1.50	310	225
番茄（小）	7 000.00	36.00	1.25	540	200
西瓜	40.00	50.00	2.00	100	15
秋葵	8.00	—	0.08	1 050	1 000
罗勒	7 500.00	20.00	0.10	720	360
黄瓜	12.00	50.00	1.00	335	65
甘薯	1 248.00	—	0.08	1 333	1 350
冬南瓜	12.00	50.00	2.50	53.3	27

图表 4
每一箱的零售价格

	餐馆	CSA	农贸市场
番茄（大）	$40.00	$36.00	$45.00
番茄（小）	26.00	36.00	40.00
西瓜	20.00	20.00	22.50
秋葵	24.00	36.00	40.00
罗勒	18.00	24.00	25.00
黄瓜	24.00	24.00	28.00
甘薯	36.00	36.00	40.00
冬南瓜	36.00	36.00	40.00

Even' Star Organic Farm

Alfred J. Nanni, Jr.
Babson College

Dessislava Pachamanova
Babson College

Julia Shanks
Babson College

The house was quiet as Brett started to brew his first cup of coffee for the day. The roosters had just started to crow as the sun was rising over the fields. It was the first week of June in 2001, but the summer season was already promising to be very difficult for the farm. Late spring had been unseasonably cool and wet. Many seedlings had been washed away during heavy rains. And the tomatoes, his feature crop, had suffered from some blossom-end rot. As a result, yields were going to be clearly lower than planned. But now, with the sun beaming into the kitchen, Brett had to make some decisions about how to sell his crops as they began to come in.

His business had grown over the years, and he was on the verge of reaching what he considered to be financial stability. He had many potential customers in three different market channels: restaurants, farmers' markets, and community-supported agriculture (CSA) subscriptions. Given his lower than usual yields, he would be unlikely to fill that potential demand in any of those three customer segments. As a result, he wondered which channels he should serve and how many customers in each.

COMPANY HISTORY

Even' Star Organic Farms was founded in 1997. Brett Grohsgal quit his job as a chef in Washington, D.C., to grow organic tomatoes for upscale D.C. area restaurants. With his wife Christine, he bought 100 acres in southern Maryland. The couple set aside 1 acre for their personal use and built a farmhouse on it. They built farm buildings (a barn and a greenhouse) and erected fencing. They spent a significant amount from their savings in the process and also assumed significant debt.

The first few years were very lean. Until the farm started showing a profit, they were reliant on Christine's limited outside earnings. Brett hoped the farm would become profitable enough to support them both comfortably in the near future. He felt his selling decisions for the approaching summer market season would be critical in pursuit of that goal.

Brett had to deal with all of the classical concerns of a farmer, which are also standard worries of any entrepreneur: his value proposition, market demand and price, production volume and quality (e. g. , his crop mix and yield), cost of operations, and cash flow.

MARKETING ORGANIC PRODUCE TO THREE SALES CHANNELS

As a small farmer, Brett markets directly to his customers. Initially, he sold exclusively to upscale restaurants. Each restaurant typically purchased a total of about eight cases of mixed varieties of produce per week. As the farm expanded, Brett began to sell at farmers' markets as well. Just last year, he began selling through community-supported agriculture (CSA). Each of the three channels has its own pricing structure. Also, each of the three channels requires different levels of support activity and resource utilization.

Brett's primary investment related to marketing is a truck he uses for his deliveries. He bought it used for $7 000 and expected that it would last him about 100 000 miles, at which point he would scrap it. The truck requires an additional $0. 13 per mile for maintenance and repair. He also monitors his fuel usage for delivery trips. Based on expected pump prices this year, he expects to have an average cost of $0. 21 per mile for fuel in the coming summer.

THE RESTAURANT CHANNEL

Restaurants require deliveries on Thursdays in order to accommodate the weekend rush of diners. Brett's round trip for the deliveries to 10 restaurants last year required 220 miles and took him a full eight-hour day. He figures each restaurant after the first adds another 5 miles and another 30 minutes to his trip.

In order to service the restaurant customers last year, Brett spent 6 hours a week calling the 10 restaurant customers. He needs to let the chefs know what produce is available and then take their orders. Chefs are not the most accessible lot, so it could sometimes take several phone calls to each chef. Still, Brett considers this to be important market development work and plans to do the same this year. Brett spent an average of $4. 10 per week on toll calls to the restaurants last year. Packing the truck for a restaurant delivery run only took 5 minutes for each customer. Last year, with 10 customers, it consumed 50 minutes of laborer time per week. The total average weekly sales mix for the restaurant customers from last year is shown in Exhibit 1.

Exhibit 1
Average Weekly Restaurant Delivery Composition
(Total for 10 Customers)

	Cases
Tomatoes (large)	21.75
Tomatoes (small)	35
Watermelon	4
Okra	1.5
Basil	2
Cucumbers	9
Sweet potatoes	3.33
Winter squash	2.25

THE CSA CHANNEL

The members of the CSA pay a subscription of $400 at the beginning of the 15-week season. Every week, each subscriber gets a box of the currently ripening produce in a mix that yields about $27 worth of produce at prices that fall somewhere between restaurant and farmers' market prices. Brett makes the decision as to what goes into the box each week. The selection is based on the availability of the crops, but Bret is committed to variety and abundance. Further, he knows that his feature crop of big tomatoes is a critical component of the CSA mix. If the customers received less than 1/8th of their seasonal content in big tomatoes, he believed that they would not be likely to return as customers in the following year.

Like restaurants, CSA orders require weekly communication. This involves much less phone time. Last year, his average CSA-related long-distance charges were only $0.70 per week. As a service enhancement for CSA subscribers, however, Brett emails them every week with recipe suggestions for the current week's produce. Invariably, his email inbox is full of questions and comments from his customers that require response. On average, Brett spent about 2.5 hours per week on CSA communication last year.

Brett makes the CSA delivery trip on Fridays. All of the subscriber boxes are dropped off at a single location. Last year, the round trip consumed 2 hours and 70 miles. Brett considers this travel and delivery time to have been a constant, regardless of the number of CSA subscribers he had.

The primary labor time effort required by the CSA simply arises from packing a variety of produce in each of the subscriber boxes. Every week, each CSA customer gets a cardboard box (not the same as a harvest case) full of the different current offerings from the farm. The customer does not get a choice in the contents, so it is a great way to dispose of the farm's excess yields. The overall seasonal ratio of the contents of a CSA box is shown in Exhibit 2.

Exhibit 2
Average Make-up of a Single CSA "Box"

	Approximate Percentage of a Standard Harvest Case	CSA Caselot Price	Extended CSA Price
Tomatoes (large)	12.50%	$36.00	$4.50
Tomatoes (small)	8.25%	36.00	2.97
Watermelon	10.00%	20.00	2.00
Okra	5.00%	36.00	1.80
Basil	5.00%	24.00	1.20
Cucumbers	16.67%	24.00	4.00
Sweet potatoes	10.00%	36.00	3.60
Winter squash	18.75%	36.00	6.75
Total CSA-rate value of box contents			$26.82

The downside in selling through the CSA is that each box takes about 8 minutes to pack and load onto the truck. Last year, Brett had 33 subscribers and the weekly process of boxing and loading CSA produce for those customers required over 4 – 1/2 hours of his laborers time. He pays his laborers $10 per hour, so this packing/loading time cost him $44 per week last year. In order to keep the enterprise income in perspective, Brett also "pays" himself $10 per hour for his "labor."

THE FARMERS' MARKET CHANNEL

The summer farmers' markets are a high-risk/high-return sort of venture. On sunny days, Brett usually returns to his farm with all of his produce sold. He could sell any of his produce in the farmers' markets, but through the course of the season he can only sell 600 cases (limited by truck capacity). Furthermore, since buyers tend to purchase in smaller quantities and select their own produce, Brett can sell at higher prices than either the restaurants or CSA subscribers pay. The downside risk comes with inclement weather. The worst case is rain. Then the customers don't come and Brett returns with as much as half the product unsold. Some unsold produce ends up spoiled and has no sales value. This is especially true of the large and small tomatoes, the okra, and the basil. Based on past experience, factoring in the likelihood of rain, resulting sales levels, and spoilage rates, Brett estimates that on average, he loses 15% of items in those four categories of produce when they are offered through the farmers' markets. The other crops (watermelon, cucumbers, sweet potatoes, and winter squash) are hearty enough to allow some pieces to be offered for sale in the following week. The overall spoilage rate for those varieties was 10% last year.

Brett sold on two market days last year. He registered with the municipal organizers for each one at the beginning of the season. Each market required him to commit to a single stall to be occupied every week for the full 15-week season. There was no further communication with those organizers except face-to-face during the market days. The Saturday farmers' market was in Chevy Chase, MD; it was about 180 miles round trip. In order to be ready for the onslaught of customers at the 9 a.m. opening, Brett had to leave by 6 a.m. He typically did not return to the farm again until 6 p.m. While the Sunday market in Arlington, VA, was closer (only 110 miles round-trip), his travel and selling time was only one hour less.

Selling at the farmers' markets consumes big chunks of Brett's time, but that is not the only aspect that is labor-intense. Preparing the truck is also time-consuming. Preparation for the farmers' markets takes Brett two hours of his own time for each market day. This is because Brett needs to bring a full "portable retail store." He has to pack signs and banners, decorations, folding tables, and a tent awning. The manner in which the truck is packed is important, since the display materials have to be accessible in a sequence that allows for a quick and efficient set-up once he arrives at the market.

THE PRODUCE

In the summertime, Brett grows 25 varieties of tomatoes in two broadly defined classes: cherry (small) tomatoes and main-crop (big) tomatoes. He also grows cucumbers, okra, watermelon, zucchini, sweet potatoes, and basil. In the springtime, Brett plants a pre-seeding cover crop, also known as clover. Just before the summer crops are planted, the clover is mowed into the ground, providing necessary nutrients to the new seedlings. Different clovers are used for the various plants. The tomatoes use a type that costs $50 per acre to plant, grow, and turn under. The sweet potatoes do not require any cover crop. All the remaining crops use a clover that provides higher levels of phosphorous and costs $60 per acre.

The tomatoes are started from seed in the greenhouse. They require careful attention and daily, gentle watering. They are gradually moved from small to medium to larger pots until they are ready to withstand the elements. Brett estimates that it costs about $1 to get each seedling from seed to planted-in-the-ground. He plants 7 000 tomato plants per acre (regardless of the size of the plant's fruit). The other crops are less expensive to get into the ground. For example, the zucchinis are direct-sowed; the seeds are put directly into the ground.

Once the seeds and seedlings are in the ground, they are covered with sheets of black plastic mulch, with holes cut out for each plant. The material required to cover an acre costs $133. The plastic prevents weeds from emerging among the crop plants, prevents evaporation of the plants' requisite water, and acts as a solar blanket. During a drought, this is essential to keeping the plants well hydrated.

During dry spells, the irrigation system provides what nature has not. Over the course of a season, Brett usually spends about $50 per acre on irrigation. As the various crops ripen, workers pick the produce and place it in wood-framed crates (cases) specific to the vegetable type. These are the cases in which items are delivered to the restaurants. They are also the containers in which the week's leftovers are taken to the farmers' markets (although they must be removed for display at the sales stall). Before delivery to the CSA subscribers, however, the vegetables must be unloaded from the cases, sorted, and then repacked into cardboard boxes.

BRETT'S DECISIONS

Crop yield is highly dependent on the weather, and the weather has not been kind this growing season. In fact, Brett expects his yield to be lower than standard for five of his eight crops this summer. Small tomatoes and okra will probably be 10% below standard yield rates. Large tomatoes will probably come in at 12.5% below standard. Watermelon crop will be about 16.7% lower than normal, and cucumber yield will be off by 25%.

Without doing the math, Brett knows he cannot satisfy all of his potential customers. He has an additional 10 restaurants interested in buying from him beyond the 10 he supplied last year and believes he can sell to any or all of them. Furthermore, he believes that, at the $400 subscription price, he could probably increase his CSA client pool from last year's 33 to as many as 90.

Brett gathered together some additional data from last few seasons. Exhibit 3 contains some additional data related to this season's crops. Exhibit 4 lists current selling prices.

All of the produce has to be harvested, regardless of his selling choices. Also, for each restaurant or CSA subscription customer he takes on, he must sell to that customer for the entire 15 – week season. If he stops in the middle of the season for any single customer, his reputation will suffer seriously and he may not be able to return to that entire customer group again next year. Similarly, he believes that the choice to sell at the farmers' markets is a season-long commitment.

Brett knows each decision he makes will be critical to his success. His immediate needs are to determine how he should apportion his sales effort for the current season's crops across the three customer channels. Which channels should he operate in and how many customers should he take on in each channel? Clearly, he needs to consider the effect of his choices on the current season's income. He therefore needs to estimate the net increment in profit for each channel/customer count combination. Yet he must also keep in mind the long-term effect of his choices on sales in future years.

Exhibit 3
Various Production Data

	Cost of Seed or Seedlings per Acre	Fertilizer Cost per Acre	Acres Planted	Standard Caselot Yield per Acre	Labor Hours per Acre (Plant, Care & Harvest)
Tomatoes (large)	$7 000.00	$36.00	1.50	310	225
Tomatoes (small)	7 000.00	36.00	1.25	540	200
Watermelon	40.00	50.00	2.00	100	15
Okra	8.00	—	0.08	1 050	1 000
Basil	7 500.00	20.00	0.10	720	360
Cucumbers	12.00	50.00	1.00	335	65
Sweet potatoes	1 248.00	—	0.08	1 333	1 350
Winter squash	12.00	50.00	2.50	53.3	27

Exhibit 4

Retail Prices per Caselot

	Restaurants	CSA	Farm Market
Tomatoes (large)	$40.00	$36.00	$45.00
Tomatoes (small)	26.00	36.00	40.00
Watermelon	20.00	20.00	22.50
Okra	24.00	36.00	40.00
Basil	18.00	24.00	25.00
Cucumbers	24.00	24.00	28.00
Sweet potatoes	36.00	36.00	40.00
Winter squash	36.00	36.00	40.00

Bridgestone 行为医疗保健中心:为编制计划和控制所作的成本—数量—利润(CVP)分析

A. Ronald Kucic
University of Denver

Lisa M. Victoravich
University of Denver

James E. Sorensen
University of Denver

简介

当年 6 月,Bridgestone 医疗保健中心的常务董事托马斯·拉塞尔(Thomas Russell)博士和会计师苏珊·史密斯(Susan Smyth),正在就更好的理解如何对该中心的经营和对财务业绩实施监督的必要性问题,展开进一步的讨论。Bridgestone 坐落在俄亥俄州克利夫兰市,为有药品滥用问题的个人提供预防、干预和治疗服务。在上一年中,虽然预期会略有盈余,却蒙受了亏损。此后,Bridgestone 的管理层开始关心它的财务业绩。尽管管理层关心并注意到 Bridgestone 的盈利能力问题,但它今年的年度预算仍然预期只有 7 000 美元的微量盈余[①](见图表 1)。

托马斯:从你所编制的财务报告来看,在过去三年中,我们曾为达到收支平衡而不断奋斗。直到最近我们才得以保本,但我仍然担心,只要经营中稍微出一点差错,看来就会把我们置于经营亏损的境地。我已积极努力管理这个中心,我不知道我们应如何做才能避免亏损!

苏珊:不幸的是,我的工作职责在于:业务发生时,把财务数据和次数记入会计账册,对如何监督业绩我没有整体认识。我现在每周工作 40 多个小时,因而我确实不知道还能再多干些什么。也许我们可以雇用个咨询师什么的人,来帮我们一下?

托马斯:事实上,为避免损失从外面请人来帮忙,未尝不是个好办法。因为我受的是心理学方面的训练,我自己在会计方面并没有什么经验。我们需要找个对非营利性的公众服务机构的财务管理有专长的人。

---

① 边际贡献 3 500 000 美元减去固定费用 3 493 700 美元。——译者

BRIDGESTONE 的背景情况

历史和任务

Bridgestone 是坐落在美国中西部的一家治疗麻醉药品滥用的综合门诊中心。自 1985 年以来，Bridgestone 提供一系列的门诊服务，包括咨询、危机干预、戒毒治疗和美沙酮维持疗法。Bridgestone 把自己的任务定为，通过向有需要的个人，提供高质量的行为健康保健，成为治疗和改变人们生活的领导者。基于这样的任务，Bridgestone 对外界承诺，它要通过一些创新的服务和逐一地丰富每一个病人的生活，来推进行为保健工作。

常务董事和员工队伍

中心的常务董事托马斯·拉塞尔博士从俄亥俄大学获得社会工作硕士、又从西北大学获得临床心理学（戒瘾辅导专业）博士学位，已经有了超过 30 年的行为健康戒瘾方面的工作经验。他是美国戒瘾考官协会的成员，并曾是俄亥俄大学心理学院的一名教师。拉塞尔博士在戒瘾领域发表了许多论文，并多次在重要的会议上发表演讲。

除了这位高素质的常务董事之外，Bridgestone 还有一个卓越的员工队伍。中心一直保持着比较低的病人对员工的人数比率；此外，员工中有许多受过良好训练的专业人员，时刻准备着在各种环境下向病人提供良好的服务。Bridgestone 的员工们就像是同一个家庭的成员，并以待人正直和服务专业著称。他们改变了数以千计的人的生活，这是中心成功的关键所在。

病人的表扬信

病人和病人家属的表扬信中包括了这样的内容：

"我要说的是，多谢你们帮助了我的女儿！我认识很多临床专家……事实上我也是其中之一。在自己执业 20 年之后，我对于把自己的女儿送去治疗的经验一直都深有沮丧的感觉，这持续到把她送到 Bridgestone 之前。尽管临床专家不乏其人，……但你们这些人才是真正的**临床专家**——这四个字要用粗体字写出。"

"今天是我恢复清醒一周年的日子。如果没有 Bridgestone 的咨询师们的帮助，我不可能恢复清醒。我真不知道怎么样来表达我的谢意！"

"我对自己在 Bridgestone 所受到的治疗，深表谢意。走向恢复的这条路，崎岖不平。为了使我复原，直到今天我仍然按照必须遵行的治疗程序，每天坚持着做。我认识到具备正直并保持开放的思想，是十分必要的。我现在完全对要求我做到的一切，举双手投降——因为我要取得真正的胜利。"

行为健康和各项戒瘾服务

为治疗不同程度的麻醉药物依赖疾病，从戒毒治疗到保持长期清醒和防止旧病复发，Bridgestone 提供的服务总共有 10 项。

病人预检——对病人的预检，是由戒瘾咨询师来做的。咨询师采用多项手段，确定酗酒或毒瘾问题是否确实存在。如果确诊如此，就有必要确定病情的严重程度，看是不是需要采用药物戒毒，需要对病人提供哪些服务和哪个程度的照料使其安全、顺利地达到清醒。

实验室尿液分析——实验室尿液分析，是为筛洗和干预而作的服务，目的是帮助病人经受住毒品的诱惑。验尿还能提供毒品服用的早期证据，从而对该病人的治疗作出适当的调节。

病历管理——病历管理是监察病情的发展，以及是否遵照所推荐的戒瘾治疗方案实施监督而提供的服务。如有需要，还向各外部单位，如法院、儿童保护服务、颁发执照的机构和雇主提供报告书。

团体心理辅导——在病人处于发病期时，一般认为打破病人被隔离的状态，也就是把他们组成一个群体，对治疗最为有效。在团体咨询的过程中，病人能有机会通过分享经验、倾听别人的自我叙述、获得他人对自己行为所作的反馈。在这样一个团体之中，病人也学会如何提高自己的社交能力。

个别心理辅导——有嗜瘾的人，往往认为自己的问题具有独特性，所以最好单独地与咨询师面谈，才能让他们觉得被更好地理解。个别心理辅导的重点包括病人在教育过程中的进展、参与团体活动、对毒品的监督、遵照医嘱的情况、12 项步骤[②]，以及了解病情有哪些改善，从而使病人获得长期清醒。

危机干预——由于嗜瘾所引起的疾病会带有暴力的性质，Bridgestone 设置了危机干预（又称紧急咨询）这个服务项目，以应对可能引起旧病复发的精神紧张状态、或者帮助病人克服可能导致旧病复发的对毒品的渴望。

重症门诊——门诊治疗的重点在于对个别和团体病人提供教育和心理辅导服务，向每个病人提供一项从嗜瘾中恢复过来，并由自己来实施的戒瘾方案。每个病人每星期需要就诊 3 次，每次 3 小时，根据各人的病情而定，持续 6~8 个星期。

药物干预[③]——这是一项对呈现有《精神失常的诊断和统计手册（第四版）》(*Diagnostic and Statistical Manual of Mental Disorders*, Fourth Edition, DSM-IV) 所述症状的成人、儿童和青少年，提供的评估和监督服务。它包括评估病人对治疗精神疾病的药物的需求并实施监督，提供与精神失常、严重的情绪疾患、冲动控制失常、双重极端性格障碍，以及其他会有碍日常生活的精神疾病有关的药物。

美沙酮维持治疗法——对有鸦片瘾的病人，要按各人的具体情况提供健康护理和处方药美沙酮，帮助他们解除失眠、减轻对鸦片的渴望、使其体内

---

② twelve-step program is 是一套引导酗酒者戒酒的原则，最初由美国匿名戒酒互助会所倡导，披露于 1939 年出版的《匿名戒酒互助会：10 多万人从酗酒中解脱出来的故事》(Alcoholics Anonymous: The Story of How More Than One Hundred Men Have Recovered From Alcoholism) 一书中。——译者

③ medical somatic，somatic 指人的躯干、肉体。这个门诊部的大部分治疗是针对人的精神的，例如提供心理辅导等。但这一项服务则指通过药物处理嗜瘾对肉体的影响。姑译为"药物干预"。——译者

达到生物化学平衡。

随访式戒毒治疗——随访式戒毒治疗（又称门诊戒毒）是使病人不必住院，就能解除对毒品和酒精的依赖。随访式戒毒这种门诊的治疗方法的优点在于给病人正常的日常生活，带来最小的影响。

为行为保健服务提供的医疗补助计划

俄亥俄是美国对行为保健服务实施医疗补助计划的少数几个州之一，虽然在联邦法律中是并不要求这样做的。凡应用医疗补助计划于行为保健服务的州必须对医疗补助计划所支付的是哪些服务项目，作出明确的规定。为了便于病人接受医疗补助计划的偿付款起见，Bridgestone 所提供的各服务项目的内容，必须与俄亥俄州所规定的支付内容相一致。

当一个接受医疗补助计划的病人接受心理健康和/或戒酒、戒毒服务时，当地的"戒酒戒毒和心理健康（Alcohol, Drug Addiction and Mental Health，ADAMH）委员会"、"戒酒戒毒机构（Alcohol and Drug Addiction Services，ADAS）委员会"和"社区心理健康（Community Mental Health，CMH）委员会"向提供服务者支付费用。这个委员会随即从联邦政府取回服务成本的 60%，这笔偿还款通过俄亥俄州工作与家庭服务部（Ohio Department of Job and Family Services，ODJFS），转给俄亥俄州心理健康部（Ohio Department of Mental Health，ODMH）和俄亥俄州戒酒和戒毒部（Ohio Department of Alcohol and Drug Addiction Services，ODADAS）。其余 40% 则从该州和当地的收入中支付。

根据下一年预期的医疗补助计划偿付的比率，编制该中心未来一年和季度的预算，按不同的服务项目，分别详见于图表 1 与图表 2。由于各季度之间对不同服务项目的需求量起伏不大，因而季度预算按年度预算的 1/4 编列。虽然医疗补助计划的偿付款是 Bridgestone 主要的收入来源，但也还有一小部分的收入是来自顾客的私人付款。

服务咨询事务所

如前所述，Bridgestone 曾经历了重大的财务压力，常务董事托马斯一直想知道如何把财务运行稳定在保本水平之上。同时，他希望能够对中心的绩效作持续的量度和监督。由于在本单位没有人能帮助他解决这个问题，托马斯遂与一家享有盛名、为非营利性单位服务的有限责任公司服务咨询事务所联系。这家事务所的业主兼经营者名叫谢里尔·马歇尔（Sheryl Marshall），她还是克利夫兰州立大学的会计教授。该事务所专攻政府和非营利性机构的管理问题。

图表 1
Bridgestone 行为医疗与戒瘾中心
次年年度预算

	预检	验尿	病历管理	团体心理辅导	个别心理辅导	危机干预	重症门诊	药物干预	美沙酮维持治疗法	随访式戒毒治疗	合计
收入											
医疗补助计划											
费率	$40	$100	$80	$30	$90	$140	$110	$200	$15	$260	
服务次数	4 000	11 550	6 000	28 000	12 000	1 500	2 000	800	8 000	1 300	
收入	$160 000	$1 155 000	$480 000	$840 000	$1 080 000	$210 000	$220 000	$160 000	$120 000	$338 000	$4 763 000
州	—	—	—	—	—	—	3 000	—	—	205 000	208 000
私人支付	10 000	500	—	5 000	10 000	—	3 500	—	—	—	29 000
合计	$170 000	$1 155 500	$480 000	$845 000	$1 090 000	$210 000	$226 500	$160 000	$120 000	$543 000	$5 000 000
变动成本											
药物检验	$30 000	$404 250	—	$140 000	$120 000	$30 000	$200 000	$200 000	$96 000	$260 000	$1 480 250
其他	2 500	2 000	$10 000	2 000	2 000	1 000	250	—	—	—	19 750
合计	$32 500	$406 250	$10 000	$142 000	$122 000	$31 000	$200 250	$200 000	$96 000	$260 000	$1 500 000
边际贡献	$137 500	$749 250	$470 000	$703 000	$968 000	$179 000	$26 250	$(40 000)	$24 000	$283 000	$3 500 000
固定费用											
工资福利											1 827 607
咨询费											174 685
租金											419 244
运费											104 811
办公用品											69 874
折旧											873 424
其他											524 055
固定费用合计											$3 493 700

图表 2

Bridgestone 行为健康与戒瘾中心

次年第一季度预算

	预检	验尿	病历管理	团体心理辅导	个别心理辅导	危机干预	重症门诊	药物干预	美沙酮维持治疗法	随访式戒毒治疗	合计
收入											
医疗补助计划											
费率	$40	$100	$80	$30	$90	$140	$110	$200	$15	$260	
服务次数	1 000	2 888	1 500	7 000	3 000	375	500	200	2 000	325	
收入	$40 000	$288 750	$120 000	$210 000	$270 000	$52 500	$55 000	$40 000	$30 000	$84 500	$1 190 750
州	—	—	—	—	—	—	750	—	—	51 250	52 000
私人支付	2 500	125	—	1 250	2 500	—	875	—	—	—	7 250
合计	$42 500	$288 875	$120 000	$211 250	$272 500	$52 500	$56 625	$40 000	$30 000	$135 750	$1 250 000
变动成本											
药物/检验	$7 500	$101 063	—	$35 000	$30 000	$7 500	$50 000	$50 000	$24 000	$65 000	$370 063
其他	625	500	$2 500	500	500	250	63	—	—	—	4 938
合计	$8 125	$101 563	$2 500	$35 500	$30 500	$7 750	$50 063	$50 000	$24 000	$65 000	$375 000
边际贡献	$34 375	$187 313	$117 500	$175 750	$242 000	$44 750	$6 563	$(10 000)	$6 000	$70 750	$875 000
固定费用											
工资福利											456 901
咨询费											43 671
租金											104 811
运费											26 203
办公用品											17 469
折旧											93 356
其他											131 014
固定费用合计											$873 425

在他们第一次见面讨论 Bridgestone 处境的会谈将要结束时，托马斯强调他并不只是要雇用谢里尔把当年的工作做好，他还想知道在此基础上如何持续地衡量和监督 Bridgestone 的绩效。了解这个情况之后，谢里尔就解释说，本量利（CVP）分析对托马斯会有用，他需要做的是收集一些与成本、销售收入和服务量有关的基本信息。她还解释道，CVP 是一项基本的管理会计方法，它对编制计划、控制和决策都有用处。它探究成本、数量或作业水平，以及利润三者之间的关系。

谢里尔要求托马斯提供以边际贡献的格式编制的 Bridgestone 的年度预计利润表。她解释道，这个格式是作 CVP 分析的基础，因为表上把收入和费用，分别按相对于与服务作业量（即各项服务的数量）呈变动或固定的习性来列示。谢里尔通过对 Bridgestone 的经营环境和边际贡献式利润表的了解，可对如何增加利润能力提供建议。她提出的三项关键性建议是：把重点放在保持目标所定的服务量、降低可自行酌定的固定成本，以及向公司和非营利性单位提供外出服务。

服务量

谢里尔从她过去为一些收入依靠医疗补助计划的保健中心提供咨询的经验中知道，达到预期的服务量水平，对于维持盈利目标，至关重要。没有达成预计的服务水平将会使中心无法实现可能的收入和边际贡献。服务水平强调了对提供服务的数量实施监督的重要性，以及确保所提供的由医疗补助计划付款的服务项目上不低于计划的数量。因此，重要的不只是把注意力放在已经达到的边际贡献和净利额上，而且还必须确保实现计划所规定的数量水平。

达成预定的数量的重要性还必须进一步加以强调，因为医疗补助计划的各项费率不能增加，从而也不是增加收入的途径。而且，每年医疗补助计划的资金是有上限的，因而试图逐步提高业务数量的做法来提高收入并不可行。

可自行酌定的固定成本

谢里尔提到，为了达成利润目标，另外一个要注意的方面是降低可自行酌定的固定成本。为此，必须了解约束性固定成本与可酌定固定成本之间的差别。每一个组织总有若干受到约束的成本，例如设施、设备、已经发生的长期债务或组织策略等的成本。租赁费用、为长期债务支付的利息、财产税和关键人员的薪酬都是不会有所变动的，除非经营的范围发生了变化。这些成本被看做是约束性固定成本。例如，为了使该组织持续经营下去，租赁费用或利息是必须付出的。如果不付租赁费用，就可能造成失去一项资产的结果；不向债券持有者支付利息，债券持有者就会接收了企业的经营权。折旧看来只是对历史成本的一个分配过程，实际上它是遵循一定的模式计算的结果，而这一模式是在固定资产购置的当时就已经确定下来了。

可酌定固定成本则不同。如何酌定，依管理层为了达成该组织的目标，如何开支这些成本的决策而定。这些成本的多少，由管理层斟酌确定。例如，从短期看，经理人员可以改变其支付的广告费、差旅费、员工培训费、办公用品或研究与开发成本。在资金短缺的时候，这些成本可以减缩；手头宽裕时，不妨增加。可酌定固定成本，通常可以依据对近期成本的考量而改变；但从长远来看，长期地完全不予开支，则属不智之举。谁愿意年复一年地在一个为了提高利润数字，而把员工培训成本降低到零的单位里工作呢？降低广告费用固然在短期内不至于损及销售收入，但对销售收入的长远影响又如何呢？也许到其他州的出差费可以在一个短时间内不予开支，但如果长期地不派人去其他州参加全国性的专业会议，最终会对该组织的业绩产生什么影响呢？

对 Bridgestone 医疗保健中心而言，折旧和租金可能属于约束性成本，而其他各项（诸如薪水和福利、咨询费用、交通运输、办公用品）则可能属于可酌定的固定成本。谢里尔鼓励托马斯把固定成本中哪些属于可斟酌确定的、哪些是约束性的，加以区别。这样，他就可以对可酌定固定成本作适当削减，以达成 Bridgestone 的利润目标。这也使他能够认识到，在某种程度上，固定成本实际是"可斟酌确定"的，以及它们的开支水平从长远或短期来看是否可以有所降低。

外出服务项目

谢里尔担任咨询的一些行为医疗保健中心，曾通过向公司、政府机关或其他非营利性公司提供外出服务项目，来增加收入。可能的项目包括为酗酒、其他麻醉药瘾或行为健康咨询等问题提供给员工辅导项目（employee assistance programs，EAP）或其他种类的项目。美国卫生与公众服务部报告称，精神疾病所引起损失的工作天数和危害，比许多其他慢性疾病（诸如糖尿病、气喘和关节炎）更多[4]。因精神疾病和滥用药物引起的效率低下而损失的工作天数，每年约达 2.17 亿天，使美国的职工每年损失 170 亿美元。

Bridgestone 可以让它的人员去到客户处或客户所指定的场所（为确保匿名起见），向这些病患者提供服务。为这些服务支付各项费用的可能是各个公司。如果这些成为经常性的服务，将会是一种有着很高边际贡献的补充和经常性的收入来源。真正大的公司可能会向员工提供员工辅导项目（EAP）或咨询性的服务项目，但小一些的公司则不能。因而这一类合约对大公司非常具有吸引力，它能提高员工的福利而所费又不多。为这些公司所提供服务的成本，属于变动成本（按服务量而变化），而不是固定成本，即不需要因这些咨询而另外雇用永久性的员工。这对 Bridgestone 可能是个优势，因为该中心已经为这些咨询师支付了固定的薪酬。

---

[4] 见 U. S. Department of Health and Human Services. Mental Health: A Report of the Surgeon General — Executive Summary. Rockville, MD: U. S. Department of Health and Human Services, Substance Abuse and Mental Health Services Administration, Center for Mental Health Services, National Institutes of Health, National Institute of Mental Health; 1999. 亦可访查网址：http://www.surgeongeneral.gov/library/mentalhealth/home.html——原注

可以提供的服务项目中包括：
- 帮助该单位的管理层，解决由于精神健康或滥用麻醉药物而影响工作效率和无故缺席问题。
- 帮助有效地实施监督管理。
- 帮助员工应对由行为或其他健康问题引起的业绩恶化的情况。
- 帮助应对导致残障与影响恢复工作有关的各项问题。
- 帮助辨识可能因工作组织的原因而造成的情绪紧张问题。
- 帮助该单位贯彻无毒品工作场所的政策和规章，以及准备应对与各项心理问题相关的恐怖主义问题。

担任该单位管理当局的内部咨询人员，就员工的行为健康问题提供咨询意见。

要求

请以业务便函的格式向 Bridgestone 行为医疗保健中心执行董事托马斯·拉塞尔博士提出，看来该中心只能勉强保本和财务业绩下降的原因所在。你会向拉塞尔博士提出哪些建议，来改善该中心当前的运营状况，他又能如何对它未来的业绩实施有效的监督？在你的信函中，应该详述下列各点：

讨论题

1. Bridgestone 来年预算的加权平均边际贡献（weighted average contribution margin，WACM）百分率是多少？

2. 对 Bridgestone 的管理层来说，边际贡献（WACM）百分率高，意味着什么？

3. Bridgestone 是不是能够为明年制订计划，做到保本或收入稍高于费用（有一点利润）？如果该中心能够达到保本或收入稍高于费用，而你担心一些事项可能造成损失，你会做些什么试图改变这个情况呢？（你可能考虑到在中心内或向中心外提供一些服务项目。）

4. CVP 分析中，服务性收入的安全边际是一项有用的内容。
此数是一个金额（$），也可以是一个百分率（%）。Bridgestone 明年的预计安全边际是多少？回答这个问题，并解释它对拉塞尔博士意味着什么？

5. 固定成本可能是可酌定的、也可能是约束性的。请根据案例中所陈述的内容，指出哪些成本是属于可以斟酌确定的。假定管理层可以把可酌定固定成本减少 10%，这将对 Bridgestone 的保本点收入产生什么影响？

6. 在 Bridgestone 第二年的经营中，需要更多地注意哪些服务项目？（提示：这些服务项目相对 WACM 的贡献百分比是多少，其总的边际贡献又是多少？来自哪些服务项目？）

7. 加权平均边际贡献（WACM）的预算百分率，可以如何用来帮助对 Bridgestone 的实际经营实施控制？

8. 如果在一个预期收入水平和固定成本数的情况下，确定了一个加权平均边际贡献（WACM），同时又确定了一个预期的收入水平和固定成本的计划数，而 WACM 的预算百分率在第二年（未来）的时间段中事实上是实现了，那么如果总收入下降到预算水平以下或固定成本的增加超过了预算水平，则该组织是不是仍然会蒙受亏损呢？你能不能解释：虽然在未来的时间段中实现了计划的 WACM 百分率，为什么仍然会亏损呢？

9. 你能否用数字来表明，财务上的亏损是如何产生的？请说明下述三种可能的前景所产生的结果：

a. 如果 Bridgestone 的团体心理辅导项目的服务量，在第一季度中减少 10%，则在财务方面会对它造成什么影响？

b. 如果 Bridgestone 的团体心理辅导服务项目的偿付比率，在第一季度减少 10%，则在财务上会对它造成什么影响？

c. 如果季度收入总额维持不变，但因病历管理从医疗补助计划所得的季度收入减少 48 000 美元（服务量为 600 次，每次 80 美元），同时为团体心理辅导从医疗补助计划所得的季度收入增加 48 000 美元（服务量为 1 600 次，每次 30 美元），则会造成什么财务影响？请注意：数量的变化会使收入总额、变动成本总额和边际贡献发生变化。假定私人在团体咨询中所支付的费率，与医疗补助计划的费率维持不变（每单位 30 美元）。

d. 如果在第一季度中，Bridgestone 的固定成本增加 1%，则在财务上会对它造成什么影响？

10. 就 CVP 分析这项工作，你会向 Bridgestone 的管理层提出哪些总体的建议？

11. 作为会计师，通常会把重点放在一个可增加企业盈利性的定量方法（如 CVP）上。但对会计师来说，善于跳出定式思维，辨识增加利润的各项途径，是很重要的。你可能提出哪些建议，来提高 Bridgestone 的盈利能力？

Bridgestone Behavioral Health Center: Cost-Volume-Profit (CVP) Analysis for Planning and Control

A. Ronald Kucic
University of Denver

James E. Sorensen
University of Denver

Lisa M. Victoravich
University of Denver

INTRODUCTION

In June of the current year Dr. Thomas Russell, Executive Director, and Susan Smyth, Accountant, at the Bridgestone Behavioral Health Center were discussing the necessity of gaining a better understanding of how to monitor the Center's operating and financial performance. Located in Cleveland, Ohio, Bridgestone provides prevention, intervention, and treatment services for individuals with substance abuse problems. Bridgestone's management is concerned about its financial performance after realizing a loss in the prior year although a small profit was projected. Despite management's concern and attention of Bridgestone's profitability troubles, the Center's annual budget once again contains a projection for a meager profit of $7 000 (see Exhibit 1).

Thomas: According to the financial reports that you have prepared, we have been fighting to reach breakeven over the past three years. We have been able to just get past breakeven recently, but I am worried—it seems like only a slight variation in our operations could throw us into an operating loss. I've been actively involved in managing the Center, and I don't understand how we avoid showing a loss!

Susan: Unfortunately, I have no oversight with respect to monitoring performance since my job is to input the financial and units of service numbers into the accounting system as they occur. I am currently working more than 40 hours a week so I am not sure what else I could do. Maybe we can hire someone like a consultant to help us?

Thomas: In reality, securing some outside assistance seems to be a good option to avoid future losses. Since my training is in psychology, I don't have the accounting background to take the task on myself. We need someone who specializes in financial management for nonprofit human service organizations.

BRIDGESTONE BACKGROUND

HISTORY AND MISSION

Bridgestone is a comprehensive outpatient substance abuse treatment center located in the Midwest United States. Since 1985, Bridgestone has offered a continuum of outpatient services, including counseling, crisis intervention, detoxification, and methadone maintenance. The Bridgestone mission is to be a leader in healing and changing lives by providing high quality behavioral health care and rehabilitation to all individuals in need. With this mission, the Center promises to advance behavioral healthcare through the creation of innovative services and enriching the lives of patients one by one.

EXECUTIVE DIRECTOR AND SUPPORTING STAFF

Dr. Thomas Russell, Executive Director, has over 30 years of behavioral health addiction experience and holds a Masters of Social Work from Ohio University and a Ph. D. in Clinical Psychology with a specialization on Addiction Counseling from Northwestern University. He is a fellow of the American College of Addiction Examiners and is a former faculty member of the Ohio University Department of Psychology. Dr. Russell is the author of numerous papers in the field of addictions and presents frequently at major conferences.

In addition to a highly qualified Executive Director, Bridgestone has an outstanding support staff. They consistently maintain a low client-to-staff ratio with highly trained professionals who are well prepared to support patients in a large array of circumstances. The staff members at Bridgestone are like a family and are defined by their integrity and expertise. They are the key reason for the Center's success in terms of the thousands of lives that they have changed.

PATIENT TESTIMONIALS

Patient and family member testimonials include:

" I wanted to say thank you for helping my daughter! I know of lots of therapists... in fact I am one. After 20 years of practice I was very frustrated sending my daughter to treatment until Bridgestone. Yes there are therapists... but your folks are THERAPISTS, with a capital T. "

" Today is my one year anniversary of sobriety, which would not have been possible without the help of the counselors at Bridgestone. I can't say thank you enough!"

" I'm thankful to Bridgestone for the treatment I received. The road to recovery was not an easy road back. I still do the same elementary things today that I had to do to achieve recovery. I realized that honesty and open-mindedness was a must. I had to surrender all—I wanted real success. "

BEHAVIORAL HEALTH AND ADDICTION SERVICES

Bridgestone offers 10 services designed to treat a large array of substance dependencies from the point of detoxification to supporting long-term sobriety and preventing relapses.

Patient Assessment—Patient assessment is performed by an addiction counselor who uses a number of methods to determine if an alcohol or drug use problem truly exists. If such a diagnosis is established, it is necessary to determine the extent or severity of disease, if there is a need for medical detoxification, and the services or level of care required to safely and successfully achieve sobriety.

Lab Urinalysis—Laboratory urinalysis services are performed for screening and intervention purposes. This is aimed at helping the patient withstand urges to use drugs. Such monitoring also can provide early evidence of drug use so that the individual's treatment plan can be properly adjusted.

Case Management—Case management serves to monitor patient progress and compliance with recommended addiction treatment plans. Reports to outside parties such as courts, children's protective services, licensing boards, and employers are provided as needed.

Group Counseling—Groups are considered the most effective method of breaking patterns of isolation, which is typical of clients during their active addiction stage. During group counseling, clients have the opportunity to examine their thoughts through sharing, listening, and receiving feedback from their peers. In a group setting, clients also learn to develop social skills.

Individual Counseling—Individuals with addictions often consider their problems unique and, therefore, are best understood in a one-on-one session with their counselor. Individual counseling sessions focus on the patient's progress in the educational process, group participation, drug monitoring, compliance, 12 - step work, and identification of areas for improvement to achieve long-term sobriety.

Crisis Intervention—Due to the volatile nature of the disease of addiction, Bridgestone provides crisis intervention or emergency counseling for stressful situations that may lead to relapse or to help patients work through cravings or urges that could lead to a relapse.

Intensive Outpatient—Outpatient care focuses on education and counseling in both individual and group settings to achieve abstinence and to develop a self-responsible plan of addiction recovery for each patient. The program lasts six to eight weeks depending on individual progress and involves three three-hour sessions per week.

Medical Somatic—The service evaluates and monitors the needs of adults, children, and adolescents exhibiting symptoms associated with a *Diagnostic and Statistical Manual of Mental Disorders*, Fourth Edition, (DSM-IV) diagnosis. (DSM-V is expected in 2013.) This consists of evaluating a patient's need for psychotropic medications associated with psychotic disorders, severe mood disorders, impulse control disorders, bi-polar disorders, and other psychiatric conditions impairing daily functioning.

Methadone Maintenance—Patients with an opiate addiction are provided with individualized healthcare and medically prescribed methadone to relieve withdrawal symptoms, reduce the opiate craving, and bring about a biochemical balance in the body.

Ambulatory Detoxification—Ambulatory detoxification (also known as outpatient detoxification) is designed to safely detoxify patients from drugs and alcohol without a hospital admission. Ambulatory detoxification as an outpatient treatment has the advantage of causing minimal disruption to a patient's normal day-to-day life.

MEDICAID FOR BEHAVIORAL HEALTH SERVICES

Ohio is one of the few states that includes behavioral health services in its Medicaid benefits package, although it is not required to do so by federal law. States that cover behavioral health services must clearly define which services are covered by Medicaid. To facilitate receiving payment for Medicaid patients, the types of services Bridgestone offers are consistent with those defined as covered services by the state of Ohio.

When a Medicaid client receives mental health and/or alcohol and drug addiction services, the local Alcohol, Drug Addiction and Mental Health (ADAMH) Board, Alcohol and Drug Addiction Services (ADAS) Board or the Community Mental Health (CMH) Board pays the provider. The Board is then reimbursed for 60% of the cost by the federal government, which flows to the Boards through the Ohio Department of Mental Health (ODMH) and the Ohio Department of Alcohol and Drug Addiction Services (ODADAS) via an interagency with the Ohio Department of Job and Family Services (ODJFS). The remaining 40% Medicaid match comes from both state and local sources.

The Medicaid reimbursement rates for each service type and the respective level of service expected for the upcoming year are used in preparing the Center's annual budget and quarterly budget as presented in Exhibit 1 and Exhibit 2, respectively. Since there is modest fluctuation in the demand for services from quarter to quarter, the quarterly budget is 25% of the annual budget. Although Medicaid reimbursement is the primary source of revenue for Bridgestone, a minimal amount of revenue is generated from private pay customers.

SERVICE CONSULTING PLUS, LLC

As identified earlier, Bridgestone has experienced significant financial stress, and the Executive Director, Thomas, was inquisitive about how to stabilize financial operations above a break-even level. As well, he would like to gain the ability to measure and monitor the Center's continuing performance. Faced with the lack of internal personnel who could help with this issue, Thomas contacted *Service Consulting Plus, LLC*, a local consulting firm with a reputation for working with nonprofit organizations. The firm is owned and operated by Sheryl Marshall, who is also an accounting professor at Cleveland State University. Her firm specializes in the management of governmental and nonprofit organizations.

At the end of their initial meeting to discuss the situation at Bridgestone, Thomas stressed that he didn't simply want to hire Sheryl to get the job done for the current year, but rather that he wanted to learn how to measure and monitor the financial performance of Bridgestone on an ongoing basis. With this in mind, Sheryl explained that Cost-Volume-Profit (CVP) analysis would be useful to Thomas after he gathered some basic information about costs, revenues, and units of service. She explained that CVP is a fundamental management accounting tool that is useful for planning, control, and decision making. It explores important relationships between costs, volume or activity levels, and profit.

Sheryl asked Thomas to provide her with Bridgestone's annual budgetary income statement in a contribution margin format. She explained that this format is the basic foundation for CVP analysis since it presents revenues and expenses based on their variable or fixed behavior in relation to service activity (namely, volume of services). Sheryl's understanding of Bridgestone's operating environment and the contribution margin income statement will enable to provide suggestions regarding how to increase profitability. The three key suggestions include a focus on maintaining targeted service volume, reducing discretionary fixed costs, and offering off-campus programs to companies and nonprofits.

SERVICE VOLUME

Sheryl's prior experience consulting for health centers that rely on Medicaid

Exhibit 1
Bridgestone Behavioral Health and Addiction Center
Next Year's Annual Budget

	Assessment	Urinalysis	Case Management	Group Counseling	Individual Counseling	Crisis Intervention	Intensive Outpatient	Medical Somatic	Methadone Maint.	Ambul Detox	Total
Revenue											
Medicaid											
Rate	$40	$100	$80	$30	$90	$140	$110	$200	$15	$260	
Units of Service	4 000	11 550	6 000	28 000	12 000	1 500	2 000	800	8 000	1 300	
Revenue	$160 000	$1 155 000	$480 000	$840 000	$1 080 000	$210 000	$220 000	$160 000	$120 000	$338 000	$4 763 000
State	—	—	—	—	—	3 000	—	—	—	205 000	208 000
Private Pay	10 000	500	—	5 000	10 000	—	3 500	—	—	—	29 000
Total	$170 000	$1 155 500	$480 000	$845 000	$1 090 000	$210 000	$226 500	$160 000	$120 000	$543 000	$5 000 000
Variable Costs											
Medications/Tests	$30 000	$404 250		$140 000	$120 000	$30 000	$200 000	$200 000	$96 000	$260 000	1 480 250
Other	2 500	2 000	$10 000	2 000	2 000	1 000	250	—	—	—	19 750
Total	$32 500	$406 250	$10 000	$142 000	$122 000	$31 000	$200 250	$200 000	$96 000	$260 000	$1 500 000
Contribution Margin	$137 500	$749 250	$470 000	$703 000	$968 000	$179 000	$26 250	$(40 000)	$24 000	$283 000	$3 500 000
Fixed Expenses											
Salaries & Benefits											1 827 607
Consulting Fees											174 685
Rent											419 244
Transportation											104 811
Office supplies											69 874
Depreciation											873 424
Other											524 055
Total Fixed Expense											$3 493 700

Exhibit 2
Bridgestone Behavioral Health and Addiction Center
Quarter 1 Next Year's Budget

	Assessment	Urinalysis	Case Management	Group Counseling	Individual Counseling	Crisis Intervention	Intensive Outpatient	Medical Somatic	Methadone Maint.	Ambul Detox	Total
Revenue											
Medicaid											
Rate	$40	$100	$80	$30	$90	$140	$110	$200	$15	$260	
Units of Service	1 000	2 888	1 500	7 000	3 000	375	500	200	2 000	325	
Revenue	$40 000	$288 750	$120 000	$210 000	$270 000	$52 500	$55 000	$40 000	$30 000	$84 500	$1 190 750
State	—	—	—	—	—	—	750	—	—	51 250	52 000
Private Pay	2 500	125	—	1 250	2 500	—	875	—	—	—	7 250
Total	$42 500	$288 875	$120 000	$211 250	$272 500	$52 500	$56 625	$40 000	$30 000	$135 750	$1 250 000
Variable Costs											
Medications/Tests	$7 500	$101 063	—	$35 000	$30 000	$7 500	$50 000	$50 000	$24 000	$65 000	$370 063
Other	625	500	$2 500	500	500	250	63	—	—	—	4 938
Total	$8 125	$101 563	$2 500	$35 500	$30 500	$7 750	$50 063	$50 000	$24 000	$65 000	375 000
Contribution Margin	$34 375	$187 313	$117 500	$175 750	$242 000	$44 750	$6 563	$(10 000)	$6 000	$70 750	$875 000
Fixed Expenses											
Salaries & Benefits											456 901
Consulting Fees											43 671
Rent											104 811
Transportation											26 203
Office supplies											17 469
Depreciation											93 356
Other											131 014
Total Fixed Expense											$873 425

reimbursement for revenue has taught her the importance of achieving projected levels of service volume in order to maintain profit targets. Missing the projected levels of service will cause centers to pass up potential revenue and contribution margin. Service levels underscore the importance of monitoring the volume of delivered service and to ensure that it doesn't fall behind the planned volume when Medicaid is involved. Thus, it's not only important to focus on the achieved contribution margin and bottom line, it's also important to ensure that the planned level of volume in achieved.

The importance of meeting the project volume is further highlighted because Medicaid rates don't increase and, as a result, aren't a means of increasing revenue. Further, annual Medicaid funding is capped, so attempting to increase volume over time to increase revenues isn't possible.

DISCRETIONARY FIXED COSTS

Sheryl mentions that another area to focus on to achieve profit targets is a reduction in discretionary fixed costs. In order to use this avenue, it's necessary to understand the difference between committed fixed costs and discretionary fixed costs. Every organization has some costs to which it is committed, for example, costs for facilities, equipment, long-term debt arrangements, or organizational strategy. Lease payments, interest payments on long-term debt, property taxes, and salaries of key personnel may only change if a major shift in the scope of operations occurs. These costs are viewed as committed fixed. The lease payments or interest payments, for example, have to be made in order for the organization to stay in operation. A failure to pay a lease payment may result in the loss of an asset or a failure to pay interest to bondholders may result in the bondholders taking over the business. Depreciation, while an allocation of historic costs, usually follows a pattern set at the time of the asset acquisition.

Discretionary fixed costs, on the other hand, are set because management has decided to incur these costs to meet organizational goals. These costs may vary at the discretion of management. Managers, in the short-run for example, could vary advertising, travel, employee training, office supplies, or research and development costs. In dire times, these costs could be decreased, and in abundant times they could be increased. Usually the discretionary fixed costs may be changed to meet short-run cost concerns, but it's usually unwise to reduce all discretionary completely or for long periods of time. Who would want to work for an organization that reduced its training costs to zero year after year just to improve the bottom line? While reducing advertising costs in the short-run might not hurt revenues, what about the long-run effects on revenues? Perhaps out-of-state travel could be trimmed in the short-run, but would the failure to attend national professional meetings out-of-state eventually have an unfavorable effect on organizational performance?

In the Bridgestone Behavioral Health Center case, depreciation or rent may be committed while others (such as salaries and benefits, consulting fees, transportation, office supplies, and other) may be discretionary. Sheryl encourages Thomas to identify which fixed costs are discretionary and which are committed. He then can make a modest reduction in the discretionary fixed costs to achieve Bridgestone's profit objective. This will also give him an idea of how "discretionary" the identified fixed costs are in reality and whether the level can be reduced in the long-term or short-term.

OFF-CAMPUS PROGRAMS

Other behavioral health centers that Sheryl has consulted for have increased revenue by offering off-campus programs to corporations, governmental departments, or other nonprofit corporations. Possibilities include employee assistance programs (EAP) to deal with alcohol or other drug disorders or behavioral health counseling or other kinds of programs. According to the United States Department of Health and Human Services, mental illness causes more days of work loss and work impairment than many other chronic condition, such as diabetes, asthma, and arthritis. [①]Approximately 217 million days of work are lost annually due to productivity decline related to mental illness and substance abuse disorders, costing Unites States employers $17 billion each year.

To provide services such as these, the idea is to use Bridgestone talent, but at the client's premises or a location selected by the client (to ensure anonymity). These would be companies that could pay for these services. If the services are used on a regular basis, they could be a supplemental and steady source of revenue with high contribution margins. Really large companies may be able to afford EAP or counseling programs, but smaller ones can't, so this type of contract would be attractive to boost employee benefits at a minimum cost. The cost to these companies could be a variable one (based on usage) without incurring the fixed cost of hiring permanent staff to do the counseling. It could be an advantage to Bridgestone because the Center is already incurring the fixed salary expense of the counselor.

Various services that could be offered include:

• Support management in addressing issues of productivity and absenteeism that may be caused by mental health or substance abuse problems.

---

① U. S. Department of Health and Human Services. Mental Health: A Report of the Surgeon General — Executive Summary. Rockville, MD: U. S. Department of Health and Human Services, Substance Abuse and Mental Health Services Administration, Center for Mental Health Services, National Institutes of Health, National Institute of Mental Health; 1999. Available online at: http://www.surgeongeneral.gov/library/mentalhealth/home.html.

- Support effective supervisory practices
- Assist employees with deteriorating performance relating to behavioral or other health problems
- Address work-related issues influencing disability or return to work
- Assist in the identification of stress-related problems that may be a result of work organization
- Assist the organization in its response to drug-free workplace policies and regulations and disaster and terrorism preparedness as it relates to psychosocial issues
- Serve as an internal consultant to management regarding issues of employee behavioral health.

REQUIREMENT

In business memo format addressed to Dr. Thomas Russell, Executive Director of Bridgestone Behavioral Health Center, describe why the Center is appearing to barely break even and what might cause decreases in financial performance. What recommendations would you offer to Dr. Russell for improving the current operation of the Center and how he can effectively monitor the Center's future performance? Included in your memo should be a discussion about the following points:

ISSUES FOR DISCUSSION

1. What is the weighted average contribution margin (WACM) percentage for Bridgestone's next annual budget?

2. What does a high weighted average contribution margin (WACM) percentage mean for the management of Bridgestone?

3. Is Bridgestone able to *plan* for breakeven or a modest over-recovery of expenses (or profit) for the next year? If the Center achieves breakeven or a modest over-recovery and you are concerned about events that could cause a potential loss, what would you try to change? (You may consider both on- and off-campus programs.)

4. A useful component of CVP analysis is the margin of safety for service revenue that can be calculated as a dollar amount ($) or as a percentage (%). What is Bridgestone's project margin of safety for next year? Interpret your answer in terms of what it means to Dr. Russell.

5. Fixed costs can be discretionary or committed. Using your judgment based on the discussion in the case, identify which costs are likely to be discretionary. Assuming that management is able to decrease discretionary fixed

costs by 10%, what would be the impact on Bridgestone's break-even point revenues?

6. As Bridgestone operates during the next year, do some services deserve more attention than others? (Hint: What is their relative contribution to the WACM % and to the total contribution margin? Which services?)

7. How can the budgetary weighted average contribution margin (WACM) percentage be used to help *control* the actual operations of Bridgestone?

8. If a budgetary weighted average contribution margin (WACM) percentage has been developed with an *expected* level of revenue and a *planned* fixed cost and the budgetary WACM percentage is in fact achieved in the next (future) time period, could the organization still face losses if the total revenue drops below the budgeted level or *total* fixed costs increase beyond the budgeted levels? Can you explain how losses still might occur even though the *planned* WACM *percentage* is being realized in the future time period?

9. Can you demonstrate with numeric examples how financial losses *might* occur? Describe the effects of the following three possible scenarios:

a. What is the financial impact if Bridgestone's group counseling unit of service *volume* decreases by 10% during the first quarter?

b. What is the financial impact if Bridgestone's *reimbursement rate* for group counseling service decreases by 10% during the first quarter?

c. What would be the financial impact, if any, if the *total* quarterly revenue remains the same but the quarterly Medicaid Revenue for Case Management *decreases* by $48 000 (600 units of service at $80 per unit) while quarterly Medicaid Revenue for Group Counseling *increases* by $48 000 (1 600 units of service at $30 per unit)? Note the change in volume changes total revenues, total variable costs, and contribution margin. Assume the unit price of Private Pay services in Group Counseling is the same as for Medicaid Services ($30 per unit of service).

d. What is the financial impact if Bridgestone's fixed costs increase by 1% during the first quarter?

10. What are your *overall recommendations* for Bridgestone's management regarding the use of CVP analysis?

11. As accountants, it is common to focus on quantitative tools such as CVP analysis to increase the profitability of a business. But it is important for accountants to think outside of the box to identify avenues of increasing profitability. What suggestions could you provide to assist Bridgestone in increasing profitability?

阿帕鲁萨县日托中心

Kristen Irwin
Truman State University

Debra Kerby
Truman State University

Sandra Weber
Truman State University

背景

阿帕鲁萨县日托中心（Appaloosa County Day Care Center, Inc., ACDC）刚开始经营时，设在一所空仓库里，经翻修改造增设了几个浴室和厨房设施。ACDC 的目标[①]在于给本社区和周围地区的居民提供优质、实惠的日托服务。它服务的区域是农村一个经济萧条的县，老是排在该州人均收入最低的 10% 之列。这个日托中心的七位董事都是志愿者，分别来自该社区的不同机构——学区、社区学院、医院、公众服务部（或社会服务部）等。这些董事有处理公众服务的各方面的经验，可以照管日托服务，但大部分都没有财会方面的经验。因为他们对日托工作在财务上是不是可以支撑得住负有责任，他们起先把注意力集中在该中心的任务——为劳工阶级的家庭提供负担得起的儿童照管服务。因此，董事会制订了照管儿童的费率，目的在于使居民负担得起；通过提供高质量的服务使日托中心达到盈亏平衡的足够收入。

从创立时起，这个中心还面对另外一个重大挑战。它是该社区提供这一类服务的第一家，因而大家对设立一个"机构"来提供日托服务，普遍存在着负面的看法。当地的一些家庭宁愿选择由朋友或亲戚提供的居家日托服务。这一类看法和偏好，加上日托的管理不善，使这家中心长期以来一直在财务上挣扎。ACDC 几乎要被迫关门。ACDC 的这种财务状况并不少见，有许多社区性的日托机构在勉强维持经营。

日托业收入和成本的一般情况

日托服务整个行业的毛利都很低。通常营利性日托的毛利大约只有

[①] mission，或译"使命"。——译者

4%,全部成本中70%用来支付工资和其他与员工有关的成本(Helburn,1995,172,176)。州政府公众服务部关于颁发服务执照的规定,使与员工有关的各项成本大幅升高。这些规定要求员工与儿童的人数成一定的比率,所有的持有执照的机构都必须遵行。例如,婴儿(年龄为2周到2岁)照管的规定是,每四个儿童必须有一位员工(见图表1中所示的规定摘要)。因此,如果中心只付给最低工资(目前联邦政府的规定是每小时7.25美元,即税前为每小时7.80美元),为每个入托的婴儿要在员工身上支付每小时1.95美元。此外,还必须考虑到,为每位员工安排照管的婴儿数少于4个时,对托儿所的收入所带来的影响。如果这个比率下降,每小时的收入就会随之下降;然而,付给员工的小时工资依然不变,这就立即造成亏损。公众服务部对不同年龄的入托儿童对员工比率的要求的摘要,请参阅图表1。

图表1

公众服务部儿童照管规定的摘要

员工比率。员工对儿童的比率应为:

儿童年龄	员工对儿童人数的最低比率
两星期到两岁	每4个儿童一人
两岁	每6个儿童一人
三岁	每8个儿童一人
四岁	每12个儿童一人
五到十岁	每15个儿童一人
十岁及以上	每20个儿童一人

资料来源:公众服务部,2008。托儿所和幼儿园执照发放标准和手续。Comm 204,8月。

除了人工以外,对日托中心的经营有影响的其他成本包括(场地)占用成本、食物、保险、物料和规划费用。占用和食物成本也在很大程度上受公众服务部的影响,因为托儿机构对每一个儿童提供的场地面积,有一个最低要求(视其年龄而定),在准备膳食和点心方面,也必须按具体的营养指导办事。

ACDC 的规划和经营

在经营了五年之后,日托中心任命了一个新的董事会,并制订了各项战略目标。董事会第一个战略行动,是更换了中心的行政班子,并制订了具体的经营规程,使这个机构能够在财务上站得住脚。为了消除社区中对"机构化"的照管儿童工作的负面看法,董事会决定把这个中心办成一个高品质的机构。在作了进一步研究之后,董事会得出结论是,为了在一个有吸引力和安全的环境中提供高质量的保育服务,最好的办法是建一个新的设施。此外,由联邦政府提供资金的社区"启蒙"规划[2]和当地校区的残障幼儿园项目也都应该设在这所新的大楼中(这些项目现在还栖居在不恰当的设施之中)。因此,ACDC 的董事会带头建造一栋 8000 平方英尺的大楼,产权属于 ACDC,一部分由联邦政府拨款,另外一部分来自当地 USDA 农村发展办公室的贷款。

在这所新大楼落成开幕之前,即在其规划和建造期间,ACDC 必须解决好几个问题。首要的是,董事会并不想要提高照管儿童的费率,担心如果这样做会阻止人们对这个设施的赞助。在另一方面,董事会又并不完全认为现行的费率足以弥付与新大楼有关的各项成本。此外,ACDC 将成为一个房东,这也成为董事会需要考量的一个新问题。ACDC 同意把大楼面积或几个房间出租给"启蒙"计划和学区,并负责维护设施和提供公用事业。ACDC 并不提供任何家具或固定装置。董事会的主要问题是:ACDC 应该向房客收取多少租金?ACDC 董事会对当地商业零售设施的租金作了研究,确定当前的费率为每 100 平方英尺 20 美元,于是决定按此向房客收取租金。由于董事们在财务和资本开支的决策方面没有经验,他们没有充分考虑到这个费率只指租用的面积;商业性的承租人通常自己支付公用事业费、环境卫生[3]费和各项维修费。这样一来,董事会一不小心就为 ACDC 埋下了未来财务危机的可能性。我们把建造以后的各项收入、成本和经营信息,列示如下。

ACDC 的成本结构

人工成本

ACDC 认为,为各个以年龄划分的教室所分派的员工都符合 DHS 规定的要求。员工的日程表在一个星期内轮流更迭,使员工对儿童的人数保持规定的比率,同时没有一个员工一周的工作时间超过 40 小时。员工的人工成本包括工资、FICA(7.65%)和 SUTA[4](1%)。ACDC 并不向员工提供其他福利。(见表 1)。

食物成本

中心为 ACDC 的主顾提供食物,但并不为点心或膳食的成本单独收费。食物成本包括为学费的一部分。此外,为了维持员工对孩童的人数比率,还要求员工在午餐时间保持在岗位上,因而员工的膳食也由中心提供。所有的孩童和教室里的员工都有早餐、午餐和每天两次的点心。

---

[2] 启蒙计划(Head Start Program)是美国健康与公众服务部的一项计划,旨在向低收入的家庭和他们的孩子提供各项健康、营养和家长参与的服务。此处按从 Google 查到的译法,可能是"从头抓起"的意思。——译者

[3] sanitation,此处主要指下水道设施。——译者

[4] 分别为"联邦社会保险捐款法(Federal Insurance Contributions Act)"和"州失业税法(State Unemployment Tax Act)"的缩写。——译者

表 1
工资表明细项目

	工资	税金	工资合计
行政	$ 13 750	$ 1 190	$ 14 940
厨房	9 000	780	9 780
婴儿照管	19 250	1 665	20 915
幼童照管	38 500	3 330	41 830
学前班照管	29 000	2 510	31 510
合计	$ 109 500	$ 9 475	$ 118 975

占用成本

大楼：在建造新大楼之前，ACDC 是和当地的学区和启蒙计划合在一起工作的，因此这栋大楼有意建得比日托单独需要的大。结果是，等到分析成本时，董事会就提出意见，认为启蒙计划和学区应该分担贷款和大楼的成本（即利息费用和折旧）。

公用事业：在 ACDC 设计该设施时，它考虑了房客的需要来设计他们的房间。然而，董事会并未预见到把房客的房间跟各自的煤气表、水表和电表配套。结果是，所有各项公用事业都只有总表，ACDC 将为整栋设施付全部账单。唯一例外的是电话费，房客都各付各的电话费。

维修等：租约规定，ACDC 付有关维修、保洁用物料和卫生设备地下管道的费用。详见表图 2。

图表 2
大楼租约摘要

阿帕鲁萨县日托中心（以下称为房东）与"启蒙"规划（以下称为房客）双方于 20XX 年 7 月约定：

房东向房客自愿出租、同时房客向房东自愿承租下列位于美国阿帕鲁萨县的大楼连同地基。对在"ACDC"日托中心中的、具体在大楼蓝图中已经指明的三个房间和一间办公室（2650 平方英尺），双方按下述的价格、规定和条件约定：

1. 租赁期。本租约的租赁期限为从 20XX 年 7 月 1 日起的 12 个月。
2. 租金。房客将为这一期间付下列租金：于 7 月 1 日付 530 美元，并在租赁期内此后每个月的 1 日付 530 美元；因此上述租金都是每月预付的。房东将支付所有在这栋大楼内的公用事业费、维修费和保管费。其余的房间，房东留作己用。

保险成本

ACDC 有四项保险成本：财产保险、一般责任保险、行政人员的责任保险⑤和职工伤害险⑥。财产险保的是整栋房子。一般责任保险，是为 ACDC 这个项目的孩子和员工投的保，保护中心免受意外或员工的索赔。房客必须为他们保责任保险。行政人员的责任保险保护中心免受因董事会处理财务事项不当而蒙受的损失。最后，职工伤害险，保的是对 ACDC 的行政人员和员工的工伤损失的补偿。

其他营业成本

这个组织的营业费用全都列在表 2 中。此前没有讨论过的成本包括行政管理或规划的成本，诸如会计、广告、继续教育和物料。这些成本全由 ACDC 负担。

表 2
营业费用

会计与法律事务	$900
广告	150
银行收费	35
继续教育	450
折旧	11 800
食物费用	5 500
保险——大楼/财产	860
保险——行政人员的责任	120
保险——一般责任	2 190
保险——员工赔偿	400
利息费用	13 085
工资单——工资*	109 500
工资单——税金*	9 475
修理与维修	5 950
环境卫生服务	2 435
物料——保洁	365
物料——电脑程序/艺术	3 675
物料——办公室	2 900
电话	1 060
公用事业	4 000
自来水/排污	1 100
费用合计	**$ 175 950**

*详见表 1

---

⑤ bond insurance，或称错误与疏漏（errors and omissions）保险，指为各种专业人士（如保险代理商、律师、建筑师等）因工作疏漏而被控诉的赔偿损失而投的保。在本案例中，指为中心的负责人或董事会成员对所作出的决策可能引起的赔偿责任而投的保。——译者

⑥ workers' compensation，北美或澳大利亚的一种为员工因工受到伤害而投的保险，如遇意外，由保险公司赔付。——译者

对会计师的挑战

董事会对在设施的建筑期间产生的各项收入和成本问题，没有进行会计处理，而是采取"走一步，算一步"的观点，即等新设施开始运转时再来仔细考虑照管儿童和房租的收费问题。在大楼投入使用一年后，ACDC 的董事会想要评估每一项日托和房客的相关成本和收入。假定你是该中心的会计师（而且是董事会成员中唯一具有相当财务知识的人），因而其他董事要求你解释一下为什么中心经营亏损。你指出，你认为照管儿童的收费和房租的费率都没有与这些收费应该弥补的成本联系起来考虑。你还说你需要一些时间，对该日托的儿童照管业务和房客租约作一全面的成本和盈利分析。为此，你决定实施一种作业成本法制度，把发生的成本分配给各项业务和房客们。

表 1~3 列示了新设施开始运转的第一年的收入和成本情况。表 4~6 列示了另外一些对成本分析和决策有用的信息。

表 3
收入

学费	
婴儿照管	$28 530
幼童照管	68 710
学前儿童照管	62 650
房租	
学区	4 200
"启蒙"	6 360
合计	$170 450

表 4
每小时儿童照管收费

婴儿照管	$2.00
幼童照管	1.75
学前儿童照管	1.75

表 5
面积（平方英尺）

ACDC	3 600
学区	1 750
"启蒙"	2 650
合计	8 000

作业成本法简述

作业成本法（ABC）常被制造业采用，因为在一般情况下它有助于改善产品成本的信息。ABC 替代了任意分配的做法，而先把成本计入各项作业，然后再按各产品耗用了多少作业，把作业成本分配计入产品。ABC 概念也适用于没有实物产品的服务行业。在服务业的组织中，先把成本分派到各项实施的作业；接着辨识用以估量各作业的动因，算出各作业的费率；最后再用各作业的费率把成本分派所提供的各项服务上去。这一过程反映了作业、作业所形成的成本和分派这些成本到各服务之间的因果关系。

成本动因的识别

在日托业中，发生成本和驱动成本的作业有许多项。例如，准备和端上食物是一道作业。把成本，如食物和直接人工计入这一作业中去，并非难事。然而，在一家日托中，要把成本分派到重要的日常作业上，那就比较困难了。有些重要的作业（如读一本书、玩一个游戏，或者教会一种技艺），是提供服务（照管孩子）的关键性组成部分，但这些作业却难以量度。因此，对于日托业而言，按照作业来辨识各项成本的驱动动因，然后按那些作业把成本分派到各项日托服务上去，在成本效益上行不通的。因此，ACDC 就只能把作业按比较宽的范围来分类。设定动因，必须既考虑到不至于引起计算过程过于繁复、费时，又能与成本的开支有因果关系，那么全体人数或按全体人数的分类，可用来作为许多作业成本归集点的动因了。全体人数可以按登记入学的人数、班级的规模、或员工的人数来计算。见表6。

表 6
全体人数

	入学总数	雇用员工总数	每天平均出席的学生数	每天平均受雇的员工数	全体人员每天平均人数
ACDC					
行政人员	—	1	—	1	1
厨房	—	1	—	1	1
婴儿照管	11	3	8	2	10
幼童照管	35	5	22	4	26
学前儿童照管	32	4	20	3	23
学区	—	—	12	6	18
"启蒙"	—	—	40	6	46
合计	78	14	102	23	125

问题

1. 请确定哪些服务或项目应该包括在成本和盈利分析中。
2. 观察对表 2 中所列示的各项成本。
a. 辨识与各项服务或项目⑦有关的直接成本。
b. 哪些成本应该列为组织与维持成本?讨论这些成本是否应该计入服务与项目。
3. 通过把表 2 中的各项成本分派到各成本归集点去,确定比较宽泛的作业分类并设定各个成本归集点。
4. 请辨识各项成本动因,成本动因与问题 3 中所设定的作业成本归集点之间有因果关系。
5. 为每一个成本归集点,算出作业费率或成本动因费率。请注意:你设定的费率只用于把各项成本分配计入 ACDC 的各项服务和/或房客。你不应该把成本分回一般行政费用中。
6. 使用在问题 1 中所确定的服务或项目,来确定服务或项目的收入、分派给服务或项目的各项成本、并计算服务或项目的盈利能力。在解答此题时,不妨编制一份电子数据表。
7. 根据你对问题 6 的计算结果,哪些服务或项目运行得比较成功?决定该服务或项目是否盈利的因素,看来是什么?
8. 请对提高该日托机构的整体盈利能力的至少三种可选用的方法,展开讨论。

参考文献

(略)

---

⑦ service or program,此处"服务(service)"指为人员提供的服务,如膳食、书籍和各项直接成本;"项目(program)"指该日托中心对外提供的各种不同的项目,如婴儿班、幼童班等。——译者

Appaloosa County Day Care Center, Inc.

Kristen Irwin
Truman State University

Debra Kerby
Truman State University

Sandra Weber
Truman State University

BACKGROUND

The Appaloosa County Day Care Center, Inc. (ACDC) began operations in a vacant warehouse retrofitted with bathrooms and kitchen facilities. ACDC's mission is to provide quality, affordable childcare to the residents of the community and surrounding area. The service area is a rural, economically depressed county that continually ranks in the lowest 10 percent of per-capita income in the state. The organization's seven-member board of directors is comprised of volunteer representatives from various agencies throughout the community – the school district, community college, hospital, Department of Human Services, etc. The board members bring a breadth of human services experience to the oversight of the day care, but most do not possess an accounting or financial background. While they were committed to the financial viability of the day care, they initially focused on the center's mission-to provide affordable childcare to working-class families. As a result, the board set childcare rates to achieve their goal of affordability rather than assuring adequate revenues to provide high-quality services while reaching breakeven points.

From its founding, the center faced another significant challenge. The center was the first of its kind in the community, so negative perceptions about using "institutionally" provided day care were prevalent. Local families preferred to use in-home childcare provided by friends or relatives. These perceptions and preferences, coupled with poor administrative practices, caused the center to struggle continually to meet its financial obligations. ACDC was almost forced to close its doors on more than one occasion. The financial performance of ACDC is not unusual, as many community-based day care facilities struggle to remain open.

DAY CARE INDUSTRY REVENUE AND COST PATTERNS

As an industry, day care facilities generally operate with very low profit margins. Typical for-profit day care profit margins are approximately 4 percent, with about 70 percent of a center's total costs attributed to wages and other employee-related costs (Helburn 1995, 172, 176). The state's Department of Human Services' licensing regulations drive a significant level of employee-related costs. These regulations mandate a strict staff-to-child ratio that all licensed facilities must follow. For example, infant care (ages two weeks to two years) regulations require at least one staff member for every four children (see excerpt from regulations in Exhibit 1). Thus, if a center pays just the minimum wage (federal wage currently $7.25 per hour, $7.80 w/taxes), at least $1.95 per hour would need to be charged for each infant just to cover the cost of the employee. Additionally, one must consider how revenues are affected when there are fewer than four infants per employee scheduled in the nursery. When the ratio drops, income per hour drops; however, the full hourly wage to the employee remains the same and an immediate loss occurs. See Exhibit 1 for the complete Department of Human Service staff ratio requirements.

Exhibit 1
Department of Human Services Excerpt from Childcare Regulations
Staff ratio. The staff-to-child ratio shall be as follows:

Age of Children	Minimum Ratio of Staff to Children
Two weeks to two years	One to every 4 children
Two years	One to every 6 children
Three years	One to every 8 children
Four years	One to every 12 children
Five years to ten years	One to every 15 children
Ten years and over	One to every 20 children

Source: Department of Human Services. 2008. Child Care Centers and Preschools Licensing Standards and Procedures. Comm. 204, August.

In addition to labor, other costs that impact day care center operations include occupancy costs, food, insurance, supplies, and programming expenses. Occupancy and food costs are also highly influenced by the Department of Human Services, as a facility must provide a minimum amount of space per child (based on age) and follow specific nutritional guidelines in preparing meals and snacks.

ACDC PLANNING AND OPERATIONS

About five years into operations, a new board of directors was appointed and strategic objectives were developed. As its first strategic actions, the board replaced the Center's administration and developed specific operating procedures to keep the facility afloat financially. In order to eliminate the community's negative perceptions of institutionalized childcare, the board decided to move the center to a higher-quality facility. After further study, the board concluded that constructing a new facility would be the best option for providing quality childcare in an attractive and safe environment. In addition, the new building would house the community's federally-funded Head Start program and the local school district's handicapped pre-school program, as these programs were housed in inadequate facilities. Thus, the ACDC board spearheaded the construction of an 8 000 - square-foot building that would be owned by ACDC, Inc., and funded in part by a federal grant and a loan from the local USDA Rural Development Office.

During the planning and construction of the new facility but prior to its opening, the ACDC board had to resolve a number of issues. First and foremost, the board did not want to raise the childcare rates, for fear that doing so would deter people from patronizing the facility. On the other hand, the board was not at all positive that the existing rates would cover the costs associated with the new building. In addition, ACDC was becoming a landlord, and this created additional concerns for the board. ACDC agreed to lease floor space or rooms to the Head Start program and school district, perform facility maintenance, and provide utilities. ACDC did not provide any furniture or fixtures. The board's main question: How much rent should ACDC charge the tenants? The ACDC board researched the lease rates charged to the area's commercial retail facilities and determined that $ 20 per 100 square feet was the going rate and decided to charge their tenants at this rate. Because the board members were not experienced in making financial and capital expenditure decisions, they did not fully consider that this rate was for floor space only; commercial leaseholders typically pay all of their own utilities, sanitation, and maintenance fees. Thus, the board had inadvertently created the potential for a future financial crisis for ACDC. Selected post-construction revenues, costs, and operational information for ACDC follow.

ACDC COST STRUCTURE

LABOR COSTS

ACDC maintains a staff of employees assigned to each age-level classroom that is in compliance with DHS guidelines. The staff schedule is rotated throughout the week so that the staff-to-child ratio is always maintained while no one employee works more than 40 hours per week. The employer's labor costs include the wages, FICA (7.65%), and the SUTA rate (1%). The facility does not offer any other employee benefits. (See Table 1)

Table 1
Payroll Detail

	Wages	Taxes	Total Payroll
Administrative	$ 13 750	$ 1 190	$ 14 940
Kitchen	9 000	780	9 780
Infant care	19 250	1 665	20 915
Toddler care	38 500	3 330	41 830
Pre-K care	29 000	2 510	31 510
Totals	$ 109 500	$ 9 475	$ 118 975

FOOD COSTS

The center provides food for ACDC patrons, but it does not charge a separate fee to recover the cost of snacks or meals. The cost of food is included as part of the tuition fee. In addition, the employees are required to remain on-site during the lunch hour in order to maintain the staff-to-child ratio, so their meals are also provided by the center. All children and classroom staff receive breakfast, lunch, and two snacks a day.

OCCUPANCY COSTS

Building: Because ACDC worked in conjunction with the local school district and the Head Start program prior to constructing the new facility, the building was purposely built larger than the space required by the day care only. Consequently, when it came time to analyze costs, it was the board's opinion that the Head Start and school district programs should share in the costs of the loan and building (i.e., interest expense and depreciation).

Utilities: When ACDC designed the facility, it considered the needs of the tenants and designed their rooms accordingly. The board did not have the foresight, however, to set up the tenants' rooms with their own gas, electric, and water meters. Therefore, all of the utilities are measured through common meters, and ACDC pays the bills for the entire facility. The only exception to this is the telephone expense, as each program contracts and pays for its own phone service. See Exhibit 2 for details.

Exhibit 2

Excerpt from Building Lease

IT IS AGREED this 1st day of July, 20xx, by and between Appaloosa County Day Care Center, Inc., hereinafter referred to as Landlord; and Head Start, hereinafter referred to as Tenants; That the Landlord hereby leases to the Tenants and the Tenants hereby lease from the Landlord the following premises situated in Appaloosa County, USA, to wit:

Three rooms and an office (2650 sq. ft.) in the "ACDC" day care center as specified in the building plans, in consideration of the mutual promises of the parties herein and upon the terms, provisions, and conditions following:

1. LEASE PERIOD. The term of this lease shall be for a period of twelve months starting July 1, 20xx.

2. RENT. Tenants shall pay rental for the period as follows; $530.00 on the 1st day of July and $530.00 on the 1st day of each month thereafter during the lease period; said rental thus at all times to be paid in advance for the month. The Landlord will pay all utilities, maintenance, and custodial services on the building. The Landlord reserves all remaining rooms for their use or lease.

Maintenance, etc.: As specified in the lease agreement, ACDC pays the entire building's expenses related to maintenance, cleaning supplies, and sanitation. See Exhibit 2 for details.

INSURANCE COSTS

ACDC has four different insurance costs: property, general liability, officer's bond, and worker's compensation. The property insurance covers the entire building. The general liability insurance covers the children and staff in the ACDC program and helps protect the center against accidents or claims against the staff. The tenants must carry their own liability insurance. The bond insurance on the officers covers the center for any inappropriate handling of financial matters by the board of directors. Finally, the worker's compensation insurance covers the administration and ACDC employees for work-related injuries.

OTHER OPERATING COSTS

A complete listing of the organization's operating expenses is shown in

Table 2. The costs not previously discussed include administrative or program costs such as accounting, advertising, continuing education, and supplies. These costs are attributable solely to ACDC.

THE ACCOUNTANT'S CHALLENGE

Rather than addressing the revenue and cost issues that arose during the facility construction, the board took a "wait and see" position and opted to review both the childcare rates and rental rates after the new facility had begun operations. After the first year of building occupancy, the ACDC board wanted to evaluate the costs and revenues associated with each of the day care's and tenants' programs. You are the center's accountant (and the only individual on the board with significant financial knowledge), so the other board members have asked you to explain why the center is running at a loss. You indicate that you believe that both the childcare rates and rental rates were set without establishing correlation to the costs that they were intended to cover. You also state that you want to take the time to complete a thorough cost and profitability analysis of the day care's childcare programs and tenant agreements. In order to do so, you decide to implement an activity-based costing system to allocate costs to the various programs and tenants.

Tables 1 – 3 provide revenue and expense information for the first year of operations at the new facility. Tables 4 – 6 provide additional information useful for the cost analysis and decision making.

ACTIVITY-BASED COSTING—A QUICK REVIEW

Activity-based costing (ABC) is used frequently in manufacturing settings because it typically improves product cost information. ABC replaces arbitrary cost allocations by first assigning costs to activities and then to goods based on how much each good uses the activities. The concepts of ABC can also be applied to service-based organizations where tangible products do not exist. In a service organization, costs are assigned to the various activities performed, cost drivers that measure the activities performed are identified, cost driver rates are calculated for each activity, and the resulting rates are used to assign activity costs to the types of services provided. This process reflects the causal relationship between the activity, the costs created by the activity, and the assignment of these costs to services.

Table 2
Operating Expenses

Accounting & legal	$ 900
Advertising	150
Bank charges	35
Continuing education	450
Depreciation	11 800
Food expense	5 500
Ins. – Bldg/property	860
Ins. – Officer bond	120
Ins. – Gen. liability	2 190
Ins. – Workers comp	400
Interest expense	13 085
Payroll-wages*	109 500
Payroll-taxes*	9 475
Repairs & maintenance	5 950
Sanitation Service	2 435
Supplies-Cleaning	365
Supplies-Program/art	3 675
Supplies-Office	2 900
Telephone	1 060
Utilities	4 000
Water/sewer	1 100
TOTAL EXPENSES	**$ 175 950**

* See detail in Table 1

Table 3
Revenues

Tuition	
Infant care	$ 28 530
Toddler care	68 710
Pre-K care	62 650
Rent	
School district	4 200
Head Start	6 360
TOTAL	**$ 170 450**

Table 4
Hourly Childcare Rates

Infant care	$2.00
Toddler care	1.75
Pre-K care	1.75

Table 5
Square Footage

ACDC	3 600
School district	1 750
Head Start	2 650
TOTAL	8 000

IDENTIFICATION OF COST DRIVERS

There are many activities present in a day care setting that create or drive costs. An example is the preparing and serving of food. It is relatively easy to assign many of the costs, such as food and direct labor, to this activity. It is more difficult, however, to assign costs to many of the most significant activities that occur regularly in a day care. These activities (like reading a book, playing a game, or teaching a skill) are key components of the service being provided—childcare—but they are difficult to measure. Therefore, identifying each of the individual activities that drive cost and then assigning cost to the daycare programs based on those activities may be cost prohibitive. For that reason, ACDC places activities into broad category classifications. When considering drivers that would be cost effective yet causally related to the costs being incurred, population or a population subset becomes the driver identified for many of the activity cost pools. Population may be measured in terms of enrollment, class size, or number of staff. See Table 6.

QUESTIONS

1. Identify the services or programs to be included in the cost and profitability analysis.

2. Examine the costs listed in Table 2.

   a. Identify the direct costs associated with each service or program.

   b. Which costs would be organization-sustaining costs? Provide an argument for or against assigning these costs to services or programs.

Table 6
Population

	Total number of students enrolled	Total staff employed	Average daily attendance of students	Average daily staffing of employees	Total average daily population
ACDC					
Administrator	—	1	—	1	1
Kitchen	—	1	—	1	1
Infant care	11	3	8	2	10
Toddler care	35	5	22	4	26
Pre-K care	32	4	20	3	23
School district	—	—	12	6	18
Head Start	—	—	40	6	46
Total	78	14	102	23	125

3. Identify the broad activity categories and create cost pools by assigning the costs from Table 2 to the pools.

4. Identify the cost drivers that have a causal relationship to the activity cost pools created in Question 3.

5. Calculate the activity or cost-driver rates for each cost pool. Note: You should develop rates that will allocate costs to ACDC programs and/or tenants only. You should not allocate any costs back to general administration.

6. Using the services or programs identified in Question 1, determine service or program revenues, assign the costs to the service or programs, and calculate service or program profitability. A spreadsheet may be helpful with this task.

7. Based upon your calculations in Question 6, which services or programs are operating successfully? What appears to be the determining factor in whether the service or program is profitable?

8. Discuss at least three alternatives for improving the overall profitability of the daycare facility.

REFERENCE LIST

Helburn, S. W. *Cost, Quality and Child Outcomes in Child Care Centers Technical Report.* Denver, CO: Department of Economics, Center for Research in Economic and Social Policy, University of Colorado at Denver, 1995.

Anderson, L. W. and D. R. Krathwohl. *A Taxonomy for Learning, Teaching, and Assessing: A Revision of Bloom's Taxonomy of Educational Objectives.* NY: Longman, 2001.

成本计算方法
Costing Methodologies

另类成本计算法：精密涂漆工厂的两难处境

Eileen Peacock
AACSB International

Paul Juras
Wake Forest University

"我们在发展作业成本法（ABC）制度上投入了大量的时间和金钱，但我现在不能肯定它是否为我们提供了作长期决策真正需要的信息，"精密涂漆工厂（Precision Paint Shop, PPS）南部工厂的经理埃米·韦斯林（Amy Wesling）对她的行政团队说。"ABC 提供的数据帮助我们更好地理解我们的成本；但现在我怀疑，它所提供的信息是否可以帮助我们来实现我们的战略目标。"

公司简介

精密涂漆工厂（根据美国中西部一家公司的实际情况写成，托名"精密工厂，Precision Paint Shop，以下简称 PPS"）是在原始设备制造商（original equipment manufacturers, OEMs）的汽车部件上，按客户要求作涂层（涂漆）的一家私有（合伙）的工厂，同时又是个一级和二级供应商[①]。公司年销售收入 9 000 万美元，其中 3 500 万美元来自专门从事喷面漆工作的南部工厂。

PPS 擅长做各种涂层。客户将金属毛坯寄存在工厂，对金属毛坯施以所需要的油漆或其他涂层之后，运返原主。各生产线包括有多种颜色的油漆、不同种类的涂层，以及各种面漆。图 1 是生产流程的图解；"PPS 的生产流程"（见侧栏 1）则是对生产流程所作的说明。

PPS 对客户的订单，一向来者不拒。价格由市场决定，管理层采用一种标准成本法，对产品的盈利作出估计。在过去三年中，市场需求显著增加；在高级涂层方面的需求，尤其如此。事实上，产品的组合发生了很大的变化。在前两年的产品中，有 80% 属于光泽度低（low-gloss, LG）的成品，

[①] 在美国汽车行业中，一级供应商（tier 1 supplier）指直接对组装汽车的工厂提供部件（assemblies）的厂商；二级供应商（tier 2 supplier）指为组装汽车的工厂提供零件（parts）和部件（assemblies）的厂商，也指为一级供应商提供零件和分部件（sub-assemblies）的厂商。本案例中的这家"精密涂漆工厂"既直接为汽车工厂提供产品，也向一级供应商提供产品。——译者

今年则有85%是光泽度高（high-gloss，HG）的成品了。不幸的是，产量提高的同时，利润却下降了。

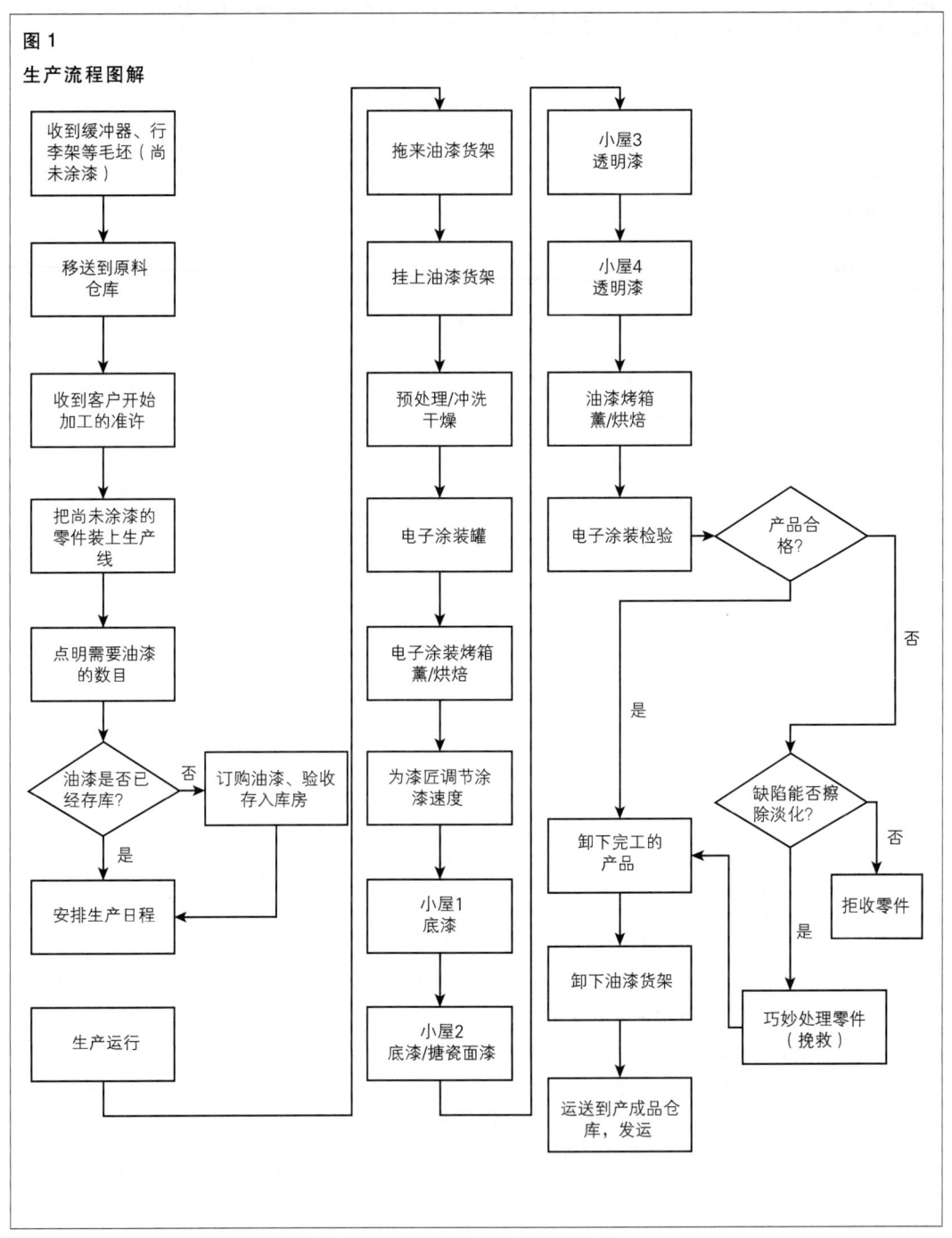

图1
生产流程图解

涂层和颜色的多种组合使公司的复杂程度也随之提高。另外，需要油漆的零件的尺寸和形状各异，更使油漆工序趋于复杂。因此，决定生产操作复杂程度的因素有四个——涂层、颜色、形状和尺寸。这一多样化，使每一项任务都各有其独特的操作方法。根据油漆工序的特点及对工序近乎

100%的完美的追求，使其对检验、返工抛光、重做和碎屑都有很高的要求。复杂程度高、间接费用也随之增加，致使直接材料仅占制造成本总额的26%。

成本计算制度

近来，PPS从原先通常采用的标准成本法制度，变革为ABC制度。这一变革是为了更好地了解与各种不同的产品有关的成本。ABC分析使人们了解，产品的各种特性的不同组合所带来的不同结果。表1列示了一个缓冲器采用两种不同工序的成本比较：一种是LG抛光的成本，另外一种是HG抛光的成本。按照ABC分析法，工厂的会计人员查德·利德斯（Chad Leaders）编写了一份报告书，列示了各个产品生产线不同的盈利情况。表2归纳了从标准成本法改为ABC法后，各项产品的毛利变化情况。如果实施了ABC法，则可以用ABC法算出的成本数字作为与客户谈判产品定价和报告财务业绩之用。

表1
受缓冲器需要高或低光泽的抛光而影响的各项目一览表

	高光泽	低光泽
不合格率	高	低
颜色数	高	低
批量大小	低	高
漆匠人数	高	低

表2
从标准成本法改为ABC，算得的毛利发生变化的产品数

负毛利	正毛利
←3项产品的负毛利增加	→5项产品的正毛利增加
7项产品→从负毛利转为正毛利	
1项产品→负毛利增加	←10项产品正毛利减少

编制产能利用计划

生产传送带显然是油漆工序的一项具约束条件性质的资源。该工厂的生产主任为曼迪·詹姆斯（Mandy James），根据她对约束理论（theory of constraints，TOC）的理解，把各道工序按对传送带的需求的不同进行分解。她用缓冲器这项产品作为一个实例，编制了一份"样板"（见表3），并对

LG 缓冲器和 HG 缓冲器作了比较。该样板首先列示的是质量问题。不合格率越高,这一道生产运行的收得率(yield rate,YR)也就越低。形状和抛光比较复杂的产品的收得率,必定低于复杂程度较低的产品。LG 缓冲器目前的 YR 为 95%,而 HG 缓冲器则为 92%。

表 3
抛光质量对盈利的影响

产品	产出率(YR)	修复率(RR)	运行系数(RF)=1/(YR+RR)	速度	复杂系数(CF)=18/速度	需求系数(DF)=(RF×CF)	每单位产品的平方英尺数(Sq. Ft.)	瓶颈需求平方英尺(BDF)=(DF/Sq. Ft.)	抛光后产品的单位利润	(P/TU) 在传送带上通过的每个单位的经调整后每平方英尺的利润额/BDF
光泽度不同的两种缓冲器的比较										
低光泽缓冲器	95%	5%	100%	15	1.20	1.20	10	.120	$10.00	$8.33
高光泽缓冲器	92%	5%	103%	12	1.50	1.55	10	.155	$12.00	$7.76
对改变流程所作的评估										
高光泽缓冲器现行流程	92%	5%	103%	12	1.50	1.55	10	.155	$12.00	$7.76
改变速度和 YR	90%	6%	104%	13	1.38	1.44	10	.144	$12.00	$8.32

有些不合格品可以在内部加以修复。缓冲器的修复率(recovery rate, RR)大约相当于投产量的 5%。由于这些缓冲器经过修复达到了合格的标准,能够满足客户要求的标准,不再加重传送带的负荷。YR 和 RR 这两个指标相结合,可以确定为获得 1 个单位的合格品,必须加工多少个产品[②],此数称为运行系数(run factor,RF)。RF 等于 1/(YR+RR)。如果 YR + RR = 1(LG 的情况就是如此),那么为最终获得 1 个单位的合格品,送上传送带的也就只是 1 个。如果 HG 缓冲器的 RF 为 103%(计算公式为 1/(92% +5%)),这就意味着 PPS 必须涂漆的缓冲器总数,等于可满足客户需要的 103%。

由于传送带是个约束条件,产品花费在传送带上的时间便成了重要的问题。传送带的速度为每分钟 10~18 英尺不等,取决于需要涂漆的产品的尺寸和形状。Mandy 把每分钟 18 英尺定为传送带的标准时间单位。复杂度系数(complexity factor,CF)在 1(最快的传送带速度)和 1.8(最慢的速

[②] 假设投产 100 个产品,收得率(YR)90%,其余 10%(10 个)需要修复;如果修复率(RR)为 5%,则成功修复的是 5 个产品,最终得到的合格品总数为 95 个。由此可见,每完成一个合格品,需要投产 100/95(即 1.053)个。这个数字就等于下面所讲的 1/(90% +5%)。——译者

度）之间，根据产品种类加上需求数算得。CF 为每分钟 18 英尺的标准传送带速度，除以该产品所需要的传送带速度之商；因此较快的传送带速度使算得的 CF 更接近于 1。HG 缓冲器现在的传送带速度为每分钟 12 英尺，因此算出的 CF 为 18/15 = 1.5。然后，把这一 CF 乘以 RF，得总约束的需量系数（demand factor，DF）。

DF 实际上是为了完成一个单位的某类零件的合格品，需要放在传送带上的零件个数。由于各类零件的形状和尺寸不同，PPS 需要一种标准的衡量单位，把放在传送带上的总的需求量加以分解，以比较各个产品的盈利。各种零件的面积（平方英尺）可用作计量单位，因为它代表每个零件需要涂漆的表面面积。把 DF 除以某一零件（例如缓冲器）总面积的平方英尺数，得出瓶颈需量系数（bottleneck demand factor，BDF），此数是具体的尺寸、形状和抛光程度下零件每平方英尺面积的需量系数。每平方英尺合格品的利润水平，除以 BDF，可得出在传送带上通过的每个单位的利润额（profit per throughput unit，P/TU）。在表 3 上，LG 缓冲器的单位利润较低（每件 10 美元，即每平方英尺 1 美元），但用传送带的需求量加以调整后，LG 缓冲器的 P/TU 就提高了。

决定点

为了使价格制订得更为合理，PPS 的管理层采用了 ABC，以求更好地了解产品的"真实"成本。现在，管理层在使用成本信息中，需要有较多的前瞻性，在市场需求超过企业现有产能的情况下，帮助发展和实施企业的战略。埃米在开头的问题中提到，PPS 的管理当局试图从单纯地把成本布置下去的做法③，转为利用成本信息推动战略性决策。具体来说，埃米想要对应该改进或继续哪几条生产线，作出战略性的决策。她注意到：通过 ABC 方法可以把资源的消耗分配到各个作业上去，但她认为这只是一个操作方法，而不是一个战略性的问题。她对 ABC 是否能帮助做出战略决策，还弄不清楚。

曼迪指出，传送带已经满负荷工作了，由于产能受限，有的订货已被拒绝。埃米认为一切战略决策都取决于产能问题，在作出战略性决策时，应该采用 TOC 和产量成本计算法的理念。曼迪用下面这个例子支撑她的主张与观点。"HG 缓冲器占生产的大部分，"她说。"当对 HG 缓冲器涂漆时，我们考虑是否需要提高传送带的速度。如果提高速度，收得率就会从 92% 降为 90%。不合格品会增加，但 RR 则会增加到 6%；而且，如表 3 所示，P/TU 会提高，'巧妙处理'的单位成本实际上也会下降。"（见侧栏 2 "巧妙处理。"）

查德不同意曼迪的建议，查德引用表 1 指出，HG 抛光的废品率较高，需要增加漆匠以及更多的颜色、更多的检验和维修成本，并减缓传送带的速

---

③ 指通过标准成本法把成本任务分配、布置给企业的各级组织去完成。——译者

度。HG 产品也需要通过工作站 3 和 4 进行处理。由于成本中有些部分所需要的资源属于固定成本性质，所以不应该采用产量成本计算法；因为在产量成本法中，这些固定成本会被忽略。他提出另外一种做法，即资源消耗会计（RCA），这是他从当地管理会计师协会（IMA）分会的一次聚会中得知的。他认为埃米所需要的可能是 RCA，但不能完全肯定。查德把这一成本计算方法向埃米作了一次简要的介绍（见侧栏 3 "RCA 的要点"）。他建议去参加 IMA 组织的一项后续教育课程，对 RCA 取得更多的了解。但埃米则想要取得更多的信息，以决定是否让查德参加该课程。

建议的阅读资料

Chwen, Sheu, Ming-Hsiang Chen, and Stacy Kovar. "Integrating ABC and TOC for Better Manufacturing Decision Making." *Integrated Manufacturing Systems*, May 2003, pp. 433 – 441.

Grasso, Lawrence P. "Are ABC and RCA Accounting Systems Compatible with Lean Management?" *Management Accounting Quarterly*, Fall 2005, pp. 12 – 27.

Keys, David, and Anton van der Merwe. "Gaining Effective Organizational Control with RCA." *Strategic Finance*, May 2002, pp. 41 – 47.

Resource Consumption Accounting Institute website, http://www.rcainstitute.org

van der Merwe, Anton, and David Keys. "The Case for Resource Consumption Accounting." *Strategic Finance*, April 2002, pp 31 – 36.

侧栏 1：PPS 的生产流程

PPS 以每班 8 小时的两班制运行，一年工作 240 天。涂漆工序有一条单轨的传送带，以每分钟 10~18 英尺的速度向前移动，具体速度视操作和零件复杂程度而定。总的涂漆生产周期约为 2.5 小时。生产日程是按照客户需求、生产线速度、最小批量和可用的货架数来安排。材料装卸工把零件毛坯和货架运送到生产线上，装货工又把每一个零件装上货架，务必做到放置稳妥，当进入电子涂装（E-coat）罐时，才能够获得电气接地[④]。

涂漆工序

第一道，对零件作化学处理（预处理阶段）；要作一系列的冲洗，去除

---

④ 这里讲的是，PPS 采用电子涂漆的工艺，要使被涂漆的零件带有某种电荷，与喷上去的漆的电荷相反，从而把漆均匀地涂上去。所以，在传送带上要放一个货架，把尚未涂漆的零件以正确的方式放在上面，使零件能带有所需要的电荷。所以需要获得"电气接地。"

油污和尘土，用磷酸化合物喷射表面，使油漆能够粘附其上。第二道是把零件浸在一个容量为 20 000 加仑的电子涂装罐中，出罐时喷上新鲜、去离子的水，冲掉所有依附于零件表面的"废酸洗液（drag out）"油漆，用以去掉外表上的缺陷。然后，该零件被送去通过四道油漆小屋。有的零件可能不需要全部经过这四道小屋[⑤]，视零件的种类而定。

- 小屋 1 有五杆上底漆的自动化喷射枪。喷底漆是为了修整表面的缺陷和防止生锈，零件不一定都需要上底漆。
- 小屋 2 有两座人工操作的和若干座自动化的喷射机，用来上底漆或搪瓷面漆。
- 小屋 3 有一座人工操作的喷射枪，另有一杆自动化喷射枪，用来上清漆。只有高光泽度的产品才需要在完工前施以有光泽的、发亮的清漆。
- 小屋 4 有两座人工操作的喷射机，另有若干杆自动化喷射枪，也是用来对需要两个涂层的零件上清漆用的。

当对低光泽的产品涂漆时，小屋 3 和小屋 4 都闲置不用，喷射枪也都被关掉。根据产品的需要，有的零件要上底漆（高光泽度的），有的则上搪瓷面漆（低光泽度的）。在经过了这些工序以后，零件置于另外一个炉子里烘干涂漆。当产品回到装卸区时，要印上日期，从货架上拿下来，放在一个地面传送带上，经过检验、卸下、然后包装起来。

准备工序

在改换油漆颜色时，需要有五分钟的间隙以做准备。这使生产线上的工人有时间来更换工具架、调节生产线的速度、清除线上的老漆，并在整个系统中改用新漆。

当间隙的五分钟时间临近结束时，盛装所需要的各种颜色的油漆容器就被运送到油漆小屋。当前一种颜色要涂的最后一个零件涂成时，要把油漆线上的老漆迅速洗清，用溶液冲洗各条涂漆线，新漆则通过喷射枪以达到预期的一致性。当这个间隙临近结束时，零件毛坯就出现，新一轮的涂漆又开始了。

质量保证或返修工序

成品被拒收的主要原因，是在手工喷射枪、老旧设备中带来的污尘和铁锈，以及这个行业必然存在的问题。高光泽度产品的再加工的费用要高得多，其废品率也要比低光泽度产品高得多。

重新加工大部分都需要打磨。产品需要经过打磨，把电子涂装的底漆磨去，移送到线上重新加工。有些产品需要送到外部去除漆。有些缺陷则可以

---

⑤ 小屋（booth）是车间的厂房内另外隔开的小室，目的是为了防尘，防止在涂漆过程中有尘埃落在涂层表面，影响质量。——译者

通过巧妙的处理方法①来纠正缺陷，不需要完全推倒重来。其做法是，用巧妙的处理方法把涂有清漆的零件表面的缺陷擦除，使零件的面漆光滑。只要能够与其他上了漆的合格零件一起装运出厂，这些零件就可以被认为是"获救"了。

侧栏 2：巧妙处理

当前，PPS 每年经过"巧妙处理"的缓冲器大约有 100 000 件，相当于运行在传送带上的缓冲器的 5%。如果线上的速度加快，产出率的降低将额外需要"巧妙处理"部处理 20 000 件缓冲器。如果以最高的产能来运行，该部每年能够处理 125 000 件；其变动成本每件低于 0.02 美元，因此即使计算出的单位成本有所变化，该部加工数量的增加仍然不会对总成本有什么影响。下表列示了这方面的详细数据。

产品在各种的不合格水平下"巧妙处理"的单位成本	年度成本	单位数	单位成本
当前不合格品水平	$480 000	100 000	$4.800
提高流水线速度下的不合格品水平	$480 400	120 000	$4.003
在处理不合格品中实际可行的产能	$480 500	125 000	$3.844

侧栏 3：RCA 的要点

资源消耗会计（resource consumption accounting，RCA），是在德国公司所发展的成本计算方法和 ABC 作业成本法理念的基础上发展起来的。RCA 采用的是企业的基础在于资源的观点，并密切地观察耗费资源的数量和这些资源的成本特性。RCA 的主要特点有：对闲置产能的处理、采用除了实际（历史）成本之外的其他成本、并在不同的层面上对成本信息进行归类和追踪的能力。这种综合的管理会计系统能够提供更正确的产品成本，以及对各道工序和各项成本互相之间的关系有更好地理解，从而帮助改进决策。

---

① 他们在用高速旋转的软纤维衬垫进行抛光时，用一种巧妙的、技术精巧的处理方法，清除表面的缺陷，而又不损及涂层。例如，在涂层变得干燥的时候，有尘埃落到表面上，质量就稍受损害。此时，旋转的衬垫，就可以把尘埃磨去。这种把尘埃除去而又不损及涂层的做法，称为"巧妙处理（finessing）"。finessing，原意指牌戏中利用手中握有的牌的情况，巧妙出牌的做法。——译者

Alternative Costing Methods: Precision Paint Shop's Dilemma

Eileen Peacock
AACSB International

Paul Juras
Wake Forest University

"We invested a great deal of time and money into developing the activity-based costing (ABC) system, and now I am not sure if it provides the information we really need for long-term decision-making purposes," Amy Wesling, plant manager of Precision Paint Shop's (PPS) Southern Plant, told her administrative team. "The ABC data helped us understand our costs better, but now I'm wondering if it's the right information to serve as the basis for helping us achieve our strategic goals."

COMPANY DESCRIPTION

Precision Paint Shop (a fictionalized version of an actual Midwest company) is a privately-held custom coater (painter) of automotive components for original equipment manufacturers (OEMs) and tier 1 and tier 2 suppliers.

The company has annual revenues of $90 million per year, with $35 million in sales from the Southern plant, which specializes in spray topcoat applications.

PPS specializes in the application of a series of coatings. Raw metal parts are received on consignment from the customer, finished with the desired application(s) of paint and other coatings, and shipped back to the same customer. The product lines consist of a large number of combinations of paint colors, types of coating, and paint finishes. Figure 1 provides a diagram of the production process, and "PPS's Production Process" (Sidebar 1) provides a narrative of the production process.

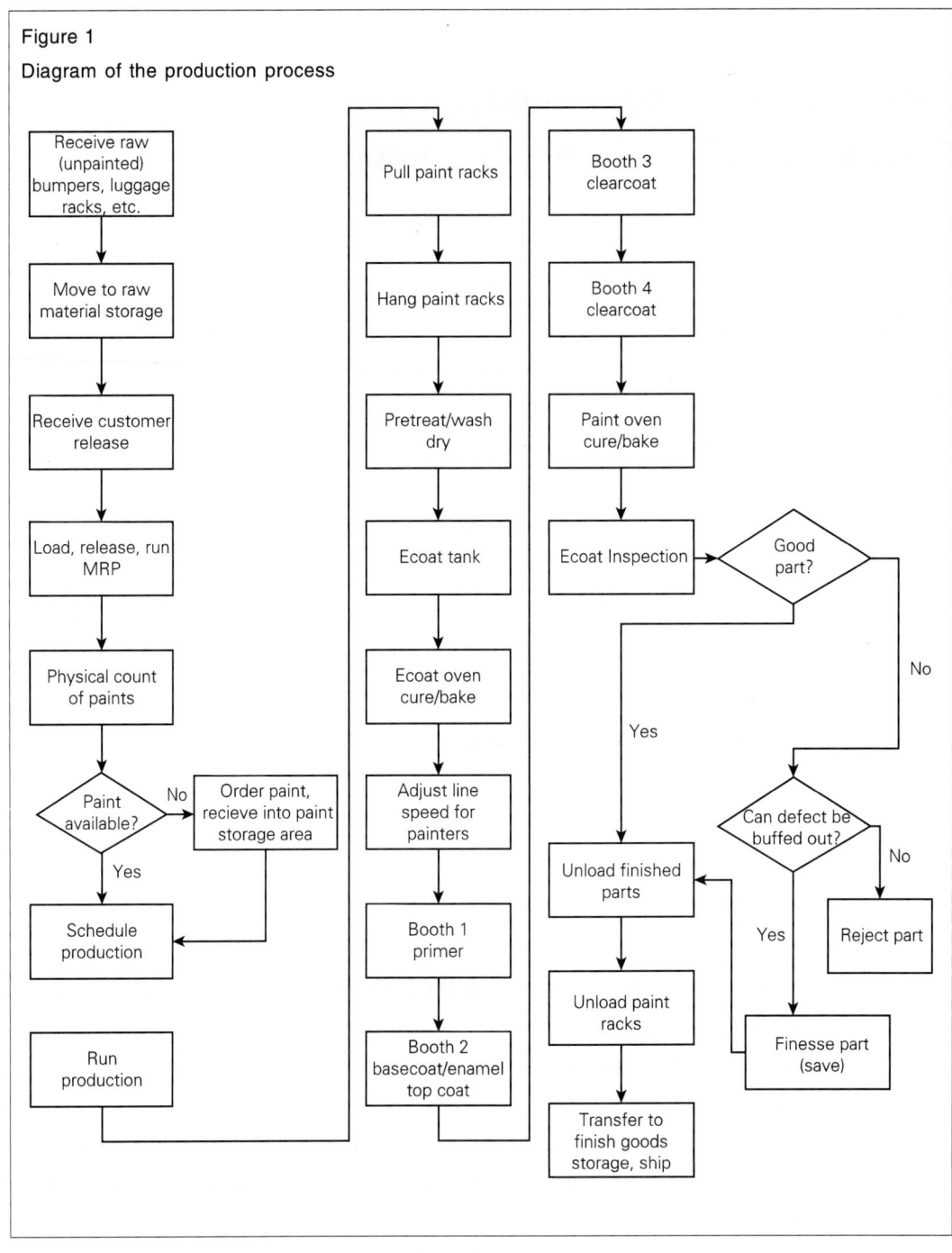

Figure 1
Diagram of the production process

Historically, PPS accepted most of the work assignments offered. Prices were market driven, and management used a form of standard costing to evaluate product profitability. Over the past three years demand had significantly increased, especially in the higher-grade coatings. In fact, the product mix flip-flopped from 80% low-gloss (LG) finish two years ago to 85% high-gloss (HG) finish in the current year. Unfortunately, along with the increase in volume came a decrease in profits.

The immense number of combinations of coatings and color created complexity for the company. Also, the parts to be painted varied in size and shape, further complicating the painting process. The end result was that four characteristics—coating, color, shape, and size—were instrumental in determining the complexity of the operation. This variety initiated a mix of activities unique to each job. The very nature of the painting process and the need for a near-100% perfection level in the industry resulted in a high level of inspections, refinishing, rework, and scrap. Complexity had driven up overhead costs, leaving direct materials accounting for only 26% of total manufacturing costs.

THE COSTING SYSTEM

Recently had PPS moved away from a conventional standard costing system to ABC. The change was made to better understand the costs associated with painting the various products. The ABC analysis revealed the fundamental differences that existed between the different mixes of product characteristics. Table 1 provides an illustrative comparison of two versions of a bumper: an LG finish and an HG finish. After the ABC analysis, Chad Leaders, plant accountant, provided a report showing a significant change in the reported profitability levels of the various product lines. Table 2 summarizes the types of changes that took place. Once implemented, the ABC information was used to negotiate product pricing and to report financial performance.

Table 1
Summary of Items Affected by the Need for High-or
Low-gloss Finish on a Bumper

	High Gloss	Low Gloss
Rejection Rate	high	low
Number of Colors	high	low
Batch Size	low	high
Number of Painters	high	low

Table 2
Number of Products That Had Changes in Calculated
Profit Margin from Standard Costing to ABC

Negative Margin	Positive Margin
←3 became more negative	→5 became more positive
7→moved from negative to positive	
1→became less negative	←10 became less positive

PLANNING FOR CAPACITY USE

The conveyor line was definitely a constraining resource of the painting process. Through her knowledge of theory of constraints (TOC), Mandy James, production supervisor, had developed a method for factoring in the various process elements into demand levels on conveyor capacity. Using bumpers as an example, she presented the template appearing in Table 3, and compared an LG bumper to an HG bumper. The template starts with the quality issue. The greater the percentage of defects, the lower the yield rate (YR) for a production run. The more complex shapes and finishes have lower yield rates than those that are less complex. LG bumpers currently have a YR of about 95%, while HG bumpers run about 92%.

Defective products can be worked on in-house, and some can be recovered. For bumpers, the recovery rate (RR) is about 5% of units started. Since the recovered bumpers are brought up to an acceptable quality level, they contribute toward meeting customer demand and put no further demand on the conveyor capacity. The YR and RR can be combined to determine how many products must be processed to generate one unit of acceptable quality, which is called the run factor (RF). The RF is equal to $1/(YR + RR)$. If $YR + RR = 1$, as with the LG bumper, then only one unit must be put on the conveyor to ultimately yield one unit of acceptable quality. The RF for the HG bumper is 103% (computed as $1/(92\% + 5\%)$), meaning PPS must paint 103% of the total bumpers required to yield enough bumpers of acceptable quality to satisfy customer demand.

Table 3
Using Capacity Demand to Rank Profitability

Product	Yield Rate (YR)	Recovery Rate (RR)	Run Factor (RF) =1/ (YR + RR)	Speed	Complexity Factor (CF) =18/ Speed	Demand Factor (DF) = (RF × CF)	Sq. Ft. per Unit of product (Sq. Ft.)	(BDF) Bottleneck Demand Sq. Ft. = (DF/ Sq. Ft.)	Profit per Unit of Finished Product	(P/TU) Adjusted Product Profit per Throughput Unit Profit per Sq. Ft. /BDF
Compare Two Bumper Finishes										
Low-Gloss Bumper	95%	5%	100%	15	1.20	1.20	10	.120	$10.00	$8.33
High-Gloss Bumper	92%	5%	103%	12	1.50	1.55	10	.155	$12.00	$7.76
Evaluate a Process Change										
Current Process High-Gloss Bumper	92%	5%	103%	12	1.50	1.55	10	.155	$12.00	$7.76
Change Speed and YR	90%	6%	104%	13	1.38	1.44	10	.144	$12.00	$8.32

Since the conveyor line is the constraint, the time a product spends on the conveyor is an important issue. Line speed can vary from 10 to 18 feet per minute, depending on the size and shape of the product being painted. Mandy considers 18 feet per minute to be the standard time unit for the conveyor line. A complexity factor (CF) ranging between 1 (for fastest line speed) and 1.8 (for slowest speed) is determined for each product family and added to the calculation of demand. The CF is computed by dividing the standard line speed of 18 feet per minute by the line speed required for the specific product, so a faster line speed results in a CF closer to 1. The line speed of the HG bumper is currently 12 feet per minute, resulting in an RF of $18/12 = 1.5$. The CF is then multiplied by the RF to get the total constraint demand factor (DF).

The DF is actually a demand placed on the conveyor per unit of finished good of a particular part type. Because parts can vary in shape and size, PPS needed a standard unit of measure to compare product profitability that factored in the total demand placed on the conveyor. The square footage of each part was chosen as the measurement unit because it represents the surface area of each part that's coated. As a result, the DF is divided by the total square footage of a particular part (e.g., a bumper) to yield the bottleneck demand factor (BDF), which is the demand factor per square foot of a particular size, shape, and finish. The profit level per square foot of finished good is divided by the BDF to yield the profit per throughput unit (P/TU) on the conveyor. Table 3 shows the LG bumper has a lower profit per unit ($10 per bumper, or $1 per sq. ft.), but after adjusting for the respective demands on the conveyor, the LG bumper has a higher P/TU.

DECISION POINT

Management of PPS used ABC to obtain a better understanding of the "true" cost of the products in order to help make better pricing decisions. Management now wants to be more proactive in the use of costing information to help develop and implement organizational strategy in an environment where the demand exceeds current productive capacity. Based on the opening question posed by Amy, PPS's management was attempting to move away from merely trying to assign costs more accurately to using the cost information to support strategic decision making. Specifically, Amy wants to make strategic decisions about which product lines to promote and pursue. She is aware of the ABC process of assigning cost of resources to activities, but considers this an operational rather than strategic issue. She isn't clear about whether ABC supports strategic decision making.

Mandy pointed out that the conveyor line was being fully utilized and jobs were being turned down because of the capacity constraint. She thought the capacity issue should drive any strategic decisions and that Amy should adopt the principles of TOC and throughput costing for strategic decision making. Mandy supported her position with the following example. "HG bumpers are a big part of production," she said. "We evaluated whether or not to increase the line speed when HG bumpers are being painted. The increase in speed will reduce the yield rate from 92% to 90%. There will be more defects, but the RR will increase to 6%, and, as Table 3 shows, the P/TU will increase and the finesse costs per unit would actually decline." (See Sidebar 2, "Finessing.")

Chad disagreed with Mandy's recommendation. Using Table 1, Chad noted that the HG finishes have higher reject rates, require additional painters, more colors, more inspections and maintenance costs, and slower line speed. The HG products are also treated as they pass through Stations 3 and 4. Since some of the costs related to resource demands are fixed costs, throughput costing shouldn't be used because these fixed costs would be ignored. He offered an alternative, resource consumption accounting (RCA), which he had heard about at a recent local IMA chapter meeting. He thought RCA might be what Amy needed, but he wasn't entirely sure. Chad presented Amy with a brief description of the costing method. (See Sidebar 3, "Basics of RCA.") He offered to learn more about RCA by attending a continuing education session offered by IMA, but Amy wanted more information before making the investment in having Chad attend the session.

SUGGESTED RESOURCES

Chwen, Sheu, Ming-Hsiang Chen, and Stacy Kovar. "Integrating ABC and TOC for Better Manufacturing Decision Making." *Integrated Manufacturing Systems*, May 2003, pp. 433 – 441.

Grasso, Lawrence P. " Are ABC and RCA Accounting Systems Compatible with Lean Management?" *Management Accounting Quarterly*, Fall 2005, pp. 12 – 27.

Keys, David, and Anton van der Merwe. " Gaining Effective Organizational Control with RCA." Strategic Finance, May 2002, pp. 41 – 47.

Resource Consumption Accounting Institute website, http: // www. rcainstitute. org

van der Merwe, Anton, and David Keys. "The Case for Resource Consumption Accounting." Strategic Finance, April 2002, pp 31 – 36.

SIDEBAR 1: PPS'S PRODUCTION PROCESS

PPS operates two 8-hour shifts, 240 days per year. The paint process involves a monorail conveyor line that moves at line speeds of 10-18 feet per minute, depending on the application and part complexity. The total paint cycle time is about 2.5 hours. The production schedule is created based on customer requirements, line speed, minimum lot (or batch) size, and the availability of racks. The material handlers bring the raw parts and racks to the line and loaders rack each part, making sure it is racked properly so that when it enters the E-coat tank a proper electrical ground is attained.

THE PAINT PROCESS

The part is first treated with chemicals (pre-treatment stage), a sequence of washing and rinsing to remove any grease or dirt and to prepare the part for paint adhesion with a phosphate spraying. Next, the part is submerged in a 20,000-gallon e-coat tank. As it comes out of the tank, it is sprayed with fresh, deionized water to rinse off any "dragout" paint clinging to the parts, thereby eliminating appearance defects. The part then moves through four paint booths. Depending on the part type, however, all four booths may not be used.

- Booth 1 has five automatic spray guns that apply primer. A part may or may not receive a primer coating, which provides additional protection against

chipping and rusting.
- Booth 2 has two manual sprayers as well as automatic sprayers that paint basecoat or enamel topcoat.
- Booth 3 has one manual sprayer and an automatic spray gun that apply clearcoat. Only high-gloss products receive the glossy, shiny clearcoat finish.
- Booth 4 has two manual sprayers and automatic spray guns that also apply clearcoat for parts that require two coats.

While low-gloss products are being painted, booth 3 and booth 4 painters are idle and the spray guns are turned off. Depending on the product line, the part receives a basecoat (high gloss) or an enamel topcoat (low gloss). After these processes, the paint is cured in another oven. As the product arrives back at the unload/load area, it is date-stamped, unracked onto a floor conveyor, inspected, unloaded, and packaged.

THE SETUP PROCESS

A five-minute setup "gap" is required when changing paint colors. This gives line workers the time to change the tooling racks, modify the line speed, purge the line of the old paint, and run the new paint through the system.

As the setup gap nears the paint booths, paint containers with the required colors are transported to the paint booth. While the last part from the prior color is painted, the paint lines are quickly purged of the old paint, flushed with solvents to clean the paint lines, and new paint is sprayed through the spray guns to obtain the desired consistency. As the gap ends and the raw parts appear, the painting begins again.

QUALITY ASSURANCE OR REWORK PROCESS

The primary sources of rejections are: dirt and dust in the manual hand sprayers, old equipment, and the nature of the industry. High-gloss products, which are much more expensive to reprocess, have substantially higher rejection rates than low-gloss products.

Rework mostly requires sanding. The product is sanded down to the e-coat primer and then moved to the line for reprocessing. Some products are sent to an outside stripper. Some defects can be corrected by finessing, which eliminates the need for complete reprocessing. Finessing allows the defect to be buffed out on parts that have the clearcoat glossy finish. Parts are considered "saved" when they can be unloaded along with the other painted good parts.

SIDEBAR 2: FINESSING

Currently PPS finesses approximately 100 000 bumpers per year, or about 5% of bumpers run on the conveyor. If the line speed is increased, the decline in the yield rate would create about 20 000 additional bumpers that the finesse department could work on. The finesse department can handle 125 000 units per year when operating at maximum efficiency, and the variable costs for finesse are less than $0.02 per unit, so the increase in units worked wouldn't generate much change in the total costs even though the computed cost per unit does change. The table provides the supporting detail.

Finesse Cost Per Unit at Various Defect Levels			
	Annual Cost	Units	Cost Per Unit
Current Defect Level	$480 000	100 000	$4.800
Defect Level with Increased Line Speed	$480 400	120 000	$4.003
Practical Capacity to Handle Defects	$480 500	125 000	$3.844

SIDEBAR 3: BASICS OF RCA

Resource consumption accounting (RCA) is based on costing methods developed by German companies and the activity costing philosophy of ABC. RCA takes a resource-based view of an organization and looks closely at the quantity of resources consumed and the underlying nature of the cost of those resources. Some of the key characteristics of RCA are the treatment of idle capacity, the use of costs other than historical, and the ability to group and track cost information at various levels. This comprehensive management accounting system can lead to improved decision support by providing more accurate product costs and a better understanding of the interrelationships between processes and costs.

平衡记分卡
Balanced Scorecard

Tri-Cities 社区银行——一则平衡记分卡的案例

Tom Albright
University of Alabama

Stan Davis
University of Tennessee
at Chattanooga

Aleecia R. Hibbets
University of Louisiana
at Monroe

案例甲：平衡记分卡的开发

Tr-Cities 社区银行（TCCB）坐落在美国中西部，共有 10 家支行，组成南方分部（SD）和北方分部（ND）两个分部。每一个分部下属五家支行，每一家支行雇有一名支行行长、支行副行长/信贷主任、若干名客服代表、信贷员、按揭贷款发放人员、出纳主任、柜面人员[①]和行政助理。所有支行间的距离不超过 60 英里。

过去几年，TCCB 已取得不俗的财务业绩，但他们还在不断寻求改进业绩的新途径。行里每年都要召集高管和外部顾问召开一次会议，审查其战略方向。会议的目的是廓清该银行的愿景和使命，以确保所有的高管都理解并赞同银行的发展方向。2004 年，TCCB 的管理层采用的总体战略是使利润与增长取得平衡，确保银行的独立地位，并向日益多元化的客户群提供优质的服务和产品。

克莉丝·比林斯（Chris Billings）最近从营销主管被提拔为南方分部（SD）的行长，这一升迁正好发生在她 2006 年 12 月份完成了 MBA 夜校课程之际。在研究生课程中，她接触了平衡记分卡（BSC），知道其是一种业绩考核制度，用于引导决策者致力于创造长期价值的各种活动。克莉丝认为，可以采用平衡记分卡来改善 TCCB 的财务业绩。在 2006 年 12 月下旬，她找 CEO 商量，请求允许她推行这个新方法。

TCCB 的 CEO 对这个新方法惴惴不安。他的犹豫来自两方面原因：一是自己不熟悉平衡记分卡，二是克莉丝接手南方分部行长一职为时过短。他

[①] ccashier，直译应作"出纳"，但中国通常称为"柜面人员"。——译者

还忧虑克莉丝的想法是否会被北方分部的行长和员工所接受。最后，他对平衡记分卡究竟能带来什么好处也拿不准。同时，这位 CEO 也不想打击积极性，因为这是她就任南方分部行长后的第一个努力尝试。为了不打击克莉丝的积极性，这位 CEO 答应了在她分部的 5 家支行中实施平衡记分卡（而非答应其在行内全面推行平衡记分卡）；而克莉丝则答应在三个月内，向 CEO 和银行的董事会作一次陈述报告。在这个会上，克莉丝将要陈述平衡记分卡的概念，及如何运用这一方案来改善她管辖支行的财务业绩。当时，要设计出一个试点计划，时间紧迫；克莉丝对于怎么样才能说服董事会允许她推行平衡记分卡，心中也没有底。她知道，自己必须说服南方分部各支行的行长们相信平衡记分卡的价值。

2007 年 1 月 7 日，克莉丝和她管辖的各支行的行长们见面，并讨论了平衡记分卡方案，以期他们在制定各支行的记分卡上能出谋划策。会议一开始，她给大家发了一份材料（见图表 A1），重点阐明平衡记分卡的主要目的。她通过这份材料告诉各支行行长平衡记分卡的四个方面（在平衡记分卡制度中所包括的四类考核指标）。她在这份资料中所列举的一些指标，来自一家已经施行了平衡记分卡制度的医院。由于她当时手头没有哪家银行采用平衡记分卡制度的现成的考核指标，所以她就想把其他一些服务行业的指标拿过来，供各位支行行长参考。如这份文字资料所示，该医院把按病例计算的营业毛利和成本，作为其主要的财务考核指标；以出院病人给予的推荐评级和让病人出院的及时性，作为有关顾客的考核指标；住院时间的长短和复诊（病人因同一病因重新入院）比率，作为内部经营的考核指标；把对员工的培训和员工的留任率，作为"学习与成长"方面的考核指标。接着，她指导支行行长们共同协作，制定针对各支行平衡记分卡的有价值的指标。虽然各家支行最终都会制定针对自身情况的记分卡，但是克莉丝认为各支行的情况很相似，因而各位行长在开始时是可以坐在一起共同协作的。这一组人将在 6 个星期以后再次会面，讨论他们在制定支行平衡记分卡制度中所取得的进展。

2 月 25 日，他们的会面情况并不像克莉丝所期望的那样理想。各个支行行长虽然对于各自需要注意的问题，有了很好的认识，但在会上陈述的内容，至多只能看作为建立平衡记分卡制度所需要的原始资料而已。在正式实施这个制度之前，还需要做很多工作。

时间日益紧迫，克莉丝逐渐感到一些忧虑，她还没有为 3 月 31 日已安排好的董事会准备好一份具体的陈述意见。她担心如果不能为董事会提出一份内容具体的报告，方案很可能就得不到批准。克莉丝的目标是要在会上陈述一组可以量化的考核指标。这些指标之间存在着因果关系，并且可以导致关键财务指标的提升。

平衡记分卡的主要好处之一在于，它可以把各项非财务指标和银行密切关注的三项主要财务指标之间的因果关系，用路径图的形式描绘出来。非财务指标分为三大类别：学习与成长、内部业务流程和以客户为中心。平衡记分卡各指标之间的因果关系如下：如果学习能力有提高，则内部业务流程会有所改进；如果内部流程有所改进，则顾客获得的价值就会有所增加；如果顾客获得的价值有所增加,则企业的财务业绩就会有所提高。财务绩效是一家公司战略追求的最终目标。如果财务业绩获得显著的提高,则企业的战略就成功了。因此,如果企业有一个优良的战略,则对非财务指标的考核,就会改善增加企业价值的各项指标,这一切最终会归结于财务指标的提高。

图表 A1
BSC 所包含的业务分类的几个方面和领先/滞后的各项指标

BSC 主要的方面:
财务方面——股东如何看待我们?

- 企业的各项财务目标是一切活动的焦点所在。平衡记分卡所选用的每一项指标,都应该是因果链中的一个组成部分,这个因果链最终导致各项财务目标业绩的改善。
- 例如医院产业财务方面的目标,可能包含营业毛利、每个病例的成本和资本金的募集。

顾客方面——顾客如何看我们?

- 在顾客方面,各个组织必须明确它的主要顾客和市场细分。各个组织还必须同时确定,它们如何让顾客得到实惠,并且按各个顾客的具体需求量体裁衣,向他们提供更好的产品和服务。
- 在医院产业中,顾客角度方面的目标包括提高推荐评级和病人出院的及时性。

内部业务方面——我们必须在哪些方面超越别人?

- 在内部业务方面,各个组织必须确定需要改进或新创的各道操作工序,以达到顾客和财务方面的各项目标。
- 在医院产业中,内部业务方面的目标包括降低(为同一医疗情况的)复诊率,和增加医生对病人的接触时间。

学习和成长方面——我们如何持续提高和创造价值?

- 为达到对上述三方面目标所确定的高标准,各组织必须投资于它们的员工和基础设施。各组织应该识别哪些资源是它所需要的,并制订一项计划,使它的员工能够达到其他各方面的目标。
- 医院产业在学习与成长方面的目标包括增加对员工的培训和留任,改善其信息技术系统,并对各个轮班配备适当的人员。

领先指标和滞后指标:

在顾客、内部业务流程和学习与成长各个方面所用的非财务考核指标(NFMs)的改进,会导致各项财务目标的提高。因为这些 NFMs 的改善,往往会"领先"于在财务指标的改善,所以把这些 NFMs 称为"领先指标"。与此相似,在财务方面被选定的各项指标,往往又比 NFMs"滞后",因而被称为"滞后指标"。

* 本图表的内容来自卡普兰(Kaplan)与诺顿(Norton)发表的《平衡记分卡:化战略为行动》(1996)和《战略中心型组织》(2001)。

图表 A2 提供了一份由各支行行长所提出的业绩指标清单,和克莉丝在开会时所作的纪要。图表 A3 是一份因果关系示例图。如图表 A3 所示,如果员工们在销售效果、客户服务、产品盈利和本地银行业务方面接受培训,他们就会有更足的底气为客户提供更优质的服务。TCCB 通过让员工参加行内组织的各项业务考试,来检验其培训项目的效果。通过提高员工的知识和技能,他们就能在向客户作推荐和交叉销售[②]方面卓有成效,从而使顾客高

---

② 交叉销售(Cross-sell):发现一位现有顾客的多种需求,并通过满足其需求而实现向其销售多种相关的服务或产品的营销方式。——译者

度满意、把顾客留住。留住现有的顾客群，就有基础增加存贷款余额了。同时，成功的推荐和交叉销售的增加又提高了非利息收入。

为了向董事会阐述，平衡记分卡是如何提高三项主要财务指标（贷款余额、存款余额和非利息收入）的业绩的，克莉丝需要编制一份各指标间的因果关系图。她知道，任何专注于提高这三项指标的方案，都很有可能获得批准。

图表 A2
TCCB 平衡记分卡中的业绩考核指标

- 未偿还贷款余额
- 存款余额
- 每位顾客平均购买产品数
- 新发展的客户数
- 非利息收入（NII）——从银行所提供的各项服务和产品中所获得的收入。NII 中包括与定期存款、银行卡、保单、保险箱、年金业务、经纪人账户、支票账户和旅行支票有关收取的费用。
- 新增贷款额
- 新开账户数
- 新推出的产品数

- 员工培训小时数
- 客户满意程度
- 顾客维系率
- 员工满意程度
- 对潜在顾客所打的促销电话
- 对新老客户发致谢电话/明信片
- 员工流动率
- 引荐——所谓引荐，指的是员工向某一客户建议找本支行的另一名员工，以获取有关某种产品更详细的信息
- 交叉销售——当一位客户仅为一项产品来到本银行时，却向他销售了多种产品，这称之为"交叉销售"

会议纪要

最重要的财务考核指标为贷款余额、存款余额和非利息收入。我们所做的一切，都应以改善这三项财务考核指标为终极目标。

必须提高客户的满意程度。我们是一家小型的社区银行，因而我们依靠打"家乡"牌，以提供优质服务，使客户有一种宾至如归的感觉。我们对口碑宣传的依赖，不亚于对电台和报纸广告的依赖。

我们的员工必须在各个方面获得培训，包括营销技巧、客户服务和产品知识/盈利性。这一类培训会提高我们的员工与客户之间的互动，使柜面人员与客户代表对顾客的需求有所认识，向客户作出更有效的引荐及提供新的产品。

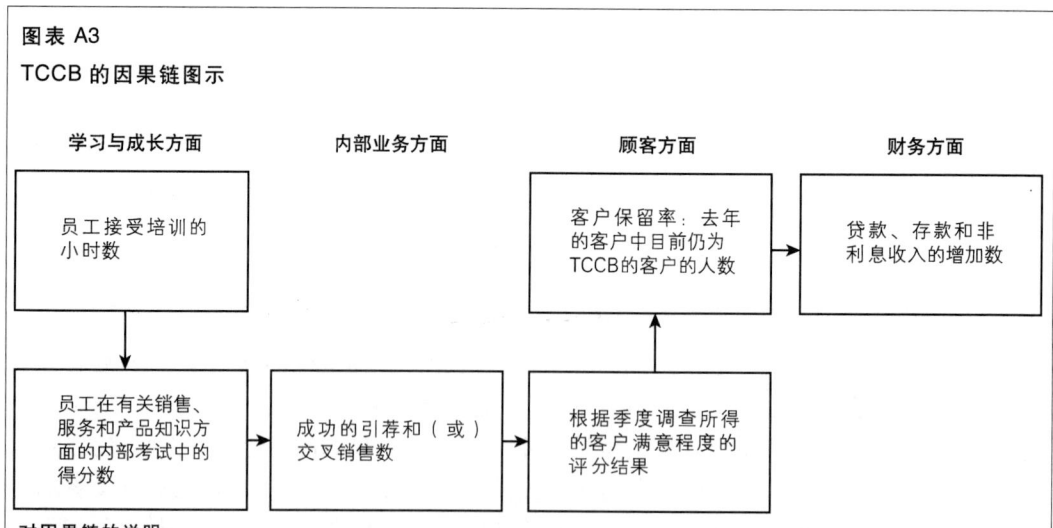

图表 A3
TCCB 的因果链图示

对因果链的说明：

如果员工接受提高营销效果、顾客服务、产品盈利性和当地银行知识方面的培训，他们就能提供更好的顾客服务，与现有客户之间有更好的互动。TCCB 的员工就能更好地摸准客户的需求，从而向他们作优良的推荐和为银行的其他部门推介业务；因此客户会更加满意，并继续与 TCCB 开展银行业务往来。而增加推荐或交叉销售，会增加非利息收入，并增加存款与贷款的余额。

要求：

编制一份对董事会的报告，说明平衡记分卡是如何来帮助 TCCB 达成其战略目标的。在你的报告书中应包括以下内容：

① 编织一张表格，把图表 A2 列示的各项指标归类至平衡记分卡的四个方面，并陈述你为何如此归类。

② 编制两份与图表 A3 相类似的因果关系链图。用图表 A2 所列示的指标清单，或者用你认为其他的合适的指标来编制这份因果链图。请务必在你的答案中把因果关系说清楚。

案例乙：对财务指标改善的评估

这次对董事会所作的陈述，受到了大家的欢迎；克莉丝获得批准，在南方分部的五个支行中试点实施平衡记分卡。她有一年时间去向 CEO 和董事会证明平衡记分卡是可以提高各支行的业绩的。在这一年中，南方分部的五个支行都实施了平衡记分卡。然而，每一位支行行长都将他或她的个人风格融入到了实施的过程中。

现在，一年的试点阶段已经过去，克莉丝已经收集了各项数据，可以确定这个方案究竟是否成功。这一年中，由于经营环境并没有发生异常情况，因而克莉丝相信，试点行在业绩上所发生的变化都应该归因于采用了平衡记分卡制度。图表 B1 分别描述了截止到 2008 年 6 月 30 日和 2007 年 6 月 30 日的贷款余额、存款余额和非利息收入的数据。图表 B1 所示南方分部的各支行（支行 A～E），是在 2007 年 7 月 1 日开始实施平衡记分卡的。

在每一个支行，克莉丝都和一些员工作了面谈，以此评价这项工作。面谈的情况，归纳如下：

支行 A：

客服代表——玛丽·理查德

实施平衡记分卡的理由之一，是要帮助我们达到支行的各项目标。每一个人都知道，我们的战略是要在贷款、存款和定期存单之间取得平衡增长。例如，为了增加贷款量，我们情愿在每一项贷款上减少毛利。平衡记分卡使我们的战略更加清晰明了。

信贷员——迈克·穆尔

我们必须为记分卡的各项指标付出努力。这些指标并不容易达成，但它们是根据现实情况而制订的。我的指标和我所看到的其他记分卡上的指标，同样地难以实现，因此它是公平合理的。当然，我同事们的记分卡上的指标，可能和我的不同，但每个人都必须全力以赴方能达成。

出纳主任——保罗·弗兰克斯

如果我们达到或超额完成我们的各项目标，我们就能获得相应的奖金。每个月业绩最好的人，都会获得表彰并给予奖金。每个季度，还对记分卡上

图表 B1
各支行主要的财务指标业绩情况

支行	2008年6月30日			2007年6月30日		
	贷款余额（百万美元）	存款余额（百万美元）	非利息收入（千美元）	贷款余额（百万美元）	存款余额（百万美元）	非利息收入（千美元）
A	39.3	85.1	476.0	35.9	77.0	411.0
B	58.1	104.5	428.0	49.7	101.4	399.0
C	63.7	136.3	529.0	56.1	124.0	474.0
D	46.7	93.1	291.0	45.1	86.7	276.0
E	54.4	109.3	343.0	53.9	108.2	344.0
F	42.9	87.5	345.0	41.9	88.5	335.0
G	64.5	115.2	498.0	64.5	114.8	477.0
H	33.2	78.2	230.0	32.7	77.8	233.0
I	51.1	93.7	293.0	50.8	91.6	280.0
J	71.2	150.8	589.0	68.0	145.0	571.0

业绩最出色的个人，发放1 000美元的奖金。

支行 B：

信贷员——帕米拉·怀兹

依我所见，平衡记分卡是衡量我们在完成管理层所确定目标方面取得进展的一种工具。就我们支行而言，我们要满足不断成长的社区在各项理财方面的需求，又让我们的服务给人一种"家乡小镇"的感觉。

柜面人员——格伦达·斯莫利

记分卡上对我考核的某些指标，富有挑战性；但并不比我曾经见过的另外一些记分卡难多少。虽然这些指标是难以达到的，但并非不可能达到。我想，平衡记分卡是用来鼓励我们工作得更好；有了进步，我们就获得奖金。例如，我们在记分卡上所表现的业绩，能帮助我们确定年终奖，也可以使我们获得提升和增加工资。

支行 C：

客服代表——比尔·索伦森

当然，我对为什么要实施平衡记分卡心中有数。其目的是要提高柜面人员、信贷主任和客服代表之间的团队协作。另外，它还帮助每一个人理解我们的目标和如何达成这些目标。

按揭贷款发放人员——黛比·汉森

只有通过营销、交叉销售、起到作为沟通枢纽的作用和让客户宾至如归，才能达成支行的目标。平衡记分卡让我们知道，在这个过程中，我们每个人都有份。当我们决定开始实施平衡记分卡时，管理层需要从员工那里获得许多反馈。他们需要确定：我们每一个人都对这个做法心中有数。

行政助理——洛乌·马丁

当我们达成了支行各项平衡记分卡季度目标时，我们开了一个盛大的派对。如果记分卡的成绩好，每一个人都会因自己的成绩获得休假，最多达到每两个月就给一天。不幸的是，我的记分卡指标因极难达成，成绩够不上要求。

支行 D：

信贷员——加里·史密斯

根据我的理解，平衡记分卡的目的在于记录或跟踪成长的过程。我们必须确定，对于公司来说，哪些指标是重要的。因此，在我们决定哪些指标应该列在记分卡上时，我们的支行行长向我们提出了几个问题。我想，她这样做是为了帮助我们对这件事有一个统一的看法。

客服代表——阿尔·泰勒

我的记分卡上的所有的指标，都是公平合理的，并非遥不可及。所有的指标难度可能都差不多。完成我们的目标，还有物质鼓励。例如，如果我们完成了个人的平衡记分卡目标，那么每个月就可以多得 50 美元。我们支行行长总是寻求更好的方法，对我们的平衡记分卡取得良好业绩，给予奖励。

支行 E：

信贷员——安·斯通

在我们的支行里，平衡记分卡追踪记录了我们所做的一切，并把我们的业绩与其他支行相比较。我并没有如临大敌的感觉。在开始实施这个做法的两个月内，我就达到了我的所有考核指标。

柜面人员——皮特·琼斯

我想记分卡只是赶时髦而已。我不敢肯定我的物质奖励是否都和我在记分卡上的业绩有关。但是，如果我做得很差，却是会被解雇的。从另一方面来看，保住我的工作，也可以看做是一种物质报酬。

行政助理——丹尼尔·休斯

在开发我们的记分卡中，我们自身并没有参与很多。只是有一天，管理层来到这里，告诉我们这种新的业绩考核制度。

信贷员——蒂姆·瓦因斯

我看到过一些资料上说，记分卡是用来帮助各个公司实现他们的战略的。要让管理层给我们如何完成自己的战略出个主意是一件困难的事情。我做的事情或许能（或许不能）帮助公司实现其战略目标。

克莉丝相信，平衡记分卡的推行已经取得了成功。她对 CEO 表示，自己有信心取得董事会的批准，同意她把平衡记分卡推广到所有支行的计划。然而，她知道在批准这一计划之前，董事会将要求她提出过硬的证据。她也明白，必须做好准备向董事会陈述，在南方分部试点平衡记分卡过程中，什么地方可取，什么地方犯了错误。

要求：

1）对平衡记分卡是否收到效果作一分析。

2）向董事会提出报告，归纳你的结论。

3）以 A~E 各支行实际业绩，说明在推行平衡记分卡上各支行之间存在的差距。

北方分部的行长们正在考虑采用平衡记分卡，你将如何向他们推荐这项做法？

Tri-Cities Community Bank—A Balanced Scorecard Case

Tom Albright
University of Alabama

Stan Davis
University of Tennessee
at Chattanooga

Aleecia R. Hibbets
University of Louisiana
at Monroe

CASE A: BSC DEVELOPMENT

Tri-Cities Community Bank (TCCB) is located in the Midwest US and has a total of 10 branches grouped into two divisions, the southern division (SD) and the northern division (ND). Each division consists of five branches; each branch employs a branch president, branch vice-president/chief loan officer, customer service representatives, loan representatives, mortgage loan originators, head tellers, tellers, and administrative assistants. All branches are located within a 60-mile radius.

TCCB has enjoyed strong financial success over the past few years but continues to look for ways to improve its performance. The strategic direction of the bank is reviewed annually at a meeting of top bank officials and outside consultants. The purpose of the meeting is to outline the vision and mission of the bank and to ensure all top managers understand and agree on the direction of the organization. In 2004, TCCB management adopted the master strategy of balancing profits with growth to ensure the bank remains an independent entity existing to provide quality service and products to an increasingly diverse customer base.

Chris Billings recently was promoted from marketing director to SD president. The promotion came just as Chris finished her evening Masters of Business Administration degree in December 2006. As part of her graduate studies, she was introduced to the balanced scorecard (BSC), a performance measurement system that directs decision-makers toward long-term value creating activities. Chris thought the BSC could be used to improve the financial performance of TCCB. In late December 2006, she approached the chief executive officer (CEO) and requested permission to implement the new program.

TCCB's CEO was apprehensive about the new program. His reluctance stemmed from his own unfamiliarity with the BSC and Chris's short tenure as SD president. The CEO also was concerned about whether Chris's ideas would be accepted by the ND president and ND branch employees. Finally he was uncertain about the BSC's benefits. At the same time, the CEO did not want to respond negatively to Chris's first efforts as SD president. To appease Chris without totally committing the bank to implement the BSC, the CEO agreed to allow Chris to begin the process of developing the BSC in the five branches of her division. In turn, Chris agreed to make a presentation to the CEO and the bank's Board of Directors in three months. In this meeting, Chris would present BSC concepts and how she planned to use the program to improve the financial performance of her branches. Given the short period of time to design a pilot study, Chris wondered how she could convince the Board of Directors to give her permission to implement the BSC. She knew she must convince the SD branch presidents of its value.

On January 7th, 2007, Chris met with her branch presidents to discuss the BSC program and enlist their help in developing balanced scorecards for their branches. She began the meeting by distributing a handout (Exhibit A1) highlighting the key objectives of the BSC. She used the handout to inform the branch presidents of the four business "perspectives" (categories of measures to be included on the BSC). The example measures she included on the handout are from a hospital that had implemented the BSC. Since she did not have example measures from a bank using the BSC, she wanted to show the branch presidents measures from another service industry for them to consider. As the handout shows, the hospital uses operating margin and cost per case as their primary financial measures, recommendation ratings from outgoing patients and discharge timeliness information as customer measures, length of stay and readmission rate (patients being admitted again for the same injury or illness) for the internal business measures, and employee training and retention measures in the learning and growth perspective. She then instructed the branch presidents to work together to develop meaningful measures to be included on branch BSCs. While each branch would eventually develop a branch-specific scorecard, she believed the branches were similar enough to allow branch presidents to work together initially. The group was to meet again in six weeks to discuss their progress in developing branch BSCs.

The group meeting on February 25th did not go as well as Chris had hoped. While the branch presidents had done a good job of identifying areas that needed attention within each branch, the information presented could, at best, only be considered as raw materials necessary to build a BSC program. Much work was needed prior to implementing the program.

Exhibit A1

Key Business Perspectives and Lead/Lag Indicators *

KEY BUSINESS PERSPECTIVES:

Financial Perspective-How do we look to our shareholders?

- The financial objectives of the organization serve as the focus of all activities. Every measure selected for a balanced scorecard should be part of a causal chain that results in improved performance on financial objectives.
- Some examples of financial perspective objectives in the hospital industry include operating margins, cost per case, and capital fund-raising.

Customer Perspective-How do customers view us?

- In the customer perspective, organizations must identify key customers and market segments. Organizations must also determine how they add value for customers and seek to deliver better products and services that are tailored to specific customer needs.
- Some examples of customer perspective objectives in the hospital industry include improved recommendation ratings and discharge timeliness.

Internal Business Perspective-At what must we excel?

- For the internal business perspective, organizations identify those processes that must be improved or created in order to reach the objectives of the customer and financial perspectives.
- Some examples of internal business perspective objectives in the hospital industry include reducing the readmission rate (for the same medical condition) and increasing the doctor-to-patient contact time.

Learning and Growth Perspective – How do we continue to improve and create value?

- To achieve the lofty standards set in the previous three objectives, organizations must invest in their people and infrastructure. For this perspective, organizations identify where resources are needed and craft a plan to enable its employees to achieve the objectives of the other perspectives.
- Some examples of learning and growth perspective objectives in the hospital industry include increased employee training and retention, improved information technology systems, and adequate staffing for all shifts.

LEAD AND LAG INDICATORS:

Nonfinancial measures (NFMs) selected in the customer, internal business process, and learning and growth perspectives serve as lead indicators of improvement in financial objectives because improvement in these NFMs often "lead" or precede the improvement observed in financial measures. Likewise, the financial measures selected in the financial perspective are often called lag indicators because improvement in these financial measures often "lags" or comes after the improvement in the NFMs.

---

* Adapted from Kaplan and Norton's 1996 *Translating Strategy into Action: The Balanced Scorecard* (1996) and *The Strategy-Focused Organization* (2001).

With time running out, Chris grew concerned about the scheduled meeting with the Board of Directors on March 31st. She had nothing concrete to present at the meeting and worried she might not receive permission to pursue the program if she did not make a solid presentation to the board. Chris's goal is to present a group of quantifiable measures that are linked through causal relationships and lead to improvement of key financial measures.

One of the primary benefits of the BSC comes through mapping the causal relationships from nonfinancial performance measures to the three primary financial measures the bank monitors. Nonfinancial measures are categorized into three perspectives: Learning and Growth, Internal Business Processes, and Customer Focus. The cause and effect linkages in the BSC will occur in the following manner: if learning improves, then internal processes will improve. If internal processes improve, then customer value will increase. If customer value increases, financial performance will improve. Financial performance is the ultimate evaluation of a firm's strategy. If financial performance improves significantly, the firm's strategy is successful. Thus, if the strategy is good, the measures of the nonfinancial perspectives will be lead indicators of increasing value that will ultimately be proven by improved financial measures.

Exhibit A2 provides a list of performance measures developed by the branch presidents and notes Chris took during meetings with them. Exhibit A3 illustrates a sample cause-and-effect chain. For example, as shown in Exhibit A3, if employees receive training in sales effectiveness, customer service, product profitability, and local bank knowledge, they will be better equipped to provide customers with higher quality service. TCCB measures the effectiveness of its training programs by having employees take in-house tests on various training topics. By increasing employee knowledge and skills, higher quality referrals and cross-sell proposals will take place, leading to higher customer satisfaction and greater customer retention. Maintaining the current customer base provides the basis for growth in deposit and loan balances, while a greater number of successful referrals and cross-sells increase non-interest income.

Chris wants to prepare a series of cause-and-effect chains to illustrate to the Board of Directors how the BSC can be used to improve performance on three key financial measures: loan balances, deposit balances, and non-interest income. She knows that any program emphasizing improvement in these three measures has a strong chance of receiving approval.

Exhibit A2
Performance Measures for TCCB Balanced Scorecards

- Outstanding Loan Balances
- Deposit Balances
- Number of Products per Customer
- Number of New Customers
- Non-Interest Income-income earned from fees on services and products provided by the bank. NII includes fees associated with CDs, ATM cards, insurance policies, lock boxes, annuities, brokerage accounts, checking accounts, and travelers'checks.
- New Loans Created
- New Accounts
- New Products Introduced
- Employee Training Hours
- Customer Satisfaction
- Customer Retention
- Employee Satisfaction
- Sales Calls to Potential Customers
- Thank-You Calls/Cards to New & Existing Customers
- Employee Turnover
- Referrals-referrals occur when an employee suggests a customer see another branch employee for more information about a product
- Cross-Sells-selling multiple products to a customer when the customer comes in for only one product

Notes from Branch Presidents' Meetings

The most important financial measures are loan balances, deposit balances, and non-interest income. Everything we do should be aimed toward improving these three financial measures.

Customer satisfaction must be improved. Because we are a small community bank, we rely on delivering quality services with a "hometown" feel. We rely on word-of-mouth advertising as much as we do radio and newspaper ads. Our employees must have training in several different areas, including sales techniques, customer service, and product knowledge/profitability. This type of training would improve the interactions between our employees and customers, allowing tellers and customer sales representatives to recognize customer needs and make more effective referrals and new product offerings.

Exhibit A3
Cause-and-Effect Chain Illustration for TCCB

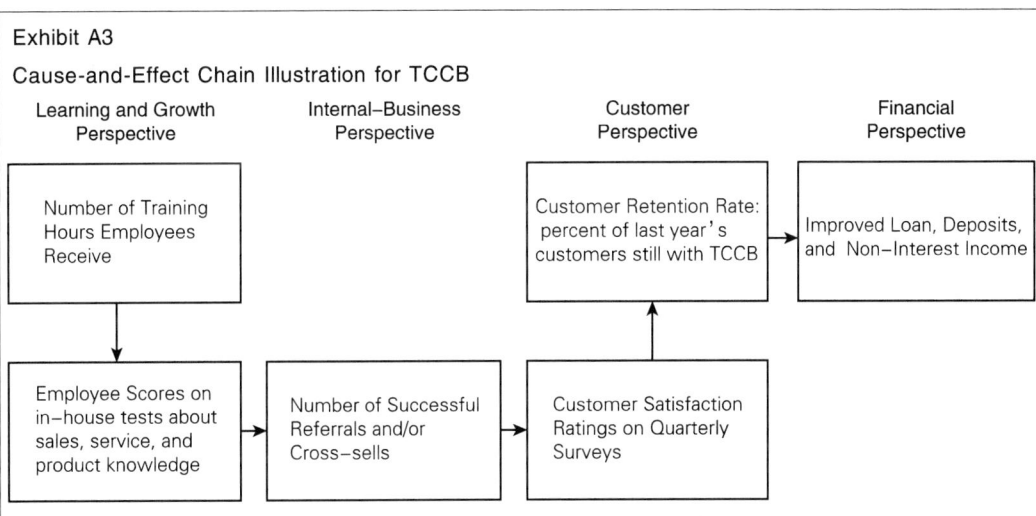

Causal Chain Explanation:

If employees receive training in sales effectiveness, customer service, product profitability, and local bank knowledge, then they can provide better customer service and higher quality interactions with existing clients can take place. TCCB employees will be better able to ascertain the needs of customers, thereby making higher quality referrals and cross-sell proposals to customers, and customers will be more satisfied and choose to continue banking with TCCB. Increased referrals or cross-sales increases non-interest income and provides the basis for growth in deposit and loan balances.

REQUIRED:

Prepare a report to the Board of Directors that explains how the BSC may be used to help TCCB achieve its strategic goals. Include the following in your report:

1) A table that categorizes each of the measures in Exhibit A2 into one of the four BSC perspectives. State why you placed a measure in a particular perspective.

2) Two cause-and-effect chains similar to the one shown in Exhibit A3. Use the measures listed in Exhibit A2 or suggest other measures you feel are appropriate. Be sure to include a causal chain explanation with your answer.

CASE B: ASSESSING FINANCIAL IMPROVEMENT

The presentation to the Board of Directors was well received and Chris secured permission for a pilot study of the BSC in the five SD branches. She had one year to convince the CEO and Board of Directors of the BSC's ability to improve branch performance. During the year, all five SD branches implemented the BSC. However, each manager brought his or her individual style to the implementation process.

Now, the one-year trial period is over and Chris has collected data to determine whether the program was successful. Because no unusual business situations occurred during the year, Chris believes any changes in performance among the adopting branches can be attributed to the BSC. Exhibit B1 reports financial data on loan balances, deposit balances, and non-interest income for the periods ended June 30, 2008 and June 30, 2007, respectively. The SD branches, Branches A-E in Exhibit B1, began their BSC programs on July 1, 2007.

As part of her program assessment, Chris interviewed several employees at each branch. The interviews are summarized below:

BRANCH A:

Customer service representative-Mary Richards

One reason for implementing the BSC is to help us reach our branch goals. Everyone understands that our strategy is to balance loans, deposits, and Certificates of Deposit with growth. For example, to create greater loan volume, we are willing to accept a lower profit margin on each loan. The BSC helps clarify our strategy.

Exhibit B1

Branch performance on key financial indicators

Branch	As of June 30, 2008			As of June 30, 2007		
	Loan Balance (Million $)	Deposit Balance (Million $)	Non-Interest Income (Million $)	Loan Balance (Million $)	Deposit Balance (Million $)	Non-Interest Income (Million $)
A	39.3	85.1	476.0	35.9	77.0	411.0
B	58.1	104.5	428.0	49.7	101.4	399.0
C	63.7	136.3	529.0	56.1	124.0	474.0
D	46.7	93.1	291.0	45.1	86.7	276.0
E	54.4	109.3	343.0	53.9	108.2	344.0
F	42.9	87.5	345.0	41.9	88.5	335.0
G	64.5	115.2	498.0	64.5	114.8	477.0
H	33.2	78.2	230.0	32.7	77.8	233.0
I	51.1	93.7	293.0	50.8	91.6	280.0
J	71.2	150.8	589.0	68.0	145.0	571.0

Loan representative-Mike Moore

We have to work at our scorecard measures. They're not easy, but they are realistic. The process seems fair because my measures are just as hard as the other scorecards I have seen. Of course, the measures on my co-workers' scorecards may be different from mine, but everyone has to work hard.

Head teller-Paul Franks

If we meet or exceed our targets, we are eligible to earn cash bonuses. Each month the top performers are recognized and rewarded. There's also a $1 000 reward per quarter to the individual who performs the best on his or her scorecard.

BRANCH B:

Loan representative-Pamela Wise

As I understand it, the BSC is a tool to measure our progress in achieving the goals established by management. In our case, we want to meet the financial needs of a growing community, yet keep a small-town feeling to our services.

Teller-Glenda Smalley

Some of my scorecard measures are challenging, but no more so than the other scorecards I have seen. The measures are difficult, but not unattainable. I think the BSC is being used to encourage us to do better. We are rewarded when we improve. For example, our performance on the BSC helps to determine our year-end bonuses, as well as promotions and raises.

BRANCH C:

Customer service representative-Bill Sorensen

Sure, I understand why we implemented the balanced scorecard. It's purpose is to promote teamwork among tellers, loan officers, and customer service representatives. Also, it helps everyone understand our goals and how to reach them.

Mortgage loan originator-Debbie Hansen

The scorecard taught us how everyone has a part in achieving branch goals by selling, cross-selling, serving as a communication port, and making customers feel welcome. Management wanted a lot of employee feedback when we were deciding to start the BSC. They wanted to be sure we knew about the program.

Administrative assistant-Lou Martin

When we reach our BSC goals as a branch on a quarterly basis, we throw a big party. Individually, we can earn time off, up to a day every two months, if we do well on the BSC. Unfortunately, some of my scorecard measures are next to impossible to achieve.

BRANCH D:

Loan representative-Gary Smith

As I understand it, the BSC is for charting growth. We had to determine which measures were important to the company. Thus, our branch manager asked a few questions when we were deciding which measures to include on the scorecards. I think she helped focus our ideas.

Customer service representative-Al Taylor

My scorecard measures are not impossible; they are fair. All of our measures are probably about the same difficulty. There are some incentives to achieve our goals. For example, we can earn $50 each month if we meet our individual BSC goals. Our branch president is always looking for better ways to reward us for good BSC performance.

BRANCH E:

Loan representative-Ann Stone

In our branch, the BSC is to keep track of what we're doing and to compare our performance with others. I don't see it as a big deal. I reached all of my goals within two months of starting the program.

Teller-Pete Jones

I think the scorecard is used just to keep up with people's activities. I'm not sure any tangible rewards are associated with my performance on the BSC. If I do poorly, I'll probably be fired, however. On the other hand, keeping my job may be considered a tangible reward.

Administrative assistant-Daniel Hughes

We didn't get to participate very much in developing our scorecards. Management just came in one day and told us about the new performance measurement system.

Loan representative-Tim Vines

I've read that the scorecard is supposed to help companies with their strategy. It's difficult to get an idea of our strategy from management. Maybe what I do helps (or does not help) us achieve our strategic goals.

Chris believed the BSC had been a success. She expressed her confidence to the CEO about winning board approval for her plan to expand the BSC to all branches. However, she understood the board would require hard evidence before approving a plan. Chris also understood she must be prepared to answer questions about what went right and what went wrong during the pilot study in the SD branches.

REQUIRED:

1) Prepare an analysis to determine whether the BSC appears to have had an effect.

2) Summarize your results in a report appropriate for the Board of Directors.

3) Identify differences in implementation quality that may explain variation in performance among branches A-E. What implementation recommendations would you make to ND managers who are considering adopting the balanced scorecard?

爱荷华州滑铁卢市：设置财务总监职位

William F. Bowlin
North Dakota State University

Margaret L. Andersen
North Dakota State University

1. 简介

爱荷华州滑铁卢市的财务主管（finance officer，FO）辞去职务，去了私营单位谋职。

在他任期之初，该市的市长曾任命一个由公民组成的咨询委员会，对这个市的财务工作提出建议。该市的财务需求不断增长，但人口却在缩减，其课税基础也就随着减少。市长认为，由公民对本市的财务状况提出意见是有益的。咨询委员会的职责包括监督本市的财务状况、提出降低成本的建议、审查审计报告书等其他与财务有关的职责。咨询委员会由本市一位债券包销人的代表、一位当地大学的会计教授、一位当地的银行家、一位滑铁卢市注册会计师事务所的代表和三位对本市的财务情况有兴趣的市民组成。

在那位财务主管辞职后不久，该咨询委员会检查本市的财务情况时，委员们注意到该市的财务职能似乎分散在本市的各个行政部门。委员会遂建议市长，趁财务主管职位现在空缺之际，对本市财务机构的设置作一检查，确定是否需要设置一个财务总监（CFO）的职位，以代替原有的财务主管，使财务工作能进行得效率更高、更为有效。在做了初步检查之后，由公民组成的咨询委员会建议，需要聘用一位 CFO 来代替原先的财务主管，扩大 CFO 在财务职能方面的权力，使财务职能的履行效率更高、更有效。

市长遂决定请一位咨询人员对设置这样一个 CFO 的职位是否为最佳选择做一评估；如果确实如此，则这位 CFO 的职责又应该是哪些。他相信，一位从外面请来的、独立的咨询人员，不但有这方面的专长，而且处于超然独立的地位，有充分的说服力向滑铁卢市的公民和市政委员会证实有必要设置 CFO 职位代替原有的财务主管职位。他认为从外面请来的咨询师提出的建议会比市政府的人员或由市长任命的委员会的建议更容易使人信服。

1.1. 滑铁卢市的背景情况

滑铁卢于 1868 年组成一个市，现在是黑鹰县（Black Hawk County）的县城所在地。它是爱荷华州第五大的城市，人口约 67 000。可是，该市的人口正在不断减少。该市是以市长—委员会形式的政府进行管理。市政府设置了 20 个业务部门，共有约 600 名员工，其任务由市长指定。这些业务部门向公众所提供的服务，包括警察、消防、图书馆、休闲服务、文化艺术活动、人权、街道维修、工程服务等。政府每年的开支约为 1.05 亿美元，此数正在增长。

2. 当前财务活动的组织结构

图 1 说明当前滑铁卢市进行财务活动的组织结构。各不同部门之间以实线连结时，表示该部门直接向在它之上的那个人报告工作。虚线则表示这些部门属于支援性质，它并不向在其上的那个人报告工作。例如，财务主管并不向财务委员会报告工作，但可能听取财务委员会的意见。另外，财务主管向各个会计职能部门（例如，簿记）提出意见，但这些会计职能部门并不向财务主管报告工作。市府秘书由市政委员会任命、并直接向市政委员会报告工作。此外，市府秘书应执行市长所布置的工作任务。

2.1. 财务主管

财务主管当前负责管理三个职能部门：（1）现金管理，（2）编制预算，（3）内部审计。现金管理的职能包括银行对账和投资。财务主管也向债券评级机构提供有关本市各项债券的评级信息，管理本市的债务，并制定与投资有关的各项政策和手续，这些都是它在投资方面所负的一部分责任。编制预算的责任包括编制年度预算，以及为这个市提出拨款的申请。内部审计职能包括：在偿付应付账款之前进行预审；要对账龄长的应收账款进行预审；监督主要的资本投资和资金来自拨款的投资项目的财务管理；做好市府固定资产的记账工作。

本案例第 6 节附录 A 中，具体列示了财务主管的各项职责的说明。从职位描述中可见，财务主管的职责包括了若干种活动，但这些活动（包括编造工资单、处理应收账款和应付账款、会计和采购等）目前并不由财务主管的管辖之下的人员所执行。在职位描述中，也要求财务主管对中央会计体系、会计控制、编制数据处理报告和编制各种财务报表等各项工作的正常运行负责。此外，他/她理应对市府的风险管理（保险）制度的管理负责，并指导对每一个保险领域的相关成本和招标技术条款的制定进行不断的分析，监督市府的采购系统，以及选择并评估市府所用的软件。

2.2. 财务委员会

市府的财务委员会支持财务主管的工作，但财务主管并不对财务委员会负责。财务委员会是一个永久性的委员会，由三位经市长任命的地方议员组成，任期 2 年。财务委员会的职责是评估并批准超过 500 美元的采购申请。

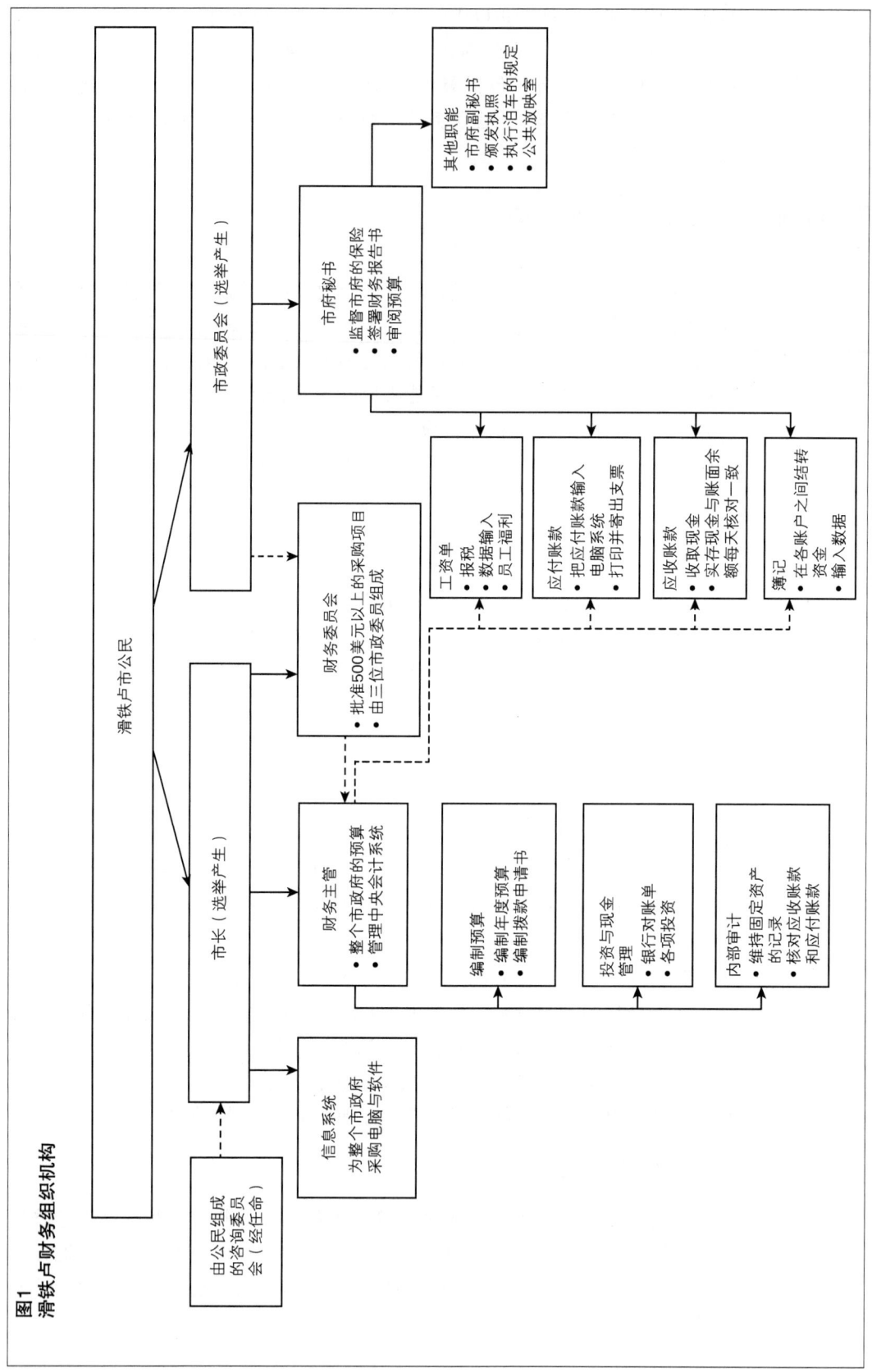

图1
滑铁卢财务组织机构

2.3. 市府秘书

市府秘书现在的职责,事实上相当于一位行政主管,包括以下内容:(1)监督市府的财政,(2)发布营业和宠物执照,(3)组织市政委员会的会议,(4)记录并保管城市各项法令,(5)管理泊车事务。市府秘书与财务有关的职责包括监督市府的债务和财产保险(这一条包括在财务主管的职位描述之中),并为市府编制各项财务报告,包括警察/消防员的养老金报告书、向市政府和联邦政府报税、IPERS[①]养老金计划的报告书和有关工人报酬的报告书。市府秘书也对市府员工的福利(包括人寿保险、健康保险和牙医保险)实施监督。最后,他还审阅预算,公告有关预算的文告,并签署各项财务报告书。

在传统上,向市府秘书报告的职能部门有应收账款、应付账款、工资单、颁发执照和簿记。虽然这些职能部门都向市府秘书提供报告书,但财务主管仍有向这些职能部门提供财务政策、规程和其他意见的责任。按现行的工作安排,管理人员向财务主管提出有关财务手续方面的问题,但如果是有关业务的日常管理问题,则向市府秘书提出。例如,当一位管理人员在本周中不能工作、病休时,是通知市府秘书的。某一个人是否完成了当天的工作,由市府秘书确定。另外,市府秘书还对这些职能部门的每一个人作出年度的考绩报告。

2.4. 其他各部门

有些职能部门自己开具账单、收取现金、小额支付、并设有可以自己支配的小额备用金。这些财务活动,是为各职能部门向辖区内的居民提供业务服务,通常每个星期需要花费两个小时来完成这些事。这些事由各部门内部的行政人员来做。这些部门所遵行的有关现金收支的会计规程,由财务主管制定。街道、警察、消防、建筑检查等部门、图书馆、机场和冰上运动场都属于这一类的机构。

2.5. 采购

滑铁卢市政府并没有一个集中管理的采购部门。所有部门都可以自由处置金额在 500 美元以下的采购项目,无须经过批准。在作此类采购时,某个人[②]可以授权、购置、收取和批准付款。超过 500 美元的采购项目,在采购之前须经财务委员会授权,但仍由该部门执行。只有少数的采购项目,例如采购办公用品,是集中办理的。

2.6. 管理信息系统

管理信息系统(management information systems,MIS)只有一个员工,直接向市长报告工作。他为市府采购所有的电脑和软件。在采购电脑和软件之前,需经电脑技术评审委员会(computer technical review committee)审查。

---

① Iowa Public Employees' Retirement System,爱荷华州公务员退休制度。——译者
② 此处的"某个人"指有订货、采购之权者,可能是经理一级,但不一定。——译者

3. 聘用咨询人员

为了确定市府财务活动的组织机构应如何设置为好，咨询人员采取了两个步骤。首先，他们研究了经典的组织行为学文献和公共行政管理文献中组织机构的各项理论和概念。其次，他们仔细查阅了爱荷华州其他各市的财务活动的机构设置情况。滑铁卢市财务主管的具体职责概要重述于附录A。

4. 考虑新闻媒体的看法

市政府的工作在很大程度上受公众的监督。市政府的商议意见、行动和决定都向当地的媒体（包括报纸和当地的电视台）报道。如果有一位重要的高级政府官员（例如滑铁卢市的财务主管）辞职，公众当然会要知道辞职的原因。由于政府官员负有保护市府财产的责任，人们可能会关心此人是不是出了什么错。虽然这些担心司空见惯，但当地政府重大的人事改变的原因还是会引起公众的兴趣。其结果是，例如这则案例来讲，市长就需要对公众提出的问题做一个交待。由于下一次的市长选举即将举行，人们期望着州政府公布对市府所作财务审计的结果，因而大家对市府的财务状况格外有兴趣。

5. 对学生的要求

问题1：滑铁卢市是否应该重组其财务与会计的职能？如果需要的话，又该如何重组？
 a. 新的财务总监（CFO）应该主管哪些职能部门？
 b. 管理信息系统和采购部门是不是应该在CFO的管辖之下？
 c. 哪些职能部门应向市府秘书报告工作？

问题2：亨利·法约尔（Henri Fayol）认为经典的机构组织原理有下述各项：权力与责任、指挥统一、方向一致。如何把这些概念应用于滑铁卢？其他"公认"的组织原则包括：控制的幅度、集思广益、效率和效果、风险管理。这些概念可以如何应用于滑铁卢？

问题3：在爱荷华州其他主要的城市中，财务职能部门是怎么样的？是不是能够用这些城市中的某一个作为滑铁卢的标杆（基准）？

问题4：管理会计师协会（IMA®）已经编写了两份管理会计公告（Statements on Management Accounting，SMAs），可供分析本案例之用："财务职能再设计（Redesigning the Finance Function）"和"财务职能再设计的工具与技术（Tools and Techniques for Redesigning the Finance Function）"。请对这两则公告作一概述，并把它们应用于滑铁卢。

问题5：平衡记分卡（balanced scorecard，BSC）是企业用来把各项业绩指标导向其战略目标的一种有用的手段。该市是不是有可能利用平衡记分卡来帮助它重组其财务职能呢?如果可能,则滑铁卢市的具体做法将是怎么样呢?

问题6:请讨论内部控制与一个政府机构有何关联之处。萨班斯-奥克斯利法案404节所规定的多项要求是不是有用,即使并未作这样的要求,是否对政府设计、实施、记录和测试内部控制有用?这项法案在该市的政府机构中应该被放在什么地位?

问题7:道德标准在政府机构中应起什么作用?制定一个道德守则是否相宜?其内容应包括什么?

问题8:市长可能如何回应媒体的问题?其他各种媒体(例如Facebook)可能起到什么作用?

6. 附录A

按该市市政府正式的职位描述,滑铁卢市财务主管的具体职责如下:

5.1. 计划、组织和指导市政府的所有各项财务活动,包括财务投资、编制市政府的全部预算、工资单、应收账款和应付账款、会计、采购、开具账单和收取款项。

5.2. 指导计划的编制、组织和维持中央会计系统的运行,包括事先审计、发布开支的公告、会计控制、编写数据处理的报告、投资的各项政策和手续、债券及其他债务的发行与控制。

5.3. 计划与指导编纂各项统计、会计、财务、月度开支和收入的报告书,供市政府所有各部门、州的和联邦政府的债券发行机构、债券咨询人员、保险精算师和投资公司之用。

5.4. 协同市府各部门领导人、市长和市政委员会编制全部预算文件、各项建议书,以及短期和长远的预算目的;从事持续性的分析,并对该市财务状况的各个方面作出评估。

5.5. 起草和修改有关该市财务问题(诸如各项投资政策和手续)和文告的草案。

5.6. 就该市各方面的财务状况和立法关注的问题,向市长、市政委员会和市府各部门的领导人提供建议和咨询意见。

5.7. 按现有的投资政策、手续和适用的本州法律,把市府所有收入的钱存储起来和作投资之用。

5.8. 管理本市的风险管理项目,包括健康保险计划、残障保险计划、财产保险计划和责任保险计划;对每一项保险计划的有关领域的成本持续地进行分析,并起草各项报价说明书。

5.9. 对本市的采购工作实施监督。

5.10. 监督、指导和检查财务人员的工作。

5.11. 评估和选择适用于财务工作的电脑软件。

City of Waterloo, Iowa:
Organizing a Chief Financial Officer Function

William F. Bowlin
North Dakota State University

Margaret L. Andersen
North Dakota State University

1. INTRODUCTION

The finance officer (FO) for the City of Waterloo, Iowa, had resigned to find a position in the private sector.

Earlier in his term, the city's mayor had appointed a citizens' advisory board to advise him on the city's finances. The city's financial needs were growing, but it was experiencing a shrinking population and corresponding decrease in its tax base. The mayor felt that citizens' input on the city's financial situation would be beneficial. The advisory board's responsibilities included monitoring the city's financial position, making recommendations for reducing costs, reviewing audit reports, and other finance related responsibilities. The advisory board consisted of a representative from the city's bond underwriters, an accounting professor from the local university, a local banker, a representative from the Waterloo office of a public accounting firm, and three other citizens interested in the city's finances.

During an advisory board review of the city finances shortly after the FO had resigned, board members noted that the city's financial functions appeared to be scattered throughout the city's administrative activities. The board recommended that the mayor take the opportunity presented by the vacancy in the FO position to review the city's financial activity structure to determine the appropriate responsibilities and activities for a chief financial officer (CFO) function. Following its initial review, the citizens' advisory board recommended that a CFO with expanded financial responsibilities be hired to replace the FO in order to provide a more efficient and effective finance function.

The mayor decided to have a consultant evaluate whether a CFO function was best, and if it was, what responsibilities the CFO should have. He believed that an outside, independent consultant would bring an expertise and independence to the situation that was needed to convince the citizens of Waterloo and the city council of the need of a CFO function and the additional cost of hiring a CFO instead of an FO. He felt that an outside consultant's recommendation would have more credence than recommendations from city personnel or a board appointed by the mayor.

1.1. BACKGROUND ON THE CITY OF WATERLOO

Waterloo was incorporated in 1868 and is the Black Hawk County seat. It is the fifth largest city in the State of Iowa, with a population of about 67 000. The city's population has been decreasing steadily, however. A mayor-council form of government runs the city. The city is organized into 20 operating departments that have nearly 600 employees whose activities are specified by the mayor. The public services provided by these operating departments include police, fire, library, leisure services, cultural and arts activities, human rights, street maintenance, engineering services, and others. Annual general government expenditures are approximately US $ 105 million and growing.

2. CURRENT ORGANIZATIONAL STRUCTURE OF THE FINANCE ACTIVITY

Figure 1 illustrates the current organizational structure for the finance activities for the City of Waterloo. A solid line connecting the different functions shows that the function is directly reportable to the person above it. The dotted line indicates that the functions are support staffs that are not directly reportable to the person above them. For example, the FO does not report to the finance committee, but may rely on the finance committee for advice. Also, the FO advises the accounting functions (e.g., bookkeeping), but these functions do not report to the FO. The city clerk is appointed by and reports directly to the city council. In addition, the city clerk does have a responsibility to perform tasks assigned by the mayor.

2.1. FINANCE OFFICER

Currently, the FO is responsible for three functional areas:

(1) cash management, (2) budgeting, and (3) internal audit. The cash management function includes bank reconciliations and investments. As part of the investment responsibilities, the FO also provides information to bond rating agencies for the city's bond rating, manages the city's debt, and develops investment policies and procedures. The budgeting function requires preparing the yearly budget and completing grant applications for the city. The internal audit function includes pre-auditing of payables before payment, aging account receivables, overseeing the financial management of major capital and grant-funded projects, and maintaining the fixed asset records of the city.

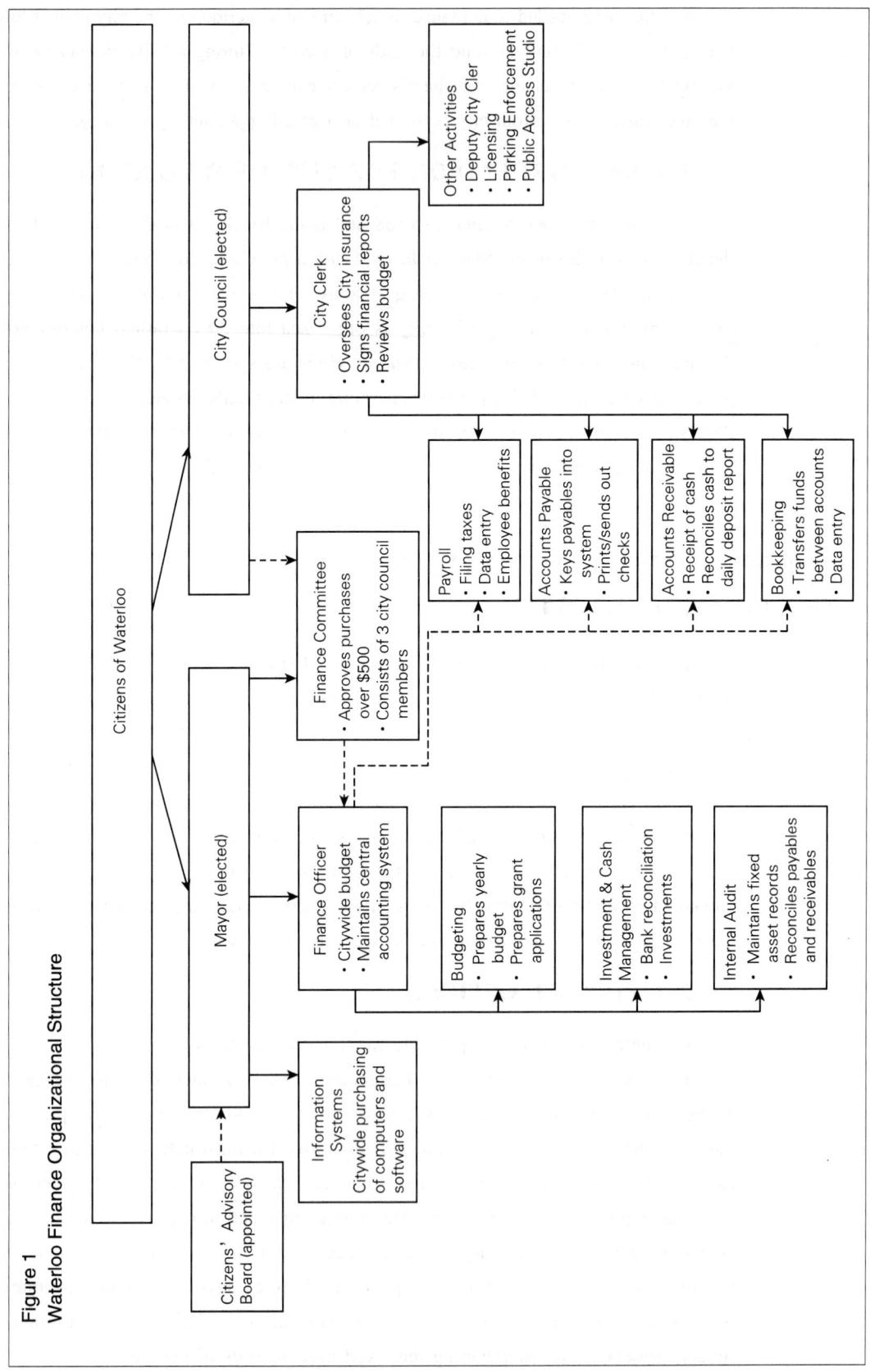

Figure 1
Waterloo Finance Organizational Structure

Specific FO duties as included in the city's job description are in section 6. As can be noted from the job description, there are several activities that are supposed to be the FO's responsibilities but currently are done be personnel not under the control and authority of the FO. This includes directing all municipal fiscal activities to include payroll, accounts receivables and payables, accounting, and purchasing. The job description also calls on the FO to be responsible for maintenance of central accounting systems, accounting controls, data processing reporting, and preparing of financial reports. Additionally, he/she is supposed to be responsible for administering the city's risk management (insurance) program and conducting ongoing analyses of the associated costs for each insurance program area and the development of bid specifications, overseeing the city's purchasing system, and selecting and evaluating software.

2. 2. FINANCE COMMITTEE

The FO is supported by, but not answerable to, the city finance committee. The finance committee is a standing committee that consists of three city councilmen who are appointed by the mayor for two-year terms. The responsibility of the finance committee is to evaluate and approve all purchase requests over US $ 500.

2. 3. CITY CLERK

The city clerk's current responsibilities are in effect those of a chief administrator and include: (1) overseeing city finances, (2) issuing business and animal licenses, (3) organizing city council meetings, (4) recording and maintaining city ordinances, and (5) managing parking enforcement. Finance-related responsibilities of the city clerk include overseeing liability and property insurance (included in FO's job description) and doing various financial reporting for the city to include police/fire pension reporting, state/federal tax reporting, IPERS pension plan reporting, and workmen's compensation reporting. The city clerk also oversees city employee benefits, including life, health, and dental plans. Finally, the city clerk reviews the budget, posts notices about the budget, and signs the financial reports.

Traditional financial functions reporting to the city clerk are the accounts receivable, accounts payable, payroll, licensing, and bookkeeping functions. Although all of these functions report to the city clerk, the FO has responsibility for providing financial policy, procedures, and other advice to these functions. Under the current arrangement, staff members question the FO about financial procedures and turn to the city clerk with any issues that affect day-to-day management of the operations. For example, the city clerk is notified when an employee cannot work during the week and approves sick leave. It is up to the city clerk to make sure that person's work gets done for the day. Also, the city clerk is responsible for the annual performance reports of the individuals working in these functions.

2.4. OTHER DEPARTMENTS

There are some departments that do their own billing and receiving of cash, make small disbursements, and have petty cash accounts at their disposal. These financial activities are for services provided by the departments to constituents and generally require only a couple of hours per week to accomplish. They are done by administrative personnel within the department. Procedures, established by the finance officer, are in place for these departments to follow in accounting for the receipt and disbursement of cash.

The street department, police department, fire department, buildings inspections department, library, airport, and ice arena are included in this category.

2.5. PURCHASING

Waterloo does not have a centralized purchasing department. All departments are allowed to make purchases up to US $500 without approval. In these purchasing situations, a single individual can authorize, procure, receive, and authorize payment for a purchase. Purchases over US $500 must be authorized by the finance committee but are still made by the department. For purchases over US $10 000, authorization must be granted by the city council prior to purchase by the department. A few purchases such as office supplies are done in a centralized fashion.

2.6. MANAGEMENT INFORMATION SYSTEMS

The management information systems (MIS) department has one employee that reports to the mayor. He handles the purchasing of all computers and software for the city. All computer and software purchases must go through the computer technical review committee before purchase.

3. CONSULTANTS ARE HIRED

In order to determine the appropriate organizational structure for the city's financial activities, consultants took two approaches. First, they researched organizational structure theories and concepts in the classical organizational behavior literature and the public administration literature. Second, they examined the organizational structure of the finance activities of other Iowa municipalities. The specific duties of the City of Waterloo finance officer are recapped in Appendix A.

4. THE VIEW FROM THE PRESS BOX

City governments are subject to a great deal of public scrutiny. Many of their deliberations, actions, and decisions are reported by local media, including newspapers and local television. When a key senior government official resigns from public office, such as occurred with the Waterloo finance officer, it is common for the public to wonder why. Given the stewardship role of city officials, there can be concerns about possible wrongdoing. Although these concerns may always be present, a major change in the local government can highlight the public's interest in the reasons for such a change. As a result, key government officials, such as the mayor in this case, need to be responsive to the public's questions. Because of an upcoming mayoral election and the expected release of a state financial audit of the city, there is additional interest in the city's finances.

5. REQUIRED

Question 1: Should the City of Waterloo reorganize its finance and accounting activities? If so, how should they be reorganized?

a. What functions should be placed under the new chief financial officer (CFO)?

b. Should management information systems and purchasing be placed under the CFO?

c. What functions should report to the city clerk?

Question 2: Henri Fayol identified the following classic principles of organizational structure: authority and responsibility, unity of command, and unity of direction. How might these concepts be applied to Waterloo? Other "generally accepted" organizational principles include the following: span of control, pooling of knowledge, efficiency and effectiveness, and risk management. How might these concepts be applied to Waterloo?

Question 3: What does the finance function look like in other major Iowa cities? Could any of them be used for benchmarking?

Question 4: The Institute of Management Accountants (IMA®) has written two Statements on Management Accounting (SMAs) that could be useful in analyzing this case: "Redesigning the Finance Function" and "Tools and Techniques for Redesigning the Finance Function." Summarize these statements and apply them to Waterloo.

Question 5: The balanced scorecard (BSC) is a useful tool for organizations to match their performance measures to their strategy. Would it be possible for a city to use the BSC to aid in reorganizing its finance function? If so, what would be an example for the City of Waterloo?

Question 6: Discuss the relevance of internal controls for a governmental organization. Could the requirements from Section 404 of the Sarbanes-Oxley Act be helpful, even if not required, as a government designs, implements, documents, and tests internal controls? Does Waterloo need an internal audit function? Where should it be placed in the city's organization?

Question 7: What role do ethics play in a government? Would a code of ethics be appropriate? If so, what would it include?

Question 8: How might the mayor respond to the media's questions? What role might other media outlets such as Facebook play?

6. APPENDIX A

Specific duties of the City of Waterloo finance officer per the city's formal job description are:

5.1. Plans, organizes, and directs all municipal fiscal activities, including financial investments, citywide budget development, payroll, accounts receivable and payable, accounting, purchasing, billings, and collections.

5.2. Directs planning, organization, and maintenance of central accounting systems, including pre-audit, posting of expenditures, accounting controls, data processing reporting, investment policies and procedures, bond and other indebtedness issuance and control.

5.3. Plans and directs the compilation of various statistical, accounting, finance, monthly expenditure, and revenue reports for all city departments, state and federal government bond writing agencies, bond consultants, actuaries, and investment firms.

5.4. Develops annual citywide budget documents and recommendations and short- and long-term budget objectives in conjunction with department heads, mayor, and city council; engages in an ongoing analysis and evaluation of all aspects of the financial status of the city.

5.5. Drafts and revises proposed ordinances and resolutions relating to city financial matters such as investment policies and procedures.

5.6. Advises and consults with mayor, city council, and department heads on the financial condition of the city and legislative concerns.

5.7. Directs receipt deposits and investments of all city monies within established investment policies and procedures and applicable state laws.

5.8. Administers the city's risk management program, including health insurance plans, disability insurance plan, property insurance program, and liability insurance programs, and conducts an ongoing analysis of the associated costs for each insurance program area and the development of bid specifications.

5.9. Oversees the city's purchasing system.

5.10. Supervises, directs, and reviews work of finance staff.

5.11. Evaluates and selects applicable computer software for the finance activity.

编制计划与预算
Planning & Budgeting

策划计划与方案
Planning & Budgeting

浦东咖啡馆

Peter Clarke
University College Dublin，Ireland

> "宁三日无粮，不可一日缺茶。"
>
> ——中国古谚

简介

有一个大国叫中国，它有许多不同的形象，其中最著名的莫过于中国的茶馆！然而，因近年咖啡馆的发展，这个形象在迅速改变。星巴克在中国开设的它第一家店（1999年1月）只不过十年，咖啡文化就已经出现在这块茶客的土地上了。例如，北京现在有8 000多家咖啡馆，十年之内增长了8倍。中国一些城市里，比较年青、富有的专业人士，则把喝咖啡看成高雅、带有异国情调之举（www.chinadaily.com）。以伦敦为基地的国际咖啡协会（International Coffee Association）的报告称，全球咖啡消费平均每年的增长略多于百分之二，据估计中国的消费却每年以两位数的速度增长。不过，令人印象深刻的增长，部分源于中国的起点很低。据估计，中国平均每人一年中只喝三杯咖啡，而一般的美国人每年要喝500~700杯（www.chinapost.com）。有理由证明，由于中国经济增长迅速、人口庞大，中国完全有可能成为世界上咖啡消费最多的国家。不过，当前咖啡消费高度集中在北京、广州、上海和深圳这样的大城市。假定中国的咖啡市场只限于其13亿人口中的20%，则其市场规模就达到美国那样大了！因此，近几年来许多国际咖啡连锁店纷纷在中国开展业务，就是完全可以理解的了。在这些连锁店中，有"咖啡豆与茶叶"、"哥斯达咖啡"、"星巴克咖啡"、"U.B.C.咖啡"等。更近一些，在2010年6月，中国最大的连锁超市中国资源公司（China Resources Enterprise，CRE）表明，它将以港币3.26亿元（约合4 200万美元）购入以香港为基地的太平洋咖啡公司（Pacific Coffee）80%的股权，把业务扩展到内地去，意欲发展内地饮用咖啡的文化。CRE宣布，它会把太平洋咖啡公司开设到它每一家主要的购物商场中去，最终在规模上成为中国最大的一家咖啡连锁店（www.FT.com）。这些国际连锁店平均每杯咖啡的成本为30~40元。因此，许多人认为，人们对于咖啡本身未必在意，年轻、富裕的顾客所要体会的是那种氛围和身份状态。这种氛围，加上咖啡馆的环境和布置，对于咖啡馆的经理人员和他们的咨询人员来说成为一种有趣的营销挑战。

王利就是这样一间咖啡馆的经理。他自认他不像一个经理，因为他在服务行业没有什么经验。几年以前他从武汉的一所大学以高分毕业，获得英语与国际关系的学位。并且他得到一份奖学金，得以去欧洲深造，攻读硕士。在欧洲的学习使王利有机会看到欧洲一些主要的首都城市。这些城市各不相同，但他记得所有这些城市都有一个共同之处——咖啡馆。实际上每一条街上都有咖啡馆，有的还并排地开设了好几家。每一家店都让老顾客在那里休闲、和朋友聊天，甚至只是"消磨时光"而已。对这些店的老顾客们来说，时间似乎毫不重要，没有人急着办什么事。王利是个幸运的人，因为他的学生签证允许他在周末时到当地咖啡馆打工。这可以让他挣点零花钱，同时他也和咖啡馆的许多老顾客成了朋友，既能提高他的英语水平、又帮助他更好地理解西方文化的各个方面。

回到中国以后，王利在各地做过多种工作，担任过英语教师、酒吧男招待员、房产推销员。其后，他的父亲（一位很成功的商人）退休并把他自己的生意盘了出去。经过家庭会议，大家同意由王利的父亲在上海浦东购入一家咖啡馆，交给王利来经营。两年前，他的父亲给这个新店提供了人民币400 000元资本，用于取得一家已经开业的咖啡馆的无形资产（商誉/顾客的信赖）。咖啡馆的房屋仍属原业主所有，但王利获得很优惠的租房条件，租期到2015年年底，每年需付固定的租金100 000元。此外，他还向银行贷款了410 000元，全用于购置新的家具、设备；贷款固定年利7%，为期5年，每年年终偿还相同的金额。接着，王利的咖啡馆开张，取名"浦东咖啡馆（The Pudong Coffee Shop）"，但他并不从店里支取薪金或红利。

众所周知，黄浦江把上海这座国际大都市一分为二，分别称为浦西（西边）和浦东（东边）。在过去这二十年中，浦东（正式的名字叫"浦东新区"）崭露头角，成为中国的金融和商业枢纽。例如，浦东现在是上海证券交易所、陆家嘴金融贸易区、外高桥保税区、金桥出口加工区、张江高科技园区的所在地，还有一条天际线[1]，包括具有象征意义的东方明珠塔、上海世界金融中心和正在建筑中的上海塔（2014年完工后将成为全中国最高的大楼）。

目前情况

浦东咖啡馆设在一栋居民公寓的底层，公寓邻近世纪公园空旷地区，附近有多栋办公大楼。所在的地方有一所私立商业学校的校园，按定额招收外国学生，还有几所国际中等学校。公寓大楼的底层即为王利这家精心设计的咖啡馆所在——占了大约60平方米——其中有顾客区、服务区，另外还有玻璃陈列柜、洗手间、厨房和储藏室。此外，还留出相当的临街位置，在天

---

[1] skyline，天际线，又称城市轮廓或全景，通俗说，天际线就是你站在城市中一个地方，向四周环顾，天地相交的那一条轮廓线就是天际线。天际线亦被作为城市整体结构的色彩、规模和标志性建筑。譬如自由女神像、东方明珠塔、悉尼歌剧院、香港会展中心，都是经典的天际线。——译者转引自《有道词典》

气条件许可的时候，供老顾客在室外小坐。总体来说，咖啡馆（室内与室外）总共可以容纳50位顾客。营业时间从早上8点到晚上9点，每周工作7天，一年365天都营业。菜单用再生纸印制，列示出价格优惠的饮料和点心。饮料包括各种咖啡——有（用汽加压煮出的）浓咖啡、卡布奇诺咖啡、拿铁咖啡、穆哈咖啡以及茶和不含酒精的饮料。它还提供早餐（小松饼、吐司等）、午餐（新鲜订做的三明治、肉馅卷②、色拉、馅饼等等）和晚餐（意大利芝士蛋糕、巧克力和其他蛋糕）。

从许多方面来说，浦东咖啡馆和中国许多家族式经营企业非常相像。作为一个家族式企业，希望通过企业的经营，使主及其家庭成员过上舒适的生活。然而，正如所有在中国的企业一样，它面临着十分剧烈的竞争。例如，公寓大楼的底层还有两家相似的店铺，一家是意大利式的餐馆，另一家是冰激凌咖啡馆。竞争者的出现，使王利的店铺最近两年的销售额差强人意。这一情况也限制了价格的提高，王利的价格与这个地区大部分店铺相近。

王利以前是个伙计的身份、而不是管理者，从他有限的行业经验中，他学到顾客的信任是经营成功的重要组成部分。因此，只要他在店里，嘴上就老是挂着"欢迎光临"，同时要求员工这样做。浦东咖啡馆待客如家人，并且禁止吸烟。店里提供各种报纸杂志，因为王利要使他的咖啡馆成为一个顾客可以坐在舒适的沙发或椅子上放松休闲的场所。店铺里不放送喇叭音乐，也没有现场表演，他希望把它办成一个"轻言细语"的地方。他不在意"打包带走"的业务。他提供优质的产品和顾客服务，并在下午的时候提供免费水果和饼干。此外，他的员工名册中还有当工作需要的时候，可以招之即来的两位全职和几位兼职员工。

2010年1月新的会计年度开始时，有一些项目引起了王利的注意。在浏览互联网时，他注意到登载在一些网址上的对咖啡馆的排名，排名依据为一些对吸引顾客很重要的评估标准（见表1）。他意识到，尽管这些评估标准的主观性很强或者难以考核，如果要使他的咖啡馆兴旺起来，他必须密切注意这方面的情况。此外，他还获得一份个人所作的对该地区各咖啡馆的调查分析，这是一篇硕士论文的一部分。王利认识那位硕士导师，因而有理由相信这份分析真实可靠。它对咖啡馆的各项活动提供了广泛的信息，包括成本的高低和其他有关的内容（见表2）。他认为，其中的部分内容对他可能有用。此外，王利刚从会计那里收到一份迄止于2009年12月31日（也就是他经营这家咖啡馆的第二年）的各项财务报表的草稿（未经审计）（见表3）。他这家店的年度营业额为930 000元，按这一年的现金交易额来看，每位顾客光顾一次的平均消费约为50元。根据这些财务数据，加上他所获得和估计的一些基本数据，他就可以为第二年编制各项预算了。王利认识到，为了对他的经营情况有一个全面的了解，他必须多关心一些财务方面的问题，尤其是因为他的现金流量情况虽然有所改善，但在前一个会计年度中却蒙受了亏损，对此他觉得很不理解。

---

② wrap，一种墨西哥点心，以玉米饼内包肉馅，姑译作"肉馅卷"。——译者

表 1
咖啡馆的评分标准
（未按重要程度排序）

1. 供应的饮料/食物必须是高品质的
2. 室内布置、温度和噪音水平
3. 免费无线网络
4. 员工态度友好细心
5. 卓越的顾客服务
6. 食物的外观和可供选择的食物品种
7. 清洁和总体卫生条件
8. 供客人使用的面积
9. 物有所值

资料来源：各网站

表 2
对当地各咖啡馆所作的调查

表 2A：
总销售收入分析

	%
饮料	40%
食物销售	60%
	100%

表 2B：
各咖啡馆供应的食物和饮料品种的百分比

饮料	%
茶与咖啡	100%
冷饮	98%
冰沙	24%

食物销售	%
三明治和肉馅卷	100%
蛋糕与餐后甜点	90%
饼干、小松饼等	70%
面包（吐司）	50%
色拉	30%

表 2C：
各咖啡馆各类营业成本占总收入的百分比（平均）

占销售额的百分比	%
食物与饮料	40%
工资与报酬	20%
租金	20%
公用事业费（照明、取暖等）	5%
有形资产折旧	5%
广告与推销	5%

表 2
对当地各咖啡馆所作的调查（续）

表 2D：
各咖啡馆为促进/改进业务而采取的措施的百分比

采取的行动	%
翻修店面	70%
员工培训	60%
增加营业时间	50%
无线网络设施	40%
提高顾客忠诚度的措施	40%
增加商品种类	35%
增加广告	30%

表 2E：
分析咖啡馆顾客各年龄段所占的百分比

顾客年龄	%
20 岁以下	20%
21～30 岁	45%
30～50 岁	25%
50 岁以上	10%
	100%

表 2F：
一天中各个时段客流量占顾客总数的百分比

时间段	星期一到星期五	星期六和星期天
早上（8 点到 11 点）	23%	20%
午间（11 点到 2 点）	33%	33%
下午（2 点到 5 点）	16%	23%
下午吃茶点和傍晚时间（5 点到 9 点）	28%	24%
	100%	100%

表3
年度财务概况草稿（未经审计）

浦东咖啡馆

年度利润表摘要（未经审计）	2009年12月31日	2008年12月31日
	¥	¥
销售收入（饮料）	485 000	465 000
销售收入（食物）	445 000	450 000
销售收入合计（食物与饮料）	930 000	915 000
销售成本	(420 000)	(389 000)
毛利	510 000	526 000
减：营业费用：		
有形资产折旧	(82 000)	(82 000)
工资与报酬	(130 000)	(110 000)
租金	(200 000)	(200 000)
公用事业费（照明与取暖等）	(48 000)	(39 000)
垃圾处理费	(10 000)	(9 000)
广告与推销	(30 000)	(25 000)
营业费用合计	(500 000)	(465 000)
本年营业利润	10 000	61 000
应付贷款利息	(23 710)	(28 700)
本年度利润（亏损）	(13 710)	32 300

浦东咖啡馆

资产负债表摘要（未经审计）：	2009年12月31日	2008年12月31日
	¥	¥
商誉	400 000	400 000
家具与设备（净额）	246 000	328 000
存货	44 000	38 000
银行存款	198 000	196 000
资产总额	888 000	962 000
所有者权益	418 590	432 300
应付银行贷款	262 410	338 700
应付账款	207 000	191 000
负债与所有者权益合计	888 000	962 000

浦东咖啡馆

年度现金流量表摘要（未经审计）	2009年12月31日	2008年12月31日
	¥	¥
营业现金流量		
本年度营业利润（亏损）	10 000	61 000
加：折旧	82 000	82 000
	92 000	143 000
营运资金增减额：		
减：存货增加额	(6 000)	(38 000)
加：应付账款增加额	16 000	191 000
	102 000	296 000
投资活动	Nil	Nil
融资活动：		
偿还贷款（包括利息）	(100 000)	(100 000)
＝本年度现金流量（短缺）总额	2 000	196 000
加：银行账户期初余额	196 000	Nil
等于：银行账户结存额	198 000	196 000

挑战

王利认为店铺的业绩应该能更好一些,然而现在这个状况也有其积极方面。例如,中国的咖啡消费市场,每年大约以超过百分之十的速率在扩张。此外,他的顾客数量虽然没有变化,但却忠诚于他这家咖啡馆,而且都是当地的专业和外籍人士。顾客投诉,难得一见;不过王利也知道,顾客即使不满意,也很少会直接向经理或员工们埋怨的。

王利相信,只要管理有方,咖啡馆一定是可以持续经营并且兴旺起来的,他认为自己既然是领导,就有责任指出企业的发展方向。他满怀信心,自己的员工一定会支持他的倡议——尤其是因为现在已经按业绩给员工计酬了。他需要考虑的事千头万绪,以致不知从何着手。因此,在1月初的时候,他参加了由当地商业学院办的一个短期的高管教育课程。课程的讲师劝说道,一个合乎逻辑的决策程序应该首先是确定咖啡馆的现状,然后决定未来的方向,最后选择应该采取什么手段来达到目的。此外,经理人员还需要制定一些适当的考核指标,来推动企业的业绩;有一位讲师在研讨会上向学员们指出,"底线"③ 之所以被放在最底下一行,有其道理。因为在这一行的上面列出了许多重要的经营活动,只有这些活动成功,企业才能获得相应的财务回报。王利记得讲师做的一份关于经营活动与成果的图解,并提出了这样一条命题:"如果有了良好的设施和合适的员工,并且我们的行动得当,顾客就会对我们忠诚,我们就会获得财务上的回报"(见图1)。简单来说,王利认识到,即使供应的浓咖啡质量极好,但服务员态度粗鲁、不称职,顾客也不会觉得在这里喝咖啡是种享受!王利知道你选修了一门管理会计课程,请求你对他提建议。具体来说,他希望你针对下列问题,准备一份报告书:

1. 使用可获得的信息,对企业当前的情况作一分析。

2. 请向王利提出建议,他今后应该怎么做来提高盈利。你所提的建议,应该以你对问题1所作的分析为根据。

3. 根据你对问题2中所提出的建议,编制一套合乎逻辑的、互相协调的成功的关键因素(critical success factors)和与之相关的重要的考核指标,以帮助管理者和员工实现你的建议。在这方面,你是否另外还有什么意见?

4. 为了编制预算,王利很快地根据他所获得的数据,为2010年提出了下列假设:

销售价格将提高3%(与竞争对手保持一致);销售量将增加5%(上一年曾达到这个增长率);由于通货膨胀率的提高,可自行酌定的现金开支将增长4%;同样地,供应商将按此比率提高其商业信用限额;存货的周转率将维持不变。不拟另外增加投资或融资活动。

根据以上假设,比照2009年的报表为迄止于2010年12月31日的会计

---

③ bottom line,这里直译作"底线",喻指利润;因为利润数被列在利润表的最底下的一行。——译者

年度编制一份利润和现金流量预测,并编制资产负债表。

5. 你另外还有什么要提请王利注意的问题?请提出你的建议或意见。另请计算已经过去的 2009 会计年度和预测的 2010 年的"保本点"。并假设该店在持续经营的情况下出售,为此编制一份该咖啡馆资产评估书。

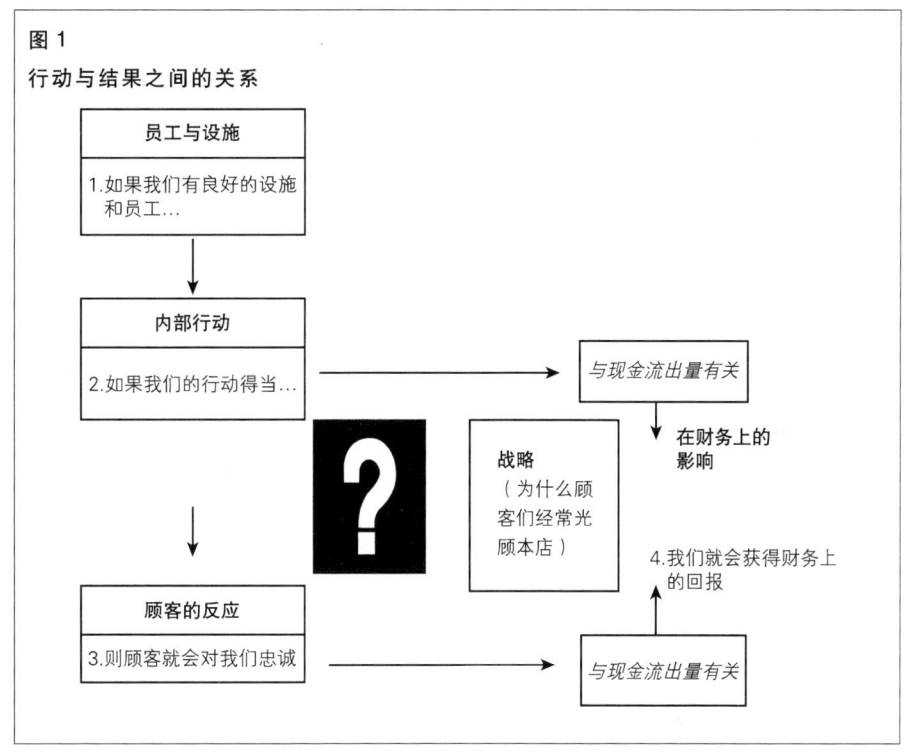

The Pudong Coffee Shop

Peter Clarke
University College Dublin, Ireland

> "Better to be deprived of food for three days, than tea for one."
> —Ancient Chinese Proverb

INTRODUCTION

The magnificent country that is China conveys a great many different images, but perhaps none more so than that of a Chinese tea house! However, that image is rapidly changing due to the recent growth of coffee shops. Just a decade after Starbucks opened their first store in China (in January 1999) a coffee culture has emerged in the land of tea drinkers. For example, Beijing now has more than 8,000 coffee shops—eight times more than just a decade ago—as the younger, affluent, urban Chinese professionals consider drinking coffee to be elegant and exotic (www.chinadaily.com). Based on reports issued by the London based International Coffee Association, it is estimated that coffee consumption in China is growing at a double-digit rate per annum, compared with a global average of slightly over two percent. However, this impressive growth is partly due to the fact that China is starting from such a low base. On average, it is estimated that each Chinese person drinks about three cups of coffee a year, compared with somewhere between 500 to 700 cups for a typical American person (www.chinapost.com). Not surprisingly, it can be argued that China has the potential to become the largest coffee consuming country in the world because of its rapid economic growth and huge population. However, coffee consumption, for the time being, is highly concentrated in the large cities such as Beijing, Guangzhou, Shanghai and Shenzhen. Thus, if one assumes that the potential Chinese market for coffee is limited to, say, 20 percent of its 1.3 billion population, that would provide a market as big as that of the United States! Therefore, it is understandable that many international coffee chains have commenced operations in China in recent years; and these include, for example, Coffee Bean & Tea Leaf, Costa Coffee, Starbucks Coffee and U.B.C. Coffee. More recently, in June 2010, China Resources Enterprise (CRE), China's biggest supermarket chain operator, indicated that it would buy 80 percent of the Hong Kong-based Pacific Coffee for HK $326m (about $42m) and expand on the mainland in an attempt to tap into China's growing coffee-drinking culture. CRE announced that it would develop Pacific Coffee by having its own coffee outlet in every one of its major shopping malls, with an ultimate goal of becoming the largest coffee chain in China in terms of size (www.FT.com). The average cost of a cup of coffee in these international chains amounts to between Yuan 30 and 40. Thus, many people believe that it is not the coffee itself that matters but rather the ambience and status experienced by its young, affluent clients. This ambience, together with location and visibility, create an interesting marketing challenge for coffee shop managers and their consultants.

Li Wang is one such coffee shop manager. He readily admits that he is an unlikely manager since he has very little experience in the hospitality sector. A few years ago he graduated from a university in Wuhan with a top class degree in English and International Relations. He received and accepted a scholarship to further his studies in Europe, where he undertook a Master's degree. This European study allowed Li the opportunity to see some of the major European capital cities. They were all different, yet he remembered that they had one thing in common-coffee shops. Virtually each street had its own coffee shop; sometimes several of them existed side by side. Each outlet allowed its patrons to relax and socialise with friends or simply 'watch the world go by'. It seemed that time was not important to patrons of these establishments, since nobody was in a hurry. Li was fortunate that his student visa allowed him to work at weekends in his local coffee shop. While this provided him with some casual spending money, it also allowed him to perfect his English and to better appreciate and absorb aspects of Western culture, since he became friendly with many of the coffee shop's clients.

On returning to China, Wang undertook a number of different jobs which included, at various times and various locations, an English language tutor, a bar-tender and a property salesperson. Thereafter, Li's father, who was a prominent businessman, retired and sold out his own business. After family discussions, it was agreed that his father would purchase and Li would manage an established coffee shop in Pudong, Shanghai. Two years ago, his father provided ¥400 000 in capital to the new business and this sum was fully used to acquire the goodwill/customer loyalty of the existing coffee shop business. (Ownership of the building remained with the landlord but Li received generous rent terms and agreed to make a fixed annual rent payment of ¥100 000 until 2015.) Furthermore, he borrowed ¥410 000 from a bank, which was entirely used to immediately purchase new furniture and equipment by way of a 5-year loan at a 7% fixed rate of interest, with constant annual repayments at the end of each year. The following day, Li opened for business under the name The Pudong Coffee Shop, but he did not take any salary or bonus from the business.

As many people know, the Huangpu river divides the giant cosmopolitan city of Shanghai into two regions, namely Puxi (West side) and Pudong (East side). Over the past two decades Pudong, which is officially known as Pudong New Area, has emerged as China's financial and commercial hub. Pudong is now home to, for example, the Shanghai Stock Exchange, the Lujiazui Finance and Trade Zone, the Waigaoqiao Free Trade Zone, the Jinqiao Export Processing Zone, the Zhangjiang Hi-Tech Park and a skyline that includes the symbolic Oriental Pearl Tower, the Shanghai World Financial Centre and the under-construction Shanghai Tower, which is set to become the tallest tower in China when it is completed in 2014.

THE CURRENT SITUATION

The Pudong Coffee Shop is located on the ground floor of a large residential apartment complex near the ample open spaces of Century Park and close to several important large office buildings. Also in the locality are the campus of a private business school, which accepts its quota of international students, and some international secondary schools. The ground floor of the apartment block includes Li's well-designed coffee shop - occupying about 60 square metres - which consists of the customer area, service area together with glass display counters, wash rooms, kitchen and storage space area. There is also considerable frontage where patrons can sit outside when the weather permits. In total, the coffee shop has (internal and external) space for about 50 customers. Its operating hours are from 8am to 9pm, seven days a week, 365 days a year. The menu, printed on recycled paper, includes a variety of competitively priced coffees-espresso, cappuccino, latte and mocha-teas and soft drinks. It provides breakfast (muffins, toast etc.), lunch (freshly made sandwiches to order, wraps, salads, pies etc.) and evening food (tiramisu, chocolate and other cakes).

In many ways, The Pudong Coffee Shop is very similar to many other Chinese enterprises that are family-owned and operated. As a family business, it is expected to provide a comfortable living for its owner and family dependants. However, as with all businesses in China, there is significant competition. For example, the ground floor of the apartment block also contains two similar enterprises, one of which is an Italian-style restaurant and the other an ice cream café. The local presence of competition has resulted in a lower than expected sales growth in the two years of Li's management. It also restricts any price increase; and Li's prices are similar to most other outlets in the area.

Wang's limited business experience, which is from an employee rather than a managerial perspective, has taught him that customer loyalty is a most important ingredient for business success. Thus, while on the premises, Li is always available to say "Huan ying guang lin" to his customers and encourages his staff to do likewise. The Pudong Coffee Shop is an intimate establishment but it is also a non-smoking area. Daily papers, ample magazines and books are provided, since Li wants his coffee shop to be a place where customers can be casual and relax on the sofas and soft chairs provided. There is no piped music playing in the background, nor are there live performances, as this facilitates what he terms "quiet whispers" to take place. The amount of "take-away" business is negligible. He provides a good quality of product and customer service and this includes providing free fruit and biscuits in the afternoon. In addition, two other full-time employees work in the business and several part-time unskilled staff are engaged as necessary and work flexible rosters each week.

In January 2010, as the new financial year started, a number of items caught Wang's attention. While scanning the Internet he noticed several sites that ranked coffee shops on the basis of several criteria which were important to potential customers (See Table 1). He realised that if his coffee shop was to thrive in the future, he would have to closely monitor performance in those areas, even if some of the criteria were very subjective or difficult to measure. In addition, Wang also received a summary of a private analysis of coffee shops in the district, which had recently been completed as part of an MBA project. Wang personally knew the supervising professor and considered it reasonable to assume that the study was both reliable and valid. It provided a wide range of information on coffee shop activities, the scale of costs and other matters (see Table 2). He believed that some of this information could be useful to him. Furthermore, Wang had just received the draft (unaudited) financial statements for the year ended 31st December 2009-the second year of operations (Table 3). The annual turnover of the shop amounted to ¥930 000 and, based on the number of cash transactions, he crudely estimated that the average spend per customer was ¥50. These financial summaries, together with some basic data that he obtained and some assumptions, would allow him to prepare budgets for the next year. Li Wang realised that he would have to take a greater interest in financial matters in order to get a comprehensive overview of the business, especially since he could not understand why the business generated a loss during the previous financial year but also improved its cash flow!

Table 1
Judging Criteria for Coffee Shops
(*not listed in order of importance*)

1. Beverages/food provided must be of good quality
2. Décor, temperature and noise levels
3. Free WiFi
4. Friendly staff
5. Excellent customer service
6. Presentation of food and food offering
7. Cleanliness and overall hygiene
8. Availability of space
9. Overall value for money

Source: Various Websites

Table 2
Survey of Coffee Shops in Local Region

Table 2A:
Analysis of Total Revenue Earned

	%
Beverages/drinks	40%
Food sales	60%
	100%

Table 2B:
Types of Food and Beverages Served in Coffee Shops %

Beverages	%
Tea and Coffee	100%
Cold Drinks	98%
Smoothies	24%
Food Sales	**%**
Sandwiches and Wraps	100%
Cakes and Desserts	90%
Biscuits, Muffins etc.	70%
Toasts e.g. Bread	50%
Salads	30%

Table 2C:
Operating Costs as % of Total Revenue in Coffee Shops (average)

Percentage of Sales	%
Food and beverages	40%
Wages and remuneration	20%
Rental	20%
Utilities (light and heat etc.)	5%
Depreciation of tangible assets	5%
Advertising and promotions	5%

Table 2
Survey of Coffee Shops in Local Region (*continued*)

Table 2D:
Steps Taken to Encourage/Improve Business in Coffee Shops %

Activities	%
Refurbishment of outlets	70%
Staff training	60%
Additional opening hours	50%
WiFi facilities	40%
Loyalty programmes for customers	40%
Wider product range	35%
Increased advertising	30%

Table 2E:
Analysis of Customers by Age in Coffee Shops %

Age of customers	%
Under 20 years	20%
21~30 years	45%
31~50 years	25%
Over 50 years	10%
	100%

Table 2F:
% of Total Customers (Footfall) Served by Time of Day

Time of Day	Monday to Friday	Saturday & Sunday
Morning (8am to 11am)	23%	20%
Lunch-time (11am to 2pm)	33%	33%
Afternoon (2pm to 5pm)	16%	23%
Tea-time and early evening (5pm to 9pm)	28%	24%
	100%	100%

Table 3
Draft (unaudited) Annual Financial Summaries

The Pudong Coffee Shop Summarised Income Statement (unaudited) for year ended:	31st December 2009 ¥	31st December 2008 ¥
Revenue (beverages/drinks)	485 000	465 000
Revenue (food sales)	445 000	450 000
Total revenue (food and beverages)	930 000	915 000
Cost of sales	(420 000)	(389 000)
Gross profit	510 000	526 000
Less Operating expenses:		
Depreciation of tangible assets	(82 000)	(82 000)
Wages and remuneration	(130 000)	(110 000)
Rental	(200 000)	(200 000)
Utilities (lighting and heating etc.)	(48 000)	(39 000)
Garbage collection	(10 000)	(9 000)
Advertising and promotions	(30 000)	(25 000)
Total operating expenses	(500 000)	(465 000)
Operating profit for year	10 000	61 000
Interest payable on loans	(23 710)	(28 700)
Profit (loss) for year	(13 710)	32 300

The Pudong Coffee Shop Summarised Balance Sheet (unaudited) at:	31st December 2009 ¥	31st December 2008 ¥
Goodwill	400 000	400 000
Furniture and fittings (net)	246 000	328 000
Inventories	44 000	38 000
Cash at bank	198 000	196 000
Total assets	888 000	962 000
Owner's equity	418 590	432 300
Bank loan payable	262 410	338 700
Trade payables	207 000	191 000
Total liabilities and owner's equity	888 000	962 000

The Pudong Coffee Shop Summarised Cash Flow statement (unaudited) for year ended:	31st December 2009 ¥	31st December 2008 ¥
Operating cash flow		
Operating profit (loss) for year	10 000	61 000
Add: depreciation	82 000	82 000
	92 000	143 000
Changes in working capital:		
Less: Increase in inventories	(6 000)	(38 000)
Add: Increase in trade payables	16 000	191 000
	102 000	296 000
Investing activities	Nil	Nil
Financing activities:		
Repayment of loan including interest	(100 000)	(100 000)
= Overall cash flow (deficit) for year	2 000	196 000
Add: Opening bank balance	196 000	Nil
Equals: Closing bank balance	198 000	196 000

THE CHALLENGE

Wang considered that his business should be performing better, but he knew there were some positive aspects. For example, the coffee consumption market in China was expanding at a rate estimated to be in excess of 10 percent per annum. In addition, his customer base, although constant, was loyal and consisted of local professionals and expats. Customer complaints were the exception rather than the rule, although Wang realised that dissatisfied customers rarely complain directly to the manager or to employees.

Li Wang believed that properly managed coffee shops would always survive and prosper, and he accepted the responsibility that he was now the leader who was needed to provide direction for the business. He was confident that the employees would support his initiatives-especially if rewards for successful performance were offered. There were so many things for him to consider that it was difficult to decide where to start. Therefore, in early January he attended a short Executive Education course delivered by the local business school. His lecturers persuaded him that a logical decision-making sequence would be to identify the coffee shop's current situation and then decide on an appropriate future direction and a means for its attainment. In addition, he would need to develop some appropriate measures to help drive business performance, since one lecturer reminded seminar participants that the 'bottom line' belongs down at the bottom for a reason. Far above it, and of much greater importance, are a number of significant activities whose successful performance is required to generate adequate financial returns. Wang remembered a simple diagram linking activities to results based on the proposition that "if we have the right facilities and employees doing the right things, then our customers will be loyal, and we will generate the financial returns" (see Figure 1). In simple terms, Wang realised the best espresso, served by a rude or incompetent barista, is not an enjoyable experience! Wang knows that you are enrolled in a managerial accounting course and has asked you to advise him. Specifically, you are required to prepare a report that addresses the following issues:

1. An analysis of the current situation of the business using the available information.

2. Advice on what Wang should do in the future in order to achieve greater profitability. Your suggestions should be embedded in your analysis of Issue #1.

3. Within your suggestions regarding Issue #2, prepare a logical, integrated set of critical success factors and related key performance indicators to assist management and employees to achieve your recommendations. What additional comments would you make in this regard?

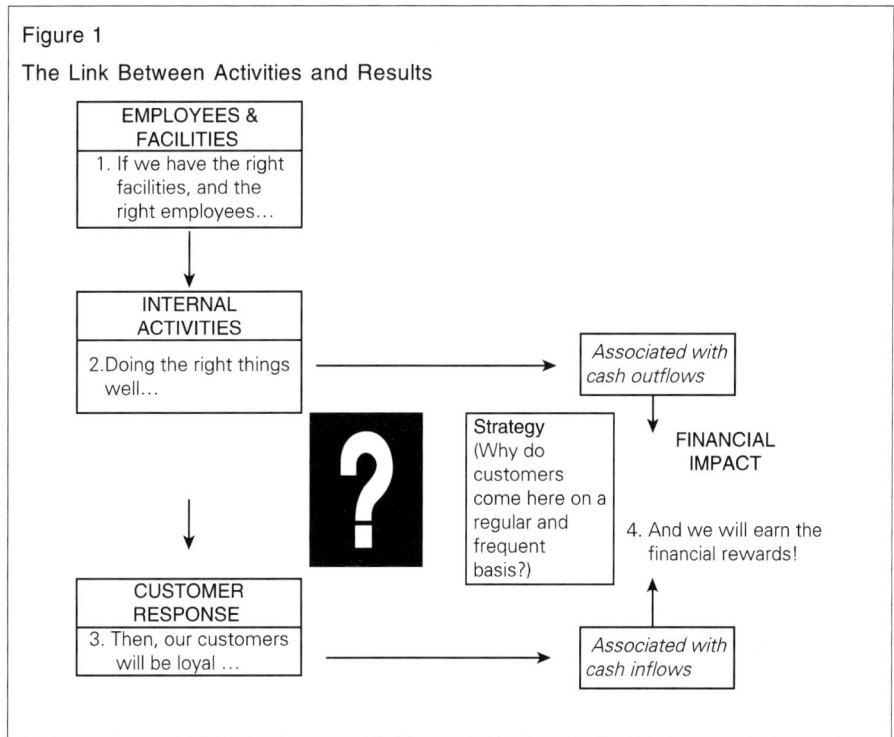

Figure 1
The Link Between Activities and Results

4. For budgeting purposes, Li has quickly made the following assumptions for 2010, based on data that he has obtained:

Sales prices will increase by 3 percent (in line with competitors) and sales volume will increase by 5 percent, which was the growth achieved in the previous year; general inflation is expected to increase discretionary cash expenses by 4 percent; suppliers will extend trade credit at the same rate and the inventory turnover rate will be unchanged. No investing or additional financing activities will be undertaken.

Prepare an income and cash flow forecast for the financial year ending 31st December 2010, together with a balance sheet at that date, based on these assumptions, compared to 2009.

5. What other issues could you bring to Wang's attention? Make suggestions or recommendations. You should include a calculation of the break-even point for the financial years ending 2009 and a forecast for 2010. You should also provide an overall valuation of the coffee shop, assuming it is to be soon sold as a going concern.

业绩考核与报酬
Performance Measurement & Compensation

通过记分为变革创造激励

Linda L. Brennan
Mercer University

D. David McIntyre
Mercer University

引言

"我们又重新开始了!"乔·菲利普斯(Joe Philips)在公司的会议后边走边对迈克·布朗(Mike Brown)说。迈克咧嘴而笑着说,"别当回事。这件事终将过去,就像我来这里以后的七年里我们所看到的其他一切'新生事物'一样。'计费小时数①'曾被看做能解决一切问题,如今又怎么了?过去如此,将来也必如此。不要相信会有什么不同!"

乔摇头、轻声的笑了笑,向他的办公室走去了。他虽然只在 Elite Engineering 公司工作了四年,却已经历了两次机构改组,一是组织了一系列的领导方法培训班,二是召集了无数次"业务小组概念②"的讨论会议——最近的管理时尚把重点放在了咨询人员方面。

作为业务小组的领导人,他负责领导分布在三个地方的十多位不同技术专业的工程师。不过,他应该领导他们做些什么,却并不明确。他知道,在原则上,业务小组理应促进不同专业之间的相互合作,开发新的业务。然而团队中的每一个人都认为,要把他们凑到一处,只是在浪费时间——昂贵的计费小时。

乔实在不能责怪他们。当你手头有工作需要完成时,有什么理由要在一些老的项目上喋喋不休呢?到年底计算奖金的时候,奖金的数额是根据你带来的业务和开出的发票来计算的。正如公司里以玩世不恭著称的鲍勃·马丁(Bob Martin)所说,"管理层推动的对象是小组,奖励的对象却是个人。"

---

① 工程师们的工作时间,一部分是直接为客户服务的,按小时数向客户计费。另外属于间接费用的部分,则不能向客户计费。(但计费小时的单价,则是包括了所有的间接费用和预计利润在内的。)公司按"计费小时"进行奖励,以鼓励员工把时间直接用于项目,提高公司的收入,并曾把这种做法视为解决一切问题的良方。——译者

② work team concept,指公司把咨询工程师组成若干个工作组的概念,它包括两个方面,一是工作组的任务是什么,二是工作组包含哪些不同专业的人员、由谁来领导、其任务和目标又是什么。此处的含义是,公司在机构改组上做了一些工作,但员工因得不到实惠而不是很乐意合作,因而收效不大。本文直译为"业务小组概念"。——译者

公司概况

Elite Engineering 公司（以下简称 EE）是一家由员工拥有的咨询公司，总共有大约 50 位工程咨询人员，是一位富有企业家精神的冶金专家保罗·约翰逊（Paul Johnson）博士于 30 多年前所创建。自从它低调创立以来，EE 已经发展成为从事十多种专业、设在美国的三个地方、拥有大量试验设施的公司了。

公司年收入约为 800 万美元，在全国享有故障分析专长的声誉。当前的收入中大约 75% 来自故障分析，主要客户是保险公司和律师。然而，瞻望未来，EE 公司的高级管理层担心已经取得的成就不能持久，其理由有二。

第一，业务小组领导会产生这种想法的原因主要是，成功创建公司的最高领导者[3]已近退休年龄[4]。一旦公司的创始人从第一把手的位置上退下来，将没有明确的接班人来担任领导。EE 任命了有经验的工程师来领导业务小组，其目的就是要培养公司的"第二代领导人"。

第二，EE 预料竞争环境会有变化。公司预测，由于侵权法的改革已初露端倪，以及在民事诉讼中对惩罚性赔偿的限制，对故障分析专家的鉴定需求会显著下降[1]。因此，继续依靠这一收入来源风险太大。建立业务小组总的目的是要鼓励工程师们相互合作，培养工业设计工作，以应付这一风险。

创始人兼第一把手保罗·约翰逊召集所有的计费员工[5]在公司总部开会，讨论去年提出的关于建立业务小组的做法迟迟不前的问题。在会上，他重申了过去提出的组成业务小组的做法，并引述了公司执行团队所拟订的五年计划中规定的下列目标：

工作质量保持卓越，年度收入达到 2 500 万美元。
- 在财务上保持健康，现金流量强劲。
- 服务多样化并保持平衡。
- 在专业和地区上保持经营业务多样化而又协调的工作。
- 积极招募并继续开发员工的工作能力，以扩大我们的业务能力。

他希望，公司的咨询人员也以此为愿景，动员他们更积极地参与到业务小组中来。不过，各组的回应如何，却是难以预测的。EE 目前的现金状况（只有 16 天）是个问题，有些人对收入达到 2 500 万美元（增长率 40%）的这一基数有疑问。大家似乎对乔·菲利普斯所提出的有关奖金计划的问题最感兴趣。保罗向他保证，奖金计划将维持不变，但如果公司达成了这些目标，奖金总额将有所增加。乔对这个答复似乎表示满意。但也仅此而已，实

---

[3] rainmaker，直译可作"呼风唤雨者"，指给企业带来业务的高管人士，或泛指成功的咨询工程师。在本案例中均意译。——译者

[4] 把公司划分成多个业务小组，也有要造就业务小组领导人、并从中选拔公司领导人的意图，这是因为最高领导人已近退休年龄，需要培养接班人。——译者

[5] billable staff，即按其工作时间向客户计费的员工，即直接向客户提供咨询服务的员工；在本案例中直译为"计费员工"。——译者

际上大家对达成五年计划或公司的目标,并不见得有多大兴趣。

过去几年里,EE 都在年底发放奖金。工程师和技术人员必须使他们当年总共的工作时间(每周 40 小时、每年 50 周)中的 80% 是向客户计费的,才有资格领取奖金。公司的执行团队按当年的利润额确定奖金总额。每个人的实际奖金是按个人总体的业绩和工资来确定的,只是如何计算的具体方法却并未向大家公布过。

保罗知道,他试图实行的改革,受到的抵触很大。每个人都忙于做他们所喜欢的按钟点计费的工作。有的业务小组的领导人说,他们虽然也知道需要朝着未来业务发展的方向去努力,但实际上小组成员不能按他所希望的那样抽出时间去做这些。对各业务小组的要求是明确的:要促进各专业之间和各地区之间的相互合作。保罗深信,合作是公司发展和多样化的关键所在——小组由来自各个地区的多种专业的技术人员组成,这意味着成员之间必须相互合作,才能达到多样化和发展的目的。但这和小组各成员的想法南辕北辙[6]。

"只要他们把从项目中获得的经验与他人分享,他们就能互相学习到许多东西,"他想。"他们完全可以找到更好的解决办法,或者通过某项故障的分析[7],由此及彼,推导出改进产品的设计以减少今后的失败的做法。或者,如果他们偶尔从另外一个地区调一名工程师过来,而不是总是同样的几个人一起工作,则调来的工程师可能会在他擅长的领域开发出类似的业务。然而现在他们却只希望能保持自己的专长、为同样的客户,并与同样的同僚共事。看来我并未能说服他们:与正式聘用本公司的律师们保持密切无间是不够的;工程师们也需要与聘用律师的保险公司建立联系,还要和雇用保险公司的制造商和建筑商建立联系。如果我们不借助于这些关系,就不可能扩大我们的工业咨询业务。"

保罗天生就是个乐观派,他那"乐观进取"的精神是 EE 取得成功的重要推动力。但他对机构惰性的厌烦感,与日俱增。他要公司在他退休之后仍然保持成功。他试过各种办法,可是并不奏效——但这一次的业务小组的新概念非成功不可。

机会

在会议之后,EE 公司的首席营运长(chief operating officer,COO)斯图尔特·魏斯曼(Stuart Weismann)在这一天的晚些时候来找了保罗。斯图尔特没有工程背景,但从一个技术公司退休下来后,却在本公司担任了开发方面咨询业务的组织工作。作为一个咨询人员,斯图尔特在三年前帮助 EE 实现了一些组织方面的变革。在面试之后,保罗决定雇用斯图尔特经管

---

[6] 为了使原文的含义更明确,译者加上了破折号后的字句。实际情况是,保罗希望各业务小组能够挤出时间来设法扩展业务范围,但员工只顾提高与奖金挂钩的计费小时数,对达成公司扩大业务范围的目标不感兴趣。——译者

[7] 如上所述,EE 公司长期从事的是故障分析。——译者

公司的日常事务。

"我能不能和你单独地谈一下？"斯图尔特问道。"当然！"保罗回答道，于是两人转向保罗的办公室走去。"你觉得这个会开得怎么样？"保罗问道。"这正是我要跟你谈的，"斯图尔特说，"我想我们有一个问题——不过应该说是一个机会。"

当他们安坐在皮革的安乐椅上后，斯图尔特继续说，"我确实有一种感觉，就是那些工程师（尤其比较成功的[⑧]工程师）们把对目标的陈述，只看做是一组字词的组合而已。他们安于现状，不愿意冒风险。他们并没有认识到，我们确实需要有这些目标来改变他们所从事的工作，以使公司有所变化。他们中有些人实际上对我们所从事的诉讼业务将要萎缩并不关心。我知道我以前已经谈到过这一点，但我要再说一遍：我们还没有达成共识。公司的目标和个人的目标并不一致。你知道，'酬劳的是 A、期盼的却是 B，那就是在干蠢事了'[2]。我们需要改变激励制度……"

"但我们已经这样做了呀！"保罗打断了他的话。"奖金也是根据各人给 EE 带来的业务量计算的，并不只根据计费的小时数。"

"是呀，"斯图尔特表示同意，"但这些指标只是短期性的，没有把他们的注意力引向比较长期的、更具战略性的业务发展上来。咨询人员仍然把注意力特别集中于获得的奖金，也就是说，他们当年的可计费小时必须达到（每周 40 小时、每年 50 周）的 80%"

看到保罗正准备反驳，斯图尔特立即继续说，"我们需要把公司的目标用比较简单的、容易考核的指标表达出来，应该让工程师们感到这些指标是可以达得到的；应该为咨询工程师所提出的有益于长远的主意支付报酬，这事不宜迟。我想这就需要一个比较平衡的激励制度，鼓励按照我们的企业发展战略进行投资，同时要保持我们的偿债能力和目前已达到的业绩。我看过一些资料，我想我们需要的就是一种'平衡记分卡'制度。这是把各项财务指标与其他业务指标结合起来的一种做法。哈佛已经出版了一本由开发这一观念的卡普兰和诺顿（Kaplan & Norton）两人合写的书。我把它带来了——看到了么？他们说，只采用财务指标就像开飞机时只用一种仪器。让我把这一段读给你听一听：

平衡记分卡（balanced scorecard，BSC）向经理人员提供了一种他们所需要的仪表装置，为他们未来在竞争中取得成功而导航……平衡记分卡将一个机构的使命和战略以一套综合性的业绩指标表达出来，这套指标提供了一套战略评估和管理体系的架构。平衡记分卡仍然把重点放在达成财务目标上，但也包括推动那些财务目标完成的其他业绩指标。记分卡用以衡量一个机构的业绩指标，有相互平衡的四个方面：财务、顾客、内部业务流程和学习与成长。平衡记分卡使公司能够在追踪财务成果的同时，监督为未来的成长建立必不可少的生产能力并取得无形资产[3]。"

"你已经把你的愿景通过五年内应达成的各项目标用语言表达了出来。

---

⑧ 也就是在现行的奖励制度下利益较多的。——译者

如果我们采用了平衡记分卡，那就能把五年的目标用可以具体衡量的指标表达出来。有些指标可能按个人考核，但有些则可能是按业务小组考核的；有些是短期性的考核指标，另外一些则可能鼓励投资于企业的发展。需要追踪的东西很多，但这样做可帮助我们鼓励咨询人员取得比较平衡的业绩。我完全相信这个做法对我们是有效的，我想试一下。"

保罗叹了口气。"我知道你说得对。工程师们本质上都是惯于挑剔问题、热爱思考的人。我们要求咨询人员解决问题，而不只是给客户打电话、建立联系。这是个难以解决的问题。我们必须使他们看到，要使这家公司生存下去并在下一代人手中兴旺起来，我们必须认真对待这件事……好，动手吧。你设计出一个记分卡来，下一步再作讨论。"

"好极了！我立即动手！"斯图尔特既兴高采烈又忧心忡忡。此举将使EE公司面目一新，把竞争力提高一步。制定一套确有实效、公司又能充分追踪其数据的指标是件十分重要的事。对一家咨询公司来讲，哪些指标才是有意义的呢？他们应该怎样做才能避免EE公司过去改革失败所遇到的问题呢？

斯图尔特走回到他的办公室，开始为EE公司起草一份记分卡。他需要有一个草稿或"原型"向其他人解释这件事的概念，并听取他们的回应。这种做法需要使不同个性的人都能接受。他想到他们中有些人的个性，不禁莞尔，漫步经过走廊，想找乔·菲利普斯。斯图尔特发现他正在电气实验室外面，和迈克·布朗与鲍勃·马丁谈话。"你们三人正是我想找来帮忙的一组人，"斯图尔特惊呼道。"我能不能明天请你们吃午餐，从你们的脑子里挖点东西出来呢？"

讨论

当服务员给他们倒咖啡时，斯图尔特向乔和鲍勃把各项问题作了一番概述。在那天上午早些时候，迈克·布朗外出对一次汽车与卡车相撞作实地检查了，所以没有参加这次的聚会。"问题在于目标一致化"，斯图尔特说。"我们对一种行为给予报酬，而期望的却是另外一种行为。我完全相信，如果我们能想出一套合理的指标，保罗会愿意为年终奖实行一种比较平衡的做法。我希望能够在你们的帮助下找到一组指标，使工程师们作出发展企业所需要的改革，同时给以他们所需要的激励。"

鲍勃说，"我知道如果我们有一个够强大的杠杆，我们是可以撬起地球的。不过，要改变这帮家伙，可难了——尤其是那些'计费小时数'高，因而在过去的奖励制度下收入可观的、成功的咨询师们，都不受公司领导的约束，独断独行。对这些人，该怎么办呢？"

乔回答说，"我猜想有些人宁愿离去，也不愿意改变他们办事的方法。如果发生这样的事，保罗能接受得了么？"

斯图尔特微笑着啜了一口咖啡。"你们俩说的都对。会有些人不愿意改变。不过，我希望我们能把重点放在愿意参与到EE新的未来的人身上。他们才是我们为之记分,并按此记分给予激励的改革者。"

"嗯,别说我没有警告过你呀,"鲍勃回答道。"好吧,那我们该如何开始设计一份这样的记分卡呢?"

斯图尔特从他上装的内口袋里取出了几张纸。他展开了这几张纸,递给鲍勃和乔每人一张。"这是一张表,上面列出了我的一些初步的想法。"

"不过请注意,这只是一个草稿而已。我希望你们俩仔细推敲一下。我希望 EE 每个成员对每一个指标都能充分了解。这些指标还应该是客观的,当然也要在短期与长期目标之间保持平衡。最重要的是,大家都能看到所做的工作、这些指标以及 EE 达成其五年目标方面所取得的成就这三者之间的联系。工程师们的目标与公司的目标,应该一致。"

两位工程师在阅读 COO 所准备的草稿(见表1)时,大家静坐着。乔抬头看的时候,看到斯图尔特也正好注视着他,等待听他的回应。乔靠后坐了一点说,"这份东西需要一些时间来消化。这里有好些指标。我初步的反应是,问题有一堆。例如,这些指标中哪一项是最重要的,还是各项指标都有同样的权数?我也并不清楚这些指标如何与我们五年目标联系起来。"

鲍勃语带嘲弄地说,"好了,乔,把你真实的想法直说了吧!斯图尔特,要考核这么多指标,我们干得了吗?像我这样的工程师真能对这些不同的事有影响吗?"

表1
EE 最初的记分卡

顾客方面的指标	• 项目结束时客户的满意度
	• 现有客户向他人推荐本公司的数目
	• 得自新客户收入的百分率
	• 工业咨询的新客户数
内部业务流程指标	• 计费率(工作小时中可以向客户计费的比率)
	• 每个业务小组对项目作回顾检查的次数
	• 多专业共同合作项目的百分比
	• 因顾客的申诉而注销的项目金额
学习与成长、创新方面的指标	• 员工流动率
	• 每个业务小组所获得的收入
	• 专业发展/后续教育的小时数
财务指标	• 营运资金
	• 营业所得现金流量
	• 收入总额
	• 收入增长率

斯图尔特微笑着。"我知道你们俩会向我提出一些不错的建议的!让我建议一两项行动计划。你们俩继续琢磨琢磨,然后再告诉我还有些什么问

题。目前还不要对外宣传。我在迈克回到办公室时会向他通报。我还要扩充这份表格，增添几栏，使你们能看到各项指标的总的权数、它与什么目标（或哪些目标）关联、有关指标的信息从何而来、分析工作要做到哪一个层次——也就是说，该指标是按个人、按业务小组还是按整个公司考核。你们认为如何？"

其他两人点头表示同意。需要做的工作还很多呢。

尾注

1 各州法庭全国中心公布的 2003 年法庭统计数字（见 http：//www.ncsconline.org）表明，经过对人口作调整之后，因侵权行为而起诉的案件在 1992 年到 2001 年之间有所减少。

各互助保险公司的全国协会 2004 年的一份报告书（见 http：//www.namic.org/newsreleases04/040108nrl.asp）称：

- 各州对涉及侵权问题的法规所作的改革，在最近几年内生效的总计 174 项。
- 大部分通过的法规改革主要为在以下五个领域的：共同及连带责任（35 个州）、担保品来源的规定和产品责任（25 个州各有一项）、非经济损害（21 个州）和惩罚性赔偿（18 个州）。
- 侵权法规改革的措施中未通过的最多是下列几类：处理常识性的科学证明（1 个州）、州内择地行诉（forum shopping，即为得到满意结果到处换法庭打官司——译者）（2 个州）、对陪审团服务的要求（3 个州）、政府与私人律师签约（3 个州）和集体起诉（7 个州）。
- 在 2003 年中，在 15 个州通过了新的侵权改革的法规，涉及上诉债券、私人律师保留、集体起诉、州内择地行诉和陪审团服务。

2003 年，在 16 个州提出的并移到 2004 年作进一步考虑的侵权改革提案，涉及共同及连带责任、产品责任、惩罚性赔偿和预断的利率。"

2 Kerr, S. (1995). "An Academy Classic: On the folly of rewarding A, when hoping for B." Academy of Management Executive, 9 (1): 7 - 14.

3 Kaplan, R. S., and D. P. Norton (1996). The Balanced Scorecard. Cambridge, MA: Harvard Business School Press.

Creating Incentives for Change by Keeping Score

Linda L. Brennan
Mercer University

D. David McIntyre
Mercer University

INTRODUCTION

"Here we go again!" Joe Philips said to Mike Brown as they were walking back from the company meeting. Mike grinned and said, "Just ignore it. This will fade away, just like every other 'new initiative' we've seen in the seven years that I have been here. It always has been, and always will be, about the almighty 'billable hour.' Don't believe any different!"

Joe chuckled and shook his head as he walked away towards his office. He had only been with Elite Engineering for four years and he had already been through two organizational restructurings, a leadership development training series, and countless meetings on the business team concept—the latest management fad being imposed on the consulting staff.

As a business team leader, he was expected to lead a dozen engineers from several different technical specialties and three locations. However, it was not clear what he was supposed to lead them to do. He knew that, in principle, the business teams were conceived to encourage multidisciplinary collaboration and were intended to promote new business development. In reality, everyone on his team felt that it was a waste of time—precious billable time—for them to get together.

Joe really couldn't blame them. Why hash over old projects when you had work that needed to be done? When it came down to bonus time at the end of the year, the dollars were going to be based on the amount of business that you brought in and billed. As Bob Martin, the company cynic, stated, "Management is pushing 'teams' but rewarding individuals."

COMPANY OVERVIEW

Elite Engineering (EE) is an employee-owned consulting company with approximately 50 engineering consultants on staff. Dr. Paul Johnson, an entrepreneurial metallurgist, founded the organization over 30 years ago. Since its modest inception, EE has grown to include more than a dozen practice areas, three locations across the United States, and extensive laboratory facilities.

With approximately $8 million in annual revenues, the company enjoys a national reputation for expertise in failure analysis. About 75% of the current revenues are based in the failure analysis area, with insurance companies and attorneys as the key clients. Looking to the future, however, EE executive management is concerned that this success is unsustainable, for two reasons.

First, the main impetus behind the business team leader concept is that the top rainmakers are approaching retirement age. There are no clear successors to lead the company, especially once the founder steps down as the chief executive. EE appointed seasoned engineers to head up business teams in an effort to cultivate the "next generation of leaders" in the company.

Secondly, EE anticipates changes in the competitive environment. The company predicts a significant decline in the demand for expert testimony on failure analysis with tort reform on the horizon and limits for punitive damages in civil lawsuits[1]. It would be extremely risky to continue to depend so heavily on this revenue stream. The business team concept is intended to address this risk by encouraging engineers to collaborate and cultivate industrial design work.

Founder and CEO Paul Johnson assembled all of the billable staff together for a meeting at the company headquarters to address the lack of traction in the business team concept from the previous year. In the meeting, he presented the following goals from the five-year plan developed by the executive team that reaffirmed the company's commitment to the business team concept:

- Achieve annual revenues of $25 million while maintaining excellence in our work.
- Maintain fiscal health with a strong cash flow.
- Diversify and balance our services.
- Operate the business with effective cross-discipline and cross-geographical teamwork.
- Expand our capabilities by aggressively recruiting and continually developing our people.

He hoped that sharing this vision with the consultants would motivate them to participate more actively in the business teams. It was hard to gauge the group's reaction, though. There was a question about EE's current cash position (16 days), and someone asked about the basis for the $25 million target (40% growth rate). The biggest interest seemed to be in Joe Philips' question about the bonus plan. When Paul assured him that it would stay the same, with the hope that the bonus pool would be larger as the company met the goals, Joe seemed satisfied. Other than that, there really did not seem like there was much interest.

For the past several years, EE paid bonuses at the end of the year. To be eligible, the engineers and technicians had to complete the year at 80% billable, based on 40 hours per week, 50 weeks per year. The executive team determined the pool based upon the year's profit. Although the formula was not published, the actual bonuses distributed were based on a combination of overall performance and pay.

Paul knew that there was a lot of resistance to the changes he was trying to institute. Everyone was busy doing what they enjoyed best, billable work. While some of the business team leaders said they understood that they needed to be working on business development for the future, they just were not making the time or engaging their team members as he had hoped. The idea of the business teams was clear: to promote that cross-discipline and cross-geographical collaboration. Paul was convinced that collaboration was the key to the company's growth and diversification.

"They could learn so much from each other, if they would just share project experiences," he thought. "They just might identify even better solutions, or a way to redefine the project from a failure analysis to a product redesign. Or if they would occasionally pull in an engineer from another location, instead of always working with the same few people, then that remote engineer might actually be in a position to develop similar business in his area. They just want to keep to their own expertise, working with the same clients and the same colleagues. I cannot seem to convince them that it is not enough to have a rapport with the attorney that officially hires the firm; the engineers need to make the connections with the insurance companies that hire the attorneys and with the manufacturers and builders who hire the insurance companies. If we do not leverage those relationships, we will never expand our industrial consulting."

Paul was a naturally optimistic person whose "can-do" attitude was an important driver behind EE's success. But he was getting tired of the inertia in the organization. He wanted to assure the company's success past his retirement. Everything else he had tried had not worked—this business team concept had to succeed.

THE OPPORTUNITY

Late in the day, after the meeting, Stuart Weismann, EE's chief operating officer (COO), approached Paul. Stuart did not have an engineering background, but had retired from a large technology corporation and went into consulting on organizational development. As a consultant, Stuart helped EE with some of the organizational changes made three years ago. After the engagement, Paul decided to hire Stuart to run the day-to-day operations of the business.

"May I speak with you privately?" Stuart asked. "Of course!" replied Paul, and the two men turned to walk back to Paul's office. "How do you think the meeting went?" asked Paul. "That's what I want to talk with you about," said Stuart, "I think we have a problem—or better yet, an opportunity."

As they settled in to the leather wing-backed chairs, Stuart continued, "I really get the feeling that the presentation of the goals was just a bunch of words to the engineers, particularly the more successful ones. They don't understand that we really need them to change what they do, in order for the company to change. Some of them don't even really buy into the concern that the litigation business is going to shrink. I know I have said this before, but I am going to say it one more time: We're missing congruence. The organization's goals and individuals' goals are not aligned. You know, "the folly of rewarding A when hoping for B^2. We need to change the incentive structure around here..."

"But we have!" Paul interrupted. "Bonuses are not only based on billable hours, but also on the amount of business brought in to EE."

"Yes," Stuart agreed, "but those are still short-term measures that don't turn their attention to longer-term, more strategic business development. The consultants are still very focused on being eligible for the bonus, which means that they have to have been 80% billable [of 40 hours/week, 50 weeks/year] for the current year."

Seeing that Paul was about to protest again, Stuart quickly continued, "We need to translate the corporate goals into simpler, more measurable targets that the engineers feel are attainable and treat as time-sensitive. I think this requires a more balanced incentive system, to encourage investment in the future according to our business strategies while still maintaining solvency and current results. I have been doing some reading, and what I think we need is a "balanced scorecard." This is a way to combine financial measures with other operational metrics. Harvard has published a book by a couple of guys, Kaplan and Norton, who developed the idea. I have it here—see? They say that just using financial measures is like flying an airplane using only one instrument. Let me read this part to you:

The Balanced Scorecard (BSC) provides managers with the instrumentation they need to navigate future competitive success... The BSC translates an organization's mission and strategy into a comprehensive set of performance measures that provides the framework for a strategic measurement and management system. The BSC retains an emphasis on achieving financial objectives, but also includes the performance drivers of those financial objectives. The scorecard measures organizational performance across four balanced perspectives: *financial*, *customers*, *internal business processes*, and *learning and growth*. The BSC enables companies to track financial results while simultaneously monitoring progress in building the capabilities and acquiring the intangible assets they need for future growth[3].

"You've articulated your vision into specific five-year goals. Using a BSC, we can try to translate the five-year goals into specific measurable objectives. Maybe some of the measures will be individually-based, but some could also be business team-based; some will be short-term performance metrics and others could reward business development investments. It would be a lot to keep track of, but it could help us reward consultants for more balanced performance. I really think it will pay off for us, and I'd like to give it a try."

Paul sighed. "I know you're right. Engineers, by nature, are critical thinkers. And our consultants are motivated by solving problems, not calling on clients and building relationships. This is going to be a hard nut to crack. We have to show them that we are really serious about this if this company is going to survive and thrive for the next generation. We have got to make this work... OK. Go for it. Come up with a scorecard, and we'll discuss next steps."

"Great! I'll get right on it!" Stuart was elated and worried at the same time. This could make all the difference in moving EE to a new level of competition. It was going to be extremely important to identify measures that had credibility and for which the company could reasonably track the data. What would be meaningful for a consulting company? How could they avoid the problems with previous attempts at change with EE?

Stuart walked back to his office and started to sketch out a scorecard for Elite. He needed a draft, or a prototype, to explain the concept and get others' input. This was an approach that needed to make sense to a broad range of personalities. Thinking of some of the personalities, he stopped, smiled, and walked down the hall, looking for Joe Philips. Stuart found him talking with Mike Brown and Bob Martin just outside the electrical lab. "You three are just the group I need to help me with something," Stuart exclaimed. "Can I take you to lunch tomorrow and pick your brains about something?"

THE DISCUSSION

Stuart summarized the issues to Joe and Bob as the waiter poured coffee. Earlier that morning, Mike Brown traveled to a site inspection of an automobile/truck collision and was not available to join the gathering. "The issue is goal congruence," Stuart stated. "We're rewarding one kind of behavior, when hoping for another. I really believe that if we can come up with a reasonable set of measures, Paul will be willing to implement a more balanced approach to the annual bonuses. What I am hoping is that with your help, these same measures will create the incentives that the engineers need in order to make the changes the company needs for business development."

Bob said, "I know if we had a lever big enough we could move the world, but changing some of these guys is going to be tough—especially the rainmakers that usually get a 'hands-off' approach from the executive team. What's going to happen with them?"

Joe responded, "It's my guess that some people will leave rather than change the way they do business. Is that an acceptable option to Paul?"

Stuart smiled and took a sip of coffee. "You are both right. There are going to be some people who will not change. What I want us to focus on, though, are the people who want to be part of the new future of EE. These are the people that we can give incentives to change by keeping score."

"Well, don't say I didn't warn you," replied Bob. "OK, so how do we start making one of these scorecards?"

Stuart took some papers out of his inside coat pocket. He unfolded them and gave a sheet each to Bob and Joe. "Here is a table with some of my initial ideas."

"Now remember, this is just a draft. I expect you two to really chew it over. I want every measure to be clear for everyone in EE to understand. The measures also have to be objective and, of course, balanced between the short and the long term. And it's most important that people see the connections between what they do, the measures, and how well EE is achieving the five-year goals. There should be congruence in the engineers' goals and the company's goals."

There was a long pause as the engineers read the draft that the COO had prepared, as shown in Table 1. Looking up, Joe saw Stuart looking at him, waiting for a reaction. Joe leaned back and said, "This is going to take some time to digest. There are a lot of measures here. My initial reaction is a bunch of questions, like which of these is most important, or are they all weighted the same? Are these all individual measures, or are some of these team-based, or location-based, or for the whole company? And I'm not clear on how these relate to the five-year goals, either."

Bob quipped, "So, Joe, tell us how you really feel! Seriously, Stuart, can we afford to measure all this? Can engineers like me really affect all of these different things?"

Stuart smiled. "I knew that you two would have some great suggestions for me! Let me suggest a couple of action items. You two continue to think this over, and let me know of any additional concerns or questions. For now, I'd like to keep it between us. I'll brief Mike when he gets back into the office. I will work on extending this table and add columns so that for each measure, you can see its overall weighting, which goal or goals it connects to, where the information is going to come from, and what level of analysis will be used—i.e., whether it is an individual, business team, or overall organization measure. Sound good?"

The other men nodded their assent. There was a lot of work to do.

Table 1
Initial Scorecard for Elite Engineering

Customer Measures	• Customer Satisfaction Ratings at Project Closings • Number of Referrals from Existing Clients • Percentage of Revenue from New Clients • Number of New Clients for Industrial Consulting
Internal Business Process Measures	• Billability • Number of Project Reviews Performed per Business Team • % of Projects with Cross-Disciplinary Collaboration • $ of Project Write-off from Customer Complaints
Learning & Growth Innovation Measures	• Employee Turnover • Revenue Generated per Business Team • Number of Professional Development/Continuing Education Hours
Financial Measures	• Working Capital • Cash Flows from Operations • Total Revenue • Revenue Growth

ENDNOTES

1 The 2003 Court Statistics project published by the National Center for State Courts (http://www.ncsconline.org) shows that population-adjusted tort filings declined from 1992 to 2001.

A 2004 report by the National Association of Mutual Insurance Companies (http://www.namic.org/newsreleases04/040108nrl.asp) reported that:

• A total of 174 tort reform laws have been enacted by states in recent years.

• The majority of the reform laws passed address five key areas of tort reform: joint and several liability (35 states), collateral source rules and product liability (25 states each), non-economic damages (21 states), and punitive damages (18 states).

• The least commonly enacted tort reform measures are those that address common sense scientific evidence (1 state), intrastate forum shopping (2 states), jury service requirements (3 states), government contracts with private attorneys (5 states), and class action (7 states).

• In 2003, new tort reform laws addressing appeal bonds, private attorney retention, class actions, the collateral source rule, intrastate forum shopping and jury service were enacted in 15 states.

Tort reform bills introduced in 16 states during 2003 addressing joint and several liability, product liability, punitive damages, and prejudgment interest rates will be carried over for further consideration in 2004. "

2 Kerr, S. (1995). "An Academy Classic: On the folly of rewarding A, when hoping for B." Academy of Management Executive, 9 (1): 7 – 14.

3 Kaplan, R. S., and D. P. Norton (1996). The Balanced Scorecard. Cambridge, MA: Harvard Business School Press.

JEA：迈向成本透明的大道

John B. MacArthur
University of North Florida

Jeffrey E. Michelman
University of North Florida

Bobby E. Waldrup
University of North Florida

Dana M. Wallace
Florida State University

背景

2006 年晚春的某一天，万永伊·肯德里克（Wanyonyi Kendrick）坐在位于佛罗里达州的杰克逊维尔（Jacksonville）JEA[1] 公司办公大楼的 15 层办公室里，寻思着她对改进"技术服务部（technology services，TS）"成本透明度方面所提出的下一步要求是否能够奏效。当她观看着午后雷阵雨正越过圣约翰河席卷而来时，这位 JEA 公司的首席信息官（chief information officer，CIO）考虑的是在未来几个月内会发生些什么事。JEA 是美国排名前八的由社区拥有的电力、水和废水处理的公用事业公司[2]。

万永伊重温过去两年中发生的所有的事，并想到明年还有什么事情可能会发生。她盼望在这个飓风季节里，不会再像 2004 年那样，飓风严重地侵袭到北佛罗里达州海岸地区。在 2004 年，四次强飓风侵袭佛罗里达州，给整个州带来了严重的破坏。虽然杰克逊维尔并没有直接受到飓风的袭击，但暴风雨还是给这个地区带来了严重的断电事故。万永伊还想到，如果 2005 年 8 月的那一次卡特里娜飓风向东而不是向西袭击了墨西哥湾的话，不知道会给这个地区带来什么灾难。2004 年发生的那次断电事故，对 JEA 为客户提供服务方面，带来了糟糕的挑战。为了防止像 2004 年的飓风那样，JEA 的网站被迫关闭，JEA 在 TS 成本方面的投入增加了很多。

不幸的是，对万永伊和其他美国人来说，气象预报并没有就 2006 年的飓风季节带来什么好消息，预报说强飓风的次数还会有所增加。对此，万永伊有许多担心的事。现在是 5 月 5 日了，此地的飓风季节在一个月之内就会开始。

万永伊担心的不仅仅是天气，公司的机构还发生了变革。在过去几年里，CEO（chief executive officer）换了人。现任 CEO 吉姆·迪肯森（Jim Dickenson）因 2004 年的那次断电事故，更加强调 JEA 有责任在营运方面做到无懈可击。他要求公司的营运要提高一步，因而对 TS 的要求比以前严格很多。对于这些新的要求会增加多少成本，万永伊心中无数。各项报告中所提供的数字相互不协调，她觉得难以把各个报告书凑到一起，得出一个比较正确的数字。看来有这种想法的，不止是她一个人。在 TS 的部门会议上，各位主任都埋怨说，由于情况在不断地变化，现在的这些报表都已陈旧、没有价值了。

万永伊回忆起 2005 年年初时，她对如何解决这个谜团束手无策。TS 部的费用没有向公司内部的各用户①公开，缺乏透明度。她需要找出一个办法，防止 TS 现行的流程成本法³（process-based costing，PBC）② 制度遭到失败。现行的 PBC 制度，是在有多道工序和分工序的情况下，为计算流程中各该工序、分工序③的作业的成本而设计的，以适应 JEA 以工序分工的流程性质⁴，但它也存在着若干设计上的缺点、所提供的信息中多数已经陈腐过时。万永伊需要的是一个能够帮助她节约成本的 PBC 制度；在严峻的飓风气候条件下，现行的 TS 制度不能够发挥出它应有的降低风险的作用。她必须不断地提高技术服务的水平和质量，在实现 CEO 的战略目标的同时，把重点继续保持在降低成本上。提高 TS 的业务对用户的价值并且不断地降低成本，在战略上有其重要意义。

在 2005 年晚春时，万永伊很高兴从著名大学聘请到三位会计教授来评估现行 PBC 作出的 TS 报表是否有用，并提出改进意见。在几年以前，她曾雇用了几位咨询人员对 TS 的成本计算制度作出评估，他们的工作质量虽高，但并没有提出可付诸实现的措施意见。

去年已匆匆逝去，现在她凝视着教授们写出的最终报告书。报告书建议下一步需要采取的措施是：完善 PBC 制度，使 TS 成本做到透明。对于她与工作组之间的互动⁵和他们的最终报告书，她感到满意，但她对整个公司是否都会同意报告书中提出的意见，心中无数。万永伊需要确定一套方案，把 PBC 的倡议和对 JEA 管理层中的其他高管们实施的平衡记分卡结合起来⁶。

PBC 倡议和方案

由于万永伊既是一位注册会计师（CPA）又是一位经过认证的注册管理会计师（CMA），看来她继续在上后续专业教育（continuing professional

---

① 本文中的"用户（users）"均指公司内部的用户，以下就迳作"用户"，不另注明"公司内部"了。——译者

② process-based costing，直译应作"以流程为基础的成本计算法"，为简约起见，比照 ABC 一般作"作业成本法"，姑译为"流程成本法"。在美国，先有"流程管理（process-based management，PBM）"一词。1994 年瑞夫·劳森（Raef Lawson，现任管理会计师协会研究副主席）在他的文章中首先采用了"流程成本法"一词（请参阅本案例尾注 3 和参考文献第 7 项）。——译者

③ 工序（processes）指一个部门中的各道工序，分工序（sub-processes）指一道工序下的若干小工序。——译者

education，CPE）的课程。2005年4月，她在一家著名的大学，选修了一门战略成本管理的CPE课程。在课间休息时，她和琼斯（Jones）教授谈及她在成本计算方面的问题，这位教授看来对此颇感兴趣。下课时，两人商定下周到她的办公室会晤。

第二个星期，琼斯博士和两位同事一起与万永伊会面，讨论TS部当前面临的问题和JEA所处的环境。在讨论中，他们一致认为应该把需要讨论的问题列出来，向万永伊的上司即公司的CEO吉姆·迪肯森汇报。虽然万永伊知道即使不经过别人的批准，也可以从她的预算中批出一笔款项来完成这个项目，但她需要把这一项目将会带来的好处，向CEO吉姆·迪肯森汇报并取得他的支持，才能取得进展。如果他们能够做成这件事，就能把从几年前开始、如今已奄奄一息的公司PBC倡议重新恢复活力。她真心希望通过使TS起到领导作用，她的部门能够成为公司各部门的一个表率。

万永伊曾经几次参与过实施PBC倡议的事，但都没有成功，PBC制度至今还未在JEA公司实施。这些倡议之所以不成功，主要是因为没有得到高管持续、充分的支持。而且在争取高管对PBC的理念作持续支持方面的努力，也做得不够；尤其是在最近CEO换了人以后，显得格外突出。万永伊明白，要使PBC这个项目取得成功，关键在于CEO的支持。要想持久解决这个问题，必须由JEA的最高领导来定调子。她还觉得，这可能是把COBIT框架结构用于TS领域，开发出一项成本计算模式的机会[7]。她特别想到COBIT的成熟度模式[8]是对这个项目作出评估的一种方法。PBC项目组的成员都同意万永伊的分析意见，并且决定要在2005年5月16日之前完成他们的提案。在此期间，万永伊同意向CEO汇报这项新的倡议。

5月16日很快就到了，琼斯博士和他的同事们如约来到万永伊的办公室。她已经反复细读了PBC方案（见图1），对这个主意感到兴奋。琼斯博士看来对提纲中所列示的步骤相当平静且有信心。万永伊很喜欢方案中把推行这个项目分为若干阶段④、几位教授和她的部下之间又多次互相沟通的做法。对于如何节约TS的费用开支，教授们提出了分三步走的计划。计划的内容是：

1. 透明度——对PBC各项指标中的有用部分加以更新，基本上把分配给各部门的TS费用额，只告知分管该部门的副总裁（VP）。

2. 最佳做法——建立一套正式的TS费用收费制度，按照这个收费制度，TS资源的用户只对其负责的部分付费。

3. 向外分包——如果公司的管理层能够从外界的供应商那里，以比较便宜的价格获得各项TS资源，那么就可以选用外部承包商提供的服务。

万永伊重申她对这一方案负责，并且从7月份开始的第一阶段起，在教授们和她的几位主任之间，约定几次接触的时间。万永伊松了一口气，希望这样做能够有助于解决缺少透明度和成本不断上升的问题。

---

④ 这若干个阶段见图1所示。——译者

图 1
流程成本法方案
目的

　　这是一项为满足 JEA 公司 TS 部在业绩考核方面的需求，而作的研究。本研究的目的，是帮助 JEA 公司的 TS 部，部署其以流程为基础的成本计算的日常工作。从 2005 年 7 月 1 日开始，以一个日历年度为期。本研究要达成的结果有五项：

1) 对 TS 部当前所用的业绩指标的成熟程度作一评估，并对通过改进流程取得切实的成本节约提出建议。
2) 对目前所收集的各项业绩指标，以及更多地把重点放在考核财务业绩方面所提出的建议，作一评估。
3) 对 TS 的管理人员，在对 PBC 价值的认识和应用方面，以及对分层次的、用于考核业绩的平衡记分卡，进行基础培训。
4) 建议采用成熟的、与管理人员报酬相结合的财务指标。
5) 就如何收集各项指标和对成绩好坏的评估方法，对 TS 管理人员进行后续教育。

对成本透明化最初的倡议将包括以下六个阶段：

1) 跟随 TS 的研究人员并进行调查
2) 对现行的各项流程和指标作一评估
   a. 对先前收集的各项业绩指标作定性评估
   b. 对先前收集的各项指标作统计检验
   c. 对有可能采用的新的定量指标作一调查研究
3) 流程成熟度模式
   a. 对 JEA 公司 TS 部要把 PBC 用作一项决策工具所作的部署的成熟程度，作一评估
   b. 所写成的成熟程度模式（包括对未来发展所提出的各项建议），是否可以呈报了
4) 对管理人员进行初步教育
   a. 与 TS 部的各位主任和经理一起，举行互动式的研讨会
   i. 对 TS 管理人员目前的认识程度，通过预试、作一估测
   ii. 讨论第 1~3 阶段研究所发现的情况
   iii. 互相讨论 JEA 的文化、价值观、PBC 的应用问题
5) 财务业绩指标
   a. 和 TS 的高管层次作面对面的讨论
   i. 把与财务有关的各项指标，向高管层次作正式的推荐
   ii. 讨论各项新指标在收集数据方面的要求
   b. 布置收集数据所用的各项技术和时限
6) 对管理人员的后续教育
   a. 与 TS 高管层次作最后一次面对面的会晤
   i. 就对于各项新指标的结果的评估，取得最终的一致意见
   ii. 在 TS 管理人员间宣传本项目成果的措词上，取得一致意见
   b. 与 TS 各位主任和经理一起，召开一次互动式的研讨会
   c. 就总的研究成果，写成一份书面报告，呈递给 TS 的高管人员

了解现有的 PBC 倡议[9]

　　这三位教授是 7 月 5 日上午 10 点来到公司的，现在准备走了。负责 TS 生产部的最大的部分即技术基础设施（Technology Infrastructure）的主任史蒂文·舒尔茨（Steven Schultz）和他们见了面。他们第一个约见的是会计部主任雷·塔尔（Ray Tull）。

　　雷：早上好。

琼斯博士：早上好。多谢你花费时间和我们一起坐下来讨论。

雷：没关系。第二季度已经结束，我稍有一些空闲了。我们一起去我的办公室如何？

琼斯博士：好呀。

在他们去雷办公室的路上，琼斯博士简略地归纳了一下要问的一些问题，和这次见面他想要讨论的是哪几个方面。

琼斯博士：我们完全需要对现行的 PBC 制度从头开始作一了解。你能不能从如何建立现行的 PBC 制度开始，给我们介绍一遍呢？

雷：嗯，从 1998 年起，我们就在这方面作了一些尝试。现行的 PBC 制度则是从 2000 年开始发展起来的。那时 JEA 公司聘用了一个外部的咨询事务所，与会计部密切合作，建立了现行的 PBC 制度。当时从事此事的 JEA 人员，如今大部分已经不在本公司工作了。当时我们大家都决定建立一些适用于整个 JEA 公司的作业成本归集点⑤、成本驱动和分配率。每一个成本归集点都与各道工序垂直对应，并且把归依的成本分配给负责该工序的主任。每一位主任对 30～50 个成本归集点负监督之责。有的资源的耗费可以直接计入某个成本归集点，但有些资源的耗费则属于共同的费用，需要分配计入若干个成本归集点。我们现行的做法是，并没有把作业成本归集点的金额分配给各个用户。

琼斯博士：JEA 公司现在是如何归集和分配各项数据的呢？

雷：我们采用 Oracle 软件，在整个公司的范围内收集和分发报表。通过一个共享服务器（shared server），向各个主任按月提供数据。

琼斯博士：现在我们明白了现行 PBC 制度的创建过程。我还希望知道现行 Oracle 系统的效率如何。不过，这多半属于史蒂文管辖的范围了。你是不是认为 Oracle 需要耗用大量资源，才能实现现行 PBC 制度下收集数据和编制报表的功能呢？

史蒂文：并非如此。我认为我们现在所做的，是设法确定在实施 Oracle 系统方面，究竟应该投入多少人力和技术资源。

琼斯博士：你能不能把现行的作业成本归集点是如何建立起来的，稍为详细一点地给我们说一说呢？

史蒂文：嗯，2002 年，我们决定不再采用传统的成本计算方法，改为采用 PBC。在 2001 年，JEA 从一个功能性的组织机构，改组成为一个精益型的、以流程为主的组织机构[10]。采用 PBC，就是为了支持这一新的、建立在流程基础上的组织机构；这样的组织机构，能够防止各个部门各自为政所带来的"地方主义"倾向，各个工序、部门之间原本就是互相依赖的关系不相容。整个企业所有的流程，都列示于各个"流程图⑥"上。每一个成本归集点都有一个相应的流程图。像这样的流程图，数以百计。部门主任对其

---

⑤ cost pools，或译作"成本库"。——译者

⑥ process map，一般译为流程图，指的是对各个业务单位的工作范围、负责者是谁、该工序完成任务的标准，以及该工序的业绩如何确定的规定。流程图一旦编出，对企业内部的各个业务单位的要求，就职责分明了。因此，对一个组织机构实施控制的第一步，在于了解它的基本流程。本案例的图 6，是对流程图的一个例示，请参阅。——译者

所管辖的各道流程负责。举例来说，我负责的成本归集点，就有35个之多。我说清楚了吗？

琼斯博士：清楚了——多谢。我的同事们和我在离开之前，希望你给我们看一个现行工序流程图的实例。间接成本是如何分配的呢？

雷：我想我能够回答这个问题。我们对11道工序部门，采用一个公司内部的标准计费制度，作为分配间接成本的依据。例如，审计、设施的服务、风险管理，都采用这个做法。如果你要知道得更具体一些，我也可以为你作深入介绍。

琼斯博士：好呀，这对我们是有帮助的。请介绍一下"作业驱动"。

雷：嗯，在JEA公司，我们把"作业驱动"称为"度量单位（unit of measure）"。我们对每一个作业归集点都确定一个"度量单位"。各个点的"度量单位"未必完全不相同，但两个点采用同一个"度量单位"的情况也是很少的。

史蒂文：我注意到一个问题：有些作业驱动现在已经不再实行了、或者没有及时修改。例如，我在PBC报表上看到，电话的台机数是"作业驱动"之一，但这个数字从来都不准确。我在报表上还看到另外一些已经过了时的"作业驱动"，例如现在TS部已经没有人在使用寻呼机了，但这一"作业驱动"却仍然出现在报表上。现在想来，那个报表该是没有什么用处了。

雷：TS的其他主任也向我提到过这个问题。

琼斯博士：我也想看一下那些报表。PRC报表中是不是还有别的地方需要分别给予解释的呢？

雷：有的。单位费率就是一例。单位费率是把计入作业成本归集点的金额除以实际作业驱动量所得之商。

琼斯博士：好了。多谢你的宝贵时间。今天我们想问的就是这些了。我希望得到一套流程图和报表的复印件。

史蒂文把三位教授带回给万永伊，他们在那里就刚才的会晤进行讨论，她补充说明了有关2002年所采用的做法中遗漏的地方。万永伊还向他们介绍了TS部的其他几位主任，相互建立了通过电邮、进一步取得所需资料的联系方法。

万永伊：是的，在2002年时我们曾试图一蹴而成地把整个系统建立起来。此事真的成了工作的重中之重。那时我们只有一个员工，也不明确高管是不是支持我们。那时好的方面是，我们能够编制出许多报表。不幸的是，报表上提供的信息大部分都是过了时的，对决策的帮助极小。从今天的情况来看，TS对企业完全是一无贡献，却又是不可或缺的一种服务；但要想取得支持这项工作的资源，却几乎是不可能的。你有没有听到过这样一种说法："TS是我们的业务，但我们忙的也仅限于TS"——TS只顾忙于自己的业务，对其他部门没有什么帮助，那就犹如追咬自己尾巴的狗，一场瞎忙而已呢？

琼斯博士：没有。我以前从未听说过。

万永伊：基本上，这种说法着重指出了这样一种观点：在今天，TS事实上与所有的各项业务都交织在一起。因此，TS所花费的钱，从成本效益的观点上来看是不是值得，是很难作出判断的。

琼斯博士：确实如此。这正是我们来这里的原因，想助一臂之力！从我们前面所作的交谈来看，我们需要把注意力集中在了解 TS 部为提供服务所耗费的资源，以及服务量与成本之间的关系。另外，看来 TS 现在所提供的信息，对主任们的决策并没有多大帮助。

万永伊：是呀，你这真是一语道破了。

在这天下午余下的时间里，教授们跟随着 TS 的几位经理人员，进一步了解他们各自的流程，其作业的驱动就是根据流程制订出来的。在往后的几个月里，教授们把他们对 TS 主任们提出的问题归纳起来，如期完成了方案的第一阶段——跟随 TS 的研究人员并进行调查⑦。按照原定的日程，对六个阶段的其余部分和它们的考核指标，逐一进行评估。

对现行的流程和考核指标的评价

在以后的几个月里，琼斯博士和他的工作组，就 TS 部的组织机构和它内部流程情况所做的笔记，开展讨论。琼斯博士还收到雷发来的几份电邮，在电邮中列示了 JEA 公司当年分类的数据。掌握了这一信息以后，教授工作组确定了 JEA 公司此前提出来的 PBC 倡议中所存在的主要缺陷，对 TS 的资源耗费作一行动分析⑧，并指出了这个研究项目目前的进行方向。教授们遂与万永伊见面讨论这些问题。

琼斯博士：我们主要发现，你们公司过去的 PBC 倡议中，存在着五项主要的缺陷。这些缺陷是：

1. 对决策没有什么用处

● 由于作业驱动已经陈旧过时，并且不符合成本习性的规律，因而经理人员和员工都对它置之不理。

2. 制订的作业驱动有欠妥当

● TS 的作业驱动主要考核的是频率——该项作业的发生次数——如果执行该作业每一次需要花费的时间并不相同，那就不能在分配费用时只按次数，而不按各次作业的不同的强度来计算。

3. 算出的作业驱动价值已经过时

● 对作业驱动所确定的度量（称为"价值"），大部分反映的是 2001 年 JEA 在全公司推行 PBC 时的实际作业情况，现在已经过时；需要按当前作业的水平，对各项作业重新确定其价值。

4. 作业驱动是按实际价值计算的

● 用实际成本作为计价的基础，就会把因效率低下而引起成本过高的后果，转嫁给用户。由于效率低下而增加的成本，理应留在 TS 部，不应分

---

⑦ 这个方案分阶段执行，具体见图 1 所示。——译者

⑧ 行动分析（action analysis）指分析说明各项成本是如何分配计入某一成本对象（某项产品或某个用户），以及某项作业发生变化成本将不容易随之升降的情况。——译者

配出去。

5. 没有把重点放在成本管理上

- 现行 PBC 的做法是把成本在宏观层次上加以分配的，这个做法只适合于确定长期的收费率，但不适用于努力降低流程成本，使成本管理更好地为内部客户服务。必须在每一个流程之内进行微观层次[9]的分析，才能做到有效的成本管理。

万永伊：这五点都很重要。那么，你建议我们如何来改正这些问题呢？

琼斯博士：嗯，我想我们不妨把重点首先放在 TS 的一个内部客户上，比方说分管某个部门的一位副总裁或该部门的领导人。我们想跟这位经理人员一起坐下来，讨论他或她的部门耗用 TS 资源的情况，最终为这位经理编制出一份报告书，在报告书中说"这就是你如何耗用 TS 资源的情况，同时也说明你可以作哪些变革，来降低这部分的成本。"

万永伊：我想告诉你，要使其他的副总裁们参与进来，表面看来是件容易的事，但事实上要比我想象的困难一些。我刚参加了一次高管会议，会上作出了一个决定，要在 12 月底在雷·塔尔的部门停止实施 PBC 制度。这个制度奄奄一息已经有相当一段时间了，但没有人愿意动手彻底结束它。正因为如此，我们需要让此事有充分的说服力，才能使公司执行委员会中的同事们接受这一倡议[11]。

琼斯博士：我充分领会这一两难处境。但是，如果他们看到了这一份改进了的报告书范例，而且我们能够向他们展示他们的部门可以如何来节约开支，也许会引起他们的兴趣。我们工作组已经草拟了报告书的提纲。这里是我们所草拟的内容（见图 2）。我们还认为，只要在开始时就采用"成熟模式"的框架，我们就可能提供一个系统的方法，来实施这一成本计算模式。

万永伊：好，那么绿色、黄色和红色成本的区别是什么呢？

琼斯博士：绿色成本是变动的或混合的、并可以通过主任一级的决策而降低的成本。绿色成本倡议，可以举降低一个部门所用的手机或 PDA[10] 的数目为实例。黄色成本则为可以斟酌处理的固定成本，并可以通过副总裁级的决策而降低的成本。黄色成本可以软件的采用为例，诸如资产管理软件系统，一个部门只采纳了该软件的一项用途，但却要支付它所备的所有三项用途的费用。副总裁有可能除去未使用部分的许可证，从而节约一些成本。最后，红色成本则是在结构上就属于固定成本，不可能因高管层次的决策而降低；这些成本的金额较大，例如整个网络的成本。

---

⑨ 这一段中所提到的宏观层次（macro level）和微观层次（micro level），均见于瑞夫·劳森 1994 年的文章的图表 1。如果一个工序（process）有若干个分工序（sub-processes）则前者称为"宏观层次"，后者称为"微观层次"；两者是相对而言的。——译者

⑩ PDA 是 Personal Digital Assistant 的缩写，字面意思是"个人数字助理"。这种手持设备集中了计算、电话、传真和网络等多种功能。它不仅可用来管理个人信息（如通讯录、计划等），重要的是可以无线方式上网浏览，收发 E-mail，可以发传真，甚至还可以当做手机来用。——译者

图 2
以工序为基础的成本计算法报告书例示[a]

2006年会计年度年底					
耗用技术服务（TS）的行动分析[b]					
公司内部用户耗用TS资源总额					$61 463 030
绿色成本					
	许可证费用和维修费				(×××,××)
	专业人员服务				(×××,××)
	物料				(×××,××)
	劳动力				(×××,××)
	个人设备				(×××,××)
	其他				(×××,××)
	资本投资				(×××,××)
黄色成本					
	许可证费用和维修费				(×××,××)
	专业人员服务				(×××,××)
	物料				(×××,××)
	劳动力				(×××,××)
	个人设备				(×××,××)
	其他				(×××,××)
	资本投资				(×××,××)
红色成本					
	许可证费用和维修费				(×××,××)
	专业人员服务				(×××,××)
	物料				(×××,××)
	劳动力				(×××,××)
	个人设备				(×××,××)
	其他				(×××,××)
	资本投资				(×××,××)
公司XX方面耗用的TS资源总额					$61 463 030

[a] 资料来源：Waldup, McArthur and Michelman（2009）.
[b] 行动分析报告中用颜色标示的部分采纳自 Garrison, Noreen and Brewer（2010）.

万永伊：这很有趣。因此我们要给每一位副总裁和/或高管人手一份这样的报告书，他或她可以从中认出有可能节约的成本支出中，哪些是属于绿色、黄色或红色部分的？

琼斯博士：没错。公司内部的每一个客户，都可以用它来作为对某一个项目采取行动的参照物。副总裁们也可以把这些成本报告书和 JEA 公司的六西格玛倡议结合起来，对各道工序作不断的改进[12]。

万永伊：我想这样做是会起到效果的。哦，我刚想到一个主意。

琼斯博士：是么？

万永伊：是呀。我想你需要把这一切都给 CEO 看一下，使他的认识能够跟上发展。那样，如果我们能够获得他的支持，他就会同意这个项目，我们就能取得副总裁们更多的支持了。一旦做到那样，你们就容易获得一位副总裁跟你们一起在某一个部门试点推行这个项目了。我想这正是重新实施

PBC 的途径。让我们计划一下，在过了新年马上就和吉姆见面。我的助手会把这事安排妥当。

琼斯博士：那就太好了。但我还是担心要想取得副总裁同意，会有困难。

万永伊：我能理解你的担心，但我已经把 PBC 的各项指标、通过成本透明化所可能节约的金额，列为明年平衡记分卡的内容了。我的这一计划，将使公司执行委员会的各位同事可据此付诸行动。这样，我希望我们能够从一个比较战略性的角度，对 TS 的资源和成本作一审视。

到了 1 月 5 日，教授们把有关成本透明度项目进展情况的五项差距、给副总裁的报告书样本，以及用三种颜色标示的成本结构图，呈送给 CEO 吉姆·迪肯森。琼斯博士向吉姆解释了成本透明度的成熟程度，也就是 JEA 公司目前实施的情况（参见图 3），以及实施节约成本的倡议后，未来可能节约的成本（参见图 4）[13]。

吉姆：琼斯博士，我真的很喜欢你给我看的这些资料。你们干得棒极了。

琼斯博士：多谢，吉姆。取得你的支持，对于这一倡议极为重要。

我们需要有一个重要的部门以及几位高层次的员工与我们合作，而他们这些日子都忙不过来。我们还听说 PBC 制度在贵公司信誉不佳。

吉姆：我完全理解你的看法。上次推行 PBC 倡议失败了，真的很糟糕。这次我要更坚决地使它能够取得成功。我全力支持你们。为了降低成本，我们必须携手努力。

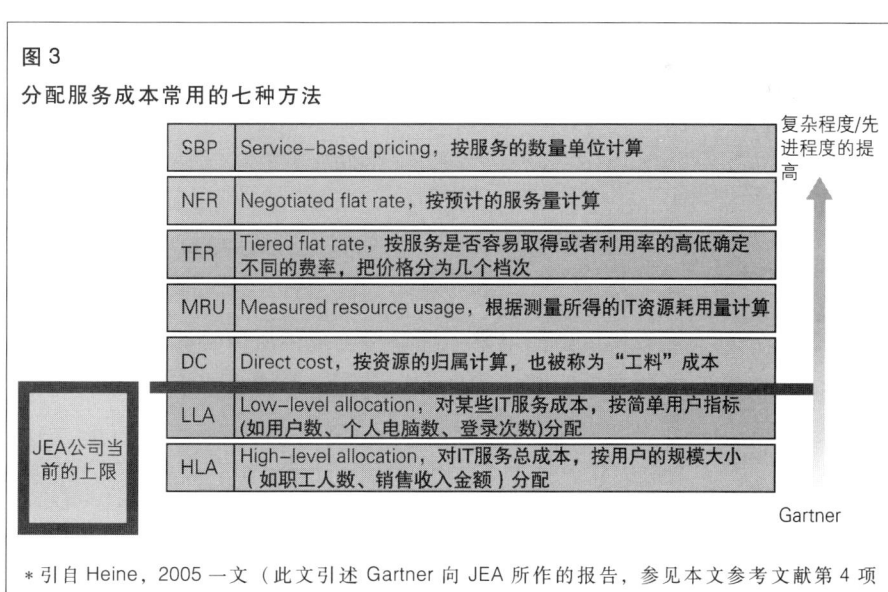

图 3
分配服务成本常用的七种方法

* 引自 Heine，2005 一文（此文引述 Gartner 向 JEA 所作的报告，参见本文参考文献第 4 项——译者）

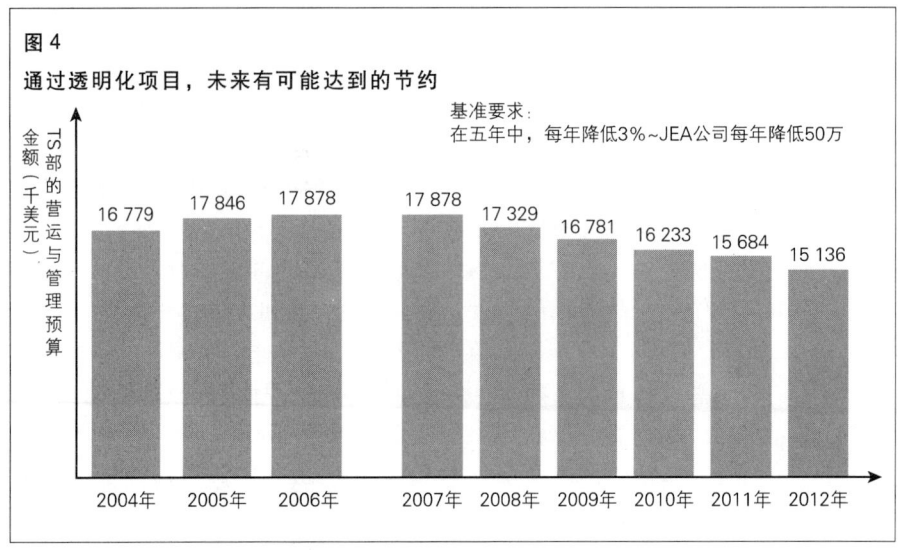

图4
通过透明化项目，未来有可能达到的节约

基准要求：
在五年中，每年降低3%~JEA公司每年降低50万

琼斯博士：对呀！等我们商量出结果后，再向你报告。

会晤后，史蒂文给琼斯博士发了一封电邮，信里说他和万永伊已经决定，车队部（车队）是一个极好的试点单位。虽然这个部门比较小（它目前消费 TS 的产品价值只有 586 212 美元），但它是一个很有希望推行 PBC 的单位；如果在一个主要的生产部门开始推行，工作组就有可能会陷入许多细节问题，难以自拔。此外，车队是"设施与后勤部"的一部分，后者则是 TS 最大的用户之一（它目前消费 TS 的产品价值达 4 090 288 美元）。

与车队部会晤

史蒂文请琼斯博士给车队的营运分析员雷切尔·戴维斯（Rachel Davis）发一封电邮，向他说明工作组正在为 JEA 公司进行一项有关成本透明化的研究，需要有关该部门的一些资料。工作组特别需要的资料，包括车队的组织机构、流程图，以及预算方面的信息。雷切尔跟她的上司讨论了这一封电邮，后者指示她用电邮向琼斯博士提供所需要的一切资料。雷切尔安排在下周三与琼斯博士和他的同事们会晤，讨论雷切尔用电邮发给琼斯博士的各项信息。

3月1日星期三上午，教授们与雷切尔在史蒂文的办公室会面。教授们向雷切尔简要地介绍了这项研究的目的，以及他们所担当的任务，接着就单刀直入地提出有关车队消费 TS 资源的问题。

琼斯博士：基本上，我们已经把你的员工在车队里所做的每一件事以及与 TS 服务之间的关系，都用线路图描绘了出来。迄今为止，我们已经绘制了你们的各项流程图，我们首先要做的是请你把这些流程图浏览一下，并告诉我们它们是不是准确地反映了当前的情况。

雷切尔：没问题。实际上，我最近刚把大部分的流程根据当前的情况作了一番修改。因此，我可以把你给我的复印件和我们最近的流程图作一对比……是呀，看来你给我的都对。我们现在有 1 426 辆车子了。其中大约 1 000 辆是可以行驶的/机动车辆，其余 400 辆则为拖车和挖掘机之类的设备。我们有 13 名员工，今年的预算为 500 万美元。

琼斯博士：好。那么你们花费在耗用 TS 的资源方面，主要是哪些费用呢？

雷切尔：我得说主要是一种称为 Maximo 的软件系统[14]。

琼斯博士：能不能请你解释一下 Maximo 是个什么意思呢？

雷切尔：当然可以。我们用它来管理资产。车队的每一辆车子都存放在那个软件里，甚至在把一辆车卖掉以后，它仍然继续作为一项退役资产保留在那里（占用着存储空间）。Maximo 不但用于资产管理，它还用于下达需要做的工作任务单——小到需要换一个灯泡，大到需要一台新的引擎。JEA 公司使用 Maximo 已经有 8 年之久了，我们这个车队是去年 12 月开始用的。

琼斯博士：哦。史蒂文，当你这个车队开始改用 Maximo 时，TS 需要做些什么？你需要购买新的许可证、新的模块、增加服务器什么的吗？

史蒂文：是的，这就要增加数据，大量的数据，从而增加了数据库的容量，也增加了采用 Maximo 所需要的电脑运算能力。我们买了一台带有 8 个处理程序的全新的服务器，但可惜目前只是利用了其中一个处理程序的一半能力，利用率只达到 9%。

琼斯博士：是吗？哦，这里正有几个关系到成本透明度的问题呢！

史蒂文：愿闻其详。

琼斯博士：在你们现行的预算制度下，把 TS 的预算成本分配给各个用户时，是用什么做分母的？

史蒂文：我不知道呀。这是什么意思？

琼斯博士：嗯，就车队而言，需要的那台新服务器的利用率只达到 9%。包括在车队预算中的服务器成本额，是按实际占用的新服务器的容量（即车队预计要占用的容量）计算出来的，还是按它的有效产能，即把它能够提供的多余的产能全都计入到车队的预算中去了呢[15]？

史蒂文：目前来说，我想应该按我们车队当前所用的服务器的 9% 来计算。

琼斯博士：这就引出了一个如何非常清晰地确定未被利用的产能容量和由谁来负责这部分产能的问题。谈到成本的透明性问题，雷切尔，能不能请你解释一下，TS 的成本是如何列示在车队预算上的？

雷切尔就 TS 的成本（包括许可证费用、维修费、专业服务费、物料、人工和个人用品等）是如何计入她的预算的，作了一番解释。取得了这一资料之后，教授们就能够为车队编出一份报告书的样本，把整个的 TS 预算分类为绿色、黄色和红色成本。这份报告书可以用作一个范本（例如，参见上面提到的图 2），编出 JEA 公司其他各个部门的报告书。

最终报告书

最后，教授们编出了可以呈交的第 3 阶段的流程成熟模式，递给万永伊。它包括几个主要的文件，帮助 TS 的经理人员重温教授们在车队对 PBC 所作的分析。教授们编制了一份"PBC 立方体"的图式，这个图把成本分配系统加以分类和归纳（见图 5）。在立方体的左侧，列示了各个业务单位；在立方体的前方，列示了提供的服务（或应用）[⑪]；在立方体的顶部，列示了成本的类别/资源。立方体中的交叉部分，实际上都记入到一份庞大的电子表格（Excel），在表格中把整个 TS 的预算，分解到 JEA 公司的所有单位。教授们准备召开最后一次会议，跟万永伊和 JEA 公司参与到这个项目中来的主任们讨论报告书。

万永伊：我理解这个立方体和它与 Excel 之间的关系。我也了解每一个业务单位（或副总裁）会收到一份报告书，标出该单位的绿色、黄色和红色成本。

琼斯博士：正是如此。通过这份报告书，副总裁们能提出自己对节约成本的倡议。

万永伊：对，我对这一点也是理解的。不过，我对于这项制度如何逐年地执行下去，还有些不够明白。我的意思是，预算是每年都有所不同的，某些成本所包括的范围更会发生变化，因而这份报告书应该只能适应这一年的实际情况。

史蒂文：我可以来解释这个问题。我认为，年度预算代表一个部门将要发生的费用。因此，我们可以把成本分配的过程和编制预算的过程联结起来，由于第二年采用的是同一个成本分配过程，这就可以编制出第二年的报告书了。我可以建立一个数据库程序，把 Excel 的各个项目"拖"到数据库中，从而"迫使"用户们把他们新的预算在每年年初就编制出来。

琼斯博士：这看来是个极好的主意。企业内部各个用户都应该照办，不能把它搁置在次要地位。在每一年的年初，就应该立即做这件事。

万永伊：正是如此。我也很喜欢这个主意。

琼斯博士：在这份可以提供出去的报告书中，我们也向你提供了一份流程图（例如，图 6 所示车队的流程图），其要点是：1）把 TS 的数据库作了更新（例如，"采用 UNIX 存储数据来更新 Maximo"），2）把对 TS 各用户分配成本的详细资料聚集在一起（例如，"由协调员输入所有需要的信息，并确认工作程序"），和 3）编制用户报告书（例如，"异常报告书"）。

[⑪] 在立方体的前方，从上至下，所列示的是 CAIR、CEMS、EIOS、FMS、GIS、IVR、JEA.COM、MAXIMO、MV90、ORACLE、NMR、PCSupport（个人电脑支持）、Oracle dB Named users（以 db 为名的用户）、Personal Communication Devices（个人通讯设备）、Growth Capatity（增长能力）、Control（控制）、Other（其他）。其中大部分的缩写体，可能是属于电脑用语，译者没有翻译这方面词汇的能力，故存原文，未译。——译者

图 5
PBC 立方体

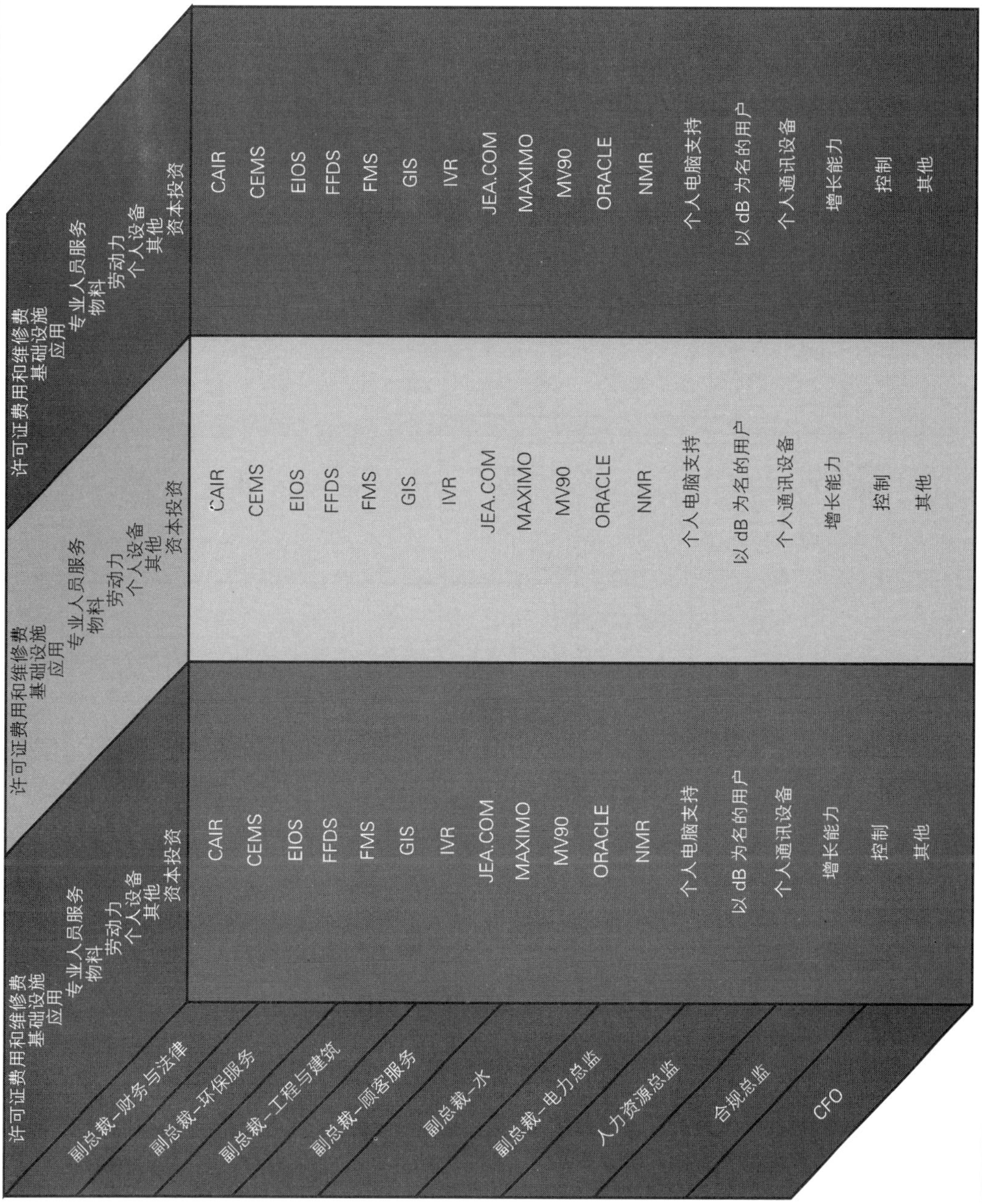
许可证费用和维修费
基础设施
应用
专业人员服务
物料
劳动力
个人设备
其他
资本投资
CAIR
CEMS
EIOS
FFDS
FMS
GIS
IVR
JEA.COM
MAXIMO
MV90
ORACLE
NMR
个人电脑支持
以 dB 为名的用户
个人通讯设备
增长能力
控制
其他
许可证费用和维修费
基础设施
应用
专业人员服务
物料
劳动力
个人设备
其他
资本投资
CAIR
CEMS
EIOS
FFDS
FMS
GIS
IVR
JEA.COM
MAXIMO
MV90
ORACLE
NMR
个人电脑支持
以 dB 为名的用户
个人通讯设备
增长能力
控制
其他
许可证费用和维修费
基础设施
应用
专业人员服务
物料
劳动力
个人设备
其他
资本投资
CAIR
CEMS
EIOS
FFDS
FMS
GIS
IVR
JEA.COM
MAXIMO
MV90
ORACLE
NMR
个人电脑支持
以 dB 为名的用户
个人通讯设备
增长能力
控制
其他
副总裁-财务与法律
副总裁-环保服务
副总裁-工程与建筑
副总裁-顾客服务
副总裁-水
副总裁-电力总监
人力资源总监
合规总监
CFO

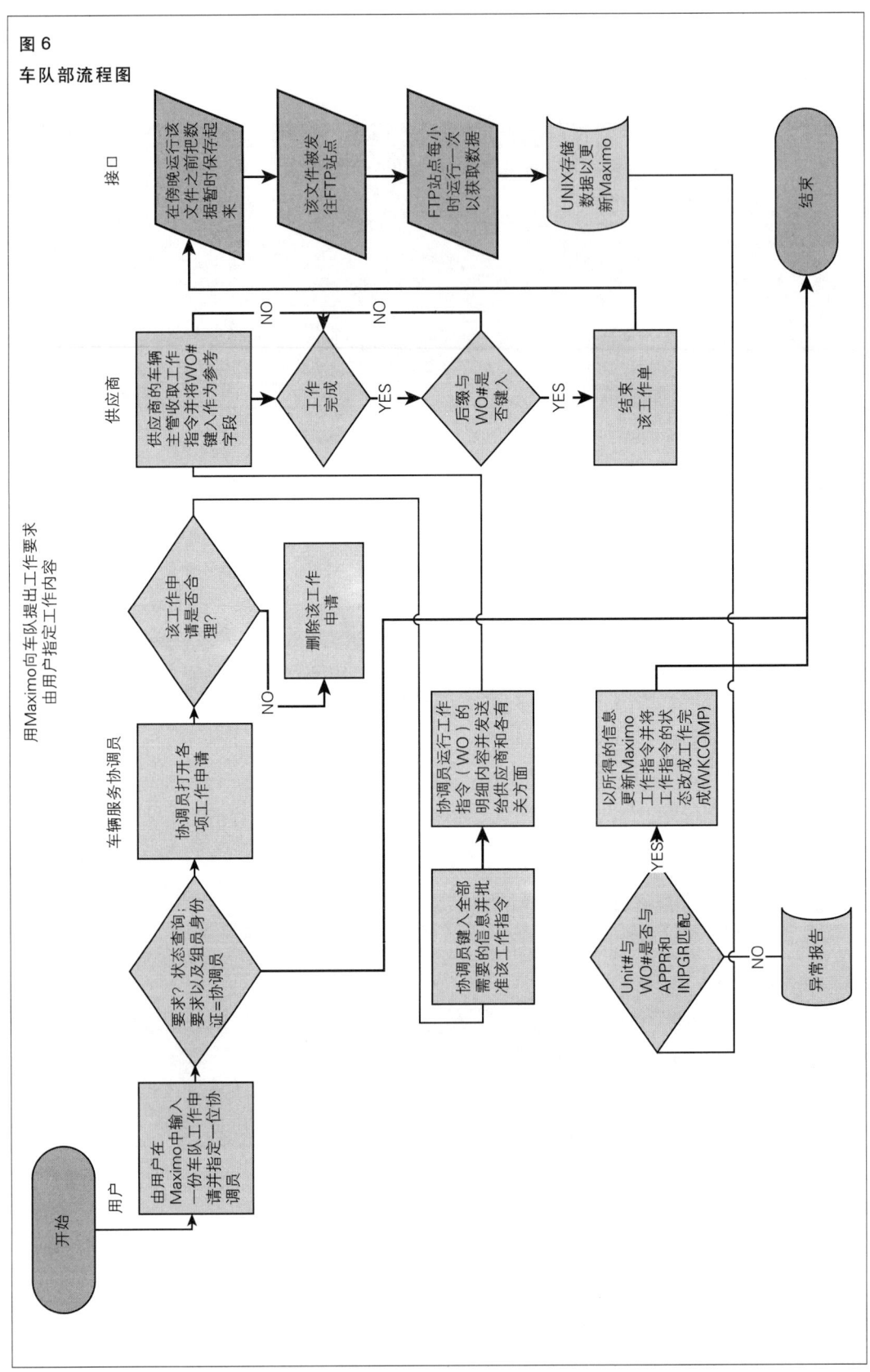

图6
车队部流程图

万永伊：好极了。这对一年一年地执行下去会很有帮助，如果一个部门的领导换了人，也不会有问题了。我想这一倡议极为成功，有助于使我们的成本透明化。谢谢你。

琼斯博士：别客气，多谢。

那一天晚些时候，万永伊坐在她的办公室里凝视着报告书，情不自禁地想着这个成本透明化项目的成败。这份最终可以提供出去的报告书是有价值的、对 JEA 公司的事业有利，但却和万永伊看到的琼斯博士最初的建议书时，所期望的大不相同。她回想起琼斯博士的行动计划，它的内容包括：

1. 透明度——对 PBC 各项指标中的有用部分加以更新，基本上只把分配给各部门的 TS 费用额，告知负责各部门的副总裁（VPs）。

2. 最佳做法——建立一套正式的把 TS 收费制度，按照这个收费制度，TS 资源的用户只对其负责的部分付费。

3. 向外分包——如果公司的管理层能够从外界的供应商那里获得比较便宜的 TS 资源，那么就可以选用外部承包商提供的服务。

大约是在一年前的这个时候万永伊读到那份建议书，当时 JEA 和教授们组成的工作组，集中分析的是行动计划中的第一个问题—透明度问题。与各部门的领导人约期会晤，对教授们来说是件难事；这件事拖后了整个项目的进度。万永伊也知道，分析讨论第二个和第三个问题都是很困难的，各有不同的难处。但是，每想到通过实现成本节约能使 JEA 公司得到发展，就使她对这个项目的未来充满希望。如何才能把 PBC 的考核结果，结合到执行委员会各位同事们的平衡记分卡中呢？如果她能做到这样，那就能大大地增加 TS 作为企业的一项战略性资源所作出的贡献了。

讨论题

1. 分析并论述 TS 的用户应该在计划、控制和成本管理上，如何利用成本结构中的绿色（短期）、黄色（中期）和红色（长期）部分。

2. 分析并论述如何把成本透明性的倡议，通过一个新的电脑程序，让公司内部所有的用户了解和接受。

3. JEA 公司如何利用 PBC 所提供的信息，才能使它的经理们、主任们和/或副总裁们改变他们开支费用的行为习惯？

4. 请说明需要有一位积极支持的高管[12]、"在最高层定调子"，对于推行像 PBC 这样的战略成本倡议的重要性。

5. 请说明如何把 PBC 制度，与 JEA 公司的六西格玛提高质量的倡议，以及考核高管业绩的平衡记分卡制度结合起来。

---

[12] executive champion，指在比较高层次的管理人员中对某项活动、政策或变革持续热心的支持者，有译作"行政冠军"的，似不妥；姑译作"积极支持的高管"。——译者

附录

有关美国公用事业行业的背景资料

美国的公用事业行业包括四个部分：电力、天然气、电话和水/废水处理。这些公用事业，按所有制还可以进一步分为三类：市政府所有、投资者所有和合作所有。美国共有598家电力公用事业，其中159家为投资者所有、251家为市政府所有、188家为合作所有。水与废水处理两项公用事业合在一起，在2009年时共有605家[16]。JEA公司的情况很独特，它同时经营电力和水/废水处理两项公用事业。它的电力系统，起先只是杰克逊维尔市政府的一个部门，后来在1967年6月1日起因市政府与郡政府合并，才组成一个独立的机构。到了1997年6月1日，从1880年起一向由市政府经营的水与废水系统，也成为JEA公司提供的一项公用事业服务。现在，JEA是佛罗里达州第一家最大的、全美国第八家最大的由社区拥有的公用事业[17]。佛罗里达州电力公用事业包括34家市政府所有的、5家投资者所有的、18家农村合作社所有的公司。由投资者所有的公司，组成一个纳税户式的企业，通常通过在自由市场上出售证券募集资金，由代表股东的董事会选出管理当局。与此相反，市政府所有的电力公用事业系统则属于市政府所有，并/或由市政府经营，向居民、商业和/或工业用户提供服务，通常以市政府的辖区为范围。最后，合作所有制的公用事业，则是为了向某一个指定的区域供应电力而联合组建起来的。市政府的和合作的公用事业通常免缴联邦所得税。大部分的合作公用事业由"乡村电气化协会（Rural Electrification Association）"提供资金（见 Florida Public Service Commission，2009，p. 1）。电力和水/废水这两种公用事业，均按各州的"公用设施委员会（public service commission）"的规定办事。所有三种——投资者、市政府和合作——所有制的公用事业，在因成本增加而提高收费价格时，事先都必须分别获得制订规定的单位批准。投资者所有的公用事业必须对其所支出的资本成本（cost of capital）提供证据（Cross，2008）。在佛罗里达州，近年成本升高的主要原因，是能源成本上升（例如，燃油）以及对飓风和热带风暴的预防和善后成本。

尾注

1　有关JEA另外的资料，请查访 http：//www.jea.com。（JEA系该公司的全称，不是首字母缩略词。）

2　有关公用事业，美国全国的一般情况和佛罗里达州的具体情况，请参阅本案例的附录。

3　有关流程成本法（PBC）在理论和实践方面的一般知识，请参阅 Lawson（1994，1996）。就其本质而言，PBC采纳了作业成本法（ABC）的概念，但把重点放在各道工序的作业的成本管理上，为顾客创造更多的价值，以达到成本控制的目的。ABC制度则把重点放在个别的各项作业上，其结果就只能使各道生产工序达到次优化，不能向用户提供最佳的产品和劳务。

4　有关JEA现行PBC制度的更具体的细节，请参阅 MacArthur et al.（2004），pp. 20 – 23。

5 工作组由三位在技术和成本计算方面有专长的会计教授、三位会计研究生和两位 TS 主任组成——一位是有技术背景且在运行 TS 方面负重要责任者,另一位则负责 TS 的预算编制和控制工作。在本案例中,三位会计教授以"琼斯博士"为代名。

6 有关 JEA 的平衡记分卡(称为"在 JEA 的公司记分卡")实例的讨论和有关各个经理的记分卡的讨论,请参阅 MacArthur et al. (2004), pp. 15 - 20.

7 有关 COBIT 的资料,请查互联网址:www.isaca.org/cobit/.

8 COBIT 以卡内基·梅隆(Carnegie Mellon)的软件工程学院(Software Engineering Institute at Carnegie Mellon)的"产能成熟度模式(Capability Maturity Model, CMM)"为依据,并把重点放在制订为继续改进开发软件的流程中的五个层次的基准点上(请参阅 Wademan, Spuches, and Doughty, 2007)。此外,CMM 是特别适用于这一情况的,因为它把组织机构的变革看作是一个需要分阶段进行的过程,而 TS 的目的则是通过应用 PBC 帮助 JEA 完成这项变革。

9 有关现有 PBC 制度的进一步细节,以及设计这一制度是为了支持质量管理的六西格玛(Six Sigma,在 JEA 被称之为"目标巧妙"Target Smart)倡议,请参阅 MacArthur et al. (2004), 20 - 23.

10 要想获得更多的信息,请阅 Hightower and Bussels, 2001.

11 JEA 近来把它的高管领导层改组成为一个小组,其成员包括 CEO、首席营运长、CFO、首席信息长、人力资源总监和首席公共事务长。分管八个方面业务的副总裁们(VPs)向这个领导小组报告工作。

12 例如,PBC 通过报告其在节约成本方面所取得的成果,和通过核算其不增值的活动,支持 JEA 的六西格玛倡议(见 MacArthur et al., 2004, p. 20)。

13 有关 Southern Company(一家大型电力公用事业)是如何通过成本透明性的倡议,改善服务并降低其信息技术(IT)成本达 1 000 万美元的详细内容,请参阅 Levinson and Pastore (2005), Pastore (2005).

14 有关 Maximo 资产管理软件的资料,请访查以下互联网址:www.ibm.com/software/tivoli/products/maximo-asset-mgmt/.

15 有关按预算的耗用量、按实际耗用量,以及按所提供的有效产能(practical capacity)来分配成本的讨论,请参阅 Horngren et al. (2009), pp. 545 - 546.

16 http://www.utilityconnection.com/index.asp.

17 http://www.jea.com/about/history/index.asp.

参考文献

(略)

作者注:这一项研究获得 JEA 公司的一笔资助。作者们对 JEA 公司的 Wanyonyi J. Kendrick(CIO)、Steven M. Schultz 和 Sharon Van Den Heuval,以及北佛罗里达州大学的研究生 Parita R. Patel 和 Delores A. Stewart 所作的贡献,谨表谢意。

JEA: On the Road to Cost Transparency

John B. MacArthur
University of North Florida

Jeffrey E. Michelman
University of North Florida

Bobby E. Waldrup
University of North Florida

Dana M. Wallace
Florida State University

BACKGROUND

In late spring 2006, Wanyonyi Kendrick sat in her 15th floor office of the JEA[1] tower in Jacksonville, Florida, wondering if the next step in her quest for improved cost transparency of technology services (TS) would work. As she watched the afternoon thundershowers roll in across the St. John's River, Wanyonyi, JEA's chief information officer (CIO), wondered what would happen over the next several months. JEA is the eighth largest community-owned electric, water, and wastewater utility in the United States.[2]

Wanyonyi was going over all that occurred in the last two years and contemplating what the next year would bring. She was hoping the hurricane season would not hit the north Florida coast as hard as it did in 2004. During 2004, the four major hurricanes that hit Florida caused devastation throughout the state. Although Jacksonville did not receive a direct hit from any of the hurricanes, the storms did bring mass power outages to the area. Wanyonyi also wondered what would have happened in August of 2005 if Hurricane Katrina had turned east instead of west when it hit the Gulf of Mexico. The power failures of 2004 made worse the challenges of providing customer service at JEA. Because of this, JEA's TS costs had increased significantly in an effort to prevent failures such as the JEA website going down during the 2004 hurricanes.

Unfortunately for Wanyonyi and the rest of the country, the forecasters were not giving her much hope for the 2006 hurricane season either and were predicting an increased number of intense storms. Wanyonyi had a lot to be concerned about. It was now May 5th and the hurricane season would be here in less than a month.

Not only did Wanyonyi have the weather to worry about, but there had been change within the organization as well. In the last several years the chief executive office (CEO) position had turned over. The current CEO, Jim Dickenson, placed increased emphasis on JEA's recommitment to operational excellence in the wake of the 2004 outages. His increased demands for excellence dramatically increased the strain on TS's resources. Wanyonyi had experienced trouble determining just exactly how much these new demands were increasing costs. There were gaps in the reports produced, and she had trouble putting the pieces together. It seemed she wasn't alone. At TS Department meetings, directors had voiced their complaints that the current reports seemed obsolete due to the ever-changing environment.

Wanyonyi reflected that in early 2005 she did not know how to solve this puzzle. The TS Department expenses were hidden from users and suffered from a lack of transparency. She wanted to find a way to prevent TS's current process-based costing[3] (PBC) system from failing. The current PBC system had been designed to cost activities in the context of processes and subprocesses to support JEA's process orientation,[4] but it contained a number of design flaws and provided largely obsolete information. Wanyonyi needed a PBC system that would help her establish cost savings despite the increased demands placed on the TS system to lower the risk that it would not be able to function in severe hurricane weather conditions. She had to continuously increase the level and quality of technology services to meet the CEO's strategic objectives while maintaining a focus on lowering costs. It was of strategic importance to increase the customer value of TS operations while reducing costs.

Wanyonyi was glad that she had hired three accounting professors from a well-respected university in late spring 2005 to review the usefulness of the existing PBC TS reports and to recommend improvements. Several years previously she had hired other consultants to evaluate TS's costing system, and although their work was of high quality, it did not produce actionable items.

The past year seemed to fly by and now she stared at the final report from the professors. It recommended the next steps to be taken to improve the PBC system to achieve transparency of TS costs. She felt good about her interaction with the team[5] and their final report, but she was not sure that she would be able to get buy-in throughout the organization. Wanyonyi needed a plan to get the PBC initiative integrated into the balanced scorecard process of other members of JEA's executive management.[6]

THE PBC INITIATIVE AND PROPOSAL

Because Wanyonyi was both a CPA and a CMA, it seemed that she was constantly taking continuing professional education (CPE) classes. She got a big surprise in April 2005 when she took a CPE course on strategic cost management at the well-respected university. During a coffee break she spoke to the instructor, Professor Jones, about her costing problems and he seemed quite interested. At the end of class they agreed to meet the following week at her office.

The following week, Dr. Jones, along with two of his colleagues, met Wanyonyi to discuss the problems currently facing the TS Department and the environment at JEA. During the discussion they all came to an agreement that a proposed agenda should be made and presented to Wanyonyi's boss and CEO, Jim Dickenson. Although Wanyonyi knew she could approve a project of this size out of her own budget, she needed to present the proposed benefits of this project to the CEO and get his buy-in before moving forward. If they could make this work, it could help invigorate the dying corporate PBC initiative that had been started several years earlier. She really hoped that by having TS take a leadership role, her Department could become a model for the rest of the organization.

Wanyonyi had been involved with several previous unsuccessful PBC initiatives at JEA, and the application of the adopted PBC system had also stalled. These initiatives had been unsuccessful largely because of insufficient executive management support on a continuing basis. Insufficient effort had been devoted to obtaining ongoing executive buy-in to the PBC concept, especially given the recent CEO turnover. Wanyonyi knew that the CEO's support was crucial to the success of this PBC project. The tone must be set at the top of JEA if this was to be a lasting solution. She also felt that this might be an opportunity for her area to use the COBIT Framework as a means to develop a costing model.[7] In particular, she thought that COBIT's Maturity Model[8] concept would be a way to evaluate the process. The PBC team all agreed with Wanyonyi's analysis and set a deadline for the proposal to be completed by May 16, 2005. In the meantime, Wanyonyi agreed to brief the CEO on the new initiative.

May 16th quickly came, and Dr. Jones and his colleagues arrived as planned at Wanyonyi's office. She had already read and reread the PBC proposal (see Figure 1) and was excited by the ideas. Dr. Jones seemed very calm and confident about the steps presented in the outline. Wanyonyi liked the structure of the phases and repeated interaction between the professors and her staff. The professors proposed a three-stage action plan to generate future cost savings in TS expenditures. The plan included:

1. **Transparency**—renewal of useful PBC metrics, which was essentially just showing the vice presidents (VPs) the magnitude of TS costs.

2. **Best practices**—creation of a formal chargeback system in which users of TS resources were accountable for TS expenses.

3. **Outsourcing**—if management could obtain TS resources cheaper from another vendor, they could utilize that option.

Wanyonyi confirmed her commitment to the proposal and set up points of contact between the professors and several of her directors to start Phase 1 in July. Wanyonyi breathed a sigh of relief and hoped that this would help to solve the lack of transparency and escalating costs problems.

UNDERSTANDING THE EXISTING PBC INITIATIVE[9]

The three faculty members arrived at JEA at 10 a.m. on July 5th, ready to go. They were met by Steven Schultz, Director of Technology Infrastructure and responsible for the largest portion of TS production departments. Their first appointment was with Ray Tull, a director in the Accounting Department.

Ray: Good morning.

Dr. Jones: Good morning. Thank you for taking the time to sit down with us.

Ray: No problem. The second quarter is closed, so I have a little breathing room. Why don't we make our way up to my office?

Dr. Jones: That sounds great.

As they made their way to Ray's office, Dr. Jones gave a brief summary of the questions he would be asking and the areas he would like to cover in the interview.

Dr. Jones: We really need to understand the current PBC system from the beginning. Can you walk us through the set-up of the current PBC system?

Ray: Well, we have made several attempts beginning in 1998. The current PBC system began development in 2000. JEA hired an outside consulting firm that the Accounting Department worked closely with to create the current PBC system. Most of the JEA folks who worked on it are no longer employed here. Together, we decided upon the activity cost pools, activity drivers, and the allocation rates that are used throughout JEA. Each cost pool is aligned vertically under processes and assigned to a director. Each director oversees anywhere from 30 to 50 activity cost pools. The costs of some resources can be traced to an activity cost pool, but the costs of shared resources have to be allocated over activity cost pools. Currently, the activity cost pool costs are not assigned to users.

Figure 1
Process-Based Costing Proposal

Statement of Purpose

This proposed study addresses the needs of the TS Department of JEA in the area of performance measurement. The purpose of this study is to assist the TS Department of JEA in its ongoing process-based costing (PBC) deployment. The timeframe is one calendar year, beginning July 1, 2005. The study will accomplish five outcomes:

1) Assessment of the current maturity state of TS's performance metrics use, and recommendations for achieving process improvements translating into tangible cost savings.

2) Assessment of the current mix of collected performance metrics, and recommendations towards greater concentration in financial measurement.

3) Primary education of TS management as to the value and use of PBC metrics and the layered balanced scorecard system for performance measurement.

4) Recommendation for the use of developed financial metrics toward directed management compensation issues.

5) Follow-up education of TS management as to how the metrics are collected and the manner in which success will be evaluated.

The first initiative of cost transparency will consist of the following six phases:

1) Researcher Shadowing and Investigating
2) Assessment of Current Processes and Metrics
    a. Qualitative evaluation of previously collected performance metrics
    b. Statistical testing of previously collected metrics
    c. Investigation of new potential quantitative metrics
3) Process Maturity Model
    a. Development of qualitative maturity-level assessment of JEA TS deployment efforts for PBC use as a decision tool
    b. Deliverable of a written maturity model, including suggestions for future growth
4) Primary Management Education
    a. Interactive Seminar with TS directors and managers
        i. Pre-test assessment of TS management's current understanding
        ii. Discussion of research findings from Phases 1-3
        iii. Interactive conversations about JEA culture, value, use of PBC
5) Financial Performance Metrics
    a. Face-to-face meeting with TS executive management
        i. Formal recommendation for financially-linked metric (s)
        ii. Discuss data collection requirements for new metric (s)
    b. Deployment of data collection techniques and time lines
6) Follow-up Management Education
    a. Final face-to-face meeting with TS executive management
        i. Finalize agreement as to outcomes assessment from new metric (s)
        ii. Agree to terms of project outcome dissemination among TS management
    b. Interactive seminar with TS directors and managers
    c. Written deliverable to TS executive management of overall study findings

Dr. Jones: How does JEA currently collect and distribute data?

Ray: We use an Oracle application to collect and distribute reports company-wide. The data is available to directors monthly on a shared server.

Dr. Jones: Now that we understand the setup of the current PBC system, I would like to know about the efficiency of the current Oracle system. This might be more in Steven's area, though. Would you say that Oracle requires significant resources to fully implement the data collection and reporting with the current PBC?

Steven: No. I would say that we are currently trying to determine the appropriate level of investment in personnel and technology with respect to Oracle.

Dr. Jones: Can you tell me a little more about how the activity cost pools are currently established?

Steven: Well, in 2002 we decided to drop traditional costing and implement PBC. In 2001, JEA changed from a functional organizational structure to a lean, process-oriented organizational structure.[10] PBC was adopted to support the new process organizational orientation, which helps to avoid local optimization of interdependent processes. The entire organization's processes were documented into process maps. Each cost pool now has a corresponding process map. There are hundreds of these process maps. Each process is then traced to a departmental director for accountability. For an example, I am over 35 cost pools. Does that help explain it?

Dr. Jones: Yes it does—thanks. My colleagues and I would like to see a sample of the current process flowcharts before we leave. How are the indirect costs allocated?

Ray: I think I can field that question. For indirect costs we use a standardized inter-corporate chargeback system of [11] processes. Examples include Audit, Facility Services, and Risk Management. If you want more information on how this is allocated, I can obtain that for you.

Dr. Jones: Yes, that might be helpful to have. What about the activity drivers?

Ray: Well, we refer to those as "units of measure" here at JEA. Each activity pool is assigned a corresponding unit of measure. They are not always mutually exclusive to the cost pools, but there is very little overlap.

Steven: One issue I notice is that the activity drivers are not always current or up to date. For example, the number of desk telephones is one of my activity drivers I see on the PBC report, but the number is never accurate. Other activity drivers I see on the report are obsolete. For example, no one in TS carries a pager anymore, yet it is still on my report. Come to think of it, there is very little in that report that is useful.

Ray: You are not the first director from TS that I have heard that from.

Dr. Jones: I would like to see a copy of those reports, too. Is there anything else that the PBC reports break out?

Ray: Yes, unit rates. They are mathematical derivations of the assigned dollars in the activity cost pools divided by the actual activity driver values.

Dr. Jones: OK. Thanks for taking the time today. That should be about it for now. I would just like to get a copy of those process maps and the reports.

Steven took the three professors back to Wanyonyi where they discussed what they discovered during their interview, and she filled in the missing pieces about the 2002 project. Wanyonyi also introduced them to other directors within the TS Department, and they established internal contacts that they could use for e-mail correspondence to obtain further input.

Wanyonyi: Yes, in 2002 we tried to do the whole system at once. It was really overwhelming. We only had one person on the staff and no clear executive support. The good news is we can produce numerous reports. Unfortunately, most of the information is obsolete, with very little decision usefulness. TS is viewed as a necessary evil in today's environment, but getting the resources to support it is almost impossible. Have you heard the saying, "TS is the business and the business is TS"?

Dr. Jones: No, I have not heard that before.

Wanyonyi: Basically, the saying highlights the idea that TS is intertwined in virtually all business processes today. Thus, it is difficult to determine the value of TS expenditures to show they are cost-beneficial.

Dr. Jones: That is so true, and that's why we are here to help! From the preliminary interviews, it appears that we will need to focus on understanding consumption of the services of the TS Department and how they drive costs. It also seems that the information that is currently produced does little to assist the directors in their decisions.

Wanyonyi: Yes, you hit the nail on the head.

The rest of the afternoon the professors shadowed several TS managers to better understand their processes, which are the root of the activity drivers. Over the next several months, the professors wrapped up their questioning of the TS directors and completed Phase 1 of the proposal as scheduled—researcher-shadowing and investigating. The next of the six phases, assessment of current processes and metrics, followed on their agenda.

ASSESSMENT OF CURRENT PROCESSES AND METRICS

During the next few months, Dr. Jones and his team reviewed their notes regarding the TS Department organization as well as its internal processes. Dr. Jones also received e-mails from Ray that illustrated JEA's current year data collection and classification. With all this information at their fingertips, the team of professors determined the major gaps in previous PBC initiatives at JEA, developed an action analysis of TS resource consumption, and also established the direction the project needed to take at that point. The professors met with Wanyonyi to discuss these issues.

Dr. Jones: We basically discovered five major gaps in your company's past attempts at PBC initiatives. These gaps include:

1. Lack of decision usefulness

- Because the activity drivers are both dated and not related to cost behavior patterns, they are being ignored by managers and employees.

2. Inadequate activity drivers

- The TS activity drivers are mainly measures of frequency—the number of times an activity occurs—which does not adequately allocate activity costs when the amount of time to perform each activity is not uniform and a time measure of intensity is needed.

3. Outdated activity driver values

- The activity driver measures (called "values") are out of date and largely represent actual activity in 2001, when PBC was implemented across JEA, rather than measuring the current level of activity.

4. Dependence of activity drivers on actual values

- Using actual costs can result in excessive costs from inefficiencies being unfairly transferred to customers rather than staying in the TS Department where they belong.

5. Lack of cost management focus

- The existing PBC model assigns costs to processes at a macro level that is suitable for determining long-run chargeback rates, but it is less suitable for cost management efforts to better serve internal customers while reducing process costs. Effective cost management requires micro level analysis of activities within processes.

Wanyonyi: The five points are all important. So what do you suggest we do to fix these problems?

Dr. Jones: Well, I think we could start by first focusing on just one internal customer of TS resources, such as a VP or officer of a specific department. We would like to sit down with such a manager to discuss his or her department's consumption of TS resources and ultimately create a report for that manager that says, "Here is how you're consuming TS resources, and here are the activities you can change to reduce costs in your area."

Wanyonyi: I would like to tell you that getting the other VPs involved will be easy, but in fact it is going to be more difficult than I envisioned. I just left an executive staff meeting and the decision has been made to shut down Ray

Tull's PBC operation at the end of December. The system has been on life support for quite some time now, but no one wanted to pull the plug. For this reason we are going to need to make a compelling business case before I can get my colleagues on the executive committee to buy into this initiative. [11]

Dr. Jones: I appreciate the dilemma, but if they saw an example of this improved report and if we showed them how they could save money in their department, maybe it would spark some interest. Our team has already established what the reports would look like. Here is an example (see Figure 2). We also believe that by using the Maturity Model framework from the outset, we may be able to provide a systematic means for implementing the costing model.

Figure 2
Process-Based Costing Report Example[a]

FYE 2006				
Action Analysis of Technology Services Consumption[b]				
Total TS Resources Consumed by Internal Customers				$61 463 030
Green Costs				
	License Fees and Maintenance			(xxx,xx)
	Professional Services			(xxx,xx)
	Supplies			(xxx,xx)
	Labor			(xxx,xx)
	Personal Devices			(xxx,xx)
	Other			(xxx,xx)
	Capital Investment			(xxx,xx)
Yellow Costs				
	License Fees and Maintenance			(xxx,xx)
	Professional Services			(xxx,xx)
	Supplies			(xxx,xx)
	Labor			(xxx,xx)
	Personal Devices			(xxx,xx)
	Other			(xxx,xx)
	Capital Investment			(xxx,xx)
Red Costs				
	License Fees and Maintenance			(xxx,xx)
	Professional Services			(xxx,xx)
	Supplies			(xxx,xx)
	Labor			(xxx,xx)
	Personal Devices			(xxx,xx)
	Other			(xxx,xx)
	Capital Investment			(xxx,xx)
Total TS Resources Consumed by XX Area of Company				$61 463 030

[a] Source: Waldrup, MacArthur, and Michelman (2009).

[b] The action analysis report with color-coding scheme was adapted from Garrison, Noreen and Brewer (2010).

Wanyonyi: OK, so what is the difference between the green, yellow, and red costs?

Dr. Jones: The green costs are variable or mixed and can be reduced directly by director-level decisions. An example of a green cost initiative would be reducing the number of cell phones or PDAs in a department. Next, the yellow costs are discretionary fixed and can be reduced by vice president-level decisions. A possible yellow cost item might be a software application, such as the asset management system, in which a department is only using one feature but is paying for three that are available. That VP could try to eliminate the unused licenses and thus realize some cost savings. Last, red costs are structurally fixed and can be reduced only by executive-level decisions. These costs are on a greater scale, such as the cost of a network.

Wanyonyi: Interesting. So we would give each VP and/or officer one of these reports, and from there he or she could identify potential cost savings, whether the savings are in the green, yellow, or red area?

Dr. Jones: Exactly. Each of the internal customers could use the report as a template for future project-related action. The VPs could also integrate these cost reports with JEA's Six Sigma initiatives aimed at continuously improving processes. [12]

Wanyonyi: I think this might work! Oh, I just had an idea.

Dr. Jones: Yes?

Wanyonyi: Yes. I think you need to show this all to the CEO to update him. That way, if we have his backing, he can essentially endorse the project in order to gain more VP support. Once that happens, it will be easier for you to get a pilot department VP working with you on this project. I think this is just what we need to get PBC back on track. Let's plan to meet with Jim right after the New Year. My assistant will set it up.

Dr. Jones: That would be great, but I am still concerned that we may have trouble getting VP buy-in.

Wanyonyi: I understand your concern, but I have already included a PBC metric, the number of dollars saved through cost transparency, as part of my balanced scorecard for next year. My plan will be to get my colleagues on the executive committee to apply these as well. In this way I hope we can look at TS resources and costs more strategically.

On January 5th the professors presented the five gaps, the sample VP report, and the tricolor costing scheme to update CEO Jim Dickenson on the cost transparency project's progress. Dr. Jones explained to Jim the cost transparency maturity levels, the level at which JEA was currently operating (see Figure 3), as well as the potential future savings that would potentially occur due to this cost savings initiative (see Figure 4). [13]

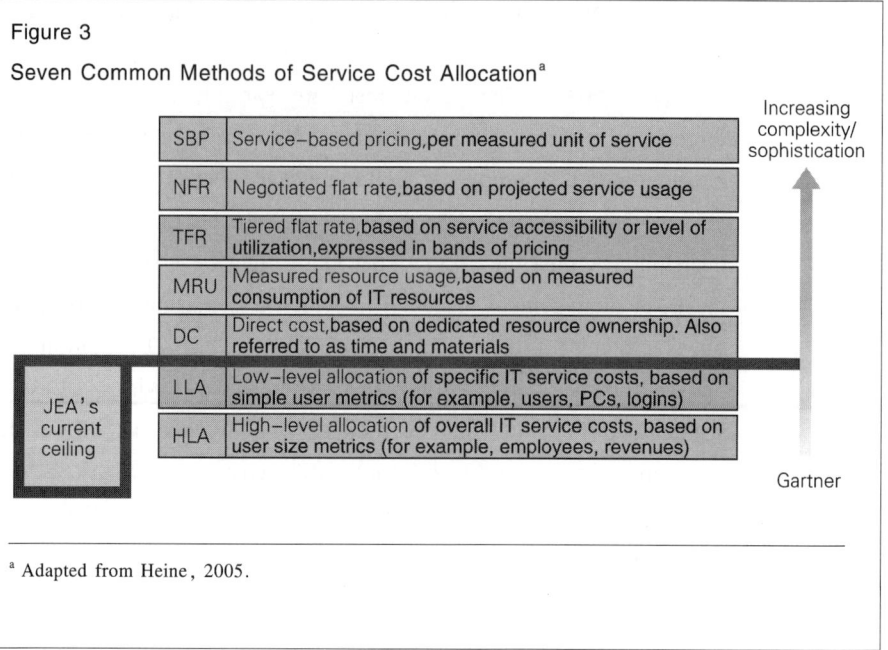

Figure 3

Seven Common Methods of Service Cost Allocation[a]

[a] Adapted from Heine, 2005.

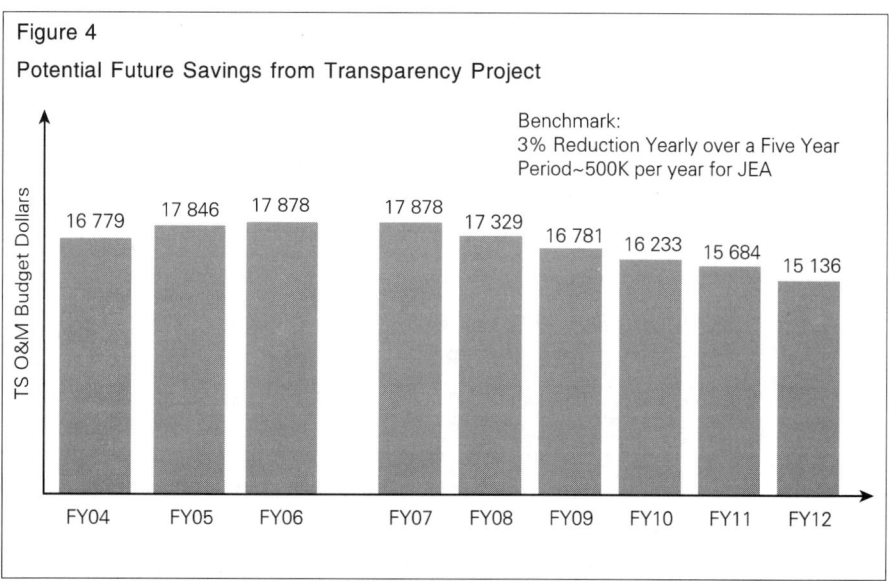

Figure 4

Potential Future Savings from Transparency Project

Jim: I really like what I see here, Dr. Jones. You all have done an excellent job.

Dr. Jones: Thanks, Jim. It was really important to gain your support for this initiative, since we are going to need the cooperation of a key department and some of the higher-level employees, when we know they already have a lot on their plates. We also know that PBC has not engendered a great reputation around here.

Jim: I totally understand. It really is too bad that the last PBC initiative failed. I am even more committed to making this one work. You have my full support. We have to work together to reduce costs.

Dr. Jones: That's right! We look forward to getting back to you with some results.

After the meeting Steven e-mailed Dr. Jones that he and Wanyonyi had decided that the Fleet Department (Fleet) would be an excellent starting point. Although the department was small (it currently consumed $586 212 of TS's products), it was a promising unit for the initial PBC pilot study and the team would not become mired in the details of a major production department. Moreover, Fleet was part of the Facilities and Logistics Group, which was one of TS's largest customers (it currently consumed $4 090 288 of TS's products).

THE FLEET DEPARTMENT INTERVIEW

Steven asked Dr. Jones to send an e-mail to Rachel Davis, a Fleet operations analyst, explaining the study that the team was conducting for JEA concerning cost transparency and the need for some information regarding the department. In particular, the team needed information on Fleet's organizational structure, process maps, and budget information. Rachel discussed the e-mail and scope of the study with her boss, who instructed her to e-mail Dr. Jones any information he needed. Rachel scheduled an appointment with Dr. Jones and his colleagues to meet on the following Wednesday to discuss all the information she had e-mailed him.

On Wednesday morning, March 1st, the professors and Rachel met in Steven's office. The professors briefed Rachel on the purpose of the study, discussed their roles, and then they jumped right into inquiries regarding Fleet's consumption of TS resources.

Dr. Jones: Basically we are taking everything your employees do in Fleet and mapping it to TS services. So what we have done so far is obtained your process maps, and the first thing we want to do with you is flip through them and have you tell us if they are current.

Rachel: No problem. I actually just updated most of the processes, so I can just make sure your copies are the most recent ones we have... Yes, they all look right! We have 1 464 vehicles right now. About 1 000 of those are drivable/motorized vehicles and the other 400 are trailers, excavators, and similar equipment. We have 13 employees, and this year we have a budget of $5 million.

Dr. Jones: Great. So what is your major expense in terms of TS resource consumption?

Rachel: I would have to say the software system called Maximo.[14]

Dr. Jones: Could you please explain Maximo to us?

Rachel: Sure. We use it for asset management. So every Fleet vehicle we have is in there, and even after a vehicle is sold it remains in Maximo as a retired asset (taking up storage space). Not only is Maximo used for asset management, but it's also used for getting needed work orders completed—anything from a light bulb to a whole new engine needing to be replaced. Maximo has actually been used by JEA for eight years, and Fleet just implemented it last December.

Dr. Jones: I see. Steven, when Fleet started using Maximo, what did that change in TS? Did you have to buy new licenses, modules, increase servers, or what?

Steven: Yes, this added data, a lot of data, which increased the database size, which increased the computing power that was needed to process using the Maximo software. We bought an entire new server that has eight processors in it, but sadly we are only using about half of one processor, which is only 9% utilization.

Dr. Jones: Really? Wow, there are some cost transparency issues there!

Steven: Tell me about it.

Dr. Jones: In your current budgeting system, what denominator base is used to assign TS's budgeted costs to users?

Steven: I don't know. What does that mean?

Dr. Jones: Well, in the case of Fleet requiring a new server which is only 9% utilized, is the budgeted server cost included in Fleet's budget based on its current actual usage of the new server space, the budgeted amount that Fleet is expected to use, or a practical capacity supplied rate that facilitates assigning to Fleet the budgeted costs of the spare capacity that its requirements generate?[15]

Steven: Right now, I think just the 9% of server space that Fleet currently uses.

Dr. Jones: This raises the issue of the identification of, and responsibility for, the cost of unused capacity in a major way. Speaking of cost transparency, Rachel, could you explain to us all the TS costs that appear in Fleet's budget?

Rachel explained how TS costs such as license fees and maintenance, professional services, supplies, labor, and personal devices were included in her budget. With this information, the professors were able to produce a sample report for Fleet, classifying its entire TS budget into green, yellow, and red costs. This report served as a model (e.g., see Figure 2 above) for the rollout of all reports for the other departments within JEA.

THE FINAL REPORT

The professors ultimately handed Wanyonyi the Phase 3 process maturity model final deliverable. It consisted of several key documents to help TS managers repeat the PBC analysis the professors had completed with Fleet. The professors developed a "PBC cube," which summarized the breakdown of the cost allocation system (see Figure 5). The business units were listed on the left side of the cube, the services (or applications) ran down the front of the cube, and the cost types/resources were listed on the top of the cube. The cross sections of this cube were actually mapped into a huge Microsoft Excel spreadsheet, which broke down the entire TS budget for all the JEA units. The professors set up one final meeting to discuss the report with Wanyonyi and the JEA directors involved in the project.

Wanyonyi: I understand the cube and how it relates to the Excel spreadsheet. I also understand that each business unit, or VP, will receive a report highlighting that unit's green, yellow, and red costs.

Dr. Jones: That is correct. And through use of this report, the VPs can develop cost-saving initiatives.

Wanyonyi: Right, I understand that. I am wondering, though, how this system will be maintained from year to year. I mean, the budget changes every year, not to mention the scope of certain costs also changes, so this report is really only good for one year.

Steven: That's where I can help. I was thinking that the annual budget is a good proxy of what departmental expenditures will be. So we could tie the cost allocation process to the budget process to ensure that our numbers for the reports are updated annually. I could create a database program, pull the Excel line items into the database, and essentially "force" users to update their budgets at the beginning of each year.

Dr. Jones: That sounds like a great idea. That way, it is not something that the internal users can ignore or just place on the back burner for a while. It becomes an immediate need at the beginning of each year.

Wanyonyi: Exactly. I like the idea, too.

Dr. Jones: Within this deliverable, we have also provided you with process maps (e. g., Fleet, Figure 6) that outline 1) updating the TS database (e. g., "UNIX stores data to update Maximo"), 2) gathering cost allocation details about TS customers (e. g., "Coordinator enters all required info and approves the work order"), and 3) producing the customer report (e. g., "Exception Reports").

Figure 5
PBC Cube

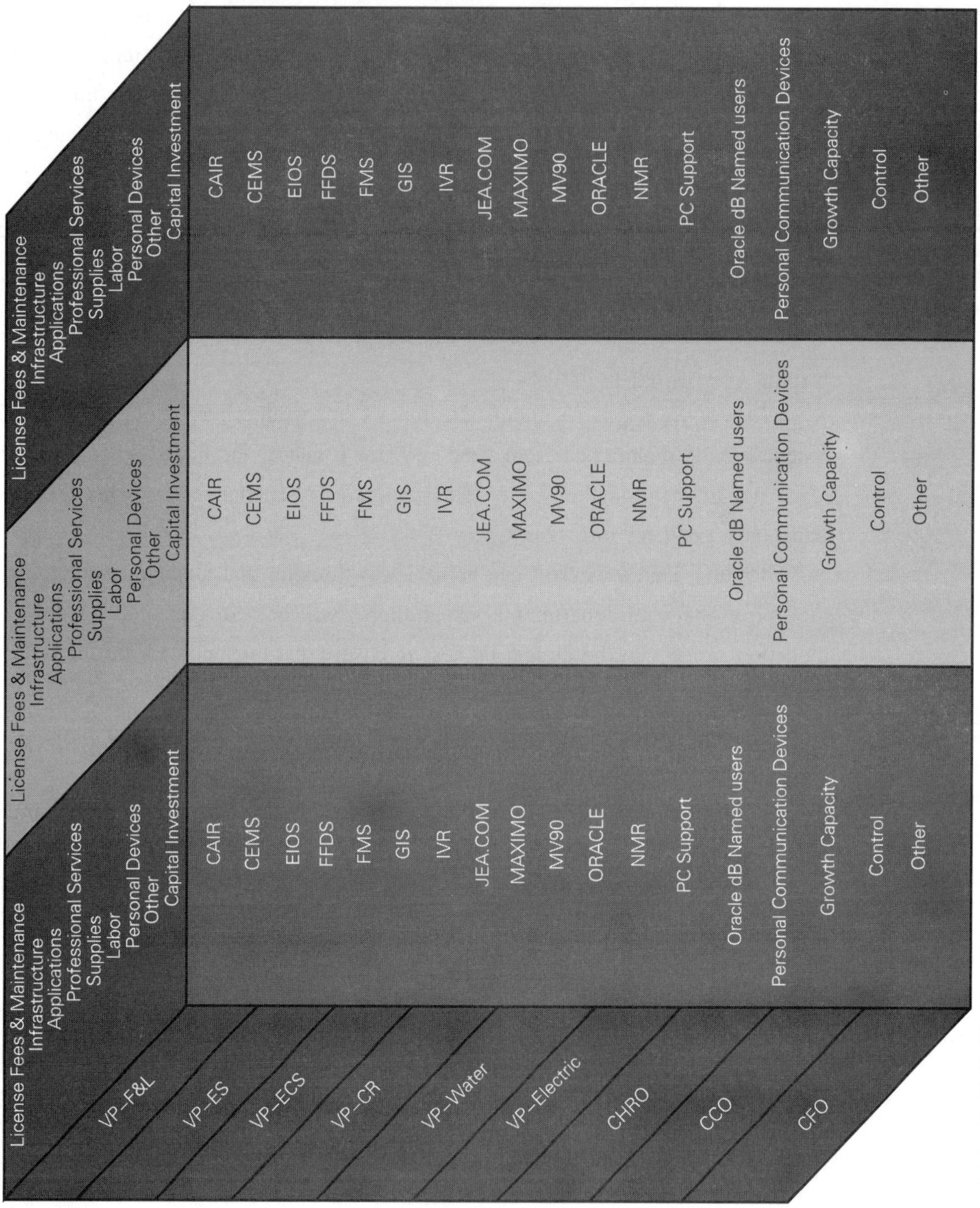

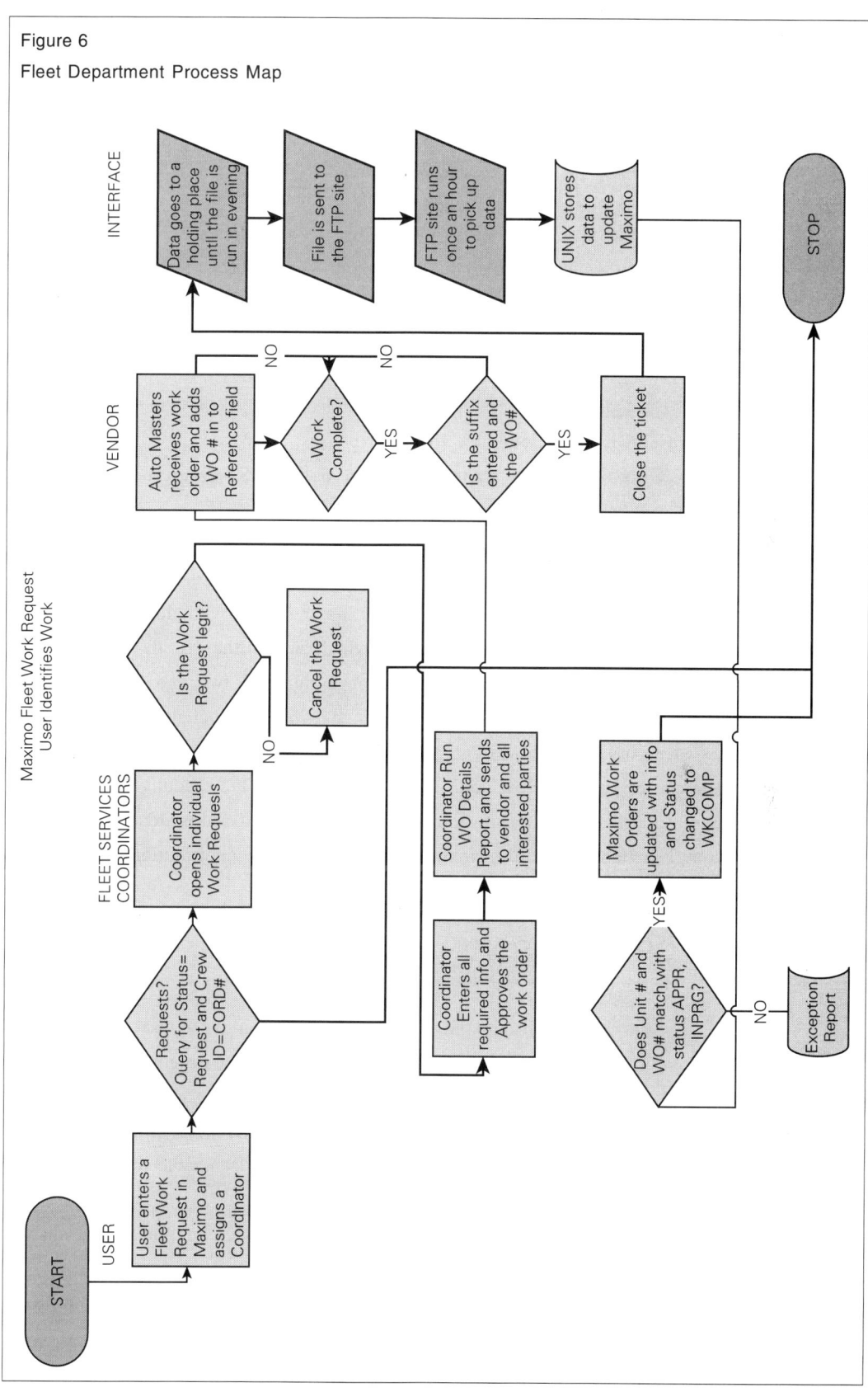

Figure 6

Fleet Department Process Map

Wanyonyi: Great. That will be helpful from year to year, and will also assist us when new leadership takes over a department. I think this initiative was a great success and will help with our cost transparency issues. Thank you.

Dr. Jones: It was our pleasure. Thank you.

Later that day, while sitting in her office and staring at the report, Wanyonyi got to thinking about the success of the cost transparency project. The end deliverable was meaningful and helpful to JEA's cause, but it was very different from what Wanyonyi had originally hoped for in reading Dr. Jones's original proposal. She recalled Dr. Jones's action plan, which consisted of:

1. **Transparency**—renewal of useful PBC metrics, essentially just showing the VPs how much TS expenses are costing them.

2. **Best practices**—creation of a formal chargeback system in which users of TS resources are accountable for TS expenses.

3. **Outsourcing**—if management can obtain TS resources cheaper from another vendor, they can utilize that option.

Wanyonyi had read this proposal approximately one year ago to the day, and the JEA/professor team had only focused its analysis on number one—transparency—of the action plan. Scheduling meetings with department leaders had been challenging for the professors, which slowed the overall progress of the project. Wanyonyi knew the journey through numbers two and three would be difficult and would present its own challenges, but the thought that JEA would grow as an organization through realized cost savings kept her hopeful about the future of this project. How could she get her peers on the executive committee to integrate the PBC results into their respective balanced scorecards? If she could accomplish this, it would significantly improve the contribution of TS as a strategic resource to the organization.

QUESTIONS FOR DISCUSSION

1. Analyze and discuss how TS customers should use the green (short-run), yellow (medium-term), and red (long-run) cost structure for planning, control, and cost management.

2. Analyze and discuss how the cost transparency initiative can be implemented by a new computer program that is understandable to and accepted by all internal users.

3. How can JEA motivate the managers, directors, and/or VPs to change their spending behavior using PBC information?

4. Explain the importance of having an executive champion to set the "tone at the top" for implementing strategic cost initiatives such as PBC.

5. Explain how to integrate the PBC system with JEA's Six Sigma quality

improvement initiative and the balanced scorecard executive performance measurement system.

APPENDIX

Background Information on the United States Public Utilities Industry

Four different subsectors comprise the public utilities industry in the United States: Electric, Natural Gas, Telephone, and Water/Wastewater Treatment. Further, these utilities are also categorized by ownership, which is broken into three groups: Municipal, Investor, and Cooperative. In the United States there are 598 electric utilities, made up of 159 investor-owned, 251 municipally-owned, and 188 cooperatives. Water and wastewater utilities are grouped together and there are a total of 605 in 2009.[16] JEA is somewhat unique in that it is comprised of both electric and water/wastewater treatment. The electric system grew from a department of the Jacksonville city government to an independent authority created by the consolidation of city and county governments in 1967. On June 1, 1997, the water and sewer systems operated by the city since 1880 also became part of JEA's utility service offerings. Today, JEA is the largest community-owned utility in Florida and the eighth largest in the United States.[17] Florida's electric utility market is comprised of 34 municipally-owned utilities, five investor-owned utilities, and 18 rural cooperatives. An investor-owned electric utility is organized as a tax-paying business usually financed by the sale of securities in the free market, with management selected by its board, which represents shareholders. In contrast, a municipally-owned electric utility system is owned and/or operated by a municipality engaged in serving residential, commercial, and/or industrial customers, usually within the boundaries of the municipality. Finally, a cooperatively-owned utility is a joint venture organized for the purpose of supplying electric energy to a specified area. Municipal and cooperative public utilities are generally exempt from the federal income tax laws. The Rural Electrification Association has financed most cooperatives (Florida Public Service Commission, 2009, p. 1). Both electric and water/wastewater utilities are regulated by individual state public service commissions. All three types of utilities—investor, municipal, and cooperative—must request permission from their respective regulators to raise rates based on increasing costs. Investor-owned utilities must also provide evidence to support their cost of capital (Cross, 2008). In Florida, a major driver of costs in recent years has been both the increasing cost of energy (e.g., oil) and the significant cost of preparing for, and cleaning up after, hurricanes and tropical storms.

ENDNOTES

1 Additional information about JEA can be found at http://www.jea.com. (JEA is the complete name and is not an acronym.)

2 For background information on the public utility industry in the United States in general and in Florida in particular, see the Appendix.

3 For general information about PBC in theory and in practice, see Lawson (1994, 1996). In essence, PBC adopts activity-based costing (ABC) concepts but focuses on cost management of activities within the context of processes in order to optimally improve value for customers and achieve cost control. ABC systems can focus on activities in isolation that can lead to suboptimization of processes and inferior products and services for customers.

4 For further details of JEA's existing PBC system, see MacArthur et al. (2004), pp. 20-23.

5 The team was made up of three accounting professors with expertise in technology and costing systems, three graduate students in accounting, and two TS directors—one who had a significant technical background and was responsible for a significant portion of TS's operations, and the other who was responsible for the budgeting and control aspects of TS. For the purposes of this case, the three accounting professors are represented by "Dr. Jones."

6 For a discussion and examples of JEA's balanced scorecard (called Corporate Scoreboard at JEA) and a discussion of individual manager scoreboards, see MacArthur et al. (2004), pp. 15-20.

7 For information about COBIT, go to the following Internet site: www.isaca.org/cobit/.

8 COBIT draws on the Capability Maturity Model (CMM) of the Software Engineering Institute at Carnegie Mellon and focuses on developing benchmarks for continuous improvement of the five levels in the software development process (cf. Wademan, Spuches, and Doughty, 2007). Further, the CMM is particularly appropriate in this context as it considers a staged approach to organizational change, which TS was intending to accomplish at JEA by using PBC.

9 For further details of the existing PBC system as well as its designed support for Six Sigma (called Target Smart at JEA) initiatives, see MacArthur et al. (2004), 20-23.

10 For further information, see Hightower and Bussels, 2001.

11 JEA had recently reorganized the executive leadership into the group comprised of the chief executive officer, chief operating officer, chief financial officer, chief information officer, chief human resources officer, and chief public affairs officer. The VPs of the eight operating areas then reported to this group.

12 For example, PBC supports JEA's Six Sigma initiatives by reporting resultant cost savings and by costing nonvalue-added activities (MacArthur et al., 2004, p. 20).

13 See Levinson and Pastore (2005) and Pastore (2005) for a discussion of how the Southern Company, a large electrical utility, was able to improve service and reduce information technology costs by $10 million with help from a cost transparency initiative.

14 For information about Maximo Asset Management, go to the following Internet site: www.ibm.com/software/tivoli/products/maximo-asset-mgmt/.

15 For a discussion of cost allocation based on budgeted usage, actual usage, and practical capacity supplied, see Horngren et al. (2009), pp. 545-546.

16 http://www.utilityconnection.com/index.asp.

17 http://www.jea.com/about/history/index.asp.

REFERENCES

Cross, P. S. 2008. "Rates, Risks & Regulators," *Public Utilities Fortnightly*, 146 (11), November, pp. 24, 26-31. Retrieved June 17, 2009, from ABI/INFORM Global database. (Document ID: 1599154661).

Florida Public Service Commission. 2009. *Facts and Figures of the Florida Utility Industry*, March, http://www.psc.state.fl.us/publications/pdf/general/factsandfigures2009.pdf.

Garrison, R. H., E. W. Noreen, and P. C. Brewer. 2010. *Managerial Accounting*, 13th Edition. NY: McGraw-Hill Irwin.

Heine, J. 2005. "Chargeback Options: One Size Does Not Fit All." Presentation by Gartner to JEA, March 15.

Hightower, M. R., and W. P. Bussels. 2001. "From the Chairman and Managing Director/CEO," *JEA Annual Report* 2001.

Horngren, C. T., S. M. Datar, G. Foster, M. Rajan, and C. Ittner. 2009. *Cost Accounting: A Managerial Emphasis*, Upper Saddle River, NJ: Pearson Prentice Hall.

Lawson, R. 1994. "Beyond ABC: Process-Based Costing," *Journal of Cost Management*, Fall, pp. 33-43.

Lawson, R. 1996. "Process-Based Costing, at Community Health Plan," *Journal of Cost Management*, Spring, pp. 31-43.

Levinson, M., and R. Pastore. 2005. "Transparency: Seeing Is Believing," *CIO Magazine*, June 1. Retrieved September 11, 2006, from: http://www.cio.com/archive/061005/transparency.html? printversion = yes.

MacArthur, J. B., M. J. Brost, and B. Doueck. 2004. "Strategic Alignment and Systems Control of Processes: The Case of JEA," *Management Accounting Quarterly*, Summer, pp. 11-24.

Pastore, R. 2005. "Case Study 2: The Price of Success," in Levinson, M., and R. Pastore. 2005. "Transparency: Seeing Is Believing," *CIO Magazine*, June 1. Retrieved September 13, 2005, from: http://www.cio.com/archive/060105/transparency _ sidebar _ three.html? printversion = yes.

Wademan, M. R., C. M. Spuches, and P. L. Doughty. 2007. "The People Capability Maturity Model: Its Approach and Potential to Improve Workforce Performance," *Performance Improvement Quarterly*, 20 (1), pp. 97-123. Retrieved December 15, 2009, from ABI/INFORM Global. (Document ID: 1619857921).

Waldrup, B. E., J. B. MacArthur, and J. E. Michelman. 2009. "Does Your Costing System Need a Tune-up? A CIO Gives New Energy to an Activity-

Based Costing Initiative," *Strategic Finance*, 90 (12), June, pp. 46 – 51.

Authors' Note: *Funding for this research was supported by a grant from JEA. The authors are thankful for the contributions of Wanyonyi J. Kendrick (CIO), Steven M. Schultz, and Sharon Van Den Heuval of JEA, as well as University of North Florida graduate students Parita R. Patel and Delores A. Stewart.*

Perelson Weiner 会计师事务所业绩管理[1]

Jan Bell
Babson College

Alfred J. Nanni, Jr
Babson College

Shahid Ansari
Babson College

简介

在 2008 年早秋的一次访谈中，罗恩·韦纳（Ron Weiner）坐在办公桌旁，眺望着东河，考虑在未来几年内如何并购其他几家会计师事务所，以提高 Perelson Weiner 会计师事务所[2]（PW）的收入。PW 是设在纽约市内一家大型的只有一个办公楼的会计师事务所。韦纳向来访者分析了这家事务所自 2004 年以来的成长情况。虽然该事务所按标准的计费单价收入，从 2004 年的 1 350 万美元增长到 2008 年大约 1 900 万美元，但韦纳仍然觉得事务所在原地踏步。他沉思地说，他应该对这一成长感到满足，因为在这一段时间内事务所已经丢了一个主要的客户（大约有 400 万美元的收入），然而在过去四年中却仍然有 40% 的增长（图表 1 与图表 2 是 PW2004 年的财务报表）。

PW 的业务，以为客户提供高质量服务和互动为重点。事务所的员工建立了客户对它的信任和信心，不但向客户提供有价值的咨询业务，而且也提供比较常规的会计服务。

战略定位

自从买下了事务所副主任萨姆·佩雷尔森（Sam Perelson）的全部股权以后，韦纳对 PW 的工作负起了主要责任。他继续把 PW 的业务重点放在事务所最擅长的方面：提供优质的税务服务、财产转移策划、审计和对富裕者和企业家们的商业咨询服务。（见图表 3 对 PW 业务的说明）。PW 的业务发

---

[1] 我们对罗恩·韦纳（Ron Weiner）、朱利亚·尚克斯（Julia Shanks）和拉里·卡尔（Larry Carr）教授在本文前几稿中给予的帮助，谨表谢意。——原注

[2] Perelson Weiner LLP，LLP 是"有限责任合伙（limited liability partnership）"的缩写，是（会计或律师）事务所常用的组织形式，在本文中都把 LLP 按中国的用法，译作会计师事务所。——译者

展以与客户建立稳定关系为基础，事务所不登广告，代之以与客户之间建立个人关系。这种关系通常始于编制报税单或财务报表，进而也为客户提供其他有价值的各项服务。韦纳对他的重点客户作如下的说明：

"我们并不谋求短期的业务；我们希望把时间花在发展能延续 40 年之久的客户关系，而不是寻求一次性的机会。"

为了确保客户能从 PW 获得所需要的价值，韦纳坚持在向客户提供服务之前，事务所的人员必须能够胜任该项工作。PW 的特长在于它能够在提供传统的填报税单、会计和审计服务中给客户以独特的价值，然后又通过积极主动地在问题发生之前，预先提供有意义的商业和税务咨询。韦纳作了一个战略性的决定，把重点放在这些客户价值之外，再增加另外一类咨询服务。事务所地处纽约市区，韦纳感到 PW 可以通过帮助它的客户在其他领域选择最擅长的专业性服务，使他们能增加其价值。例如，PW 的员工帮助客户找到所需要的最好的资产管理事务所和保险代理人。如果 PW 不是在纽约，它就很可能自己设置这些服务项目。但因为在纽约已经有了相当多高质量的专门从事保险和资产管理的公司，PW 显然只要把它的客户介绍给这些方面的公司，不必自己来提供这些服务。

韦纳认为，PW 能够与提供报税单和房地产规划服务的会计公司（如 Fidelity）相竞争。Fidelity 的主要收入来自代其客户作资金投资，而不是提供专业报税业务。Fidelity 让它的员工花尽量少的时间向客户提供服务，从而获得较高利润。PW 的核心哲理，是向其客户提供高质量的个人服务。与 Fidelity 的做法相反，韦纳认为按工作小时数对其服务收费、并花费时间为客户创造价值，至关重要。也就是说，PW 不想要在一位客户的办公室里为他作例行的服务，尽管这样做的效率较高。相反地，PW 把重点放在向客户提供增值较多的会计和商业咨询服务。

韦纳对 PW 的哲理身体力行，使过去几年中事务所的工作重点有所改变。例如，诉讼业务几乎全都被逐步淘汰了。诉讼业务主要是事务性的，而不是以与客户的关系为基础的业务活动。为获得办理诉讼业务的客户，需要经常开展营销活动。此外，在法院中作对辩的人，往往倾向于以自我为中心，需要别人为他提供特别多的支持，而未必就能向客户开出比较高额的账单。诉讼业务每小时计费标准与事务所其他业务相近。按照同样的逻辑，PW 并不为上市公司提供审计业务。上市公司通常是由规模较大的注册会计师事务所进行审计，在价格上竞争激烈。这些上市公司通常并不把他们的审计业务对外招标，从中选择开价较低者，因为这些公司的董事会通常都把审计看做为一项商品。

专业人员管理

韦纳在对 PW 是否能够开展这种以与客户的关系为基础的业务方面，主要关心的是招募人才的问题。当前优质人才短缺，而且韦纳相信，从学校会计专业毕业的大部分学生，都把重点太多地放在审计和最近发表的技术规范上，对实际商业工作所知较少。他的事务所需要的是受过广泛训练的、求知欲强、对业务决策有兴趣，并且除了传统的会计业务以外，还可以对客户提供节税增利方面的建议的会计人员。

PW 每年招募八到十位毕业生，通常正如这个行业的惯例，大部分工作 3 年左右就请辞而去。PW 偶尔从其他事务所招募担任中层职位的员工，以适应特殊客户的需要，但韦纳的经验是，这些人员在他们的职业生涯中经常流动，在比较短的时期内就会另有高就。PW 的合伙人/经理人员的团队的情况很好，这个团队的留职率相当高。

PW 意欲有三分之一的合伙人、三分之一的管理人员具有 3 年以上的工作经验，另有三分之一的管理人员只有 3 年或 3 年以下的工作经验。介于两者之间的三分之一流动率最高，这是因为这些人并不从开始工作时起就在这个事务所工作，所以不相适应。流动频率高的，是只有 3 年或 3 年以下的工作经验者。这些人中有许多之所以离去，是因为他们不能成为注册会计师所需要的多面手，特别不具备 PW 的业务所需要的向客户提供咨询的能力。上述留住干练人手方面的实际情况，加上 PW 盼望着增大收入，使它谋求通过兼并来扩展自己的业务。

管理哲理

有许多服务行业的企业采用了通过数据进行管理的方法，诸如作业成本法（ABC）或平衡记分卡，并且建立了一些管理控制制度。韦纳认为，这些制度过于复杂，炮制出大批用处不大的数据。他强烈地认为，大部分经理人员如果不理解这些数据，就不能有效地利用它们。韦纳解释说，要把一个公司经营得成功，必须熟悉这一行业和成功之道。韦纳对管理的认识，使他对需要建立一套复杂的业绩考核制度，采取排斥态度。

事实上，韦纳坚信，通过建立一个牢固的企业文化、考核并管理少量关键性的变量、并对本单位的员工给予报酬以鼓励企业所期望的表现，企业的成员就会按对他们的期望做出成绩来。用韦纳的话来说，"为取得成就，有多种可供选择的途径——换句话说，有两种截然不同的方式。如果企业文化管用，你可以对企业文化加以管理（就是采用"软"管理的技巧）。这是一项强有力的工具，因为你创造了一种渗透到各个方面的价值系统，公司每一个成员都会把它发扬光大。如果你通过控制来管理，它自上而下、强加于下面各层次，而下层则自然会采取规避的行动。这就会产生适得其反的效果。我们力求避免这种情况。企业文化和市场（我们的客户）是我们所要控制的，它推动公司成绩的增长。"

韦纳创造了一种控制方法：不需要对 PW 的员工进行日常、仔细的管理；大家都知道他们应该完成的工作，因为存在着公司的企业文化，也因为存在着它的报酬制度。这就使韦纳在领导、而不是在管理他的团队。韦纳是这样解释管理与领导之间差别的："管理是要查明应该发生的事都如所期望的那样实现了。领导则是先设想出应该发生的事，并学会如何促其实现。不过，除非有人追随着你，否则你就不能成为领导了。"

韦纳的领导的方法，来自他为一家大的会计师事务所担任管理咨询师时所获得的经验，也得自于他的父亲，他的父亲也曾是一位会计师。从他担任咨询师取得的经验，从与多次光顾的老客户们的接触中知道，在向他们提出了详尽的分析之后，他们感兴趣的只是综合报告书的概要而已。这使他懂得，服务是一个与信任息息相关的过程，而信任则不是靠一次性交易、而是要通过一段时间才能建立起来的；从中他也学习到"考核什么，就得到什么结果"。从他的父亲那里，韦纳学会了如何建立期望。在他的父亲管理的事务所中，他总是把注意力放在目标实现率③达到80%上；其结果是，不论收费单价定为多少，他父亲的事务所的实现率总能达到目标所定的百分率即80%。韦纳从中得出的结论是，达不到比较高的实现率所付出的代价是，对最终获得的利润会产生直接的影响；从他的观点来看，这是因为不论开单率是否按预期实现，产生1美元收入的服务所花费的成本总是个固定的数字。这使韦纳得出两个结论。第一，把注意力集中在实现率上，对指导和影响员工的努力，是一个很有效的方法。第二，韦纳从中明白，他父亲的雇员们无论如何都决心要达到所定的80%的目标。（也许该行业的其他事务所也完全是这样做的。因为据TSCPA所作的"全国会计实务调查"，在2006年度，该行业公认为优秀的实现率，徘徊在80%上下④。）但为什么又是80%呢？按韦纳的看法，如果事务所的工作人员不相信把他们所有的工作时间都列在账单上，那么他们就不会按照制定的费率来估算自己的价值了。提供有价值的服务，然后对其服务开出账单，是PW成功的关键性要素。⑤

PW相信，开出的账单必须完全公道，账单上的收费由合伙人共同商定，并预期达到此数。合伙人每年闭门集会一次。议题之一是讨论达到的实现率情况。韦纳深信应该保持透明性："如果目标是清晰的，那就要最大限度地实现它；如果达到的实现率在公开的讨论会上加以检查，合伙人更有可能实现这个目标。"韦纳对事务所的实现率始终达到90%或以上，感到自傲。

该事务所不让合伙人以下的员工知道它设定的实现率目标数。因为在合

---

③ 此处的"实现率（realization rate）"指的是经过与客户在折扣上的讨价还价、扣除有争议的账单和没有付款的账单后，实际开出账单的百分率。韦纳的报表上把造成这一问题的不同原因分别列出。在韦纳父亲确定80%这个比率的当年，该行业达到的比率大约是70%。——原注

④ 据2006年PCPS/TSCPA全国MAP调查数据，附录3，第5页。此资料可从网址获得（pcpsmapsurvey@intellisurvey.com/），也可以向他们索取。——原注

⑤ 这一段是要说明，合伙人对所引入的业务项目上所花费的工作小时数和每小时的计费率（小时单价）之间的关系，不易处理。如果单价定得比较高、按实际的工作小时数列出，合伙人担心客户会在这个价格上犹豫。因此，合伙人会故意少报工作小时数，从而压低收费金额，使客户愉快接受。然而，合伙人的报酬是与其开出的单价、同时又和实际工作小时数（而不是与列在账单上的工作小时数）挂钩的。在合伙人压低开具在账单上的工作小时，而他的报酬却按实际小时数计算，则事务所就会蒙受损失（向客户收费减少了，而给合伙人的报酬却并不减少）。因此，PW事务所就采用另外一个指标即"实现率"（开具在账单上的小时数/合伙的实际工作的小时数）要求账单上的小时数与实际工作小时数之间的比率，不小于某一个百分比（例如80%或90%），来控制合伙人压低开具的账单上的小时数的倾向。合伙人对此心知肚明，所以在报告其实际工作小时数时，会有意识地控制其实现率不低于要求的百分比。——译者

伙人以下的管理人员并不负有开具账单和收取账款的责任。专业人员仅对他们工作的质量负责，韦纳要他们把注意力集中在这一问题上。事务所要求专业人员把时间花费在工作上、把工作做好。管理人员不应该顾及事务所对他们所做的工作开出账单和收集账款的事。按韦纳的说法，"我们并不向管理人员施加压力，要求他们少做一些。我们要求他们做分内之事，提供优质服务。如果你告诉他们，完成预算是最重要的事，他们就不会报告预算超支的事。于是，你就不可能收到你确实已经提供的服务所应该收到的价款。向客户提供良好的服务，是事务所的责任。这是事务所价值系统的核心所在。"

开具账单制度

会计师事务所开具账单有两种做法：按工作小时计算或是按项目计算。多年以前，PW 不赞同按项目开账单。按项目开账单的做法，往往鼓励事务所人员走捷径，尽快完成项目。由于价格是固定的，成本就成为决定利润的唯一因素。作为一个以服务顾客为导向的单位，PW 需要采用一种鼓励员工提供优质服务花费所需要的时间。按所花费的时间开账单，也能向顾客显示所花费的时间的价值，因为顾客能够知道总共需要多少时间来完成这项任务。这个方法需要对每项工作所花费的时间作出正确的记录，也有助于未来从事类似的工作时，估计出需要花费多少成本。

韦纳把与客户之间的关系看成是一条双向的道路。如果客户对 PW 的服务评价高，他们就会通过付酬来表达他们的谢意。但有时客户又会对最终的账单讨价还价，客户与事务所合伙人之间的个人关系的性质就是如此。由于合伙人和事务所的员工与客户之间关系密切，他们觉得对客户负有一种责任。他们与客户共同合作，以确保在完成这个项目中，保证服务的质量。他们要把增值额低的工作留给客户自己的员工来做，这样就能降低他们所执行的那一部分工作的成本。尽管如此，事务所的合伙人（客户是由他们带到 PW 来的）必要时有权调节账单上的收费价格。例如，有时向客户提供的服务原本只需要由报酬低的员工来执行，但实际上由报酬高的员工来做了。在这种情况下，引进这一项目的合伙人可能要考虑对客户的实际价值，把费率调低。

即使费率降低了，PW 的制度仍要求管理人员把为客户工作的小时数记录下来，会计系统则按标准的收费单价记录工作小时。PW 认为，如果员工不把所有的工作小时数记录下来，那他们就会低估自己的价值。这对事务所的健康发展不利，因为与客户之间的关系，归根到底是建立在客户对事务所的服务的评价之上。韦纳已经注意到，新来的员工，有少记他们工作时间的倾向。于是通过制订监督方法，鼓励他们不要漏记任何工作时间。

客户偶尔也会拒绝对事务所开出账单付款，以表达为他或她提供的服务的不满。在这样的情况下，原先引进这一服务项目的合伙人，可能会"炒掉"这个客户。像这样的事，在过去的几年中，曾发生过两三次。

Perelson Weiner 的业绩管理

PW 通过对专业人员的报酬制度来管理业绩。PW 对每一位员工制订一个标准的收费单价，此费率随该员工的报酬而变化。每小时的收费单价大约相当于每一位员工年度报酬的 0.0024 倍[⑥]。事务所是在如果每个人都获得公道的报酬，则为他们的服务所制订的市场收费单价也就公道合理了的这一假设下经营的。相反地，如果市场认为收费单价不合理，那就说明付给个人的报酬过高了；这一情况是会通过实现率下降而表现出来的。合伙人确定他们自己的收费单价，其结果也就是确定了他们自己的工薪，因为工薪决定于他们的收费单价。如果客户认为合伙人的服务价值不值他们自己的收费单价那么高，那么其实现率就会下降。这会阻止合伙人提高收费单价，他们未来的工薪也会因而受到影响。

这一市场机制对合伙人既期望提高他或她自己的收入，同时又期望减少对客户的收费来保持并加强其与客户之间的关系，起到调整平衡作用。韦纳宁愿形成这一动态的紧张局面，是为了要对合伙人说："你应该按 300 美元收费，"而合伙人却会回答说，"不，我只想按 250 美元收费。"韦纳认为，如果由他来制订每小时的收费单价，则合伙人们会少记工作小时数，理解为这一每小时的单价是他们的工作所值，而他们所得的工薪却没有反映这一市场价值了。

这一"市场经济"，也扩展应用到专业人员。合伙人对他们所引入的项目，选择让哪些员工来做。如果一位专业人员的工薪和他或她给一项任务所带来的价值不相称，这一情况就会反映到此人可以开列在账单上的工作小时数（billable hours），和/或他或她所服务的客户的实现率（realization rate）中。这一控制制度给 PW 带来了一种"能力主义"的风气。韦纳能够审视员工的工时利用率，并且看到给予的报酬是否合理。如果多位合伙人都争着要使用某一位员工，这就说明这位员工应得到更高的工薪、并按比较高的单价向客户收费，因为他/她创造的价值高于市场现值。

反映在 PW 的控制制度上，韦纳认为，"比较赶时髦的人，会把我们的管理方法称之为平衡记分卡制度。推动我们这样做的，是我们的企业文化；我们必须通过管理为客户创造价值、对客户提供良好的服务、并且相信我们的收费单价是公道的。因此，我们理应按此取得报酬。然后，我们还要回顾所提供的服务是否起到应有的作用，因而我们完全并不是在寻找'超前变量'和设想出我们应该收到多少钱。我们的企业文化价值是，我们的收费单价是和所提供的服务价值相称的，我们向客户提供价值高的服务。我们并不

---

⑥ 工薪、收费单价和实现率之间的关系。合伙人订立他们自己未来某一时期的收费单价，并预期获得至少 90% 的实现率。按照每小时的收费单价相当于其工薪的 0.0024，确定他们的工薪。例如，某合伙人的年薪为 150 000 美元，则其收费单价大约相当于每小时 360 美元。某一年薪为 80 000 美元的管理人员的收费单价，则相当于每小时 192 美元。合伙人的报酬包括一份基本工资、另加红利。平均而言，基本工资相当于总报酬额的 1/3。详细情况请参阅图表 8。——原注

抱消极等待的态度。相反地，推动我们业务向前发展的，是我们提供服务的那种企业文化价值。提供了这样的服务，才在经济上取得如此的成就。"

业绩考核

对 PW 的业绩考核应该走哪条路，韦纳曾仔细规划过。他对行业中当前的某些趋向有意识地抱抵制态度。（见图表9对那些趋势的概述。）考虑到 PW 的战略定位清晰，而且他已经对其他服务性公司所使用的定价和业绩考核制度中存在的缺陷了如指掌，韦纳的结论是，他的制度简单、花费不多、而且有效。

该事务所的计时和开具账单的制度，能够追踪记录账单上列出的实际小时数和实现率，也为每一个客户作出记录。同时，它也按账单上的内容，列出 100 种不同分类编码（见图表4）。每月要编制一份报告书，使合伙人都能看到在账单上向他们的客户列出了多少小时数，事务所从中获得的收入和实现率又是多少。然而，韦纳却认为，尽管有了这一工具，对它充分利用的人却不多。

该事务所期望每一位员工、每年列在账单上的工作时间约为 1 750 小时，每一位合伙人约为 1 500 小时。韦纳每月收到一份按各专业人员的报表，表上分别列出其实际列在账单上的和预期的小时数（见图表5）。

事务所按月度预期可以开列在账单上的小时数，是该员工上一年度列在账单上的小时数加以调整后，所得出的在图表 5 上的月度预期数。韦纳记得，在有一份月度报表上，他注意到实际开列在账单上的小时数低于预期的小时数。在对此进行调查研究时他发现，有些新雇用的会计人员把一部分的小时数"吃掉了"，没有把他们对客户服务的全部时间都列在账单上[⑦]。对此，事务所采取了一些行动，包括对新员工进行培训，向他们灌输本事务所的企业文化。

韦纳也对月度财务报表进行分析，查明所获收入是否与专业人员的工薪呈恰当的倍数（见图表6）。如果呈不恰当的倍数，他就要调查其原因。出现差额的原因主要有三：

1. 开具账单中发生差异，有可能员工没有把他/她所有的小时数都记录在任务上。

2. 计价中发生差异，有可能对所提供的劳务的计价存在问题。

3. 执行某一项任务的员工组合与预期的有差异，有可能某项服务对客户的价值并不高，原应派出薪酬较低的员工执行该项任务，但却由薪酬较高的员工来执行了。

[⑦] 为了在小时数上达到预算数字，新员工往往不管一项任务实际花费了多少时间，总是把预算上的小时数列作实际小时数。于是就把他们多耗用的时间"吃掉"了。把时间吃掉，就意味着为了完成这项任务，做了必需的工作，却不把所花费的时间记在任何客户的账上。这种行为使时间记录不正确，并使记在账上的历史数据在编制未来的预算中的参考价值极为有限了。——原注

韦纳对利润表的审阅到此结束，因为他的经营方针建立在这样一个观念之上：即所有各项营业费用（包括租金和公用事业费）都属于变动费用，因而都是随着专业人员工薪额的变动而变动的。用韦纳的话来说，那就是"所有成本都是变动的"，因而 PW 并不需要采用 ABC 这一类复杂的成本分配方法。

韦纳认为，PW 的营业费用与专业人员的报酬直接相关。事实上，韦纳说，在他的业务中，所有的成本中至少有 80% 受专业人员的工薪所驱动，其余部分则可能受人头数驱动。例如，报酬高的人员占用房屋的面积较多、电话费较高、一般来说其消耗的间接费用也比较高。韦纳的经验是，按时间计费的标准额（即账单上的单价）的每 1 元钱中，有 0.65 美元用于支付专业人员的工薪和其他营业费用，有 0.10 美元应该用于减低资产账面价值和坏账（实现数），剩下的部分应该就是利润。

韦纳熟悉一家建筑师事务所的工作，这家事务所对考核业绩和开具账单采用一种以作业为基础的分配制度。建筑师们对从事了哪些作业或其成本都并不了解，他们埋怨说成本分配制度过于复杂、生成大量数据。这些建筑师并不相信、也不采用这一费时、费力的费用制度，其结果徒劳无益。韦纳认为并不需要编制出对 PW 和业务毫无帮助的报表。

韦纳知道，有许多别的服务企业采用 ABC 式的成本控制方法。那些企业通常按列在账单上的小时数分配变动成本，但按人头数分配其他成本。韦纳不同意以这些数字为基础来分配，因为报酬高的员工通常耗用较多的资源。因此，韦纳的结论是，这一类 ABC 式的分配制度所采用的分配基础不正确，其所生成的报表也就缺乏可信性。

韦纳进而又想到 PW 所提供的服务，并且得出结论认为：PW 所提供的产品是单一的，即列示在账单上的、对同一个客户所采用的标准（划一）的单价。因此，PW 不需要采用 ABC 制度[8]。如果 PW 开始提供完全不同的服务，例如对客户按项目收昂贵的费用、或像为商品市场上某种商品价格作出预测这样的复杂的业务、对不同的业务项目向客户收不同的费用，则 PW 可能需要采用 ABC 了。如果 PW 是经营像对商品价格作出预测这样的业务的话，它开具账单的小时数会非常高，经过与客户的讨价还价，最后会要压低付款，实现率会很低。在这样一个竞争市场下，客户会到各个事务所去询价，PW 就需要成为提供成本最低的服务者。然而，PW 的经营环境却与此不同。该事务所提供的服务有别于其他竞争者的，是它的服务所实现的价值。韦纳说，PW 所定的战略是把所有的服务，无论是税务、审计或其他服务，都不区别对待，而看成为单一的产品。

韦纳就 PW 编制报表的做法提供了一个实例，他们的做法是把全年发生

---

[8] 如果采用作业成本法（ABC）来计价，当客户委托的一个项目涉及若干种作业时，就需要按各项作业不同的单价来计算、得出该项目的总价。这就需要分别计算出各项作业的成本，在会计手续上显然比较复杂；而且，不同的项目之间，虽然工作小时数相同，但因各项作业的构成不同，账单上的金额就会有差距。在 PW 工作的会计人员会从事不同的业务（审计、税务、咨询等），这些员工的工薪相似，各项业务每小时的成本和费率也都相近，所以不见得需要采用复杂的成本计算方法。——译者

的总成本额,除以总共的标准小时数,计算出每小时服务所花费的金额。即使PW在3月份的业务量相当于7月份的3倍,这一成本与服务时间之间的关系式依然不变。在理论上,PW如果要想在收费上反映产品成本之间的区别,它就会对3月份服务的收费高过于7月份[9]。按变动成本法的理论,PW会把7月份所发生的全部成本作为固定成本来看待,而把3月份的发生额全部视为变动成本。这样,合伙人会在激励之下,对7月份给事务所引入的业务给予很高的折扣。然而,PW却在战略上不采取这种做法,因为这会使其他月份的业务受到影响;这样做会使PW的传统的定价方法受损,不能维持其定价政策了。

PW的战略是对它所提供的服务,以其价值加以区分。该事务所的文化,重点在于提供这样一个价值。合伙人知道客户的需求所在,并且知道客户从PW所提供的服务获得的价值。此价值是确定所提供服务的价格、也是确定PW报酬制度的基础。事务所的人员是按他们对客户所创造的"市场"价值来付酬的。

韦纳认为,这一企业文化本身,为简单的收益导向考核指标提供了强有力的战略控制。PW的企业文化,是其开展业务的推动力。如果PW采用平衡记分卡来考核,那就需要引入一套复杂、分散注意力的分析制度。这会得到什么结果呢?例如,"学习与成长"方面的考核指标,是能把注意力引到在员工中发展PW的企业文化的。然而,韦纳却认为,在收费单价、实现率和成本之间的这一简单的关系式,就能保证这一企业文化的实施,所以不需要引入平衡记分卡上的那一套考核指标了。韦纳以国际会计师事务所协会的数据(参见图表7所示的实例)为基准点,确保事务所能够获得与这个行业其他事务所相称的营业成果。

通过并购扩大业务

在以前,PW的业绩考核制度比较成功,但现在事务所的战略是要通过并购、扩大其营业收入,这种制度是不是依然能像过去那样有效呢?合并进来的新员工有可能习惯于其他比较"流行"的控制制度,对PW的企业文化感到陌生。PW能否使新来的员工接受它的企业文化呢?韦纳怎么样才能确保及时变革其企业文化,不至于使其对客户的服务受到影响呢?PW是不是有必要改变其业绩考核和管理制度呢?

案例要求

1. 韦纳认为,ABC模式对PW没有什么用处。试通过案例所示在标准

---

[9] 意指在对3月份的业务定价时,3月份的费用被视为变动成本,在提供的业务量间分配;而7月份发生的费用总额会维持3月份的水平不变,因而单位成本会降低很多,所以可以给予巨额折扣。之所以对7月份(业务比较淡的季节)给予巨额折扣的原因是,在这个淡季吸引更多客户。——译者

的收费单价和工薪之间的关系式,编制出一个分业务部门的利润表、选定各项费用的分配率、并把成本分配计入各个部门。通过这种方法编出的报表,能否更好地反映盈利情况?在你的分析中,假定在2004年中该事务所有员工57~19人从事行政管理和专业人员的助手工作,24人从事审计、14人从事税务。

2. 韦纳曾经就季节性业务和变动成本法说过这样的话:"我们假定提供服务的成本与按时间计算的标准成比例。我们7月份的业务量相当于3月份的3倍。从理论上讲,如果我们承认不同服务之间存在差别,我们对3月份服务的计费就应该高于7月份。如果我们把7月份的成本全部作为固定成本,而把3月份的成本又全部作为变动成本,给7月份获得的业务以高折扣率,那就不公平了。我们的价值观不应该包含有这种不公正的偏见,因为这样做就会使其他月份受到损害。"

3. 在做这一道题之前,请先阅读卡普兰和诺顿(Robert S. Kaplan 和 David P. Norton)的《"难以确定你的战略?那就先画出它的路径图吧"》(Harvard Business Review, Sep./Oct. 2000, Vol. 78, Issue 5, pp. 167-176)。

最近,平衡记分卡已被服务行业所采用。以下是一些服务企业为考核其业绩所采用的几个方面的指标:

i. **财务**——从股东的角度来看,财务方面的战略在于获得成长、盈利和规避风险。包含以下几项要素:

1. 收费收入
2. 毛利
3. 专业人员薪酬
4. 应收账款周转率

ii. **顾客**——从顾客的角度来看,它的战略在于创造价值和区别对待。包含以下几项要素:

1. 留住老客户
2. 来自客户的增收
3. 从客户那里获得任务的周转时间
4. 开出账单上的小时数与预期的小时数的对比
5. 客户投诉数

iii. **内部业务流程**——与使客户和股东满意有关的各项业务流程有关的占优策略。包含以下几项要素:

1. 间接费用的变化
2. 在行政管理上所耗用的小时数的减少
3. 实现率
4. 工时利用率

iv. **学习与成长**——在促使机构的变革、创造性和未来的成长方面的氛围的占优策略。包含以下几项要素:

1. 由合伙人讲授的培训小时数

2. 降低新雇人员的减员率[10]

如果韦纳要采用平衡记分卡方法，是不难从佩雷尔森或者从事务所的资深合伙人那里"获得"其具体做法的。但韦纳坚信任何事情都是越简单越好，除非别人使他相信平衡记分卡确实比较好，他是不会采用这种方法来管理业绩的。

请考虑当前采用平衡记分卡这一新的趋势和 PW 的成长战略，并对为什么 PW 应该（或不应该）采用平衡记分卡制度，提供充分论据。为了帮助你作出决策，请为 PW 画出一个策略图形[11]，并提出你认为为了使 PW 的战略获得成功，应该采用哪些考核指标的建议。

---

[10] 减员率是员工请辞而去的比率。在平衡记分卡制度中，对员工的学习与成长是考核内容之一，新雇的员工感觉在业务上有长进，就会促使他们继续留任，减少新手的减员率。——译者

[11] strategy map，即描绘因果联系关系的图。——译者

图表 1
Perelson Wiener 利润比较表（单位：千）

		2004 年 1~12 月	2003 年 1~12 月
收入			
	收费净额	$ 12 455	$ 11 869
	其他	10	5
	减记		(462)
收入合计		$ 12 465	$ 11 412
费用			
薪酬	审计	$ 1 923	$ 1 910
	诉讼	22	151
	税务	1 620	1 388
	其他		25
		3 565	3 474
	行政管理	899	901
		$ 4 464	$ 4 375
佣金	审计		
	税务		$ 16
	诉讼		88
外来劳动力	审计	84	38
	税务	47	—
	行政管理	42	27
	诉讼		147
	咨询人员	18	12
	其他		3
直接费用合计		$ 4 655	$ 4 706

图表 1
Perelson Wiener 利润比较表（续）（单位：千）

		2004 年 1~12 月	2003 年 1~12 月
数据处理	税务	$ 73	$ 49
	软件	118	61
	工资单/工资支票	5	5
	其他	6	12
员工福利与工资税		730	814
员工招募		156	14
其他员工费用（培训、执照等）			
审计		71	70
税务		34	30
其他		116	87
杂项行政费用		46	48
房屋占用成本		769	522
宣传费用	审计	6	7
	税务	14	1
	其他	16	29
其他业务发展		404	371
保险负债		48	50
保险——工人的补偿金		4	8
其他保险		68	62
文库	审计	15	12
	税务	79	76
	诉讼	5	7
	其他	7	4
办公费，包括设备租金		243	226
办公用品与邮费		107	133
电话与互联网		127	128
管理人员费用（旅差、停车、午餐费等）	审计	116	114
	税务	47	39
	其他	35	36
其他营业费用		169	13
营业费用合计		$ 8 289	$ 7 734
营业收益		4 176	3 678
其他收入（费用）		17	(3)
所得税		87	147
收益净额		$ 4 106	$ 3 528

图表2
Perelson Weiner
简明资产负债表（单位：千）

	2004/12/31	2003/12/31
流动资产合计	$ 5.3	$ 4.9
固定资产净额	0.3	0.2
其他资产	0.1	0.1
资产总计	$ 5.7	$ 5.2
负债	$ 0.4	$ 0.1
合伙人权益	5.3	5.1
负债与权益总计	$ 5.7	$ 5.2

图表3
PW 执业范围说明

取自 PW 网页 http：//www.pwcpa.com/brochure.pdf，2009年4月3日

会计与审计 我们把业务的重点放在数字工作方面，以实际的财务数据为工具和起始点，向客户提供价值。事务所的合伙人具有广泛的观点，并通过对事物的长期观察，形成了公司记忆库[12]，在当今要求高、不断变化的现实世界中，这是实施管理所不可或缺的。

客户把我们看做为一项资源，我们和客户一起来处理各项具体的问题，诸如为客户年复一年地编制计划和应对企业作出的经济决策所带来的影响。我们把自己的角色定位于"合伙人士"，与客户企业共同合作，利用和诠释信息的内容，并且与企业的管理层共同找出提高经营效率的机遇所在。通过对每一项受托的任务提出的需求配置恰当的人员，并且帮助提高客户企业人员的技能，帮助他们成长和降低成本。

我们 Perelson Weiner 事务所为我们人员的质量和专业水平而自豪。我们是美国证券交易委员会（SEC）和美国注册会计师协会私有公司实务部的成员之一，也是国际会计事务所联合会（International Group of Accounting Firms，IGAF）的成员。IGAF 是一个在美国各地和80多个国家有通过通讯联系的会计事务所的联合会。通过这一全球高质量的事务所的联络网，我们向全国、全世界所有地区的客户提供成本低廉的解决问题的方法。

税务与物业 我们对客户关注的问题、他们各自的目的和财务状况有深入的了解，从而使我们能够在为企业编制总体的财务计划时，把企业和个人问题结成一体。我们把编制纳税规划看做为一项持续的任务，与客户其他专业顾问人员一起，对各项纳税规划给企业的经营和生活中的重大事件所带来的影响，作出评估。

我们通过对国际的、全国的、州的和当地对该行业和客户的具体情况所定的税收法规的全面了解，能够预期税收变动引起的财务后果，使客户做好思想准备。我们所做的一切，能够使客户节省日常开支，以及税务机关前来检查的费用开支。

为本国和国际公司作税务策划，是件复杂的工作；我们必须参与跨境交易、确定结转价格、国际税收方面的争论和向 SEC 递交报告书等事务。客户对我们的人员在这方面的专长敬仰有加；有关的管理部门和同行们也都对我们表示认可。

诉讼与评估 诉讼与评估部门是本事务所的一个组成部分，它是我们的品牌服务：把我们的知识和专长应用到富有创造性地解决企业存在的各项问题中去。Perelson Weiner 的合伙人都积极参与每一个受托事项各个阶段的工作。

我们从本事务所审计和税务方面的主力中抽调人员组成工作队，他们的工作对客户作出有效的决策起到良好的影响。我们评估工作涉及企业各方面的委托事项，包括对有形和无形资产、优先股、认股权证和员工认股权、合伙纠纷、少数股东权益、以房地产抵押作担保的证券、物业审计和帮助信用机构解决其在贷出款项中遇到的各种问题。

在案件的整个诉讼过程中，提供持续的专家服务：从对案件的评估开始，在审讯之前的谈判，并且为审讯本身做好准备。我们把大量的财务数据加以浓缩，归纳写成具体的概述，梳理突出问题所在。在法院召集作证时，我们参与作证，把掌握的信息写成陪审团能一目了然的资料。

涉及若干行业的诉讼咨询包括对财务和欺诈的调查、损失的计算（包括知识产权的争端、在 SEC 的调查中采用会计和审计准则、对会计人员处置不当的索赔、购/销争端和利润损失的计算）。

业务咨询 在我们参与的每一个项目中，提供咨询是工作不可分割的一部分。在处理每一个问题时，我们并没有定则可循。正因为如此，我们与客户之间的关系也没有一定之则。作为替别人解决问题者，我们不时受客户之召，提供各种各样的服务。我们谨慎、迅速地完成任务。

在执行这样的任务时，我们与处理日常业务者的看法不同。我们对自己的业务、税务和会计工作有广泛深入的经验，我们能够有效地处理正在着手进行的任务，同时又时刻记住我们的长远目标。

本事务所合伙人的视野广阔，能帮助企业的管理层更好地利用其人力和机构的各种资源。我们也对各种不同的交易事项和因某个事件而引起的问题（例如对投资或可能发生的并购行为作尽责调查、是否采用某种技术、对高管的报酬制度、购售股票、企业内部的会计手续和与审计无关的其他事务）提供咨询意见。

我们对客户的服务，贯穿各个发展阶段：从创业到经营成熟的企业；同时，也对经济的各个领域提供服务。作为咨询人员，我们经常帮助他们与银行家、律师和其他专业人士建立关系。

---

[12] corporate memory，或称为机构记忆库（organizational memory），指该机构成立以来所积累的数据、信息和知识。它有两种形式，一是该机构的档案资料（包括电子数据库），二是机构成员的个人记忆。——译者引自《维基百科》

图表 4——账单代码

收入与费用分析
A51 销售额/收入
A52 工资
A53 费用

A55 分析审阅
A56 编制财务报表
A57 管理建议书
A58 有关 SEC 事项
A59 预测/预报
A60 研究（说明）
A 72 现场检查
A73 质量控制检查
A74 由具体参加该项目的合伙人所作的审查
A75 由未具体参加该项目的合伙人所作的审查

编写报告书
A81 打字
A82 校对
A83 装订

A99 差旅时间

税务
行政管理
T02 讨论/会议（说明）
T03 信函/备忘录
T04 聘书
T08 监管/培训

遵守法规
T10 收集信息
T15 编制报税单
T16 审核报税单
T17 修改报税单（说明）
T20 补充
T21 估计
T25 编制养老金/福利计划的报税单
T26 审阅编制养老金/福利计划的报税单
T30 编制其他报税单（说明）
T31 审阅其他报税单（说明）
T35 工资/销售/租金税
T40 通知书（说明）
T45 其他（说明）

T50 检查（说明）
T60 研究（说明）

编制计划
T70 预测
T75 物业/礼品
T80 其他（说明）

T90 校对/邮递
T99 差旅时间

咨询服务
行政管理
C02 讨论/会议（说明）
C03 信函/备忘录
C04 聘任书
C08 监管/培训

C10 编制业务计划（说明）
C15 融资（说明）
C20 业务估价（说明）
C25 诉讼支持（说明）
C30 经营审计（说明）
C35 微机服务（说明）
C40 个人理财计划（说明）
C45 人力资源（说明）
C50 遗嘱执行人/受托人职责（说明）
C55 合同审阅（说明）
C60 研究（说明）
C65 其他（说明）
C73 质量控制评估
C74 参与项目的合伙人的评估

编写报告书
C81 打字
C82 校对
C83 装订

C99 差旅时间

不列在账单上的项目的代码
办公室
N01 数据输入
N02 邮件
N03 文件保管
N04 文库保管
N05 税务日程表
N06 客户前景报告
N07 电话
N08 打字

N09 复印
N10 网络维护
N11 记账
N12 事务所管理
N13 开具账单
N14 收集款项
N15 合伙人其他职责（说明）

人事招聘
N21 招聘
N22 面试
N23 评估与审查
N24 安排日程
N25 培训

会议
N31 合伙人会议
N32 事务所会议
N33 其他会议（说明）
N34 专业组织
N35 慈善/营销活动组织
N36 后续专业教育

客户发展
N41 现有客户
N42 预期的客户
N43 银行家
N44 律师
N45 其他（说明）

其他
N51 节假日
N52 假期
N53 病休
N54 宗教节日
N55 积假调休
N56 未派职务的
N57 无薪假
N58 注册会计师考试
N59 差旅（非工作时间）
N60 献血活动
N61 其他（说明）

图表 5

姓名缩写	PERELSON WEINER 会计师事务所	雇用日期	账单小时数 12/04	账单小时数 12/03	月度差额	账单小时数 12/04	账单小时数 12/03	到现在为止的一年差额	合计小时数 12/04	合计小时数 12/03	合计小时数差额
	会计与审计部										
JJB	JJB		125	180	(55)	1 609	1 735	(126)	2 409	2 417	(8)
SYC	SYC		119	88	31	1 542	1 368	174	2 288	2 174	114
GC	GC		156	116	40	1 689	1 768	(79)	2 135	2 077	58
RC	RC		4	15	(11)	463	257	206	524	348	176
YE	YE		126	56	70	1 698	1 502	196	2 215	2 135	80
JME	JME		145	154	(9)	1 815	1 613	202	2 723	2 483	240
MG	MG		96	100	(4)	1 900	1 793	107	2 331	2 272	59
BMH	BMH		129	118	11	1 548	1 362	186	3 056	2 999	57
AK	AK		122	40	82	1 443	1 192	251	2 255	2 264	(9)
MK	MK		89	61	28	1 073	897	176	1 130	922	208
EL	EL		156	93	63	1 863	1 583	280	2 748	2 461	287
TP	TP		77	0	77	1 149	918	231	2 030	1 781	249
RSQ	RSQ		139	114	25	1 708	1 620	88	2 672	2 505	167
PZ	PZ		139	149	(10)	1 668	1 558	110	2 205	2 151	54
	小计		1 622	1 284	338	21 168	19 166	2 002	30 721	28 989	1 732
	到现在为止的一年中开列在账单上的小时数的百分比					68.90%	66.11%				
14	平均小时数/每人		116	92		1 512	1 369		2 194	2 071	
SA	SA	10/18/04	13	0	13	140	0	140	282	0	282
VB	VB	01/20/03	0	115	(115)	1 924	1 557	367	2 334	2 130	204
TG	TG	11/30/04	0	0	0	0	0	0	0	0	0
JH	JH	08/13/03	126	130	(4)	1 988	600	1 388	2 392	846	1 546
EK	EK	11/30/04	31	0	31	31	0	31	200	0	200
SK	SK	08/31/04	79	0	79	339	0	339	719	0	719
AL	AL	10/07/04	102	0	102	280	0	280	491	0	491
SR	SR	09/08/03	61	45	16	1 388	192	1 196	2 270	687	1 583
JBS	JBS	11/22/04	119	0	119	121	0	121	256	0	256
VS	VS	11/15/04	17	0	17	17	0	17	30	0	30
MZ	MZ	09/01/03	133	116	17	1 829	351	1 478	2 273	692	1 581
	小计		681	406	275	8 057	2 700	5 357	11 247	4 355	6 892
EB	EB		0	0	0	0	545	79	0	850	(850)
HC	HC	02/02/03	0	0	0	0	77	(77)	0	249	(249)
BE	BE		0	0	0	0	475	(475)	0	1 039	(1 039)
JG	JG		0	69	(69)	0	1 664	(1 664)	0	2 217	(2 217)
LJG	LJG	05/24/04	0	0	0	327	0	327	426	0	426
SMG	SMG	01/22/04	0	0	0	400	473	(73)	400	572	(172)
JK	JK		0	0	0	0	1 724	(1 724)	0	2 231	(2 231)
SL	SL	07/15/03	0	76	(76)	789	294	495	1 500	1 026	474
YM	YM	06/10/04	0	0	0	510	0	510	823	0	823
NM	NM	09/03/02	0	0	0	0	627	(627)	0	852	(852)
MR	MR		0	73	(73)	1 511	1 606	(95)	1 869	2 264	(395)
SS	SS	09/09/02	0	0	0	0	443	(443)	0	510	(510)
CS	CS	07/06/04	0	0	0	0	0	0	97	0	97
YY	YY		0	0	0	0	1 023	(1 023)	0	1 260	(1 260)
	小计		0	218	(218)	3 537	8 951	(4 790)	5 115	13 070	(7 955)
	会计与审计部总计		2 303	1 908	395	32 762	30 817	1 945	47 083	46 414	669
	到现在为止的一年中会计与审计部开列在账单上的小时数的百分比					69.58%	66.40%				

图表5(续)

姓名缩写	PERELSON WEINER 会计师事务所	雇用日期	账单小时数 12/04	账单小时数 12/03	月度差额	账单小时数 12/04	账单小时数 12/03	到现在为止的一年差额	合计小时数 12/04	合计小时数 12/03	合计小时数差额
	诉讼部										
LIT	各种临时雇员	差额	0	0	0	0	0	0	0	0	0
KB	KB		0	110	(110)	58	997	(939)	58	1 411	(1 353)
CL	CL		0	68	(68)	89	986	(897)	89	1 764	(1 675)
JP	JP	07/07/03	0	0	0	0	92	(92)	0	134	(134)
RW	RW		0	5	(5)	11	447	(436)	175	1 747	(1 572)
	诉讼部合计数		0	183	(183)	158	2 522	(2 364)	322	5 056	(4 734)
	迄今为止的一年中可开具账单的百分比——诉讼部					49.07%	49.88%				
	业务连续部										
ML	ML	03/04/02	0	0	0	0	27	(27)	0	367	(367)
	业务连续部合计数		0	0	0	0	27	(27)	0	367	(367)
	迄今为止的一年中可开具账单的百分比					#DIV/0!					
	税务部										
MJE	MJE		126	140	(14)	1 467	1 435	32	2 668	2 619	49
JAF	JAF		190	146	44	1 756	1 682	74	2 710	2 665	45
JMJ	JMJ		104	94	10	1 428	1 359	69	1 504	1 451	53
LL	LL		86	69	17	1 470	1 119	351	3 107	2 820	287
RN	RN		151	128	23	1 793	1 643	150	2 368	2 244	124
AWS	AWS		101	126	(25)	1 548	1 504	44	2 310	2 165	145
CS	CS		130	142	(12)	1 830	1 930	(100)	2 297	2 334	(37)
RES	RES		134	135	(1)	1 722	1 735	(13)	2 753	2 661	92
BW	BW		101	141	(40)	1 658	1 651	7	2 347	2 327	20
	小计		1 123	1 121	2	14 672	14 058	614	22 064	21 286	778
	迄今为止的一年中可开具账单的百分比					66.50%	66.04%				
9	平均小时数		125	125		1 630	1 562		2 452	2 365	
SK	SK	11/06/04	92	0	92	92	0	92	169	0	169
BK	BK	11/01/04	130	0	130	224	0	224	368	0	368
KL	KL	02/11/04	119	0	119	1 418	0	1 418	1 988	0	1 988
RL	RL	01/01/04	65	0	65	1 151	0	1 151	2 366	0	2 366
TR	TR	01/16/04	118	0	118	1 726	0	1 726	2 236	0	2 236
	小计		524	0	524	4 611	0	4 611	7 127	0	7 127
MB	MB		0	0	0	0	904	(904)	0	1 385	(1 385)
JG	JG		0	0	0	0	613	(613)	0	781	(781)
SL	SL		1	0	1	8	16	(8)	8	17	(9)
PS	PS	08/31/04	0	0	0	77	0	77	89	0	89
HS	HS		0	0	0	0	1 557	(1 557)	0	2 134	(2 134)
SM	SM		0	0	0	0	608	(608)	0	815	(815)
MS	MS	01/05/04	0	0	0	639	0	639	642	0	642
EV	EV	12/03/03	0	65	(65)	560	64	496	784	169	615
GW	GW	02/17/04	0	0	0	532	0	532	618	0	618
	小计		1	65	(64)	1 816	3 762	(1 946)	2 141	5 301	(3 160)
	税务部合计数		1 648	1 186	462	21 099	17 820	3 279	31 332	26 587	4 745
	迄今为止的一年中可开具账单的百分比——税务部					67.34%	67.03%				
SSP	SSP		28	7	21	251	217	34	1 648	1 640	8
RGW	RGW		72	46	26	720	619	101	2 830	2 830	0
	小计		100	53	47	971	836	135	4 478	4 470	8
	行政管理合计		69	110	(41)	4 936	3 876	1 060	36 362	36 121	241
	事务所合计		4 120	3 440	680	59 926	55 898	4 028	119 577	119 015	562
						50.11%	46.97%				

图表 5（续）

姓名缩写	PERELSON WEINER 会计师事务所	雇用日期	账单小时数 12/04	账单小时数 12/03	月度差额	账单小时数 12/04	账单小时数 12/03	到现在为止的一年差额	合计小时数 12/04	合计小时数 12/03	合计小时数差额
	股东										
JJB	JJB		125	180	(55)	1 609	1 735	(126)	2 409	2 417	(8)
SYC	SYC		119	88	31	1 542	1 368	174	2 288	2 174	114
MJE	MJE		126	140	(14)	1 467	1 435	32	2 668	2 619	49
JME	JME		145	154	(9)	1 815	1 613	202	2 723	2 483	240
JAF	JAF		190	146	44	1 756	1 682	74	2 710	2 665	45
BMH	BMH		129	118	11	1 548	1 362	186	3 056	2 999	57
JMJ	JMJ		104	94	10	1 428	1 359	69	1 504	1 451	53
RL	RL	01/01/04	65	0	65	1 151	0	1 151	2 366	0	2 366
EL	EL		156	93	63	1 863	1 583	280	2 748	2 461	287
LL	LL		86	69	17	1 470	1 119	351	3 107	2 820	287
RN	RN		151	128	23	1 793	1 643	150	2 368	2 244	124
SSP	SSP		28	7	21	251	217	34	1 648	1 640	8
RSQ	RSQ		139	114	25	1 708	1 620	88	2 672	2 505	167
AWS	AWS		101	126	(25)	1 548	1 504	44	2 310	2 165	145
RES	RES		134	135	(1)	1 722	1 735	(13)	2 753	2 661	92
RGW	RGW		72	46	26	720	619	101	2 830	2 830	0
	小计		1 870	1 638	232	23 391	20 594	2 797	40 160	36 134	4 026
	前股东		0	110	(110)	58	1 499	(1 441)	58	2 817	(2 759)
	合计数		1 870	1 748	122	23 449	22 093	1 356	40 218	38 951	1 267
	会计部和审计部合计数 迄今为止的一年中可开具账单的百分比					68.90%	66.11%				
14	平均小时数		116	92		1 512	1 369		2 194	2 071	
	诉讼部合计 迄今为止的一年中可开具账单的百分比					49.07%	49.88%				
#REF!	平均小时数		#REF!	#REF!		#REF!	#REF!		#REF!	#REF!	
	税务部合计数 迄今为止的一年中可开具账单的百分比					66.50%	66.04%				
9	平均小时数		125	125		1 630	1 562		2 452	2 365	
	事务所合计		4 120	3 440	680	59 926	55 898	4 028	119 577	119 015	562
	事务所到现在为止的一年中开列在账单上的百分比					50.11%	46.97%				
					员工小时合计数						
	事务所小时数合计		4 120	3 440	680	59 926	55 898	4 028	119 577	119 015	562
	事务所到现在为止的一年中开列在账单上的百分比					50.11%	46.97%				
		减:行政管理	(69)	(110)	41	(4 936)	(3 876)	(1 060)	(36 362)	(36 121)	(241)
		小计	4 051	3 330	721	54 991	52 022	2 968	83 215	82 894	321
	迄今为止的一年中可开具账单的百分比					66.08%	62.76%				
		减:合伙人	(1 870)	(1 748)	(122)	(23 449)	(22 093)	(1 356)	(40 218)	(38 951)	(1 267)
		小计	2 181	1 582	599	31 542	29 930	1 612	42 997	43 943	(946)
	迄今为止的一年中可开具账单的百分比					73.36%	68.11%				

图表 5（续）

RC			31	29	93	44	40	53	28	8	54	50	28	4	1	463	257
YE	A&A	05/24/04	122	181	212	114	119	144	145	149	131	120	135	126	1	1 698	1 502
LG	A&A		0	151	207	0	20	136	148	23	0	0	0	0		327	0
SG	LASS	01/22/04	42	151	207	0	0	0	0	0	0	0	0	0		400	473
MG			141	182	233	185	133	152	161	166	150	175	126	96		1 900	1 793
JH			153	219	254	192	166	166	159	151	151	133	118	126		1 988	600
AK			32	173	226	157	108	124	107	70	134	96	94	122		1 443	1 192
MK	A&A	11/30/04	63	76	112	122	71	86	76	73	108	126	72	89	(1)	1 073	897
EK			0	0	0	0	0	0	0	0	0	0	0	31		31	0
SK	TAX	01/06/04	0	0	0	0	0	0	0	0	0	0	0	92		92	0
BK	TAX	01/01/04	0	0	0	0	0	0	0	0	0	0	94	130		224	0
SK	A&A	08/31/04	0	0	0	0	0	0	0	0	58	83	118	79	1	339	0
SL	A&A	07/15/03	30	210	140	32	56	70	131	119	0	0	0	0	1	789	294
AL	A&A	01/07/04	0	0	0	0	0	0	0	0	0	67	110	102	1	280	0
KL	TAX	02/11/04	0	128	222	117	77	94	106	126	194	146	89	119	1	1 418	0
YM	A&A	06/01/04	0	0	0	0	0	117	131	91	109	63	0	0	(1)	510	0
TN			61	118	168	65	78	118	88	87	104	78	109	77	(2)	1 149	918
SR			51	211	254	82	108	110	120	145	106	63	76	61	1	1 388	192
TR	LASS	01/16/04	92	195	237	177	121	99	122	150	151	169	96	118	(1)	1 726	1 606
MR			138	205	216	170	133	130	145	129	160	86	0	0	(1)	1 511	0
JS	A&A	11/22/04	0	0	0	0	0	0	0	0	0	0	2	119		121	0
CS	A&A	11/15/04	123	146	242	201	141	148	134	101	172	171	120	130	1	1 830	1 930
VS	LASS	01/05/04	0	0	0	0	0	0	0	0	0	0	0	17		17	0
MS	LASS	12/03/03	153	218	181	87	0	0	0	0	0	0	0	0		639	0
EV	TAX		71	146	197	146	0	0	0	0	0	0	0	0		560	64
GW			0	103	283	147	0	0	0	0	0	0	0	0	(1)	532	0
BW	LASS	02/17/04	100	172	264	208	116	107	101	122	155	138	73	101	1	1 658	1 651
MZ			131	149	251	191	131	178	151	160	94	150	109	133	1	1 829	351
PZ			193	161	199	166	95	129	144	88	82	140	131	139	1	1 668	1 558
新/老员工——净数			0	11	89	0	0	0	0	0	77	0	0	0		177	0
小计			2 021	3 524	4 717	2 927	2 011	2 451	2 456	2 268	2 490	2 403	2 082	2 180	0	31 533	11 309
行政管理			181	433	1 536	1 040	216	233	180	258	291	319	149	69	31	4 936	29 912
员工小时合计数			2 202	3 957	6 253	3 967	2 227	2 684	2 636	2 526	2 781	2 722	2 231	2 249	34	36 469	33 788

图表5（续）

员工姓名	雇用日期	1月 实际	2月 实际	3月 实际	4月 实际	5月 实际	6月 实际	7月 实际	8月 实际	9月 实际	10月 实际	11月 实际	12月 实际		2004 实际	2003 实际
JB		167	173	233	176	81	91	93	96	135	128	111	125		1 609	1 735
SC		121	186	229	153	107	100	81	140	137	120	49	119		1 542	1 368
ME		70	149	226	131	65	106	131	124	128	101	109	126	1	1 467	1 435
JE		109	180	258	158	143	130	142	149	161	138	102	145		1 815	1 613
JF		83	174	253	181	92	94	135	113	180	166	95	190		1 756	1 682
BH		102	149	247	185	82	83	92	109	118	134	121	129	(3)	1 548	1 362
JJ		85	116	204	164	91	115	135	81	118	150	66	104	(1)	1 428	1 359
RL	01/01/04	76	130	155	96	92	43	104	86	128	105	72	65	(1)	1 151	0
EL		132	210	260	156	126	149	113	111	139	164	146	156	1	1 863	1 583
LL		66	124	223	143	72	115	115	97	170	170	102	86		1 470	1 119
RN		80	144	240	186	121	158	138	183	184	157	49	151	2	1 793	1 643
SP	税	12	15	30	26	17	28	23	13	14	31	12	28	2	251	217
RQ		102	149	209	176	101	118	127	106	195	186	101	139	(1)	1 708	1 620
AS		109	176	230	166	92	121	108	87	128	117	115	101	(2)	1 548	1 504
RS		102	184	253	206	113	130	102	126	131	142	100	134	(1)	1 722	1 735
RW		49	39	98	72	62	50	57	60	53	35	72	72	1	720	619
前任合伙人		28	30	3	1	—	—	—	—	2	—	—	—		66	1 516
合伙人合计小时数		1 493	2 328	3 351	2 376	1 457	1 631	1 683	1 681	2 121	2 045	1 422	1 871	(2)	23 457	22 110
管理人员合计小时数		2 202	3 957	6 253	3 967	2 227	2 684	2 636	2 526	2 781	2 722	2 231	2 249	34	36 469	33 788
合计小时数		3 695	6 285	9 604	6 343	3 684	4 315	4 319	4 207	4 902	4 767	3 653	4 120	32	59 926	55 898
X母小时平均单价		218	218	218	218	218	218	225	225	225	225	225	225		221	212
标准小时数		805 510	1 370 130	2 093 672	1 382 774	803 112	940 670	971 775	946 575	1 102 950	1 072 575	821 925	927 000		13 238 668	11 878 521
到现收为止的一年的累计小时数		805 510	2 175 640	4 269 312	5 652 086	6 455 198	7 395 868	8 367 643	9 314 218	10 417 168	11 489 743	12 311 668	13 238 668			
实际开出账单的小时数——2004		854 536	1 396 506	2 069 681	1 392 461	820 249	937 338	990 955	971 367	1 194 807	1 150 585	859 022	0		12 637 507	
减去系列入账单的小时数		(9 357)	(14 583)	(8 206)	(12 334)	(1 076)	(23 857)	(20 852)	(16 198)	(13 817)	(6 035)	(21 287)	0		(147 602)	
到商未完成的项目已花费的小时数		845 179	1 381 923	2 061 475	1 380 127	819 173	913 481	970 103	955 169	1 180 990	1 144 550	837 735	0		12 489 905	
到现收为止的一年的累计实际小时数		845 179	2 227 102	4 288 577	5 668 704	6 487 877	7 401 358	8 371 461	9 326 630	10 507 620	11 652 170	12 489 905	12 489 905			

	每小时收费标准												平均比率		小时数	标准时间
		2004	$220.92										4 120		59 926	13 238 668
合计小时数——2004	3 695	6 285	9 604	6 343	3 684	4 315	4 319	4 207	4 902	4 767	3 653	4 120	3.96%	增加的百分比-2004/2003	7.21%	11.45%
合计小时数——2003	4 422	5 890	7 811	5 847	4 116	4 046	4 173	4 987	4 987	4 543	3 155	3 440	8.37%	增加的百分比-2003/2002	-15.37%	-8.28%
合计小时数——2002	5 628	6 667	7 671	6 808	6 078	4 269	4 555	4 776	6 081	5 781	3 902	3 831	6.93%	增加的百分比-2002/2001	-17.85%	-12.15%
合计小时数——2001	6 183	7 222	9 672	8 551	6 380	7 103	6 744	7 387	5 341	5 807	5 052	4 952	7.97%	增加的百分比-2001/2000	4.25%	12.56%
合计小时数——2000	5 552	7 440	9 792	6 877	5 468	6 126	5 595	6 101	6 374	6 869	5 643	5 282	4.14%	增加的百分比-2000/1999	17.20%	22.06%
合计小时数——1999	4 515	6 325	9 147	7 386	4 626	5 162	4 548	4 183	5 521	5 370	4 189	4 827	0.76%	增加的百分比-1999/1998	17.12%	18.02%
合计小时数——1998	3 979	5 296	6 893	5 726	4 137	3 878	4 265	3 985	4 925	4 948	4 361	3 786	5.40%	增加的百分比-1998/1997	12.79%	18.88%
合计小时数——1997	3 879	4 536	5 922	4 976	3 567	3 741	3 826	3 787	4 645	4 408	3 037	3 485	7.89%	增加的百分比-1997/1996	1.98%	10.03%
合计小时数——1996	3 549	4 978	6 404	5 257	3 363	3 025	3 234	3 449	4 223	4 867	3 143	3 351	5.36%	增加的百分比-1996/1995	-0.07%	5.29%
合计小时数——1995	3 304	4 832	6 291	5 026	3 368	3 557	3 226	3 963	4 082	4 680	3 272	3 276	5.64%			
													平均			

新任/前任管理人员/合伙人		28	41	92	1	0	0	0	0	79	0	0	1			
		KKB-28	KKB-30	SJL-3	SJL					SJL-2	SJL-1		SJL-1			
			RW-11	CL-89						S-77						

图表 6
Perleson Weiner 费用占标准计费额的百分比（2004 年 12 月 31 日）

		2004 年	2003 年	差额百分比	2004 年	2003 年	差额百分比
费用总额		781 703.29	697 629.84		8 289 560.91	7 473 206.29	
占标准计费额的百分比		76.44	83.39	-6.95	61.35	62.91	-1.57
专业人员报酬	a	360 890.66	312 689.61		3 713 930.34	3 674 228.04	
占标准计费额的百分比		35.29	37.38	-2.09	27.49	30.93	-3.45
其他人员报酬	b	98 029.66	96 018.77		940 822.17	927 942.52	
占标准计费额的百分比		9.59	11.48	-1.89	6.96	7.81	-0.85
其他费用		322 782.97	288 921.46		3 634 808.40	2 871 035.73	
占标准计费额的百分比		31.56	34.54	-2.97	26.9	24.17	2.73
标准计费额		1 022 620.05	836 597.25		13 512 524.85	11 878 520.75	

图表 7
PW 内部所用的标杆管理数据

资料来源："2006 年实务管理调查（2006 Practice Management Survey）"，图表 7-27，国际会计师事务所协会（International Group of Accounting Firms，IGAF）第 79~81 页

	事务所	各事务所的平均数 > $8 000 000	纽约州纽约市 相差百分比
执业范围的人数	21 000 000	7 022 675	67%
员工人数			
合计	57	180	-216%
持股合伙人/负责人	4	13	-215%
非持股合伙人/负责人	11	8	26%
0~1 年专业人员	5	25	-394%
2~4 年专业人员	4	27	-581%
5~6 年专业人员	1	16	-1 512%
6 年以上专业人员	13	43	-229%
专业人员的助手	2	17	-746%
文员、非专业人员	17	37	-118%
合伙人/管理人员比率	3	8	-183%
年度收费总额——各事务所的平均数为当年数字	17 580 286	32 914 757	-87%
增长的百分比	30%	13%	57%
年度收费的净额——各事务所的平均数为当年数字	16 040 795	25 787 594	-61%
增长的百分比	27%	18%	34%
列在账单上的小时数——本年度	72 771	190 655	-162
增长的百分比	21%	11%	49%
年度收费总额——各事务所均自 6 月 30 日算起	20 809 695	35 918 042	-73%
年度收费净额——各事务所均自 6 月 30 日算起	18 312 532	28 740 547	-57%
列在账单上的小时数——各事务所均自 6 月 30 日算起	81 921	202 647	-147%
每一位全职人员的年度收费额	281 417	148 045	47%
每一位（权益）合伙人的平均报酬	1 263 861	512 317	59%
每一位（非权益）合伙人的平均报酬	319 114	234 191	27%
每一位（权益与非权益）合伙人的平均报酬	571 046	402 710	29%
单个合伙人所引入业务所得到的收费额			
最高占比	32	16	50%
最低占比	1	2	-144%
担任非技术性工作的管理人员的平均每人的年度报酬			
事务所行政管理人员	123 850	119 320	4%
营销主任		87 696	—
专业人员的助手	46 932	40 142	14%
文员、非专业人员	48 728	43 224	11%
会计与审计部担任技术工作的管理人员的年度平均报酬			
0~1 年工作经验	48 327	46 314	4%
2~4 年工作经验	57 118	54 893	4%
5~6 年工作经验	53 934	67 606	-25%
6 年以上工作经验	87 767	89 003	-1%
税务部担任技术工作的管理人员的年度平均报酬			
0~1 年工作经验		47 013	—
2~4 年工作经验	56 934	54 553	4%
5~6 年工作经验	61 111	69 277	-13%
6 年以上工作经验	93 588	94 883	-1%

图表 7
PW 内部所用的标杆管理数据（续）

	事务所	各事务所的平均数 > $8 000 000	相差百分比
管理咨询服务部担任技术工作的管理人员的年度平均报酬			
0～1 年工作经验		46 409	
2～4 年工作经验		60 635	
5～6 年工作经验		73 404	
6 年以上工作经验		105 478	
专业人员的平均起薪（工作经验一年以下者）	45 000	41 918	7%
每小时收费单价：			
专业人员每年工薪 $50 000 者	120	116	3%
专业人员每年工薪 $75 000 者	180	170	6%
专业人员每年工薪 $100 000 者	240	222	7%
从收费的小时中所得的收入：	220	141	36%
待命时间的收费单价：			
合伙人/负责人	368	307	17%
专业人员 0～1 年	120	105	12%
专业人员 2～4 年	153	129	16%
专业人员 5～6 年	165	159	4%
专业人员 6 年以上	258	211	18%
专业人员助手	130	87	33%
文员、非专业人员	100	74	26%
本年度收费中按标准收费单价实现的百分率	91	83	8%
平均每小时收费单价	220	141	36%
合伙人和负责人本年度平均每小时实现的收费单价	335	240	28%
在过去的会计年度中收费单价提高的百分率			
合伙人/负责人	3	4	－47%
专业人员 0～1 年	8	8	6%
专业人员 2～4 年	8	7	9%
专业人员 5～6 年		7	—
专业人员 6 年以上	6	6	1%
专业人员助手	4	6	－44%
文员、非专业人员		5	—
每一个事务所年度平均列入账单的小时数（按专业人员总人数计算）	1 801	1 475	18%
每人平均列入账单的小时数：			
合伙人/负责人	1 575	1 034	34%
专业人员 0～1 年	1 742	1 420	18%
专业人员 2～4 年	1 821	1 507	17%
专业人员 5～6 年	1 819	1 481	19%
专业人员 6 年以上	1 823	1 355	26%
专业人员助手	1 251	1 325	－6%
文员、非专业人员	277	278	0%
简明平衡表——资产（6 月 30 日，占总额的百分比）			
现金	22%	12%	46%
应收账款——开出账单	53%	37%	30%
在产品	18%	21%	－15%
其他流动资产	3%	4%	－36%
家具、设备	2%	7%	－261%
其他资产	2%	7%	－312%

图表 7
PW 内部所用的标杆管理数据（续）

	事务所	各事务所的平均数 > $8 000 000	相差百分比
简明资产负债表——负债/权益（6 月 30 日，占总额的百分比）			
应付账款	1%	2%	-117%
应计费用	1%	12%	-843%
应付票据	0%	7%	—
其他负债	6%	4%	33%
权益	92%	63%	31%
应收账款（月度平均数，占销售额的百分比）	25%	16%	36%
在产品（月度平均数，占销售额的百分比）	10%	11%	-4%
应收账款（占应收款总额的百分比）			
本月	18	43	-138%
31~60 天	31	20	34%
61~90 天	6	11	-87%
90 天以上	45	26	43%
在产品账龄分类（占在产品总额的百分比）			
本月	80	49	39%
31~60 天	15	21	-43%
61~90 天	5	12	-145%
90 天以上	0	17	—
本年度收费所得的分配情况（占销售额的百分比）			
专业人员（不包括合伙人）工薪	16%	31%	-96%
与人员有关的各项费用	8%	8%	8%
其他人员工薪	7%	6%	3%
外部服务	2%	2%	27%
营销费用	3%	2%	28%
设施费用	5%	6%	-20%
权益合伙人的工薪	4%	13%	-194%
非权益合伙人的工薪	10%	4%	54%
权益合伙人的工资税	1%	0.18%	65%
非权益合伙人的工资税	1%	0.11%	83%
所得税（公司与州）	1%	0.20%	81%
其他营业费用	5%	11%	-100%
可供向权益合伙人分配的结余额	27%	15%	43%
可供向非权益合伙人分配的结余额	11%	2%	82%
总金额	16 040 795	25 787 594	-61%
每位合伙人平均所获金额:			
退休福利	10 000	11 015	-10%
"汽车额外津贴"		1 962	—
"俱乐部会员津贴"	2 022	1 207	40%
"保险额外津贴"	3 343	6 306	-89%
后续专业教育费用:			
会计与审计部（占销售额的百分比）	0.43%	0.42%	3%
税务部（占销售额的百分比）	0.14%	0.19%	-39%
管理咨询服务（占销售额的百分比）	0.00%	0.13%	—

图表 8

PW 的激励工薪制度

为了激发员工的积极性并付给报酬，PW 实施了一种激励薪酬制度，对它的专业员工（包括管理人员、经理人员和权益与非权益合伙人）付给奖金。

管理人员（包括经理人员）的奖金按开出账单的小时数计算，但分配的金额和每个人的奖金额则是逐年主观确定的。除了这些主观确定的奖金以外，给 PW 带来客户的管理人员，还能获得按他所引入的客户收费总额的 10% 为酬劳。管理人员升到经理这一级后，就不是经理以下人员所获得的这一 10% 之数了；他可以获得按他所引入的客户的任务项目的盈利额的 50% 为酬劳。迄今为止，按这一激励薪酬制度所付出的奖金为数不大。

对合伙人的薪酬制度比较复杂，其内容包括基本工资、奖金、佣金和利润分成。在确定合伙人当年的工薪时，他/她参与其事，工薪以他/她"标准收费单价"的某一倍数计算。各人的标准收费单价由事务所的"政策委员会"批准确定。

为确定工薪额，每一位成员都需要向事务所提供示范性的计算结果。

合伙人的职责，除了其他内容以外，包括：

- 可以开具账单的工作时间达 1 500 小时
- 对与客户之间的关系（包括开具账单与收取账款）进行有效的管理
- 对管理人员的培训、监督和评估
- 积极参与事务所和部门的会议、活动、委员会、项目、后续专业教育、招聘、适当地参与专业学会的委员会活动
- 发展新客户、保留老客户
- 保证事务所的记录/税务按规定办事

计算合伙人的奖金有五个因素。下表对该制度作一详细的说明。

奖金制度的定义	**合伙人的实现率** = 该合伙人所引入的项目所实现的或可能实现的金额/按标准的每小时单价计算的金额 **合伙人的利润率** = 事务所毛利率 * （1 – 该合伙人的实现率）
奖金元素	（除与收费小时数相关的金额以外，其他金额均四舍五入为最近的 $1 000）
（1）从新的业务所得	（本年向该合伙人所引入的客户收费的标准小时数，减去向该合伙人前一年所引入的客户收费的标准小时数）* 该合伙人的利润率
（2）从所引入的客户所得的实现率	如果该合伙人所引入的客户按标准开具的账单金额为 25 000 美元或更多，而该合伙人的实现率又高于 88%，则在原数上添加 5 000 美元；如高于 92%，则再添加 5 000 美元
（3）对其他合伙人所引入的客户提供的服务	由其他合伙人所引入的客户按标准时间开具账单的小时数 * 1%
（4）可以开具账单的收费小时数	如果该合伙人所引入客户收费超过 1 500 小时，则 [（收费小时数 – 1 500）/ 1 500] * 薪水
（5）主观确定的部分	岗位工资/在正常职责以外所担负的工作/职责 总共所得的报酬不能超过上列 1~4 项奖金的 50%。如果各人所得的加总数，不超过对总数的限额，则对各人所得并不设限

图表 8
PW 的激励薪酬制度（续）

为详细说明奖金制度的做法，假定某一位合伙人的薪水为 155 000 美元，其当年的各项有关情况如下：
1. 本年为其所引入业务开具账单，按标准时间收费的总额为 500 000 美元（此数去年为 420 000 美元）。
2. 实际的实现率为 93%（此数在本事务所并非最高的）。
3. 由他人引入的客户所提供的服务为 250 000 美元。
4. 共开具账单 1 575 小时。
5. 因开发了一个新的培训项目，另给一份主观奖金。
6. 本事务所的毛利率为 62%。
7. 全体合伙人主观奖金的总额（全体合伙人从 1~4 项获得的该项奖金的总额，乘以 50%）超过了 100 000 美元。

奖金元素	
(1) 从新的业务所得	1/3 * ($500 000 - $420 000) * [62% - (100 - 93%)] = $14 667 因四舍五入，计作 $15 000
(2) 从所引入的客户所得的实现率	开具账单超过 $25 000，因而按实现率 93% 得 $10 000
(3) 对其他合伙人所引入客户提供的服务	($250 000 * 1%) = 2 500，因而为 $3 000
(4) 可以开具账单的收费小时数	[(1 575 - 1 500) / 1 500] * $155 000 = $7 750
(5) 主观确定的部分	$30 000
(6) 奖金合计	$15 000 + 10 000 + 3 000 + 7 750 + 30 000 = $65 750

权益合伙人还要按照他们的权益份额，分享事务所的利润；非权益合伙人则取得佣金。下表是 2004 年参与工作的（权益与非权益）合伙人的工薪总额的详细情况。

项目	平均	高	低
基本工资	$144 922	$177 083	$117 708
奖金	$41 773	$150 000	0
佣金	$110 311	$263 176	$20 796
利润分成	$249 350	$1 199 019	$3 752
报酬合计	$546 356	$1 789 278	$142 256

图表 9
业绩管理的流行趋势

作业成本法/管理。近十年来,许多服务企业采用了作业成本法/管理(ABC/M)作为一种标准化的管理方法,并以此确定盈利程度。

平衡记分卡法。对服务性事务所的关键因素进行日常的分析,能够收到在其他行业同样的效果。根据企业的机构、经营目标和战略而发展起来的一套关键业绩指标,能够为企业提供一个明确的方向。提高管理人员的水平,是平衡记分卡中"学习与成长"的一个重要方面。

围绕员工价值的关键业绩指标(KPI)。服务行业中的企业重点关注服务人员和下列各项指标:

- 平均收入/全职约当员工,和平均工资/全职约当员工(前者应该是后者的两倍以上)。
- 实际工作的月数对为学习这项技能所花费的月数之比(如果这个比例数上升,那就意味着该项技能正在逐渐变得陈旧、销路渐窄)
- 可以开具账单的工作小时数(最好能占总的工作时间的90%~95%)
- 毛利率(为某些软件服务企业所用,把从维护和咨询业务所得的收入之和,减去提供服务者的工资,即得毛利额)

精益生产与标杆管理。具有类似的流程的服务行业的企业对照基准,以及客户参与其事的程度;确定企业适用的业绩考核指标并对成本进行分析,以确定成本差异的主要原因。精益管理的内容,包括通过对需求进行管理、对流程实施标准化、把适当的资源分配给每一项任务,以控制提供服务中所存在的差异。

Performance Management at Perelson Weiner LLP[1]

Jan Bell
Babson College

Alfred J. Nanni, Jr
Babson College

Shahid Ansari
Babson College

INTRODUCTION

During an interview in early fall 2008, Ron Weiner sat at his desk, gazing out onto the East River and reflecting on plans to grow Perelson Weiner LLP's (PW) revenue base in the next few years through strategic acquisitions of other CPA firms. PW is a large single-office CPA firm located in New York City. Weiner analyzed the firm's growth since 2004 for his visitors. While standard time charges had grown from $13.5 million in 2004 to about $19 million by 2008, Weiner felt that the firm was in a holding pattern. He mused that perhaps he should be satisfied with this growth; after all, the firm had lost a major client (revenues of about $4 million) during this time and had still grown over 40% in the four years. (Exhibits 1 and 2 contain 2004 financial statements for PW.)

PW's practice focuses on a high level of client service and interaction. Its personnel build the trust and confidence of clients and provide valued business advice as well as more conventional accounting services.

STRATEGIC POSITIONING

Since the buyout of his co-chairman, Sam Perelson, Weiner has had the primary responsibility for PW's future. He has continued to focus PW's business on what the firm does best: providing tax services, wealth transfer planning, auditing, and business advisory services to high net worth individuals and

---

[1] We are grateful to Ron Weiner, Julia Shanks, and Professor Larry Carr for assistance and suggestions on prior versions of this document.

entrepreneurs. (See Exhibit 3 for a description of PW's business.) PW's business development is relationship-based; the firm doesn't advertise for business. Instead, personnel develop long-term relationships with clients. These relationships typically start with tax return or financial statement preparation and then grow to include services that provide value to the client in other ways. Weiner explains his client focus this way:

"We don't seek short-term transactional services; we want to spend our time developing client relationships that last 40 years rather than seeking one-time opportunities."

To ensure that clients receive value from PW's services, Weiner insists that personnel have unique expertise before offering services to clients. PW's expertise and its ability to add unique value lie in providing traditional tax preparation, accounting, and auditing services, which are then enhanced by meaningful proactive business and tax consulting advice. Weiner has made a strategic decision to focus on these sources of client value plus one other sort of advice. With a New York City location, Weiner feels that PW can also add value for its clients by assisting them in the selection of the best specialized professional service firms in other areas. For example, PW personnel help clients find the best asset management firms and insurance brokers for their needs. If PW had been located somewhere other than New York, the firm probably would have included those service lines in its own practice. But given the number of quality specialized insurance and asset management firms in New York, it is clear that PW can add more value to its clients by "matchmaking" in those service areas than by providing the services itself.

Weiner knows that PW can compete effectively against companies such as Fidelity that offer estate and trust planning as well as tax preparation. Since Fidelity's primary revenue comes from investing its clients' capital and not from providing professional tax services, Fidelity's profit is higher when its personnel minimize the time spent providing client services. PW's core philosophy is to deliver a high level of personal service to its clients. Contrary to the Fidelity approach, Weiner feels that it is important to charge by the hour for services and spend the time it takes to deliver value to the client. That means PW does not want to perform routine work for a client that can be performed more efficiently in the client's own office. Instead, the focus is on providing high value-added accounting and business consulting services.

Weiner's dedication to PW's philosophy has brought about a shift in the firm's practice-area focus over the past several years. For instance, litigation support has been almost phased out. Litigation support is principally a transactional, not a relationship-based, business activity. Obtaining litigation clients requires constant marketing and selling. Further, people who work in forensics tend to be highly egocentric and require disproportionate support. This is not reflected in higher billing. Forensic work has about the same standard hourly rate as the other practice areas. Using similar logic, PW does not seek to audit publicly-listed companies. Audit services for publicly-held companies are typically provided by larger CPA firms and are very competitively priced. Firms often put their audit work out to bid and select the lowest bidder, since boards of directors of client firms typically view an audit as a commodity product.

PROFESSIONAL STAFF MANAGEMENT

Weiner's principal concern about being able to deliver PW's relationship-based business is about acquiring talent. There is a shortage of qualified talent, and Weiner believes that accounting graduates from most accounting programs are too focused on auditing and the latest technical pronouncements and not enough on understanding business. His firm needs broadly trained, intellectually curious accountants who are interested in business decision making and want to provide tax-saving and profit-enhancing suggestions along with traditional accounting functions.

PW hires eight to ten new entry-level recruits per year and, typical for the industry, most stay about three years. PW occasionally hires employees from other firms for mid-level positions to meet special client needs, but Weiner's experience has been that these people are in motion in their careers and will leave relatively quickly. PW's best result is with the partner/manager group. Retention in that group is very high.

PW tries to maintain a ratio of one-third partners, one third-staff with more than three years' experience, and one-third staff with three years' or less experience. The turnover rate is the highest in the middle third because their cultural values, as a result of having not been with the firm from the beginning of their careers, do not fit. The next highest turnover occurs in the group with three years' or less experience. Many of those people leave because they have not been able to develop the broad skills needed for public accounting, especially the ability to offer advice as required by PW's practice. These retention facts, coupled with the desire to grow revenue, are causing PW to seek growth through acquisition.

MANAGEMENT PHILOSOPHY

Many service organizations have adopted data-driven management tools, such as activity-based costing (ABC) or a balanced scorecard, and have created management control systems that, in Weiner's opinion, have become overly complicated, generating tomes of little-used data. He feels strongly that most managers neither understand the data generated by these tools nor effectively utilize them. As Weiner explains, the key to running a successful company is to understand the business and the drivers of success. Weiner's management view rejects the notion that complex performance measurement systems are needed to do this.

In fact, Weiner is a firm believer that, by establishing a strong organizational culture, measuring and managing a few key variables, and rewarding the members of the firm in a way that motivates proper behavior, firm members will deliver results consistent with expectations. As Weiner puts it, "There are alternative paths to getting results—two extreme management styles, if you will. You can manage culture (using soft management skills) and if the culture takes, it's a very powerful tool because you create a pervasive value system that is furthered by every member in the firm. If you manage through control, it is top-down and imposed on lower levels, and there is the natural action of avoidance at lower levels. It breeds contrarian reactions. We try to avoid this. Culture and the market [our clients] are our controls that drive results."

Weiner has created a control process such that PW's members do not have to be actively managed on a routine basis; they know what they need to deliver because of the firm's cultural values and its reward system. This enables Weiner to lead his team rather than managing it. Weiner explains the difference between managing and leading: "Management is making sure that the things that should have happened actually happened as expected. Leadership is figuring out what should happen and learning how to encourage the process. But, you can't lead unless you have followers."

Weiner's approach to leadership came from his prior work experience as a management consultant for a major accounting firm and from his father, who was also an accountant. From his experience as a consultant, he learned that many of his repeat clients, after being provided extensive analyses of their operations, were only interested in his executive summary. This taught him that service is a process involving trust that doesn't come from a single transaction but develops over time; and that "you are what you measure." From his father, Weiner learned about establishing expectations. In managing his own firm, his father had always focused on a target realization[②] rate of 80%, and, regardless of the billing rates he established, his father's firm always achieved the 80%

---

② Realization rate, as used here, is the percentage of billings that are ultimately collected from clients after they negotiate discounts, dispute billings, and fail to pay. Weiner's reporting system does not distinguish between these causes. At the time Weiner's father set his 80% rate, the industry rate was approximately 70%.

realization rate. Weiner concluded that the cost of not achieving higher realization rates directly affected the bottom line since, in his view, the cost to produce a dollar of service was the same whether the billing was realized or not. This led Weiner to two important conclusions. First, focus on realization rate can be a powerful way to direct and influence personnel effort. Second, Weiner understood that his father's staff set out to achieve this established 80% rate regardless of what they might have been able to deliver. (Perhaps other firms in the industry did exactly the same, because in 2006, the industry standard realization rate, according to the TSCPA National Accounting Practice Survey, hovered somewhere around 80%.[3]) But why 80%? In Weiner's opinion, if staff members don't believe in billing for all their work hours, then they do not value themselves at their stated rates. Providing valued service and then billing for it are key factors for success at PW.

Believing that you will bill only what you believe is fair, PW has its partners set their own billing rates, which they are expected to achieve. Once a year the partners gather for an annual retreat. One topic is the discussion of realization rates achieved. Weiner is a firm believer in maintaining this transparency: "If the goal is clear, to achieve maximum realization, and if achieved realization rates are reviewed in this public forum, partners are more likely to achieve this goal." Weiner is proud that the firm consistently delivers realization rates of 90% or better.

The firm does not directly share the realization rate goal with anyone below the partner level, because below that level, staff members do not have billing and collection responsibility. Professional staff control the quality of work they do, and that is what Weiner wants them to focus on. The firm wants the professional staff to work the hours it takes to do the job well. Staff should not worry about what the firm bills or collects for their work. In Weiner's words, "We don't want to pressure the staff to do less. We want them to do what is necessary to deliver good service. If you tell them the budget is the most important thing, they won't report anything above the budget. Then you really don't have any chance to collect for the value of the services you truly provide. It is the firm's responsibility to deliver good value to its clients. This is central to the value system."

THE BILLING STRUCTURE

Accounting firms bill in one of two ways: by the hour or by the project.

---

[3] 2006 PCPS/TSCPA National MAP Survey Data, Appendix 3, p. 5, obtained through contacting website, pcpsmapsurvey@intellisurvey.com/ and requesting data.

Years ago, PW opted against project-based billing. Too often, project-based billing encourages firm personnel to take shortcuts to get the job done as quickly as possible. At a fixed price, profit becomes solely a function of cost. Being customer-service-centric, PW wants a billing model that encourages professional staff to work the hours required for superior service. The practice of billing for hours worked also shows clients the value of that time, since they can understand the hours required. It also helps personnel estimate the cost of future work, because an accurate record of hours exists.

Weiner views a client relationship as a two-way street. If clients value PW's services, they show respect by paying for them. But because of the nature of personal client-partner relationships, occasions arise when the client will negotiate final bills. Partners and staff feel a responsibility to their clients because of the close relationships that exist. They work with the clients to ensure that the services rendered are completed with attention to the client's needs. They attempt to drive low-value tasks back to the client's personnel, where the work can be performed at lower cost. Still, the originating partner (who brought the client to PW) has autonomy to adjust the billing rate if it makes sense. For example, on occasion a highly-paid staff member may perform low-value tasks for a client. In that case, the originating partner may adjust the rate downward for those hours in consideration of the value to the client.

Even when rates are reduced, PW's policies require that staff members record all hours worked for clients, and the accounting system records hours worked at standard billing rates. PW believes that if personnel do not record all time worked they are devaluing their own worth. This is not healthy, since client relationships are ultimately based on the clients valuing the firm's work. Weiner has noticed that staff accountants new to the firm tend to under-record their time. Part of the mentoring process encourages them to record all their time.

Every once in a while, a client demonstrates that he or she does not value the services provided by resisting payment of the firm's charges. In these cases the originating partner may choose to fire the client. This has happened two or three times in the past few years.

PERFORMANCE MANAGEMENT AT PERELSON WEINER

PW manages performance through professional compensation. PW establishes a standard billing rate for each employee that is a function of that employee's compensation. Hourly billing rates are approximately .0024 times annual compensation for each employee.④ The firm operates under the assumption that if people are paid fairly then the market rate is fair for their services. Conversely, if the market says the rate is unfair, then the individual's compensation is too high, and this will show up because the firm's realization rate will drop. Partners set their own billing rates, and, consequently, their own salaries, which are purely a function of their billing rates. If the client believes that the partners' services are not worth their billing rates, then the realization rate will go down. This will inhibit the ability of those partners to raise their own billing rates and salary in the future.

This market mechanism counterbalances a partner's desire to increase his or her own income with the partner's desire to minimize client charges in order to preserve and strengthen client relationships. Weiner prefers this dynamic tension to telling a partner, "You should charge $300 an hour" and have that partner say, "No, I only want to charge $250." Weiner feels that if he sets hourly billing rates, partners will understate hours equal to the rate they think they are worth while receiving a salary that doesn't reflect market value.

This "market economy" extends to the professional staff. Partners select staff for their engagements. If a professional staff person has a salary inconsistent with the value he or she brings to a job, it shows up in that person's billable hours and/or in the realization rates of the clients he or she services. Overpaid people have trouble getting assignments and do not get the billable hours they need. The control system drives a meritocracy at PW. Weiner can look at utilization rates of people and see if they are compensated correctly. Partners competing for a staff member's time means that staff member merits a higher salary and billing rate, because he/she is creating value in excess of current market worth.

Reflecting on PW's control system, Weiner offered, "People who are more trendy might call how we manage a balanced scorecard approach. Our culture is our driver, we have to manage to give value, service clients well, and believe that our rates are fair. Thus we should get paid for it. Then we look backward and see if it worked, so it really isn't looking for lead variables and figuring out what we should get in dollars. Our cultural value is that we are worth our rates and we deliver high value to our clients. We aren't passive, but the driver of our business is in the cultural value of service delivery; the

---

④ Links among Salary, Billing and Realization Rates. Partners establish their own billing rates for the upcoming period and are expected to achieve at least a 90% realization rate. Their salary becomes set once their billing rate is established using the idea that the billing rate per hour is .0024 times salary. For example, a partner with a salary of $150 000 annually would have a billing rate of about $360 per hour. A staff person earning $80 000 annually would have a billing rate of about $192 per hour. Compensation for partners includes a base salary and a bonus. Base salary, on average, accounts for one-third of total compensation. See Exhibit 8 for details.

economics are the consequences of that delivery."

PERFORMANCE MEASUREMENT

Weiner has carefully planned his route to performance measurement at PW. He has consciously rejected some recent trends in the industry. (See Exhibit 9 for an overview of those trends.) Given PW's clear strategic positioning, and considering the flaws he has identified in the pricing and performance measurement systems used by other service companies, Weiner has concluded that his system is simple, inexpensive, and effective.

The firm's time and billing system tracks the hours and standard time charges incurred for each client as well as the actual amounts billed and realization rates. It also contains time coded according to 100 different billing categories (see Exhibit 4). Each month a report is generated that partners can use to see how many hours have been billed to their clients, and what their revenues and realization rates are. Despite having access to this tool, Weiner said, few utilize it fully.

Each staff member is expected to generate about 1 750 billable hours per year, while each partner should generate about 1 500 billable hours. Weiner receives a monthly report by individual professional that shows actual hours billed versus projected hours (see Exhibit 5).

The firm develops the monthly projections in Exhibit 5 for individual employees based on monthly expectations for billable hours modified by the employee's billed hours from the prior year. Weiner recalls a monthly report in which he noticed that actual billed hours were lower than projected hours. When he investigated, he realized that some of the newly hired accountants were "eating their hours" and not billing for all their time servicing clients. ⑤Actions taken included training the new employees in the values of the firm.

Weiner also analyzes monthly financial statements to make sure that revenues are coming in at the appropriate multiple of professional salaries (see Exhibit 6). If they are not, he investigates the reasons. Three major reasons for variances exist:

1. There is a deviation in billing; perhaps a staff member has not charged all his/her hours to the job.

2. There is a deviation in the pricing structure; perhaps a problem exists

---

⑤ To meet time budgets, new staff members often record budgeted hours as their actual time, regardless of the time taken on the task. They then "eat" their extra hours. Eating hours means that you perform the necessary work to get the job done without recording those hours on any client's job. This behavior creates inaccurate time records and limits the usefulness of historical data in creating budgets for future jobs. This is an age-old problem that exists in many service firms.

with the value of services rendered.

3. The mix of staff is not the same as expected; perhaps highly paid staff members have performed work that has lower client value than their pay grade warrants.

Weiner's review of the income statement stops there because his business model is predicated on the idea that all other operating expenses, including rent and utilities, are variable, and, therefore, a function of professional salaries. In Weiner's terms, "All costs are variable," so PW does not need a complicated cost allocation system like ABC in order to work.

Weiner feels that PW's operating expenses are directly related to professional compensation. In fact, Weiner states that in his business at least 80% of all costs are driven by professional salaries, while the rest are probably driven by headcount. For example, a more expensive person uses more space, creates more telephone expenses, and generally consumes more overhead. Weiner's experience is that for every dollar of standard time charges (i.e., billing rates), about $.65 should cover professional salaries and other operating expenses, not more than $.10 should cover write-offs and bad debts (realization), and the remainder should be profit.

Weiner is familiar with an architecture firm that uses an elaborate activity-based allocation system for performance measurement and billing. The architects do not understand the underlying activities or their costs, and they complain that the allocation system is overly complicated, generating reams of data. Accordingly, the architects do not believe in or use the expensive system and do not get value out of it. Weiner does not believe in generating reports that are not needed to understand PW's business.

Weiner knows that many other service firms use an ABC style of cost control. Those firms usually allocate variable costs according to the number of hours billed and allocate other costs based on headcount. Weiner disagrees with these drivers because a higher paid employee will require more resources. Thus, Weiner concludes that this kind of ABC system uses incorrect drivers that cause the resulting reports to lack credibility.

Weiner further reflects on services that PW provides and concludes that PW offers aunitary product, a standard billable dollar of service. Therefore, PW doesn't need an ABC system. If PW began offering radically different services, such as high fixed-price or commodity client services and variable-rate client services, then PW might need ABC. To make money in the commodity environment, PW would have very high levels of billable hours to offset low realization rates. To compete in a commodity market, the firm would need to be the lowest cost service provider. The environment in which PW operates is different. The firm differentiates its services on value provided. Weiner says that

PW has made a strategic decision to treat all services as a unitary product and doesn't differentiate between tax, audit, or other work.

Weiner provides an example of PW's reporting system, which calculates the cost to produce a dollar of service by dividing total costs by total standard time charges throughout the year. This cost assessment relationship holds, even though PW does three times the volume in March that it does in July. In theory, if PW wanted to recognize product cost differences, it would charge more for March services than for those performed in July. Using this variable costing approach, PW would say all costs in July are fixed, and all in March are variable. In such a situation, partners would have an incentive to bring in work on a highly discounted rate in July. To maintain its value system, PW has strategically chosen not to do this, because it will leach into other months and erode PW's pricing culture.

PW's strategy is to differentiate its services based on value. The organization's culture is focused to provide that value. The partners know their clients' needs and the value their clients receive from the services PW provides. That value is the foundation of both pricing and compensation at PW. Personnel are paid for the client "market" value they create. The role of the performance measurement system at PW is to reveal the alignment between value provided and compensation paid.

Weiner believes that the culture itself provides strong strategic control based on simple income-oriented measures. Culture is the driver in PW's business. If PW were to use a balanced scorecard, complicated and distracting analyses would need to be introduced. But to what end? For example, the learning and growth dimension would focus on the development of the PW culture in employees. Instead of developing these unnecessary metrics for a scorecard, however, Weiner feels that the simple relationships among billing rates, realization, and cost ensure that culture. Weiner uses benchmarking data from the International Group of Accounitng Firms (see Exhibit 7 for an example) to assure that his company's results are in line with the industry.

GROWTH THROUGH ACQUISITION

PW's performance system has worked well in the past, but now that the firm's strategic plan calls for growth through acquisition, will the system continue to work as well? Firm members from newly merged CPA firms will be accustomed to other, perhaps more "trendy" control systems and will be unfamiliar with the PW culture. Will it be possible to get new firm members to accept PW's culture? How can Weiner assure that cultural change is occurring before client service is impacted? Are changes necessary to PW's performance measurement and management system?

CASE REQUIREMENTS

1. Weiner believes that PW will not benefit from an ABC model. Using the relationship between the standard billing rate and salaries provided in the case, create a product line income statement. Select resource drivers and assign costs to product lines. Will the results of your statement provide better feedback on profitability than the existing income statement? For your analysis, assume that there are 57 employees in 2004—19 in administration and paraprofessional assignments, 24 in auditing, and 14 in tax.

2. Evaluate Weiner's quote about seasonal business and variable costing: "We say that the cost to produce is borne pro rata over our total standard time charges. We do three times the volume in March that we do in July. In theory if we wanted to recognize product differences, we'd charge more for March services than for those performed in July. We'd say all our costs in July are fixed and all in March are variable, and we'd bias ourselves to bring in work on a highly discounted rate in July. We've chosen not to include this in our value system, because it will leach into our other months."

3. Prior to working this question, read Having Trouble with Your Strategy? Then Map It, by Robert S. Kaplan and David P. Norton (Harvard Business Review, Sep/Oct 2000, Vol. 78, Issue 5, pp. 167-176).

The balanced scorecard has recently been adapted for the service sector. Below are sample dimensions and metrics some firms use for measuring performance:

i. **Financial**—the strategy for growth, profitability, and risk viewed from the perspective of the shareholder. These can include factors such as:

1. Fee revenue
2. Profit margins
3. Professional salaries
4. Receivables turnover

ii. **Customer**—the strategy for creating value and differentiation from the perspective of the customer.

These can include factors such as:

1. Customer retention
2. Increased revenue from customers
3. Job turnaround time
4. Billed hours vs. estimated hours
5. Customer complaints

iii. **Internal Business Processes**—the strategic priorities for various business processes that create customer and shareholder satisfaction. These can include factors such as:

1. Overhead expense changes
2. Reduction in administrative hours
3. Realization rates
4. Utilization rates

iv. **Learning and Growth**—the priorities to create a climate that supports organizational change, innovation, and future growth. These can include factors such as:

1. Training hours provided by partners
2. Reduced attrition rate by new hires

If Weiner wants to use a balanced scorecard approach, he would have to get "buy-in" from Perelson as well as the senior partners of the firm. Weiner is a firm believer that simpler is better and isn't inclined to pursue using a balanced scorecard approach to performance management unless he is convinced that it is truly better.

Consider the new trend toward using balanced scorecards and PW's growth strategy. Provide a convincing argument for why a balanced scorecard approach should or should not be implemented at PW. To assist your decision-making process, create a strategy map for PW and suggest what metrics you believe are necessary for PW's strategy to succeed.

Exhibit 1

Perelson Wiener

Profit and Loss comparison—YTD (in thousands)

		Jan-dec 2004	Jan-dec 2003
Income			
	Fees, net	$12 455	$11 869
	Other	10	5
	Writedowns		462
Total Income		$12 465	$11 412
Expenses			
Salaries	Audit	$ 1 923	$ 1 910
	Litigation	22	151
	Tax	1 620	1 388
	Other		25
		3 565	3 474
	Administration	899	901
		$ 4 464	$ 4 375
Commissions	Audit		
	Tax		$ 16
	Litigation		88
Outside Labor	Audit	84	38
	Tax	47	—
	Administration	42	27
	Litigation		147
	Consultants	18	12
	Other		3
Total Direct Expenses		$ 4 655	$ 4 706

Exhibit 1
Perelson Wiener
Income Statement—YTD (in thousands)

		Jan-Dec 2004	Jan-Dec 2003
Data Processing	Tax	$ 73	$ 49
	Software	118	61
	Payroll/Paychex	5	5
	Other	6	12
Employee Benefits & Payroll Taxes		730	814
Employee Recruitment		156	14
Other Employee Expenses (training, licenses, etc.)			
Audit		71	70
Tax		34	30
Other		116	87
Miscellaneous Administrative		46	48
Occupancy Costs		769	522
Promotional Expenses	Audit	6	7
	Tax	14	1
	Other	16	29
Other Practice Development		404	371
Insurance Liability		48	50
Insurance-Workman's Compensation		4	8
Other Insurance		68	62
Library	Audit	15	12
	Tax	79	76
	Litigation	5	7
	Other	7	4
Office Expenses, Including Equipment Rentals		243	226
Office Supplies & Postage		107	133
Telephone & Internet		127	128
Staff Expenses (Travel, Parking, Meals, etc.)	Audit	116	114
	Tax	47	39
	Other	35	36
Miscellaneous Operating Expenses		169	13
Total Operating Expenses		$ 8 289	$ 7 734
Operating Income		4 176	3 678
Other Income (Expense)		17	(3)
Income Tax		87	147
Net Income		$ 4 106	$ 3 528

Exhibit 2
Perelson Weiner
condensed Balance Sheet (In thousands)

	31-Dec 2004	31-Dec 2003
Total Current Assets	$ 5.3	$ 4.9
Net Fixed Assets	0.3	0.2
Other Assets	0.1	0.1
Total Assets	$ 5.7	$ 5.2
Liabilities	$ 0.4	$ 0.1
Partners Equity	5.3	5.1
Total Liabilities & Equity	$ 5.7	$ 5.2

Exhibit 3

description of PW's Practice areas

Taken from PW webpage, http://www.pwcpa.com/brochure.pdf, April 3, 2009

ACCOUNTING AND AUDIT We focus on the business behind the numbers and use historical financial data as a tool and starting point for providing value. Partners have a broad perspective and through continuing attention develop a corporate memory, a necessary ingredient to manage in this demanding and ever changing world.

Clients draw on us as a resource and together we address specific issues such as succession planning and the impact of economic decisions.

We view our primary role as "partners" in the utilization and interpretation of information and with management identify opportunities for increasing operational efficiency. By matching our staff to the demands of each assignment and developing the skills of clients' personnel, we help them grow while reducing costs.

At Perelson Weiner, we pride ourselves on the quality of our people and professional standards. We are a member of the SEC and the Private Company Practice Sections of The American Institute of Certified Public Accountants and The International Group of Accounting Firms (IGAF), an association with correspondent firms across the U.S. and in over 80 countries. Through this worldwide network of high quality firms we provide clients with both geographic coverage and cost effective solutions.

TAX AND ESTATE In-depth knowledge of the client's concerns, personal objectives and finances enables us to integrate business and individual issues in overall financial planning. We view tax planning as a continuous process and participate with the client's other professional advisors to evaluate the impact of business and life events on tax plans.

Applying a comprehensive understanding of international, federal, state and local tax regulations to industry and client specific situations, we are able to anticipate financial consequences and mitigate surprises. These activities have translated into substantial savings for clients on a day-to-day basis and in examinations by tax authorities.

The intricate tax planning for domestic and international companies includes our involvement in activities such as cross border transactions, transfer pricing, international tax controversies and SEC reporting. The expertise of our professionals has earned the respect and appreciation of clients and favorable recognition among regulatory bodies and peers.

LITIGATION AND VALUATION Functioning as an integral part of the Firm, the Litigation and Valuation departments mirror our trademark: knowledge and expertise applied innovatively to business issues. Perelson Weiner partners are actively involved in each phase of every engagement.

Our team draws on the Firm's substantial resources in audit and tax to arrive at results that impact effective decision making. The scope of our valuation practice is diverse and includes engagements for assessment of tangible and intangible assets, preferred stock, warrants and employee stock options, partnership disputes, minority interest, mortgage backed securities, estate audits, and assisting lending institutions in troubled loan situations.

Consistent, expert service is provided throughout the litigation process from case evaluation, pretrial negotiation, and assistance in deposition preparation to the trial itself. We distill vast amounts of financial data into concise summaries, illuminating the issues at hand. When called to testify, our expert witnesses translate this information into terms readily understood by the jury.

Multi-industry litigation consulting includes financial and fraud investigations, damage calculations including those for intellectual property disputes, application of accounting and auditing standards in SEC investigations, accountants' malpractice claims, purchase/sale disputes, and computations of lost profits.

BUSINESS CONSULTING In every engagement, advising the client is an integral part of what we do. Just as there is no formula for how we approach a problem, there is no typical client relationship. As problem solvers, we are also often called upon to provide a discrete service. Projects are performed expeditiously with serious intellectual commitment.

In this role, we bring a different perspective from those with ongoing responsibilities. Drawing on the depth and breadth of our business, tax and accounting experience, we effectively address the task at hand, always keeping in mind the long-term objectives.

Partners focus on the large picture, assisting management to optimize human and organizational resources. We also consult on a variety of transaction and event driven issues such as due diligence for investments or potential acquisitions, technology implementation, executive compensation programs, purchase and sale of stock, internal accounting procedures and other non audit related activities.

We serve clients in various stages of growth from start-ups to well established businesses, and in all sectors of the economy. As advisors, we frequently assist in relationship building with bankers, attorneys and other professionals.

Exhibit 4 – Billing codes

INCOME & EXPENSE ANALYSIS
A51 Sales/Revenue
A52 Payroll
A53 Expenses

A55 Analytical Review
A56 Financial Statement Preparation
A57 Management Letter
A58 SEC Matters
A59 Projection/Forcast
A60 Research (describe)
A72 Field Review
A73 Quality Control Review
A74 Engagement Partner Review
A75 Concurring Partner Review

REPORT PROCESSING
A81 Typint
A82 Proofreading
A83 Binding

A99 Travel Time

TAX

ADMINISTRATION
T02 Discussions/Meetings (describe)
T03 Correspondance/Memo
T04 Engagement Letter
T08 Supervision/Training

COMPLIANCE
T10 Information Gathering
T15 Prepare Tax Return
T16 Review Tax Return
T17 Amended Return (describe)
T20 Extensions
T21 Estimates
T25 Prepare Pension/Benefit Plan Tax Return
T26 Review Pension/Benefit Plan Tax Return
T30 Prepare Other Tax Return (describe)
T31 Review Other Tax Return (describe)
T35 Payroll/Sales/Rent Taxes
T40 Notices (describe)
T45 Other (describe)

T50 Examination (describe)
T60 Research (describe)

PLANNING
T70 Projections
T75 Estate/Gift
T80 Other (describe)

T90 Collating/Mailing
T99 Travel Time

CONSULTING SERVICES
ADMINISTRATION
C02 Discussions/Meetings (describe)
C03 Correspondance/Memo
C04 Engagement Letter
C08 Supervision/Training

C10 Business Planning (describe)
C15 Financing (describe)
C20 Business Valuation (describe)
C25 Litigation Support (describe)
C30 Operational Audit (describe)
C35 microcomputer Services (describe)
C40 Personal Financial Planning (describe)
C45 Human Resources (describe)
C50 Executor/Trustee Duties (describe)
C55 Contract Review (describe)
C60 Research (describe)
C65 Other (describe)
C73 Quality Control Review
C74 Engagement Partner Review

REPORT PROCESSING
C81 Typing
C82 Proofreading
C83 Bindings

C99 Travel Time

NON-BILLABLE CODES

OFFICE
N01 Data Entry
N02 Mail
N03 File Maintenance
N04 Library Maintenance
N05 Tax Calendar
N06 Client Prospect Report
N07 Telephone
N08 Typing

N09 Photocopying
N10 Network Maintenance
N11 Bookkeeping
N12 Firm Administration
N13 Billing
N14 Collections
N15 Oter Partner Function (describe)

PERSONNEL
N21 Recruiting
N22 Interviewing
N23 Evaluations & Review
N24 Scheduling
N25 Training

MEETINGS
N31 Partner Meeting
N32 Firm Meeting
N33 Other Meeting (describe)
N34 Professional Organization
N35 Charitable/CMo Organization
N36 CPE

CLIENT DEVELOPMENT
N41 Existing Client
N42 Prospective Client
N43 Bankers
N44 Attorneys
N45 Other (describe)

OTHER
N51 Holiday
N52 Vacation
N53 Sick
N54 Religious
N55 Overtime Bank
N56 Unassigned
N57 Time Off Without Pay
N58 CPA Examination
N59 Trave (non-business hours)
N60 Blood Drive
N61 Other (describe)

Exhibit 5

INIT	PERELSON WEINER LLP	D/O/H	BILL HRS 12/04	BILL HRS 12/03	MONTH VAR	BILL HRS 12/04	BILL HRS 12/03	YTD VAR	TOTL HRS 12/04	TOTL HRS 12/03	TOTL HRS VAR
	A & A DEPT										
JJB	JJB		125	180	(55)	1 609	1 735	(126)	2 409	2 417	(8)
SYC	SYC1		119	88	31	1 542	1 368	174	2 288	2 174	114
GC	GC		156	116	40	1 689	1 768	(79)	2 135	2 077	58
RC	RC		4	15	(11)	463	257	206	524	348	176
YE	YE		126	56	70	1 698	1 502	196	2 215	2 135	80
JME	JME		145	154	(9)	1 815	1 613	202	2 723	2 483	240
MG	MG		96	100	(4)	1 900	1 793	107	2 331	2 272	59
BMH	BMH		129	118	11	1 548	1 362	186	3 056	2 999	57
AK	AK		122	40	82	1 443	1 192	251	2 255	2 264	(9)
MK	MK		89	61	28	1 073	897	176	1 130	922	208
EL	EL		156	93	63	1 863	1 583	280	2 748	2 461	287
TP	TP		77	0	77	1 149	918	231	2 030	1 781	249
RSQ	RSQ		139	114	25	1 708	1 620	88	2 672	2 505	167
PZ	PZ		139	149	(10)	1 668	1 558	110	2 205	2 151	54
	SUBTOTALS		1 622	1 284	338	21 168	19 166	2 002	30 721	28 989	1 732
	YTD % BILLABLE					68.90%	66.11%				
14	AVG HOURS/PER		116	92		1 512	1 369		2 194	2 071	
SA	SA	10/18/04	13	0	13	140	0	140	282	0	282
VB	VB	01/20/03	0	115	(115)	1 924	1 557	367	2 334	2 130	204
TG	TG	11/30/04	0	0	0	0	0	0	0	0	0
JH	JH	08/13/03	126	130	(4)	1 988	600	1 388	2 392	846	1 546
EK	EK	11/30/04	31	0	31	31	0	31	200	0	200
SK	SK	08/31/04	79	0	79	339	0	339	719	0	719
AL	AL	10/07/04	102	0	102	280	0	280	491	0	491
SR	SR	09/08/03	61	45	16	1 388	192	1 196	2 270	687	1 583
JBS	JBS	11/22/04	119	0	119	121	0	121	256	0	256
VS	VS	11/15/04	17	0	17	17	0	17	30	0	30
MZ	MZ	09/01/03	133	116	17	1 829	351	1 478	2 273	692	1 581
	SUBTOTALS		681	406	275	8 057	2 700	5 357	11 247	4 355	6 892
EB	EB		0	0	0	0	545	79	0	850	(850)
HC	HC	02/02/03	0	0	0	0	77	(77)	0	249	(249)
BE	BE		0	0	0	0	475	(475)	0	1 039	(1 039)
JG	JG		0	69	(69)	0	1 664	(1 664)	0	2 217	(2 217)
LJG	LJG	05/24/04	0	0	0	327	0	327	426	0	426
SMG	SMG	01/22/04	0	0	0	400	473	(73)	400	572	(172)
JK	JK		0	0	0	0	1 724	(1 724)	0	2 231	(2 231)
SL	SL	07/15/03	0	76	(76)	789	294	495	1 500	1 026	474
YM	YM	06/10/04	0	0	0	510	0	510	823	0	823
NM	NM	09/03/02	0	0	0	0	627	(627)	0	852	(852)
MR	MR		0	73	(73)	1 511	1 606	(95)	1 869	2 264	(395)
SS	SS	09/09/02	0	0	0	0	443	(443)	0	510	(510)
CS	CS	07/06/04	0	0	0	0	0	0	97	0	97
YY	YY		0	0	0	0	1 023	(1 023)	0	1 260	(1 260)
	SUBTOTALS		0	218	(218)	3 537	8 951	(4 790)	5 115	13 070	(7 955)
	A & A TOTALS		2 303	1 908	395	32 762	30 817	1 945	47 083	46 414	669
	YTD % BILLABLE-A&A					69.58%	66.40%				

Exhibit 5 (continued)

INIT	PERELSON WEINER LLP	D/O/H	BILL HRS 12/04	BILL HRS 12/03	MONTH VAR	BILL HRS 12/04	BILL HRS 12/03	YTD VAR	TOTL HRS 12/04	TOTL HRS 12/03	TOTL HRS VAR
	LITIG DEPT										
LIT	VARIOUS TEMPS	VAR	0	0	0	0	0	0	0	0	0
KB	KB		0	110	(110)	58	997	(939)	58	1 411	(1 353)
CL	CL		0	68	(68)	89	986	(897)	89	1 764	(1 675)
JP	JP	07/07/03	0	0	0	0	92	(92)	0	134	(134)
RW	RW		0	5	(5)	11	447	(436)	175	1 747	(1 572)
	LITIG TOTALS		0	183	(183)	158	2 522	(2 364)	322	5 056	(4 734)
	YTD % BILLABLE-LITIG					49.07%	49.88%				
	BIZ CONTINUITY DEPT										
ML	ML	03/04/02	0	0	0	0	27	(27)	0	367	(367)
	BIZ CONT TOTALS		0	0	0	0	27	(27)	0	367	(367)
	YTD % BILLABLE					#DIV/0!					
	TAX DEPT										
MJE	MJE		126	140	(14)	1 467	1 435	32	2 668	2 619	49
JAF	JAF		190	146	44	1 756	1 682	74	2 710	2 665	45
JMJ	JMJ		104	94	10	1 428	1 359	69	1 504	1 451	53
LL	LL		86	69	17	1 470	1 119	351 3	107	2 820	287
RN	RN		151	128	23	1 793	1 643	150	2 368	2 244	124
AWS	AWS		101	126	(25)	1 548	1 504	44	2 310	2 165	145
CS	CS		130	142	(12)	1 830	1 930	(100)	2 297	2 334	(37)
RES	RES		134	135	(1)	1 722	1 735	(13)	2 753	2 661	92
BW	BW		101	141	(40)	1 658	1 651	7	2 347	2 327	20
	SUBTOTALS		1 123	1 121	2	14 672	14 058	614	22 064	21 286	778
	YTD % BILLABLE					66.50%	66.04%				
9	AVG HOURS/PER		125	125		1 630	1 562		2 452	2 365	
SK	SK	11/06/04	92	0	92	92	0	92	169	0	169
BK	BK	11/01/04	130	0	130	224	0	224	368	0	368
KL	KL	02/11/04	119	0	119	1 418	0	1 418	1 988	0	1 988
RL	RL	01/01/04	65	0	65	1 151	0	1 151	2 366	0	2 366
TR	TR	01/16/04	118	0	118	1 726	0	1 726	2 236	0	2 236
	SUBTOTALS		524	0	524	4 611	0	4 611	7 127	0	7 127
MB	MB		0	0	0	0	904	(904)	0	1 385	(1 385)
JG	JG		0	0	0	0	613	(613)	0	781	(781)
SL	SL		1	0	1	8	16	(8)	8	17	(9)
PS	PS	08/31/04	0	0	0	77	0	77	89	0	89
HS	HS		0	0	0	0	1 557	(1 557)	0	2 134	(2 134)
SM	SM		0	0	0	0	608	(608)	0	815	(815)
MS	MS	01/05/04	0	0	0	639	0	639	642	0	642
EV	EV	12/03/03	0	65	(65)	560	64	496	784	169	615
GW	GW	02/17/04	0	0	0	532	0	532	618	0	618
	SUBTOTALS		1	65	(64)	1 816	3 762	(1 946)	2 141	5 301	(3 160)
	TAX TOTALS		1 648	1 186	462	21 099	17 820	3 279	31 332	26 587	4 745
	YTD % BILLABLE-TAX					67.34%	67.03%				
SSP	SSP		28	7	21	251	217	34	1 648	1 640	8
RGW	RGW		72	46	26	720	619	101	2 830	2 830	0
	SUBTOTALS		100	53	47	971	836	135	4 478	4 470	8
	ADMIN TOTALS		69	110	(41)	4 936	3 876	1 060	36 362	36 121	241
	FIRM TOTALS		4 120	3 440	680	59 926	55 898	4 028	119 577	119 015	562
						50.11%	46.97%				

Exhibit 5 (continued)

INIT	PERELSON WEINER LLP	D/O/H	BILL HRS 12/04	BILL HRS 12/03	MONTH VAR	BILL HRS 12/04	BILL HRS 12/03	YTD VAR	TOTL HRS 12/04	TOTL HRS 12/03	TOTL HRS VAR
	SHAREHOLDERS										
JJB	JJB		125	180	(55)	1 609	1 735	−126	2 409	2 417	(8)
SYC	SYC		119	88	31	1 542	1 368	174	2 288	2 174	114
MJE	MJE		126	140	(14)	1 467	1 435	32	2 668	2 619	49
JME	JME		145	154	(9)	1 815	1 613	202	2 723	2 483	240
JAF	JAF		190	146	44	1 756	1 682	74	2 710	2 665	45
BMH	BMH		129	118	11	1 548	1 362	186	3 056	2 999	57
JMJ	JMJ		104	94	10	1 428	1 359	69	1 504	1 451	53
RL	RL	01/01/04	65	0	65	1 151	0	1 151	2 366	0	2 366
EL	EL		156	93	63	1 863	1 583	280	2 748	2 461	287
LL	LL		86	69	17	1 470	1 119	351	3 107	2 820	287
RN	RN		151	128	23	1 793	1 643	150	2 368	2 244	124
SSP	SSP		28	7	21	251	217	34	1 648	1 640	8
RSQ	RSQ		139	114	25	1 708	1 620	88	2 672	2 505	167
AWS	AWS		101	126	(25)	1 548	1 504	44	2 310	2 165	145
RES	RES		134	135	(1)	1 722	1 735	(13)	2 753	2 661	92
RGW	RGW		72	46	26	720	619	101	2 830	2 830	0
	SUBTOTALS		1 870	1 638	232	23 391	20 594	2 797	40 160	36 134	4 026
	FORMER SHAREHOLDERS		0	110	(110)	58	1 499	(1 441)	58	2 817	(2 759)
	TOTALS		1 870	1 748	122	23 449	22 093	1 356	40 218	38 951	1 267
	A & A TOTALS										
	YTD % BILLABLE					68.90%	66.11%				
14	AVG HOURS/PER		116	92		1 512	1 369		2 194	2 071	
	LITIG TOTALS										
	YTD % BILLABLE					49.07%	49.88%				
#REF!	AVG HOURS/PER		#REF!	#REF!		#REF!	#REF!		#REF!	#REF!	
	TAX TOTALS										
	YTD % BILLABLE					66.50%	66.04%				
9	AVG HOURS/PER		125	125		1 630	1 562		2 452	2 365	
	FIRM TOTALS		4 120	3 440	680	59 926	55 898	4 028	119 577	119 015	562
	YTD % BILLABLE-FIRM					50.11%	46.97%				
					STAFF HOURS						
	Total Firm Hours		4 120	3 440	680	59 926	55 898	4 028	119 577	119 015	562
	YTD % Billable-Firm					50.11%	46.97%				
		Less:Admin	(69)	(110)	41	(4 936)	(3 876)	(1 060)	(36 362)	(36 121)	(241)
		Subtotal	4 051	3 330	721	54 991	52 022	2 968	83 215	82 894	321
	YTD % Billable					66.08%	62.76%				
		Less:Partners	(1 870)	(1 748)	(122)	(23 449)	(22 093)	(1 356)	(40 218)	(38 951)	(1 267)
		Subtotal	2 181	1 582	599	31 542	29 930	1 612	42 997	43 943	(946)
	YTD % Billable					73.36%	68.11%				

Exhibit 5 (continued)

RC			31	29	93	44	40	53	28	8	54	50	28	4	1	463	257
YE			122	181	212	114	119	144	145	149	131	120	135	126		1 698	1 502
LG	A&A	05/24/04	0	0	0	0	20	136	148	23	0	0	0	0		327	0
SG	LASS	01/22/04	42	151	207	0	0	0	0	0	0	0	0	0		400	473
MG			141	182	233	185	133	152	161	166	150	175	126	96		1 900	1 793
JH			153	219	254	192	166	166	159	151	151	133	118	126		1 988	600
AK			32	173	226	157	108	124	107	70	134	96	94	122		1 443	1 192
MK			63	76	112	122	71	86	76	73	108	126	72	89	(1)	1 073	897
EK	A&A	11/30/04	0	0	0	0	0	0	0	0	0	0	0	31		31	0
SK	TAX	11/06/04	0	0	0	0	0	0	0	0	0	0	0	92		92	0
BK	TAX	11/01/04	0	0	0	0	0	0	0	0	0	0	94	130		224	0
SK	A&A	08/31/04	0	0	0	0	0	0	0	0	58	83	118	79	1	339	0
SL	A&A	07/15/03	30	210	140	32	56	70	131	119	0	0	0	0	1	789	294
AL	A&A	10/07/04	0	0	0	0	0	0	0	0	0	67	110	102	1	280	0
KL	TAX	02/11/04	0	128	222	117	77	94	106	126	194	146	89	119		1 418	0
YM	A&A	06/01/04	0	0	0	0	0	117	131	91	109	63	0	0	(1)	510	0
TN			61	118	168	65	78	118	88	87	104	78	109	77	(2)	1 149	918
SR			51	211	254	82	108	110	120	145	106	63	76	61	1	1 388	192
TR	LASS	01/16/04	92	195	237	177	121	99	122	150	151	169	96	118	(1)	1 726	0
MR			138	205	216	170	133	130	145	129	160	86	0	0	(1)	1 511	1 606
JS	A&A	11/22/04	0	0	0	0	0	0	0	0	0	0	2	119		121	0
CS			123	146	242	201	141	148	134	101	172	171	120	130	1	1 830	1 930
VS	A&A	11/15/04	0	0	0	0	0	0	0	0	0	0	0	17		17	0
MS	LASS	01/05/04	153	218	181	87	0	0	0	0	0	0	0	0		639	0
EV	TAX	12/03/03	71	146	197	146	0	0	0	0	0	0	0	0		560	64
GW	LASS	02/17/04	0	103	283	147	0	0	0	0	0	0	0	0	(1)	532	0
BW			100	172	264	208	116	107	101	122	155	138	73	101	1	1 658	1 651
MZ			131	149	251	191	131	178	151	160	94	150	109	133	1	1 829	351
PZ			193	161	199	166	95	129	144	88	82	140	131	139	1	1 668	1 558
NEW/FORMER STAFF-NET			0	11	89	0	0	0	0	0	77	0	0	0		177	11 309
SUBTOTALS			2 021	3 524	4 717	2 927	2 011	2 451	2 456	2 268	2 490	2 403	2 082	2 180		31 533	29 912
ADMINISTRATION			181	433	1 536	1 040	216	233	180	258	291	319	149	69	31	4 936	3 876
TOTAL STAFF HOURS			2 202	3 957	6 253	3 967	2 227	2 684	2 636	2 526	2 781	2 722	2 231	2 249	34	36 469	33 788

Exhibit 5 (continued)

EMPLOYEE	D/O/H	JAN ACTUAL	FEB ACTUAL	MAR ACTUAL	APR ACTUAL	MAY ACTUAL	JUNE ACTUAL	JULY ACTUAL	AUG ACTUAL	SEPT ACTUAL	OCT ACTUAL	NOV ACTUAL	DEC ACTUAL	2004 ACTUAL	2003 ACTUAL
JB		167	173	233	176	81	91	93	96	135	128	111	125	1 609	1 735
SC		121	186	229	153	107	100	81	140	137	120	49	119	1 542	1 368
ME		70	149	226	131	65	106	131	124	128	101	109	126	1 467	1 435
JE		109	180	258	158	143	130	142	149	161	138	102	145	1 815	1 613
JF		83	174	253	181	92	94	135	113	180	166	95	190	1 756	1 682
BH		102	149	247	185	82	83	92	109	118	134	121	(129) (3)	1 548	1 362
JJ		85	116	204	164	91	115	135	81	118	150	66	104 (1)	1 428	1 359
RL	01/01/04	76	130	155	96	92	43	104	86	128	105	72	65 (1)	1 151	0
EL	Tax	132	210	260	156	126	149	113	111	139	164	146	156 1	1 863	1 583
LL		66	124	223	143	72	115	102	97	170	170	102	86	1 470	1 119
RN		80	144	240	186	121	158	138	183	184	157	49	151 2	1 793	1 643
SP		12	15	30	26	17	28	23	13	14	31	12	28 2	251	217
RQ		102	149	209	176	101	118	127	106	195	186	101	139 (1)	1 708	1 620
AS		109	176	230	166	92	121	108	87	128	117	115	101 (2)	1 548	1 504
RS		102	184	253	206	113	130	102	126	131	142	100	134 (1)	1 722	1 735
RW		49	39	98	72	62	50	57	60	53	35	72	72	720	619
FORMER PARTNERS		28	30	3	1	0	0	0	0	2	1	0	1	66	1 516
TOTAL PARTNER HOURS		1 493	2 328	3 351	2 376	1 457	1 631	1 683	1 681	2 121	2 045	1 422	1 871 (2)	23 457	22 110
TOTAL STAFF HOURS		2 202	3 957	6 253	3 967	2 227	2 684	2 636	2 526	2 781	2 722	2 231	2 249 34	36 469	33 788
TOTAL HOURS		3 695	6 285	9 604	6 343	3 684	4 315	4 319	4 207	4 902	4 767	3 653	4 120 32	59 926	55 898
X AVERAGE RATE/HOUR		218	218	218	218	218	218	225	225	225	225	225	225	221	212
STANDARD TIME		805 510	1 370 130	2 093 672	1 382 774	803 112	940 670	971 775	946 575	1 102 950	1 072 575	821 925	927 000	13 238 668	11 878 521
CUMUL YTD STD TIME		805 510	2 175 640	4 269 312	5 652 086	6 455 198	7 395 868	8 367 643	9 314 218	10 417 168	11 489 743	12 311 668	13 238 668		
ACTUAL TIME CHARGES-2004		854 536	1 396 506	2 069 681	1 392 461	820 249	937 338	990 955	971 367	1 194 807	1 150 585	859 022	0	12 637 507	
LESS NON BILL TIME		(9 357)	(14 583)	(8 206)	(12 334)	(1 076)	(23 857)	(20 852)	(16 198)	(13 817)	(6 035)	(21 287)	0	(147 602)	
NET WORK IN PROCESS TIME		845 179	1 381 923	2 061 475	1 380 127	819 173	913 481	970 103	955 169	1 180 990	1 144 550	837 735	0	12 489 905	
CUMUL YTD ACTUAL TIME		845 179	2 227 102	4 288 577	5 668 704	6 487 877	7 401 358	8 371 461	9 326 630	10 507 620	11 652 170	12 489 905	12 489 905		

										AVERAGE HRLY RATES					
TOTAL HOURS-2004		3 695	6 285	9 604	6 343	3 684	4 315	4 319	4 207	4 902	4 767	3 653	4 120	59 926	HOURS STD TIME
TOTAL HOURS-2003		4 422	5 890	7 811	5 847	4 116	4 046	4 173	3 467	4 987	4 543	3 155	3 440	55 897	2004 $220.92	% INCREASE-2004/2003 3.96%	7.21%	11.45%
TOTAL HOURS-2002		5 628	6 667	7 671	6 808	6 078	4 269	4 555	4 776	6 081	5 781	3 902	3 831	66 047	2003 $212.51	% INCREASE-2003/2002 8.37%	-15.37%	-8.28%
TOTAL HOURS-2001		6 183	7 222	9 672	8 551	6 380	7 103	6 744	7 387	5 341	5 807	5 052	4 952	80 394	2002 $196.09	% INCREASE-2002/2001 6.93%	-17.85%	-12.15%
TOTAL HOURS-2000		5 552	7 440	9 792	6 877	6 468	6 126	5 595	6 101	6 374	6 869	5 643	5 282	77 119	2001 $183.38	% INCREASE-2001/2000 7.97%	4.25%	12.56%
TOTAL HOURS-1999		4 515	6 325	9 147	7 386	4 626	5 162	4 183	4 548	5 521	5 370	4 189	4 827	65 799	2000 $169.83	% INCREASE-2000/1999 4.14%	17.20%	22.06%
TOTAL HOURS-1998		3 979	5 296	6 893	5 726	4 137	3 878	4 265	3 985	4 925	4 948	4 361	3 786	56 179	1999 $163.08	% INCREASE-1999/1998 0.76%	17.12%	18.02%
TOTAL HOURS-1997		3 879	4 536	5 922	4 976	3 567	3 741	3 826	3 787	4 645	4 408	3 037	3 485	49 809	1998 $161.85	% INCREASE-1998/1997 5.40%	12.79%	18.88%
TOTAL HOURS-1996		3 549	4 978	6 404	5 257	3 363	3 025	3 234	3 449	4 223	4 867	3 143	3 351	48 843	1997 $153.56	% INCREASE-1997/1996 7.89%	1.98%	10.03%
TOTAL HOURS-1995		3 304	4 832	6 291	5 026	3 368	3 557	3 226	3 963	4 082	4 680	3 272	3 276	48 877	1996 $142.33	% INCREASE-1996/1995 5.36%	-0.07%	5.29%
															1995 $135.09	AVERAGE 5.64%		

NEW/FORMER STAFF/PTR		28	41	92	1	0	0	0	0	79	1	0	1		
		KKB-28	KKB-30	SJL-3	SJL1					SJL-2	SJL-1		SJL-1		
			RW-11	CL-89						S-77					

Exhibit 6

Perleson Weiner expenses as a % of Standard time charges
december 31, 2004

		YTD 2004	YTD 2003	% diff	YTD 2004	YTD 2003	% Diff
Total Expenses		781 703.29	697 629.84		8 289 560.91	7 473 206.29	
% to STC		76.44	83.39	-6.95	61.35	62.91	-1.57
Professional Compensation	a	360 890.66	312 689.61		3 713 930.34	3 674 228.04	
% to STC		35.29	37.38	-2.09	27.49	30.93	-3.45
Other Compensation	b	98 029.66	96 018.77		940 822.17	927 942.52	
% to STC		9.59	11.48	-1.89	6.96	7.81	-0.85
Other Expenses		322 782.97	288 921.46		3 634 808.40	2 871 035.73	
% to STC		31.56	34.54	-2.97	26.9	24.17	2.73
STC		1 022 620.05	836 597.25		13 512 524.85	11 878 520.75	

Exhibit 7

Benchmarking Data Used Internally By PW

Source: "2006 Practice Management Survey", Exhibit7-27, International Group of Accounting Firms (IGAF) pp. 79-81

	YOUR FIRM	AVERAGE OF FIRMS > $8 000 000	New York, NY % OF DIFFERENCE
Population of Practice Area	21 000 000	7 022 675	67%
Number of Personnel:			
Total	57	180	-216%
Equity partners/principals	4	13	-215%
Non-Equity partners/principals	11	8	26%
Professionals 0-1 years	5	25	-394%
Professionals 2-4 years	4	27	-581%
Professionals 5-6 years	1	16	-1 512%
Professionals over 6 years	13	43	-229%
Para-professionals	2	17	-746%
Clericals, Non-professionals	17	37	-118%
Partner/Staff Ratio	3	8	-183%
Gross annual fees-current year for accounting firms	17 580 286	32 914 757	-87%
% of growth	30%	13%	57%
Net annual fees-current year for accounting firms	16 040 795	25 787 594	-61%
% of growth	27%	18%	34%
Charged hours-current year	72 771	190 655	-162%
% of growth	21%	11%	49%
Gross annual fees-as of June 30 for accounting firms	20 809 695	35 918 042	-73%
Net annual fees-as of June 30 for accounting firms	18 312 532	28 740 547	-57%
Charged hours-as of June 30 for accounting firms	81 921	202 647	-147%
Average fees per full-time person	281 417	148 045	47%
Average per partner compensation (equity)	1 263 861	512 317	59%
Average per partner compensation (non-equity)	319 114	234 191	27%
Average per partner compensation (equity and non-equity)	571 046	402 710	29%
Annual fees controlled by a single partner:			
highest%	32	16	50%
lowest%	1	2	-144%
Annual per person compensation for non-technical staff:			
firm administrator	123 850	119 320	4%
marketing director		87 696	—
Para-professionals	46 932	40 142	14%
Clericals, Non-professionals	48 728	43 224	11%
Annual per person compensation for A&A technical staff:			
0-1 years experience	48 327	46 314	4%
2-4 years experience	57 118	54 893	4%
5-6 years experience	53 934	67 606	-25%
over 6 years experience	87 767	89 003	-1%
Annual per person compensation for TAX technical staff:			
0-1 years experience		47 013	—
2-4 years experience	56 934	54 553	4%
5-6 years experience	61 111	69 277	-13%
over 6 years experience	93 588	94 883	-1%

Exhibit 7

Benchmarking Data Used Internally By PW (continued)

	YOUR FIRM	AVERAGE OF FIRMS > $8 000 000	% OF DIFFERENCE
Annral per person compensation for MCS technical staff:			
0-1 years experience		46 409	—
2-4 years experience		60 635	—
5-6 years experience		73 404	—
over 6 years experience		105 478	—
Average starting salary for professionals (less than 1 year experience)	45 000	41 918	7%
Hourly billing rate:			
for a $50 000 per year professional employee	120	116	3%
for a $75 000 per year professional employee	180	170	6%
for a $100 000 per year professional employee	240	222	7%
Net revenue per charged hour	220	141	36%
Standby houry billing rate			
Partners/principals	368	307	17%
Professionals 0-1 years	120	105	12%
Professionals 2-4 years	153	129	16%
Professionals 5-6 years	165	159	4%
Professionals over 6 years	258	211	18%
Para-professionals	130	87	33%
Clericals, Non-professionals	100	74	26%
Percentage of annual fees realized at standard rates	91	83	8%
Average net billing rate per hour	220	141	36%
Average realized hourly billing rate for partners and principals	335	240	28%
Pertcentage of rate increases within the last fiscal year:			
Parners/principals	3	4	-47%
Professionals 0-1 years	8	8	6%
Professionals 2-4 years	8	7	9%
Professionals 5-6 years		7	—
Professionals over 6 years	6	6	1%
Para-professionals	4	6	-44%
Clericals, Non-professionals		5	—
Annual average chargeable hours per firm (based on total professionals)	1 801	1 475	18%
Average chargeable hours worked per person:			
Partners/principals	1 575	1 034	34%
Professionals 0-1 years	1 724	1 420	18%
Professionals 2-4 years	1 821	1 507	17%
Professionals 5-6 years	1 819	1 481	19%
Professionals over 6 years	1 823	1 355	26%
Para-professionals	1 251	1 325	-6%
Clericals, Non-professionals	277	278	0%
Condensed Balance Sheet as of June 30-ASSETS (% of total):			
Cash	22%	12%	46%
Accounts Receivable-billed	53%	37%	30%
Work-in-process	18%	21%	-15%
Other current assets	3%	4%	-36%
Furniture, equipment	2%	7%	-261%
Other assets	2%	7%	-312%

Exhibit 7

Benchmarking Data Used Internally By PW (continued)

	YOUR FIRM	AVERAGE OF FIRMS > $8 000 000	% OF DIFFERENCE
Condensed Balance Sheet as of June 30-LIAB./EQUITY (% of total):			
Accounts payable	1%	2%	-117%
Accrued expenses	1%	12%	-843%
Notes payable	0%	7%	—
Other liabilities	6%	4%	33%
Equity	92%	63%	31%
Accounts Receivable (based on monthly avg. as a percentage of sales)	25%	16%	36%
Work-in-process (based on monthly avg. as a percentage of sales)	10%	11%	-4%
Accounts Receivable (% of total receivables)			
current	18	43	-138%
31-60 days	31	20	34%
61-90 days	6	11	-87%
over 90 days	45	26	43%
Work-in-process aging schedule (% of total WIP):			
current	80	49	39%
31-60 days	15	21	-43%
61-90 days	5	12	-145%
over 90 days	0	17	—
Breakdown of annual fees earned (as a percentage of sales):			
Professional staff salaries (excluding partners)	16%	31%	-96%
Personnel Expenses	8%	8%	8%
Other salaries (excluding partners)	7%	6%	3%
Outside services	2%	2%	27%
Marketing expenses	3%	2%	28%
Facilities expenses	5%	6%	-20%
Equity Partners' salaries	4%	13%	-194%
Non-Equity Partners' salaries	10%	4%	54%
Equity Partners' P/R Taxes	1%	0.18%	65%
Non-Equity Partners' P/R Taxes	1%	0.11%	83%
Income taxes (corporate & state)	1%	0.20%	81%
Other operational expenses	5%	11%	-100%
Amount remaining for distribution to equity partners	27%	15%	43%
Amount remaining for distribution to non-equity partners	11%	2%	82%
Total-in dollars	16 040 795	25 787 594	-61%
Average dollar amount received per partner for:			
retirement benefits	10 000	11 015	-10%
for "automobile perks"		1 962	—
for "club membership perks"	2 022	1 207	40%
for "insurance perks"	3 343	6 306	-89%
Amount spent on:			
A&A CPE (% of sales)	0.43%	0.42%	3%
TAX CPE (% of sales)	0.14%	0.19%	-39%
MCS CPE (% of sales)	0.00%	0.13%	—

Exhibit 8

PW Incentive Pay System

To motivate and reward its employees, PW offers an incentive pay system that provides bonuses to its professional employees including staff, managers, and equity and non-equity partners.

Staff (including managers) bonuses are based on billable hours, but the dollar amount distributed and individual bonus amounts are subjectively determined each year. In addition to these subjective bonuses, staff members who bring clients to PW get 10% of all fees earned on the clients that they originate. Staff members who have earned the rank of manager receive 50% of the profits on jobs performed for clients that they bring to the firm rather than the 10% of revenues that lower level staff members receive. To date, payments under this incentive system have been small.

A partner's total compensation package is more complex and includes base pay, a bonus, commissions and profit sharing. Partners participate in establishing his/her own salary for the year, based on a multiple of his/her standard billing rate. All member standard hourly rates are subject to approval by the policy committee.

In exchange for his/her salary, each member is expected to provide the firm exemplary results.

Partners' responsibilities include, among other things:

- 1 500 chargeable hours
- Effective management of the client relationship including billing and collection of fees
- Staff training, mentoring and evaluations
- Active participation in firm and department meetings, events, committees, programs, CPE, recruiting, appropriate participation in professional society committees
- Client development and retention
- Firm recordkeeping/tax compliance

Five factors go into a partner's bonus calculation. The table hows the details of that system.

Definitions for bonus system	Partner's Realization Rate = Amounts realized or realizable from partner originated clients/Standard time charges to partner originated clients
	Partner's Profit Rate = Firm's gross profit rate- (1partner's realization rate)
Bonus Elements	(all rounded to the nearest $1 000 except for amounts related to billable hours)
(1) On New Business	1/3 * (Standard time charges to a partner's originated clients this year minus standard time charges to that partner's prior-year originated clients) * Partner's Profit Rate
(2) Realization from originated clients	If partner's originated client standard billing is $250 000 or more, then, if a Partner's Realization Rate greater than 88%, add $5 000; greater than 92%, add an additional $5 000. Additional amounts possible
(3) For Service to clients originated by others	(Standard time charges billed to clients that were originated by other partners) * 1%
(4) Billable Hours	If partner bills more than 1 500 hours, then [(Hours billed – 1 500) /1 500] * Salary
(5) Subjective portion	Paid for duties/responsibilities taken on outside normal duties/responsibilities. Total pool cannot exceed 50% of the bonus quantified in 1-4 above. Individual bonuses within this pool are not limited beyond the constraint that, in total, they do not exceed the pool limit

Exhibit 8
PW Incentive Pay System (continued)

To illustrate the bonus system, assume the following facts about a sample partner with a salary of $155 000:
1. Originated business at standard time charges of $500 000 compared to $420 000 last year.
2. Actual realization rate 93%, not the highest in the firm.
3. Service to clients originated by others was $250 000.
4. Billed 1575 hours.
5. Was given a subjective bonus due to developing a new training program.
6. The company's gross profit rate was 62%.
7. The subjective portion of the bonus pool for all partners (sum of amounts paid in items 1-4 across all partners times 50%) exceeded $100 000.

Bonus Elements	
(1) On New Business	$1/3 * (\$500\,000 - \$420\,000) * [62\% - (100 - 93\%)] = \$14\,667$ yields $15 000
(2) Realization from originated clients	Charges above $250 000 so, 93% yields $10 000
(3) For Service to clients originated by others	($250 000 * 1%) = 2 500, so $3 000
(4) Billable Hours	[(1 575 - 1 500)/1 500] * $155 000 = $7 750
(5) Subjective portion	$30 000
(6) Total Bonus	$15 000 + 10 000 + 3 000 + 7 750 + 30 000 = $65 750

Equity partners also receive profit sharing based on their equity share and the firm's net profit, while non-equity partners earn commissions.

The table below provides details on the total pay to active partners (equity and nonequity) in 2004.

Item	Average	High	Low
Base Salary	$144 922	$177 083	$117 708
Bonus	$41 773	$150 000	0
Commissions	$110 311	$263 176	$20 796
Profit Sharing	$249 350	$1 199 019	$3 752
Total Compensation	$546 356	$1 789 278	$142 256

Exhibit 9

Trends in Performance Management

ACTIVITY BASED COSTING/MANAGEMENT. In the past decade, many service organizations have adopted ABC/M as a method of standardizing processes and determining profitability of service offerings.

BALANCED SCORECARD APPROACHES. Regular analysis of critical factors in service firms can be as effective as it is in any other business sphere. KPIs developed on the basis of firm structure, operating goals and strategies provide a purposeful direction. Development of staff is an important learning and growth dimension of a scorecard approach.

KPI'S AROUND WORTH OF EMPLOYEES. Service organizations are focusing on the individual service employees and focusing on metrics such as:
- average revenues/full time equivalent employees & average wages/full time equivalent employees (the former should be at least twice the latter.
- average age in months of skills earned (when this climbs, skills are getting old, dated and less marketable)
- Billable time (best in class in the low 90% range)
- Gross margin percentages (used by some software service organizations and combines maintenance and consulting revenue less providers' wages)

LEAN MANUFACTURING & BENCHMARKING. Benchmark against service firms with similar transformations processes and degree of client/customer involvement; define performance metrics appropriate for organization and perform cost analysis to determine main sources of cost variance. Lean methods involve controlling the variance within service delivery by managing demand, standardizing transformation, and allocating appropriate resources to each task.

公司治理与职业道德
Corporate Governance & Ethics

Ace 肥料公司：
合乎道德规范的成本分配和定价方法

Jerry Kreuze
Western Michigan University

Sheldon Langsam
Western Michigan University

简介

阿比·康罗伊（Abby Conroy），注册管理会计师（CMA），在大学本科时主修会计和集成供应链管理（Integrated Supply Management），其后又在一家著名的商学院获得工商管理硕士学位（MBA），因而被 Ace 肥料公司聘用。她在 Ace 肥料公司已任职三年，受到大家的尊敬。她工作勤奋、细心，在很短的时间内接连得到提拔。现在，阿比担任制造部的助理经理，主要负责特殊客户的订单。在制造特殊订货中，让客户满意已成为 Ace 业务中重要的盈利要素。Ace 主要经营草坪和花园用的肥料；这些特殊的订货对其主营业务属于补充性质、有时甚至毫不相干。Ace 肥料公司在竞争剧烈的市场上积极争取特殊订单，靠的是保证质量和及时交货而不是降低价格。因能不断满足客户预期，Ace 已确立了其在行业中的领导地位。

通过生产特殊订单满足客户需要是由 Ace 的创始人詹姆斯·斯特格因克（James Stegink）和诺曼·莱特（Norman Light）提出的，他们都是学设计出身，被很多人奉为"思想家"，现在二人已退出管理一线，只做 Ace 的所有者。Ace 肥料公司的制造业务由 CEO（Chief Operating Officer）汤姆·布伦南（Tom Brennen）主持。阿比的顶头上司、制造部的经理则为乔治·斯米利（George Smilee）。

作为助理经理，阿比负责从设计、开价、制造到最终向特殊订单客户发货的一系列流程。所有的特殊订单合同从起草到最后完成都由她全权负责。这些订单合同先由乔治·斯米利审阅草签，然后递交给汤姆·布伦南最后批准和签字。

Ace 肥料公司为所有的特殊订单开具发票，都按一套规定的程式办理。这些特殊订单在发票上的价格都必须比成本高出 80%（只有当取得汤姆·布伦南本人的特别授权，才可以有所松动）。由于市场的需求高于公司的产能，因而汤姆·布伦南极少同意不按这一程式办事。虽然 Ace 的材料存货经常保持充裕，但偶然也会因这些特殊订单需要阿比专门为该订单而定购材料。这些材料都是按最经济的订购量购得的。即便有时购入的专用材料有所剩余，特殊订单也要为全部材料买单。顾客可以选择取走它们，但实际上所有客户都不会再要这些剩余材料。这种做法也偶有例外，有时前面一份用该材料的订单已被签订，却有另外一份经过确认的订单需要耗用那些多余的材料。在这种情况下，汤姆·布伦南坚持认为，两份订单共用的材料的成本，应该按比例分配计入各自订单，以示公允。

阿比尤其喜欢 Ace 肥料公司的家庭氛围。她曾多次受乔治·斯米利之邀参加他的家族聚会。乔治和他的家族成员关系亲近，他们大部分都住在半径 10 英里的范围内。乔治和他的两个兄弟会定期把家人召来聚会。自从乔治的父亲去年突然逝世以来，乔治的家族成员就变得非常亲近。他的两个兄弟都在不同的行业中独立经营，Ace 公司有时也接受他们的特殊订单。

阿比在计算特殊订单的成本上已经很熟练了。她完全了解一份特殊订单所包含的多项成本，包括直接和间接成本。阿比知道必须把所有这些成本都包括进去，才能确定一项订单的成本。

直接成本与间接成本

直接成本是能够简单而且容易地计入于某一特殊订单的成本。对阿比来说，大部分的直接成本是直接材料和直接人工。直接材料就是组成产品实体的各种材料。直接人工有时称为"接触人工（touch labor）"，包括了在制造过程中直接"接触"产品的劳动者的成本。由于机械故障而停止工作的一般生产工人的工资，记作间接成本。

直接成本通常是变动性的，随产量的变动而变动。因此，直接材料和直接人工通常都属于变动成本。但对特殊订单来说，有些直接成本可能是固定性的。与专门生产一种产品的设备有关的成本（包括折旧、电力和日常维修），都是这一产品的直接成本。

间接成本不能简单容易地计入某项特殊订单。这些成本都属于共同成本，其所以称为共同成本，是因为它是因生产多项特殊订单所需要的产品而引起的费用。对通用设备的维修成本、管理人员的薪酬和公用事业费，是生产所有特殊订货所需要的直接成本，但对某一项特殊订单而言，却是该特殊订单的间接成本。此外，一般的生产成本（包括财产税、保险、草坪护理、员工食堂成本和生产中耗用的零星物料）属于间接成本，需要适当地分配计入所生产的各项特殊订单。

间接成本的分配

阿比可以用全公司统一的间接费用分配率，把间接成本分配计入各项特殊订单。这些间接成本往往是采用选定的适用于全公司产品或服务的一项分配基础来分配的。有许多公司把直接工时或机器工时确定为间接费用的分配基础。但阿比认为这种分配方法很麻烦，因为要把间接费用追踪计入各项特殊订单，碍难实现。

还有一种做法是，阿比可以采用作业成本法（ABC）将间接成本分配到各项特殊订单上。与仅应用全公司通用的分配率把间接成本分配到各项特殊订单上去的做法相比，作业成本法承认不是所有的成本都是由产量驱动的。借助作业成本法，可以确定从哪些订单和客户中盈利最多，在哪些作业和流程会产生增值，应该在哪些方面作出改进。阿比特别喜欢采用作业成本法把间接成本分配到各项特殊订单。

BREELAND 有限公司的特殊订单

成本估计。阿比从 Breedland 有限公司收到了一份订单，要求生产一种独特的、化学性质不太稳定的洗涤溶剂，应用于该公司的特殊钢板生产过程。Ace 肥料公司是全国仅有的五六家能够生产这种溶剂的企业之一。该客户需要的这种溶剂数量有限，对这笔订单之后是否还会有更多的订货毫无把握。为了生产这种溶剂，阿比必须购买一种称作 XO-1600 的特殊酸性物质。而那种物质只有 50 加仑桶装的，每桶 80 000 美元。然而，这笔订单只需 40 加仑的量。开桶之后，XO-1600 只能存放 20 天。20 天之后，这种物质变得非常不稳定，只能丢弃了。由于这种物质的化学性质，弃置时还必须经过特殊的处理。阿比估计弃置成本为 10 000 美元。阿比还查看了所有已经收到的订单，确定在未来的 20 天之内没有需要 XO-1600 的。经过向 Breedland 有限公司代表询问，他们对于把用剩下的这种物质转交给他们并不感兴趣。

阿比还确定了与完成该项溶剂特殊订单有关的其他成本与作业如下：

1. 直接材料（除 XO-1600 之外）：20 000 美元。
2. 直接人工：30 000 美元。
3. 该项特殊订货的数量：4 000 加仑。
4. 生产批量数：4（由于搅拌工序的制约）。

在开始采用 ABC 计算成本时，阿比对五项作业层次得出以下的成本数字：

a. 单位层次的作业：每单位 40 美元。
b. 批量层次的作业：每批 5 000 美元。
c. 产品层次的作业：每项产品 80 000 美元。
d. 顾客层次的作业：每个客户 30 000 美元。
e. 机构维持作业：直接材料、直接人工、单位层次作业成本和批量层次作业成本合计数的 100%。

到星期五下班时，阿比为这一特殊订单作出了下述的成本估计和定价数字：

直接材料：	
XO-1600 之外的材料	$ 20 000
XO-1600：购入成本	80 000
处置成本	10 000
直接人工	30 000
单位层次作业的成本（$40 * 4 000 加仑）	160 000
批量层次作业的成本（$5 000 * 4 批）	20 000
产品层次作业的成本	80 000
顾客层次作业的成本	30 000
机构维持层次作业的成本	
（20 000 + 80 000 + 10 000 + 30 000 + 160 000 + 20 000）	320 000
Breedland 有限公司这份特殊订单的总成本	$750 000
在成本基础上的利润加成（$750 000/0.80）	900 000
Breeland 有限公司这份特殊订单的定价	$1 650 000

  阿比跟乔治·斯米利讨论了上述的成本估计和报价的建议，后者初步表示同意。阿比完全相信 Breeland 有限公司会接受这个报价。现在需要的只是汤姆·布伦南的正式批准和签字了。在阿比和乔治离开公司去度周末之前，他们俩都一致认为 Breeland 的这份特殊订单将在下周得到批准。对生产和完工日期的细节将在获得批准之后定夺。

  周末的家族聚会。斯米利家族安排在星期六傍晚聚会，乔治通知阿比说，他很期盼她也能参加这次聚会。可惜阿比事先已有了别的安排，不能参加。

  对乔治的家族来讲，这是一次很特殊的聚会。因为斯米利老奶奶刚度过八秩寿辰。当天的气候绝佳，宜于这样的聚会。乔治和他的家族在一起，觉得非常惬意。在进餐和笑谈之后，乔治和他的两个兄弟静坐下来，把有关这项溶剂的特殊订单的细节告诉他们。当他的一位兄弟乔希（Josh）听到乔治提到 XO-1600 这种化工产品时，显得很感兴趣。原来他最近刚接触到一位需要某种喷射防锈剂的客户，这种防锈剂需要用 XO-1600 做原料。那项订单需要耗用 8 加仑，而乔希还认为他可以说服那位客户增加订货到耗用 10 加仑。乔希走开去给那位客户打电话，把那笔订货确定了下来。乔希笑容满面地把此事通知了乔治。他们俩约定在下星期内把这件事定下来。

  乔希对该项目的定价决策。星期一的一早，乔治来到阿比的办公室，把周末与乔希对这个项目的进展的情况告诉了她。他说明乔希有意购买剩余的 10 加仑 XO-1600。乔治指出，这项协议的细节将在本周内商定。阿比稍微停顿了一下，寻思此事的细节，她想起了上周五她在把该项目开价的事告诉乔治时，曾提及那剩余未用的 10 加仑将被弃置，因而对该订单所开的价格将包括购买 XO-1600 的全部成本再加上强制性弃置所需要的费用。阿比建议说，给 Breeland 公司的报价，不妨稍微推迟一些；如果

Breeland 同意推迟，则协议草稿可以等到乔希的订单确定下来后作一修改。

然而，乔治对于推迟起草协议的建议表现非常冷淡，这使阿比感到惊讶。乔治争辩说，就今天来讲，并没有哪一项订单确实需要那剩余的10加仑 XO－1600。事实上，到周末乔治与乔希再次晤面，核实上周末提到的建议时，才能把那份订单确定下来。乔治坚持该项特殊订单应该按现在所开的价格转交给汤姆·布伦南签署；等收到乔希的正式订单时，对他那份订单的定价应该仅仅包括10加仑 XO－1600 的成本与在该成本基础上的利润加成数之和。乔治很得意地把此事看作一笔意外横财，因为这样一来，这10加仑 XO－1600 可以重复计入账单，而且也不会发生账单上列及的处置成本。这一意外的好事，使公司的利润平白地增加了 93 600 美元（10加仑 XO－1600 的价值 16 000 美元，节省的处置费用 10 000 美元，机构维持作业的成本 26 000 美元，以及10加仑 XO－1600 成本基础上的加成利润 41 600 美元）。

阿比完全明白她已经在一个星期之前起草了对 Breeland 公司的订单的报价，而乔治·斯米利对此也已表示同意。由于迄今为止对剩余部分的 XO－1600 还不存在经过确认的订单，按公司的政策，阿比理应把购入成本加上处置费用全部列入成本估计数内。但是阿比现在已经知悉，在剩余的10加仑 XO－1600 的20天弃置期内，完全有可能获得订单。根据这一新的情况，阿比认为她应该修改并推迟对 Breeland 公司特殊订单的报价。

阿比认同的做法是，如果乔希的订单在20天内能够获得确认，她就应向 Breeland 有限公司递交一份修改后的报价。这份报价只应包括40加仑 XO－1600，去掉弃置费用，修改机构维持费用和按成本加成的利润数。然后，把多余的10加仑 XO－1600 售给乔米。与乔治的意见相反，阿比认为在开给乔希的账单中不但应该包含按成本加成的利润数，还应该加上适量的机构维持费用。但这样定价，会使该项特殊订单的毛利减少，并且使公司达不到它的月度利润目标。看来，乔治·斯米利对他的决定相当固执，并已指示阿比起草一个给乔希的报价，这份报价应该与 Breeland 的特殊订单毫无干系。乔治将在星期三一早就与汤姆·布伦南晤面，取得这特殊订单的签字认可。阿比正在考量她应该采取什么行动。她计划部分地按照管理会计师协会的"职业道德行为公告（Statement of Ethical Professional Practice）"（见表1）的指引行事。阿比对乔治为什么不按同一个指引行事，觉得诧异。她想，如果乔治也是一位注册管理会计师（Certified Management Accountant, CMA），他是会持类似立场的。

要求回答的问题

1. 阿比在乔治的周末家族聚会**之前**所计算的 Breeland 有限公司特殊订单的成本是否正确？如果不正确，其成本估算和/或者报价的错误何在？

2. 你认为对这项特殊订单所作的成本估算，谁做得对——是乔治·斯米利还是阿比·康罗伊？也就是说，乔治与乔希的谈话是否应该对阿比所作的有关 Breeland 有限公司特殊订单的成本估计产生影响？请说明你的理由。

3. 在确定 Breeland 有限公司特殊订单的成本中，是否涉及任何职业道德问题？如果涉及，则问题何在？阿比应该如何来解决这些冲突？阿比是不是应该为新发生的情况直接去找汤姆·布伦南？阿比可以怎样应用管理会计协会的职业道德行为公告来作为她行动的指引？

4. 如果阿比准备修改她为 Breeland 有限公司特殊订单原先所作的成本估计，把乔希购买剩余的 10 加仑 XO - 1600 这个因素考虑进去，则她得出的定价将是多少？这对 Ace 肥料公司的利润会产生什么影响？

表 1
管理会计师协会《职业道德行为公告》①

管理会计和财务管理从业人员应该道德地行事。对职业道德行为的承诺,包括了表述我们的价值观的基本原则,以及指导我们的行为的具体准则。

原则
管理会计师协会的基本道德原则包括:诚实、正直、客观和责任。从业人员应该遵守这些原则并鼓励组织中的其他人共同遵守。

准则
如果从业人员未能遵守下列准则,就会受到惩戒。

I. 胜任能力
每一名从业人员都必须遵守以下责任:
1. 不断拓展知识与提升技能,保持适当水平的专业知识。
2. 遵照相关法律、法规和技术标准履行职责。
3. 提供准确、清晰、简要和及时的决策支持信息及建议。
4. 确认并报告那些可能会对一项活动的合理判断或成功执行造成妨碍的专业局限或其他约束。

II. 保密
每一名从业人员都必须遵守以下责任:
1. 对获取的信息保密,除非经授权披露或者法律要求披露。
2. 告知所有相关方要正确使用保密信息。监督下属的活动,以确保其遵照执行。
3. 不得利用保密信息获取不道德的或非法的利益。

III. 正直
每个从业人员都必须遵守以下责任
1. 缓解现实利益冲突。同商业伙伴定期沟通,以避免利益冲突显化。告知所有利益相关方一切潜在利益冲突。
2. 不从事任何可能会妨碍遵照道德规范履行职责的行为。
3. 不从事或支持任何有损职业声誉的活动。

IV. 诚信
每个从业人员都必须遵守以下责任:
1. 公允、客观地报告信息。
2. 披露所有那些人们合理地认为会影响目标使用者对报告、分析或建议的理解的相关信息。
3. 遵照组织政策或适用法律披露在信息、及时性、流程或内部控制上的延误或缺陷。

道德冲突的解决之道
在应用道德行为准则公告时,管理会计和财务管理从业人员可能会遇到辨识不道德行为或解决道德冲突的问题。在面对道德问题时,从业人员应该遵循组织关于如何解决此类冲突的既定政策。如果组织的政策无法解决道德冲突,从业人员就应该考虑下列行动:
1. 与直接上司讨论所遇到的问题,但直接上司也牵涉其中时除外。如果牵涉直接上司,就应该呈报更高级别的管理人员。如果未得到满意的答复,也应该呈报更高级别的管理人员。如果直接上司是首席执行官(CEO)或同等职务的人,那么拥有审查、复核权限的机构就是审计委员会、执行委员会、董事会、理事会或股东等。如果未牵涉直接上司,那么只有在通知直接上司之后才能联系更高级别的管理人员。从业人员不宜将道德冲突情况报告给组织之外的权力机构或个人,除非其认为该状况明显触犯了法律。
2. 同管理会计师协会的道德顾问或其他处于中立位置的顾问进行机密地讨论,明晰相关道德问题,从而更好地理解可能采取的行动。
3. 向自己的律师咨询与道德冲突相关的法律义务和权利。

---

① IMA Statement of Ethical Professional Practice,本公告由刘霄仑译、王立彦审校。谨致谢。——译者

Ace Fertilizer Company:
Ethical Cost Allocations and Price Determination

Jerry Kreuze
Western Michigan University

Sheldon Langsam
Western Michigan University

INTRODUCTION

Having a double undergraduate major in Accounting and Integrated Supply Management and an MBA from a renowned business school qualified Abby Conroy, CMA, for her position at Ace Fertilizer Company. She has been employed at Ace Fertilizer for the past three years, and is a highly respected employee. Her hard work and dedication to detail resulted in a series of rapid promotions. Currently, Abby is assistant director of manufacturing and is primarily responsible for special customer orders. Meeting the needs of customers in manufacturing special orders has become a very profitable portion of Ace's operations. These special orders sometimes complement, but more frequently are totally unrelated to, Ace's principal business of producing lawn and garden fertilizer. Ace Fertilizer actively seeks special orders in a highly competitive market, driven more by quality and on-time completion than price. Ace has established itself as an industry leader by consistently meeting customer expectations.

The ability to meet the needs of customers through manufacturing special orders was the concept of Ace's founders, and now passive owners, James Stegink and Norman Light. Both have engineering degrees and are considered by many to be quite the "tinkerers." Abby reports to the director of manufacturing, George Smilee. The manufacturing operations are managed by Tom Brennen, the chief operating officer of Ace Fertilizer.

In her role as assistant director, Abby is responsible for the design, bidding, manufacture, and ultimate delivery of special orders to customers. Abby develops and completes all special order contracts. George Smilee initials his approval of these contracts. Completed, initialed customer contracts then proceed to Tom Brennen for his ultimate approval and signature.

All special orders at Ace Fertilizer follow a prescribed billing formula. These special orders, unless specific authorization is obtained from Tom Brennen himself, must be billed at 80 percent over the cost of the order. Tom Brennen rarely allows exceptions to this formula, as sufficient demand exists for Ace Fertilizer's operating capacity. Although Ace maintains an extensive raw materials inventory, on occasion these special orders require Abby to order materials specific to the order. These materials are acquired in the most economical order quantity available. The special order is billed for the entire cost of the specially ordered materials, even if unused quantities remain. Customers are given the option of keeping these unused materials, but virtually all companies decline. An exception to that policy is only allowed when another confirmed order exists when the initial order is signed that requires the use of those excess materials. In that case, Tom Brennen, as a matter of fairness, insists that the cost of those materials be prorated among special orders.

What Abby likes especially about Ace Fertilizer is its family atmosphere. In fact, Abby has been invited several times by George Smilee to his family get-togethers. George is close to his family, most of whom live within a 10-mile radius. The family has regular get-togethers attended faithfully by George and his two brothers. George's family has become very close since the untimely death of George's father last year. His brothers are all self-employed in a variety of businesses, and on occasion Ace Fertilizer does special orders for them.

Abby has become very skilled at computing the cost of special orders. She fully realizes a special order includes a variety of costs, including direct and indirect costs. Abby knows that proper project cost determination mandates inclusion of all of these costs.

DIRECT COSTS VS. INDIRECT COSTS

Direct costs are those costs that are easily and conveniently assigned to a special order. Major direct costs for Abby are direct materials and direct labor. Direct materials are those materials that become an integral part of the finished product. Direct labor, sometimes referred to as "touch labor," includes the cost of those laborers who directly touch the product while it is being made. The wages of general production employees who are idled due to machine breakdown are classified as indirect costs.

Direct costs are usually variable and change as production volumes change. Thus, direct materials and direct labor are typically variable costs. For special orders, some direct costs can be fixed, however. The costs (depreciation, electricity, and routine maintenance) associated with a machine dedicated to one product are direct costs of that product.

Indirect costs cannot be easily and conveniently assigned to a special order. Rather, these costs are common costs, in that they are incurred to produce a variety of special orders. Maintenance costs of general purpose equipment, the supervisor's salary, and utilities are direct costs needed to produce special orders in general, but are indirect costs for a particular special order. Moreover, general production costs, including property taxes, insurance, lawn care, cafeteria costs, and miscellaneous supplies consumed in production are indirect costs properly allocated to special orders manufactured.

ALLOCATION OF INDIRECT COSTS

Abby could allocate indirect costs to special orders using a company-wide overhead rate. Frequently, these indirect costs are allocated by selecting an allocation base common to all of the company's products or services. Many companies base overhead allocations on direct labor-hours or machine-hours. Abby realizes, however, that this allocation process is troublesome as it is impractical to trace these costs to specific orders.

Alternatively, Abby could allocate indirect costs to special orders using activity-based costing (ABC). Rather than simply allocating indirect costs among special orders using a company-wide rate, ABC acknowledges that not all costs are driven by output volume. As a result, information is available to help determine the most profitable special orders and customers, which activities and processes are value-added, and where efforts toward improvements can be made. Abby especially likes this latter approach when assigning indirect costs to special orders.

BREELAND LTD. SPECIAL ORDER

The Cost Estimate. Abby has received a request from Breeland Ltd. to produce a unique, somewhat unstable cleaning solvent for use in Breeland's specialized steel plating process. Ace Fertilizer is one of only a handful of companies across the country capable of producing such a solvent. The customer has a limited need for this solvent, and does not foresee requiring quantities of it beyond this special order. To produce this substance, Abby must purchase a specialty acid ingredient known as XO-1600. That substance is only available in 50-gallon drums. The 50-gallon drum costs $80 000. This special order will only require the use of 40 gallons. XO-1600 has a shelf life of only 20 days after the drum is opened. After those 20 days, the substance becomes very unstable and must be discarded. Because of the chemical nature of the substance, it requires proper disposal. Abby estimates the cost of this disposal at $10 000. Abby has checked existing, confirmed orders and found none that will require XO-1600 within the next 20 days. Inquiries with representatives at Breeland Ltd. reveal that they have no interest in taking possession of the unused gallons.

Abby also determines that several other costs and activities will be associated with the completion of the special order for the solvent. These costs and activities are:

1. Direct materials, in addition to XO-1600: $20 000.
2. Direct labor: $30 000.
3. Unit measure of special order: 4 000 gallons.
4. Number of batches for production: 4 (due to constraints during the mixing process).

Using ABC at the beginning of the costing period, Abby arrives at the following costs for each of the five activity measures:

a. Unit-level activities: $40 per unit of measure.
b. Batch-level activities: $5 000 per batch.
c. Product-level activities: $80 000 per project.
d. Customer-related activities: $30 000 per customer.
e. Organization-sustaining activities: 100% of direct materials, direct labor, unit-level activity costs, and batch-level activity costs.

Toward the end of the day on Friday, Abby works up the following cost estimate and price determination for this special order:

Direct materials:	
Non-XO-1600	$ 20 000
XO-1600: Purchase cost	80 000
Disposal cost	10 000
Direct labor	30 000
Unit-level activity cost ($40 * 4 000 gallons)	160 000
Batch-level activity cost ($5 000 * 4 batches)	20 000
Product-level activity cost	80 000
Customer-level activity cost	30 000
Organization-sustaining level activity cost	
(20 000 +80 000 +10 000 +30 000 +160 000 +20 000)	320 000
Total costs of Breeland Ltd. special order	$ 750 000
Markup on cost ($750 000/.80)	900 000
Total Price Determination for Breeland Ltd. Order	$1 650 000

Abby discusses this estimate and price quote with George Smilee, who expresses preliminary approval. Abby fully believes that Breeland Ltd. will accept this price quote. All that is needed now is Tom Brennen's formal approval and signature. Before Abby and George leave for the weekend, they both concur that it is highly probable that Breeland's special order will be approved next week. Details as to production and completion dates will be finalized upon approval of the special order.

The Weekend Family Get-Together. The Smilee clan has a get-together planned for Saturday afternoon, and George informs Abby that he is really looking forward to it. Unfortunately, Abby has prior plans and cannot attend.

This is a very special occasion for George's family, as Grandma Smilee has just turned 80 years old. The weather is just perfect for the gathering. George mingles with his family and is truly enjoying himself. After the meal and games, George spends some quiet time with his brothers. He is sharing some of the details of the special order for the solvent. When one of his brothers, Josh, hears George mention the chemical XO-1600, he becomes very interested. It turns out that he has recently been approached by a customer to manufacture a spray-on rust inhibitor that requires XO-1600 as an ingredient. The quantity needed for that order is 8 gallons, but Josh thinks he can convince the customer to expand his order to use all of the 10 gallons. Josh briefly walks away from the group, calls his customer, and confirms the order. Smiling, Josh informs George of the news. The two agree to finalize this arrangement later in the coming week.

Josh's Project Price Determination. Early Monday morning, George goes to Abby's office to inform her of the development with Josh over the weekend. He explains Josh's intent to purchase the remaining 10 gallons of XO-1600. George indicates that the details of that agreement are to be finalized later in the week. Pausing for a moment to fully understand the details of this arrangement, Abby remembers and informs George that the price quote last Friday assumed that the extra 10 gallons would remain unused and would require disposal, and accordingly the order included the entire cost of the XO-1600 plus the mandated disposal costs. Abby suggests that Breeland Ltd. be informed of a slight delay in the price quote and if Breeland agrees to the delay, then the initial order can be revised in light of Josh's forthcoming order.

To Abby's surprise, George is very cold to the idea of delaying the initial order. George contends that as of today, there are no confirmed orders that would require the extra 10 gallons of XO-1600. In fact, there will be no confirmed orders until later this week, when Josh meets with George to finalize the weekend arrangement. Consequently, George maintains that the special order as presently priced should be forwarded to Tom Brennen for his approval and signature, and if and when a formal order is received from Josh, that order should simply include a prorated cost for the 10 gallons of XO-1600 plus a profit markup on cost. George, in fact, is elated and sees this as a windfall, as the 10 gallons of XO-1600 can be billed twice and the billed disposal costs would not be incurred. This pleasant turn of events adds $93 600 ($16 000 for the 10 gallons of XO-1600, $10 000 of eliminated disposal costs, $26 000 for organization-sustaining level activity costs, and $41 600 for markup on the cost of the 10 gallons of XO-1600) to the company's bottom line.

Abby fully realizes that she had already developed the price quote for Breeland's order the week before, and George Smilee had expressed his approval. Since there were no confirmed orders existing at that time for the unused portion of the XO-1600, Abby, according to company policy, included the entire acquisition cost plus disposal costs in the cost estimate. Abby now knows that an order in all likelihood will be obtained within the 20-day disposal period for the remaining 10 gallons of XO-1600. Given this new information, Abby believes that her original cost estimate should be amended pending approval of a delay by Breeland Ltd.

Alternatively, Abby would like to submit a revised quote to Breeland Ltd. if Josh's order is finalized within 20 days. Specifically, she would like to only bill Breeland Ltd. for 40 gallons of XO-1600, delete the disposal costs, and modify the organization-sustaining and profit on cost amounts. Josh would then be shipped the product and be billed for the cost of the 10 gallons of XO-1600. Contrary to George's suggestion, Abby believes that Josh should also be billed an appropriate organization-sustaining cost amount in addition to a profit on cost. Even these amounts, however, would result in a smaller profit margin for the special order and would not allow the company to meet its monthly profit goal. George Smilee seems adamant in his determination and has instructed Abby to develop a quote for Josh independent of the cost determination for the Breeland special order. George is meeting with Tom Brennen the first thing on Wednesday morning to get his approval and signature on the special order. Abby is contemplating what course of action she should take. She plans to rely, in part, on the guidance provided by the Institute of Management Accounting (IMA) in its *Statement of Ethical Professional Practice*, found in Table 1. Abby is wondering why George Smilee is not using this same guidance. She wonders if George would be taking a similar position if he also were a Certified Management Accountant (CMA).

REQUIRED QUESTIONS

1. Did Abby compute the cost of the Breeland Ltd. special order correctly **before** the weekend get-together? If not, how was her cost estimate and/or price determination flawed?

2. Whose assessment of the costing of this special order do you believe is correct—George Smilee's or Abby Conroy's? That is, should George's conversations with Josh impact Abby's cost estimate of the Breeland Ltd. special order? Explain your answer.

3. Are there any ethical issues related to the cost determination on the Breeland Ltd. special order? If so, what issues are present? How should Abby resolve these conflicts? Should Abby go directly to Tom Brennen about this new development? How can Abby use the IMA *Statement of Ethical Professional Practice* as a guide for her actions?

4. If Abby were to modify her original cost estimate of the Breeland Ltd. special order to include Josh's purchase of the remaining 10 gallons of XO-1600, what price determination would she have arrived at? What impact would that have had on Ace Fertilizer's bottom line?

Table 1

IMA *Statement of Ethical Professional Practice*

Members of IMA shall behave ethically. A commitment to ethical professional practice includes overarching principles that express our values, and standards that guide our conduct.

Principles

IMA's overarching ethical principles include: Honesty, Fairness, Objectivity, and Responsibility. Members shall act in accordance with these principles and shall encourage others within their organizations to adhere to them.

Standards

A member's failure to comply with the following standards may result in disciplinary action.

I. Competence

Each member has a responsibility to:
1. Maintain an appropriate level of professional expertise by continually developing knowledge and skills.
2. Perform professional duties in accordance with relevant laws, regulations, and technical standards.
3. Prepare decision support information and recommendations that are accurate, clear, concise, and timely.
4. Recognize and communicate professional limitations or other constraints that would preclude responsible judgment or successful performance of an activity.

II. Confidentiality

Each member has a responsibility to:
1. Keep information confidential except when disclosure is authorized or legally required.
2. Inform all relevant parties regarding appropriate use of confidential information. Monitor subordinates' activities to ensure compliance.
3. Refrain from using confidential information for unethical or illegal advantage.

III. Integrity

Each member has a responsibility to:
1. Mitigate actual conflicts of interest, regularly communicate with business associates to avoid apparent conflicts of interest. Advise all parties of any potential conflicts.
2. Refrain from engaging in any conduct that would prejudice carrying out duties ethically.
3. Abstain from engaging in or supporting any activity that might discredit the profession.

IV. Credibility

Each member has a responsibility to:
1. Communicate information fairly and objectively.
2. Disclose all relevant information that could reasonably be expected to influence an intended user's understanding of the reports, analyses, or recommendations.
3. Disclose delays or deficiencies in information, timeliness, processing, or internal controls in conformance with organization policy and/or applicable law.

RESOLUTION OF ETHICAL CONFLICT

In applying the Standards of Ethical Professional Practice, you may encounter problems identifying unethical behavior in resolving an ethical conflict. When faced with ethical issues, you should follow your organization's established policies on the resolution of such conflict. If these policies do not resolve the ethical conflict, you should consider the following courses of action:
1. Discuss the issue with your immediate supervisor except when it appears that the supervisor is involved. In that case, present the issue to the next level. If you cannot achieve a satisfactory resolution, submit the issue to the next management level. If your immediate superior is the chief executive officer or equivalent, the acceptable reviewing authority may be a group such as the audit committee, executive committee, board of directors, board of trustees, or owners. Contact with levels above the immediate superior should be initiated only with your superior's knowledge, assuming he or she is not involved. Communication of such problems to authorities or individuals not employed or engaged by the organization is not considered appropriate, unless you believe there is a clear violation of the law.
2. Clarify relevant ethical issues by initiating a confidential discussion with the IMA Ethics Counselor or other impartial advisor to obtain a better understanding of possible courses of action.
3. Consult your own attorney as to legal obligations and rights concerning the ethical conflict.

我的注册会计师为我省下了数百万美元……他为我省下了吗?
关于职业道德和 SC2 税务筹划的一则案例研究

Robin Boneck
Southern Utah University

David S. Christensen
Southern Utah University

引言

　　这是一家国际会计事务所,它是世界最大的几家会计事务所之一。税务部作为该事务所的一个主要分部,提供税务筹划和守法纳税服务。从 20 世纪 90 年代后期到 21 世纪初,由于竞争的压力,该事务所需要增加税收服务方面的收入,而为了实现这一目标,投入了大量资源来开发、推广和销售复杂的税收筹划策略。

　　该事务所在其国内业务办公室中,成立了一个"纳税创新中心",这个中心只有一个目标就是制定满足公众要求的新型税务筹划策略。该中心拥有税务领域的专业人员为其提供纳税创见,这些专业人员需要在每季度提交一定量的纳税创见。中心还准备了一份表格,要求创见提出者填报某些信息,诸如提出的创见如何为客户节税,事务所又可能从中增加多少收入。

　　中心对提出的每一项创见进行筛选,看是否有可能发展成为一项税务筹划方案,并带来一定的收入。如果通过了最初筛选,将由中心的"全国税务工作组"作进一步的审查,该工作组负责确定这项创见是否符合现行法规的各项技术要求。通过了这项审查分析的方案,要再进一步由中心的"实务与专业部"进行复审,以确保其符合本事务所的专业实务和风险管理标准。

　　一项名为"SC2"的节税策略,通过了上述的筛选流程,但是在是否要向联邦政府注册为一种合法的避税手段方面尚存争议。作非属必需的登记,有可能节外生枝、招来美国国税局(IRS)对这一方案的注意,引来审计和被禁止的风险。另外,如果一个策略得以注册,它更可能落入竞争者的手中。如果登记是必要的,不去登记而被发现,就可能招致罚款;不过,从销售这项方案中预期可能获得的销售收入会远远超过因未登记而引致的罚款。此外,从这项交易报税所采用的方法来看,IRS 发现这项方案未登记的风险极低。于是,事务所决定不去登记。

事务所很快地把 SC2 发布给其税务专员,并在 2000 年和 2001 年这两年中兜售给许多委托人(客户)。销售主要通过两个途径。一是在美国的中西部成立一个电话推销中心,向全国范围所确认的潜在顾客打电话。"呼叫中心"的任务是为每位潜在客户就近安排一位税务专员进行洽谈。二是将该节税策略传授给税务专员,然后教他们如何从现有的客户群体和审计部门的客户群体中,识别潜在的纳税客户,并培训他们如何向客户介绍这项节税策略。每位税务专员每个季度都需对一定数量的潜在客户推荐这项税务筹划。

客户

在这一要求之下,一位任加利福尼亚州办公室经理的 CPA(注册会计师)[1],本月需要把 SC2 介绍给一位新的潜在客户。凑巧的是,他和一位现有的客户已约好明天会晤,这似乎是个好的推销机会。这位顾客名叫 John,是一家私有小型企业 Outfield 公司的独资业主。Outfield 公司制造和销售棒球商业卡片与体育纪念品,每年净利润约为 50 000 000 美元。CPA 认为约翰(John)会对这项计划有兴趣,因为他非常在乎每年要交给联邦税务局的所得税。在与客户晤谈的前晚,CPA 重温了当初在接受 SC2 培训时所拿到的"常见问题解答"。第二天上午,CPA 与约翰晤面,讨论来年可能实行的纳税计划。在晤谈中,CPA 告诉约翰,他们事务所有一项方案,可以帮助约翰省下几百万美元所得税。约翰悉心倾听。

交易事项

接下来,CPA 花费了半个小时详细说明了为 Outfield 公司制订的下述方案。

第 1 步:资本重组。 Outfield 公司将发行无投票权的股票和可以转换成无投票权股票的认股证书。对每一股发行在外的有投票权的股票,发行 9 股无投票权的股票。由于约翰持有 1 000 股有投票权的股票,公司将向他发行 9 000 股无投票权的股票。此外,对每一股无投票权的股票,公司将发行 10 张可以转换成无股票权股票的认股证书[2],这样将发行 90 000 张认股证书。约翰可以在以后三年中的任何时候行使认股证书的所有权(即认股权)。

第 2 步:公司的决定。 Outfield 将宣布一项决定,在未来三年中暂停分配收益。

第 3 步:估价。 Outfield 公司将雇用一家独立的资产评估事务所,按财政部法规 §20.2031-2(f)和税务规则 59-60,确定无投票权股票的价值。由于这 9 000 股的股份并无投票权而且可以因认股证书的所有者行使其所有

---

[1] 作者用 CPA 来代替他的姓名,下文均以 CPA 作为此人的代名。——译者
[2] warrant,此处指一种证券,发行的公司允许持有者按某一低于或高于发行时的股票价格换兑该公司的股票,现按财会术语译作"认股证书"。——译者

权而被稀释，因而这些股份将按很低的公允市场价估价（例如，100 000美元）。

第4步：捐助。接着，约翰把Outfield公司9 000股无投票权股份捐给一家慈善机构，因此可获得与这些股票市价同等的税收减免，为100 000美元。该事务所把凡已经同意参与这一项目、具减税条件的慈善捐款都已记录在册，因此约翰不必担心去哪里找捐款对象。此外，获赠股份的慈善机构需要签订一份返还合约，保证其于第三年年末将受赠股份按公允的市场价值返销给公司。如果慈善机构到期没有返还股权，约翰将行使他90 000张认股证书的权利，有效地稀释该慈善机构在公司的所有权。

第5步：收益分配。在接下来的三年中，该慈善机构拥有9 000股无投票权的股份，Outfield公司将按约翰和该慈善机构分别持有股份的比例（10%和90%）分配其年度净利润。这样一来，约翰的课税额（年度收入）仅为5 000 000美元（50 000 000美元×10%）；但按先前生效的公司暂停分配收益的决定，约翰将不从Outfield公司获得任何收入。该慈善机构将公司年度利润的90%即45 000 000美元（50 000 000美元×90%）列报为收入，按照Outfield公司的决定，慈善机构同样无法从该公司获得收入。慈善机构必须把这项收入列入其税单之中，但它不需要缴税，因为按照美国国内税收法规，它是免税机构。

第6步：返还。在第三年年底，该慈善机构将返还它的所有权，按返还的这笔无投票权股票的公允市场价值，获得100 000美元。

第7步：分配。在第四年中，Outfield公司将发布一项决定，撤回以前发布的暂停分配收益的决定，并决定分配所累积的收益。作为独资股东，约翰将获得未分配收益150 000 000美元。按现行税法，按照他之前股权（10%）已将缴过税的部分不再重新缴税。收购慈善机构90%股权从而分得的公司收益，按资本利得缴税，税率为15%，这样一来，与按边际所得税税率35%缴税相比，可节省所得税27 000 000美元。

能够激发兴趣的讨论

虽然约翰不大明白这个方案的细节，但他对会有什么结果是理解的。他对这个建议的合法性不太放心，他问CPA这个方法是不是合法。CPA告诉他说，他的事务所在研究这些税务问题上花费了大量的时间和资源，并没有发现税法中有明显禁止这类交易事项的条款。

约翰是个精明的生意人，他要求把这句话用书面写出来。CPA向约翰保证，他会提供一份可以完全信赖的书面意见。意见书将包括以下对该方案的陈述。

本方案使纳税人在将股票赠予一家慈善机构的当年，有资格获得相当于该捐赠的市场公允价值（在本例中为100 000美元）的慈善性捐助扣税额。每一位股东将按持股比例（在本例中，个人股东持股10%）将以后三年的公司收入列报为应税收入。在公司购回慈善机构所持股份后，原本属于慈善机构而尚未实际分配的收益均作为已纳税收益处理。在该小型企业公司分配利润时，个人股东将把分得的利润作已税收益申报。在股东的股票基价③范围内分配的利润，在当年并不需要缴税。超过股票基价的分配数，将按资本利得优惠税率缴税，不按通常的所得税率缴税。

此外，为了保证这一方案的可信度，该事务所在它的意见书中将包括一份声明，声明中说这一方案"多半可能"实现所预期的效果，即使美国国税局对此提出异议，这一交易事项仍将对减少纳税产生预期的效果。CPA 告诉约翰说，他的事务所深信对这一方案所作出的这一结论是正确的，因而也用同样的意见书帮助事务所在全国范围内对类似的企业业主开展促销活动。此外，CPA 还解释说，如果美国国税局觉察到这一交易事项，他的事务所也并不介意。这一交易事项对所得税申报表的影响，并无引人注意之处。在小企业的所得税申报表上，没有产生亏损，也没有引人高度注意的其他项目。公司所有的利润都分配给适当的所有者，每个所有者都把按持股比例分得的收益报告给了美国国税局，尽管所有者之一是免缴联邦所得税的慈善机构。

因为担心事务所分析有误或者事务所因急于增加销售额而提供过于激进的方案，约翰询问 CPA 这个方案是否已经过法律顾问的审查。CPA 遂递给约翰一份列有全国公认的三家法律事务所的名单，这三家中的任何一家都可以就这一交易事项的合法性提供独立的意见书。这些法律事务所的费用昂贵，但他们会提供所需要的意见，而且事实上也曾向其他委托人在类似情况下提供过意见书。

约翰发现事务所并没有对这一事项若被美国国税局提出异议从而产生的后果提供保证，遂向 CPA 提出了这个问题。对这个问题，CPA 早有准备。他在前一夜就查阅了他该如何把这一做法陈述得当的谈话要点。约翰提出的问题正好是"常见问题解答"的内容之一。CPA 立即充满信心地告诉约翰说，他可以推荐一家保险公司。虽然美国国税局未必会对这项交易提出异议并使约翰发生损失，但万一发生这样的事，这家保险公司是能够按要求提供一切风险保障的。事务所与同意开具这一类交易的财务事项保单的两家全国性保险公司有联系，如有需要，它们可以出具这样的保单。在保单上写明，如果美国国税局或州税务机构确定从上述交易事项获得的赋税优惠是不被允许的话，保险公司将提供包括利息和罚款在内的一切补偿。这一类保单的保

---

③ 这里，需要对"股票基价（stock basis）"及此基价与这则案例之间的关系作一解释，也许对美国税法不够了解的读者有点帮助。按美国对小企业的规定，小企业与个人所得税实施同一个税率，最高为 35%，超过某一个纳税等级的所得，需按此税率纳税。按此，约翰以 100 000 美元买回股份后，他在第四年将公司全部的未分配利润分配给自己，总共分配了 150 000 000 美元。约翰的所得税情况是这样的：他始终拥有公司 10% 的股权，这即所谓的"股票基价"。在过去三年的每年年末他已按这一比例对公司利润中属于自己的部分支付正常的所得税，每年均缴 1 750 000 美元（按 35% 的纳税等级）。在第三年年末原先捐赠给慈善机构的股权回到了他的手中，由于该慈善机构在过去三年的每年年末对公司利润中属于其的部分进行报税，只是因其组织性质才以报税不交税，其申报收入总共 135 000 000 美元（45 000 000 美元），因此在慈善机构返销约翰股份时，约翰购得的这部分股份无需再纳所得税。在第四年分配公司全部未分配利润时，这部分从慈善机构购得的股份需纳资本利得税，纳税额为 20 250 000 美元（135 000 000 × 15%），相对于按 35% 的税率缴纳所得税，他省下了 27 000 000 美元的税金，即 135 000 000 美元 × （35% − 15%） = 27 000 000 美元。——译者

险费高昂，但为取得安心，也是值得的。

约翰对这一答复感到满意，又问到这个交易事项有关慈善机构方面的问题。他疑惑为什么一家慈善机构会愿意接受一笔得不到任何好处的暂时性捐助。CPA 提醒约翰，在它的股票兑现时，这家慈善机构会从 Outfield 公司获得 100 000 美元。事务所已与三家具有资质的慈善机构作了安排，一家是市立的，另两家是大的养老基金所资助。这三家都对该交易事项作过仔细的研究，认为可以以这种形式参与其事。

约翰直觉地感到，这笔交易事项中必有什么东西被遗漏了，他不能对这项看来毫无风险的交易不起疑心。这笔交易好得简直令人难以置信。另外，约翰也注意到这笔交易的费用，相对于它所带来的好处，是过高了。CPA 告知约翰，对这一类复杂的交易事项，事务所按统一价格计费。这笔交易的费用大约为 500 000 美元。约翰很快就计算出，在支付 CPA 的费用（500 000美元）、律师费（100 000 美元）、保险费（3 500 000 美元）和捐赠成本（100 000 美元）④ 后，他净得的赋税优惠近 26 000 000 美元。他认为这是一笔相当可观的节省。

两星期后，CPA 寄给约翰一份委托书，详细说明事务所将执行工作的内容。同时寄出的还有附件，其中包括一份声明，说明这项交易事项是一项高风险的方案，并具体揭示了涉及的各项风险。约翰在原件上签了字并退回给 CPA。他表示收到该附件，但由于事务所对他许诺过的防护措施，他对风险的存在并不介意。

审计

大约在一年之后，约翰收到事务所分管税务的一位合伙人打来的电话，通知他说事务所被要求把他的姓名告诉美国国税局。美国国税局已经把这一交易事项认定为一笔"避税交易"。显然，美国国税局打算对该事务所参与的所有这类交易作一审查。约翰很快就打电话给他的保险公司，确认他的保单有效，如果交易的情况恶化，是可以由保险来弥补损失的。

六个月以后，约翰接到美国国税局的一个通知，说美国国税局正在审查该项交易。此后不久，美国国税局通知他说，这项交易所称赋税优惠是不允许的。缺额之数相当于他从这一笔交易所省下的税金，加上一笔可观的利息和罚金。他请 CPA 指点应该如何处理此事。事务所的一位合伙人通知他说，事务所正忙于就过去两年间它参与的所有 SC2 交易事项与美国国税局作旷日持久的诉讼；事务所不能就此事对他提出任何建议。这位合伙人建议他找法律顾问来咨询。约翰很快地就找了一位有经验的税务律师来处理这一缺额之说。他向保险公司提出请求，以期按他的保险单的条款获得保险补偿。保险公司拒绝了。此后，约翰与美国国税局协议，补缴欠税和利息共 8 000 万美元。约翰现在正在控告保险公司和 CPA 事务所。

---

④ 捐赠成本即该公司回购慈善机构所持本公司股票所需支付的代价。——译者

案例要求

问题 1. 税法有哪些规定支持 CPA 事务所在这项交易中所采取的立场？请尽量引证有关的美国国内税法、规定，或被引用的司法原则以支撑你的论点。把这些作为 CPA 事务所是按"法律条文"行事的根据，在讨论中提出来。重点应放在该交易事项是符合国内税法 §1361(c)(4)、§170、§1366 和 §1368 所有的技术性条款的。

问题 2. 有哪些税法会支持美国国税局作出决定，不承认从获取该交易事项可能得到的赋税优惠？请在你的讨论中包括尽可能多的法律原则（诸如"经济实质"、"实质重于形式"等），也包括可能支持这一立场的任何法律或规定。重点应放在这项交易中把认股证书看作为次等的股票⑤，是违反了"法律精神"和美国财政部规定 §1.1361-1(1)(40)(iii)(A)的。

问题 3. 在考虑了上述问题 1 与问题 2 的正反两方面立场后，还应该考虑到你自己对税法的观点和价值观，并判定哪一方面的意见比较有理。请对你的结论提供分析的依据。你不妨采用八步法。这个分析方法可获自《管理商业道德——实话直说该如何做才对》（*Managing Business Ethics - Straight Talk About How To Do It Right*，Trevino and Nelson 2007：103 - 109），也可以采用其他方法步骤来解决这一两难的问题。

1. 收集事实
2. 明确道德问题何在
3. 确定哪些是利益相关者
4. 确定有什么后果
5. 确定有哪些义务
6. 考虑你的品格和廉正问题
7. 创造性地思考可能采取的行动
8. 自我衡量是否有此胆识

回答问题 4~7 时，请应用最近公布的第 230 号通知。

问题 4. 该事务所在其 SC2 税务筹划这件事上，是否必须依据第 230 号通知⑥的规定行事？请予说明。

问题 5. 请阅读第 230 号通知 §10.33(a)(1) - (4)，并思考一下该事务所是否对有关联邦税收的各项问题，遵循典范做法，向客户提供了最高质量的代理服务。请根据你的理解，对这一节规定作出分析，以支持你的论点。

问题 6. 请阅读第 230 号通知 §10.34(a)，并思考事务所提出的交易事

---

⑤ 这种做法目的在于控制 9 000 股无选举权的股票的价格。过去，约翰是公司的唯一持股人，公司的价值除以他持有的股份数额 1 000 股，即得每股价值。发行 9 000 股无选举权的股票，就会稀释了原有股份的价值，会使新发行的无选举权的股份价格升高。现在另外发行 10 倍于无选举权股票的认股证书，约翰就可以在任何时候行使换购无选举权股票的权利，从而压低后者的价格。这一做法应该是美国对小型企业的规定所不允许的。——译者

⑥ 此后提到第 230 号通知时，将引证其 2008 年 4 月修订的版本上，在 31 CFR Subtitle A，Part 10 中所注明的章节号码。

项的建议是否符合通知的这一节的规定。请说明你的论点。

问题 7. 由美国国税局判定违反相关规定，有什么后果[7]?

问题 8. 请阅读税务服务准则公告 No.1（Statement on Standards for Tax Services No.1）、税单情况和说明 No.1-1（Tax Return Positions and Interpretation No.1-1），以及美国注册会计师协会（AICPA）"税收服务准则公告"的"现实可能性准则"（"Realistic Possibility Standard" of the AICPA's Statement on Standards for Tax Services）。请讨论这项交易是否符合这些规定。

问题 9. 违反美国注册会计师协会有关税务服务的准则将有什么后果？

---

[7] 该会计事务所有可能被禁止执行有关税收的业务。——译者

MY CPA SAVED ME MILLIONS...OR DID HE?
A Case Study of Professional Ethics and the SC2 Tax Planning Strategy

Robin Boneck
Southern Utah University

David S. Christensen
Southern Utah University

INTRODUCTION

An international accounting firm is one of the largest public accounting firms in the world. Its tax practice is a major division of the firm, providing tax planning services and tax compliance services. In the late 1990s and early 2000s, the firm was under competitive pressure to enhance its tax practice revenue. In an attempt to substantially boost its revenues from tax services, the firm devoted substantial resources to developing, marketing, and selling sophisticated tax planning strategies.

At its national office the firm established the Tax Innovation Center, whose sole purpose was to develop new tax strategies that could be sold to the public. The Center generated tax ideas from its professional staff in the field. Professionals in the field were expected to submit a certain number of tax ideas to the Center each quarter. A form was provided by the Center that required the submitter to explain certain information, such as how the idea would save a client taxes and what the potential revenue to the firm would be.

The Center screened each idea for potential development as a tax planning strategy with possible revenue generation. If the proposal survived the initial screening, it was reviewed by the National Tax Practice Group, which was responsible for assuring that the strategy met the technical requirements under current tax law. If the strategy survived this analysis, it was reviewed by the Department of Practice and Professionalism to insure the strategy met the firm's standards of professional practice and risk management.

A tax savings idea the firm named "SC2" was one of several strategies that survived all the processes, although there was some debate about whether or not the strategy should be registered with the federal government as a tax shelter.

Unnecessary registration would draw the attention of the IRS to the strategy and create the risk of audit and disallowance. Furthermore, if the strategy was registered, it was more likely to fall into the hands of competitors. If registration was required, failure to do so could result in some fines, if it was discovered, but the anticipated revenue generated from sales of the strategy would far outweigh the potential fines associated with the failure to register. In addition, the risk of the IRS discovering the strategy was extremely low because of the manner in which the transaction was reported for tax purposes. In the end, the firm decided to forgo registration.

SC2 was quickly released to the field professionals and was successfully sold for two years, 2000 and 2001. The marketing plan consisted primarily of two approaches. The first was to create a telemarketing center in the Midwest to make nationwide calls to identified prospects. The call center's duty was to set appointments for each prospect with a tax professional in the office located near the prospect. The second was to educate the field professionals about the strategy, teach them how to identify prospective taxpayers from their existing client pool and from the audit division's client pool, and train the professionals how to present the strategy. Each tax professional would then be required to present the strategy to a set number of prospects quarterly.

THE CLIENT

CPA, a manager in the firm's California office, is under pressure to present SC2 to one more prospect this month. Fortunately, tomorrow he has a meeting with an existing client who looks like a good candidate for SC2. The client, John, is the sole owner of a privately held S corporation, the Outfield Company. On average, Outfield Co., a maker and seller of baseball trading cards and sports memorabilia, produces net income of approximately $50 000 000 a year. CPA thinks John will be interested in the strategy since he is very sensitive about his annual federal income tax liability. The night before the client meeting, CPA reviews the FAQs on SC2, which he received in his initial training on the strategy. The following morning CPA meets with John to discuss potential tax planning for the upcoming year. During the course of the meeting CPA informs John that his firm has a strategy that could save John millions of dollars in income tax. John is all ears.

THE TRANSACTION

CPA spends the next half hour describing the following plan for Outfield Company.

Step 1: Recapitalization. Outfield Co. will issue nonvoting stock and warrants that are exercisable into nonvoting stock. Nine nonvoting shares will be issued for every voting share outstanding. Since John owns 1 000 shares of voting stock, the company will issue 9 000 shares of nonvoting stock to him. Additionally, for every share of nonvoting stock issued, the company will issue 10 warrants exercisable into nonvoting shares, resulting in the issuance of 90 000 warrants. The warrants can be exercised by John any time over the next three years.

Step 2: Corporate Resolution. Outfield Co. will issue a resolution suspending income distributions for the next three years.

Step 3: Valuation. Outfield Co. will employ an independent valuation firm to assign a value to the nonvoting shares in accordance with Treasury Regulation § 20.2031-2(f) and Revenue ruling 59-60. Because the 9 000 shares have no voting rights and can be diluted by the exercise of the 90 000 warrants, the shares will be assessed a very low fair market value (e.g., $100 000).

Step 4: Donation. John will then donate the 9 000 nonvoting shares of Outfield Co. to a charity and receive a current year charitable deduction equal to the fair market value of the shares, $100 000. The firm maintains a list of qualifying charities that have agreed to participate in this program, so John does not have to concern himself with identifying an appropriate charity. Furthermore, the charity will enter into a redemption agreement providing it with the right to sell its shares back to the corporation at fair market value at the end of three years. If the charity fails to redeem, John will exercise his 90 000 warrants, effectively diluting the charity's ownership in the company.

Step 5: Income Allocation. Over the next three years, the period in which the charity owns the 9 000 nonvoting shares, Outfield Co. will allocate its annual net income to the shareholders based on proportionate ownership, 10% to John and 90% to the charity. Thus, John will only be taxed on annual income of $5 000 000 ($50 000 000 * 10%), but will not receive any income from Outfield pursuant to the previously enacted corporate resolution to suspend income distributions. Likewise, the charity will report 90% of the net annual income, $45 000 000 ($50 000 000 * 90%), but it will not receive a distribution pursuant to the same corporate resolution. Even though the charity must report the income on its tax return, it is not subject to taxation on this income because it is a qualifying income-tax-exempt entity under the Internal Revenue Code.

Step 6: Redemption. At the end of three years, the charity will redeem its ownership and receive $100 000, the fair market value of the nonvoting shares redeemed.

Step 7: Distribution. In year four, Outfield Co. will issue a resolution revoking the suspension of distributions and resolve to distribute accumulated income. John will receive the entire undistributed income of $150 000 000 as the sole shareholder. To the extent of his stock basis, the distribution will be currently tax-free. The distribution in excess of his basis will be taxed to John at 15%, capital gains rates, rather than at the marginal income tax rate of 35%, creating approximately $27 000 000[①] in income tax savings.

THE COMPELLING DISUSSION

Although John doesn't catch all the details of the plan, he understands the end result. Feeling somewhat concerned about the legitimacy of this proposal, he asks CPA if this technique is legal. CPA informs him that his firm spent a great deal of time and resources researching the tax issues and found no provision in the tax code expressly prohibiting the transaction.

John, being a savvy businessman, requests that this assertion be put in writing. CPA assures John that the firm will provide him with a written opinion that he could rely upon. It will contain the following statements.

This arrangement entitles the taxpayer to a charitable deduction in the year the stock is gifted to a charity equal to the fair market value of the donation ($100 000 in this case). Each shareholder will report as income, over the next three years, a proportionate share of the S corporation's income generated each year (10% to the individual shareholder in this case). All income allocated to the charity is treated as previously taxed after the corporation buys back the shares owned by the charity. The individual shareholder will report this previously taxed income upon distribution from the S corporation. To the extent of the shareholder's stock basis, the distribution will not be currently taxable. The distribution in excess of stock basis will be taxed at the preferred capital gains tax rate and not at the ordinary income tax rates.

Furthermore, the firm will include a statement in its opinion letter providing a confidence level that it is "more likely than not" that the described tax consequences of this transaction would be sustained if challenged by the IRS. CPA informs John that his firm is so confident about its conclusions that it uses this opinion letter to aid in its national marketing campaign targeting similarly situated business owners. Additionally, CPA explains that his firm is not concerned about the IRS detecting this transaction. Nothing about the transaction attracts attention on the income tax return. It does not generate losses or other highly visible items on the S corporation tax return. All income of the company

---

① Distribution of $150 000 000 less $15 000 000 ($5 000 000 × 3 years) previously taxed to John leaves $135 000 000 of the distribution to be taxed, assuming the distribution is a capital gain and none of it is return of basis. The taxable distribution of $135 000 000 multiplied by the 20% savings rate equals a savings of $27 000 000. The 20% savings rate is determined by subtracting the applicable 15% capital gains rate from the highest individual income tax rate of 35%.

is allocated to the appropriate owners and each owner reports its proportionate share of income to the IRS, albeit one owner is a charity that is exempt from federal income taxation.

Concerned that the firm might have erred in its analysis of the arrangement or is taking an overly aggressive position in order to generate sales, John asks if this arrangement has been examined by legal counsel. CPA responds by offering John a list of three nationally recognized law firms, any of which could provide him with an independent opinion letter regarding the validity of the transaction. The law firms are not cheap, but they will provide the desired opinion, and, in fact, have provided opinions to other clients similarly situated.

John notices that the firm stopped short of actually guaranteeing the results of the transaction in the event of an IRS challenge and brings this to the attention of CPA. Fortunately, CPA is ready for this question. Just last night he had reviewed the talking points on how to best present this structure. Coincidentally, John's question is one of the FAQs covered in the material. Quickly and confidently, CPA informs John that he could recommend an insurance company that provides protection in the unlikely event the IRS challenged the transaction and John lost. The firm has a relationship with two national insurance carriers that have agreed to issue a fiscal event insurance policy covering the transaction, if requested. The policy compensates for a determination by the IRS or state tax authorities that any part of the tax benefits resulting from the above-described transaction are disallowed, including interest and penalties. The premium on such a policy is expensive but well worth the peace of mind.

Satisfied with this response, John inquires about the charitable aspect of the transaction. He wonders why a charity would be willing to receive a temporary donation without any benefit. CPA reminds John that the charity would receive $100 000 from Outfield Co. when its stock is redeemed. It's kind of like a fee for accommodating the transaction. The firm has an arrangement with three qualified charities: one municipality and two large pension funds. Each has closely scrutinized the transaction and is comfortable participating in this manner.

Although John has a gut feeling that there is something amiss about this transaction, he cannot ignore the fact that this transaction appears risk-free to him. It is almost too good to be true. Also, John is concerned that the cost of the arrangement might outweigh the benefit. CPA informs John that the firm charges a flat fee for this sort of sophisticated transaction. In this case the fee would be roughly $500 000. John quickly calculates that his net tax saving after CPA fees ($500 000), attorney fees ($10 000), insurance premiums ($3.5 million), and redemption cost ($100 000) would be close to $26 000 000. He considers that to be a substantial savings.

Two weeks later, CPA sends John an engagement letter describing the work the firm would perform. CPA makes sure he attaches the addendum, which includes a statement describing the transaction as a high-risk strategy and disclosing the risks involved. John signs and returns the original document. He acknowledges the addendum, but is not concerned about the risk because of all the protection the firm promised him.

THE AUDIT

Approximately one year later, John receives a phone call from the tax partner at the firm informing him that the firm was required to disclose his name to the IRS. The IRS had identified this transaction as a "tax avoidance transaction." Apparently the IRS intended to review all such transactions the firm had participated in. John quickly calls his insurance company and confirms that his policy is in place and that it would cover the situation if the transaction soured.

Six months later, John receives a notice from the IRS that it is examining the transaction. Soon thereafter, he is informed that the claimed tax benefits of the transaction were disallowed. The amount of deficiency equaled the tax he saved on the transaction plus substantial interest and penalties. He seeks advice from CPA. A partner at the firm informs him that the firm is occupied with protracted litigation with the IRS regarding all SC2 transactions it had advised on over the last two years. The firm would be unable to advise him any further regarding the matter. The partner suggests he seek legal counsel. John quickly retains the services of a seasoned tax attorney to challenge the deficiency. He files a claim with his insurer seeking reimbursement under the terms of his policy. The insurance company denies his claim. Thereafter, John settles with the IRS, paying $80 million in back taxes and interest. John is now suing the insurance company and the CPA firm.

CASE REQUIREMENTS

Question 1. What tax laws support the positions taken by the CPA firm regarding this transaction? Please provide supporting arguments for any relevant internal revenue codes, regulations, or judicial doctrine cited. Include as part of the discussion the argument that the CPA firm followed the "letter of the law." Focus on the fact that the transaction adhered to all technical provisions of Internal Revenue Code § 1361(c)(4), § 170, § 1366, and § 1368.

Question 2. What tax laws support the IRS's decision to disallow the tax benefits of the transaction? Please include in the discussion any relevant judicial doctrine (such as "economic substance," "substance over form," etc.)

as well as any code or regulations supporting the position. Focus on the arguments that the transaction violated the "spirit of the law" and Treas. Reg. § 1.1361-1(1)(40)(iii)(A) regarding warrants as a second class of stock.

Question 3. After considering the laws supporting the opposing positions in questions 1 and 2 above, consider your personal views and values on tax law and determine which party should prevail. Please support your conclusion with analysis. You may use the following eight-step method found in *Managing Business Ethics - Straight Talk About How To Do It Right* (Trevino and Nelson 2007: 103 – 109), or any other method to solve this dilemma.

1. Gather the facts
2. Define the ethical issues
3. Identify the stakeholders
4. Identify the consequences
5. Identify the obligations
6. Consider your character and integrity
7. Think creatively about potential actions
8. Check your gut

Answer questions 4 through 7 applying the most recent version of Circular 230.

Question 4. Is the firm subject to the regulations of Circular 230[2] for its activities with regard to the SC2 tax planning strategy? Please explain.

Question 5. Read § 10.33(a)(1) – (4) of Circular 230 and consider whether or not the firm provided the client with the highest quality representation concerning federal tax issues by adhering to best practices. Please support your conclusions with analysis of this section based on your understanding of it.

Question 6. Read § 10.34(a) of Circular 230 and contemplate whether or not the advice provided by the firm regarding the transaction met the standards required in this section. Please explain your conclusions.

Question 7. What are the repercussions for violating the regulations governing practice before the IRS?

Question 8. Read the Statement on Standards for Tax Services No. 1, Tax Return Positions and Interpretation No. 1 – 1, "Realistic Possibility Standard" of the AICPA's Statement on Standards for Tax Services. Discuss whether or not the transaction met these standards.

Question 9. What are the repercussions for violating the AICPA's standards for tax services?

---

[2] References to Circular 230 will be referred to hereafter by their section number in 31 CFR Subtitle A, Part 10, revised as of April 2008.

可持续发展
Sustainability

强生公司：一则关于编制可持续发展报告书的案例研究

Susan Borkowski
La Salle University

Mary Jeanne Welsh
La Salle University

Kristin Wentzel
La Salle University

> 试设想一个前景，企业会像现在编制财务报表那样，把环境和社会方面的业绩作为常规的内容包括在报表之中。
>
> ——吉尔伯特（Gilbert, 2002, 26）

简介

"可持续发展的企业"一词可能与企业提出的许多倡议有关，这些倡议对公司各方面的行为，即对环境、帮助员工使其生活得更为健康、使社区有所发展、使顾客得到安全保障，以及公平交易等活动产生影响。反过来，利益相关者又会关注与这些倡议有关的信息，例如投资者会关注对社会有益的投资、消费者会选择购买"绿色"产品、社区居民会关注邻近的企业对环境带来的影响。克利凯曼（Clikeman, 2004, 24）对"可持续发展"一词提出了一个通常惯用的定义[①]："将当前所作所为的经济利益与对后代的影响相权衡的一种哲理。"换言之，对社会负责任的公司不仅要关注当前行为所造成的短期和长期的经济利益，也要关注这些行为对环境和社会带来的长期影响，从而使企业的报表上需要列示的绩效包括环境、社会和经济三个方面的内容。

除了在某些国家（如日本、瑞典、挪威），其他国家的企业都不需要就公司的社会责任提供单独的报表。然而，由于利益相关者的信息需求，以及越来越多的人认识到传统的会计报表并不能提供这类信息，使得越来越多的企业开始发布单独的关于可持续发展的报告书。在涉及可持续发展的大量倡议中，企业应如何按主次分批执行？公司如何收集、评估和发布有关其社会责任活动的信息？强生公司在提供可持续发展报告方面有比较久远的历史，

[①] working definition，直译应作"工作定义"，指虽不精确但尚可一用的定义，姑意译为"通常惯用的定义"。——译者

为我们探究这些问题提供了很好的案例素材。强生公司最初设定其环保目标是在1990年，从1993年起断断续续地向公众发布这方面的报告书，并从1998年起编报可持续发展的年度报告书。

可持续发展会计的重要性日渐显现

迄今为止，并没有正式的规定，要求上市公司提供单独的报告书，详细说明其在可持续发展方面的各项倡议；但是自愿披露其三重底线[②]（triple bottom lines, TBL, 即环保、社会和经济三方面业绩）的公司在全球范围内越来越多。克利凯曼（Clikeman, 2004）认为，一家公司实施、记录并向其利益相关者披露其在可持续发展方面的活动，使公司受益良多；这些好处不一定与在年度财务报表中公布的数据有关。克利凯曼根据全球可持续发展协会（World Council for Sustainable Development）所发布的一份比较详细的清单（见表1），总结归纳了如下好处：

- 为与利益相关者之间交流和对话，提供一个良好的基础；
- 把有关的信息传递给利益相关者，从而提高他们对公司情况的了解，有助于实现透明化；
- 有助于提高企业知名度，从长远来讲，将有助于提高品牌价值、顾客忠诚度和市场份额；
- 鼓励并有助于实施严格的管理制度、更好地对环保和社会风险进行监督；
- 帮助公司向外界展示其企业价值和有关处理环保和社会问题的原则；
- 有助于吸引具有长远目光的"有耐性"的股东，并有助于使投资者和债权人确信，投资于该公司所获得的风险报酬较低是合理的[③]（Clikeman, 2004, 24）。

对公司编报可持续发展报告书不但缺少统一的规定，而且在公认会计原则对报表的规定中也没有可以参照的准则。不过，自1997年以来，为编报可持续发展报告书，曾作了不断的努力。1997年，在波士顿的非营利对环境负责的经济体联盟（Coalition for Environmentally Responsible Economies, CERES）[④] 建立了一个全球报告倡议组织（Global Reporting Initiative, GRI）。联合国环境规划署（United Nations Environment Programme）于1999年参加该联合会，成为其中的一个合伙人；同年，GRI公布了一份《编报可持续发展报告书指导准则》的征求意见稿。2002年，CERES把GRI定为

---

② 底线（bottom line）指账本上结出的末行数字，即财务报表上最终列示的盈亏净额，代表企业经营的最终成果。可持续发展报告书上表现的业绩有三个方面，于是就是有三个底线，姑译为"三重底线"。——译者

③ 这里的意思是，企业如果以对社会和环境负责的方式来经营，可能并不给投资者或债权人带来直接的好处，但他们知道自己投入的资金通过公司的经营，对社会和环保有益；环保和社会情况的改善，也是他们所获回报的一个组成部分。——译者

④ CERES是一个美国投资者、环保组织和其他对公众利益有兴趣的团体的联络网。它与各公司和投资者共同努力来应对可持续发展的各项（如全球气候变化等）挑战。该组织成立于1989年，其主要任务是要把可持续发展结合到资本市场中去。——译者引自《维基百科》。

一个独立的机构⑤。GRI 的使命是"把在市场上的许多准则整合和统一成为一项单独的、公认的可持续发展报告书编制框架，将环保、社会和经济方面的业绩都包罗在内"（Gilbert，2002，p. 21）。GRI 于 2000 年发布了编制可持续发展报告书框架和指导准则的第一稿，于 2002 年发布了修正后的第二稿（G2），接着，在 2006 年又发布了修正后的第三稿（G3）（GRI，2006）。

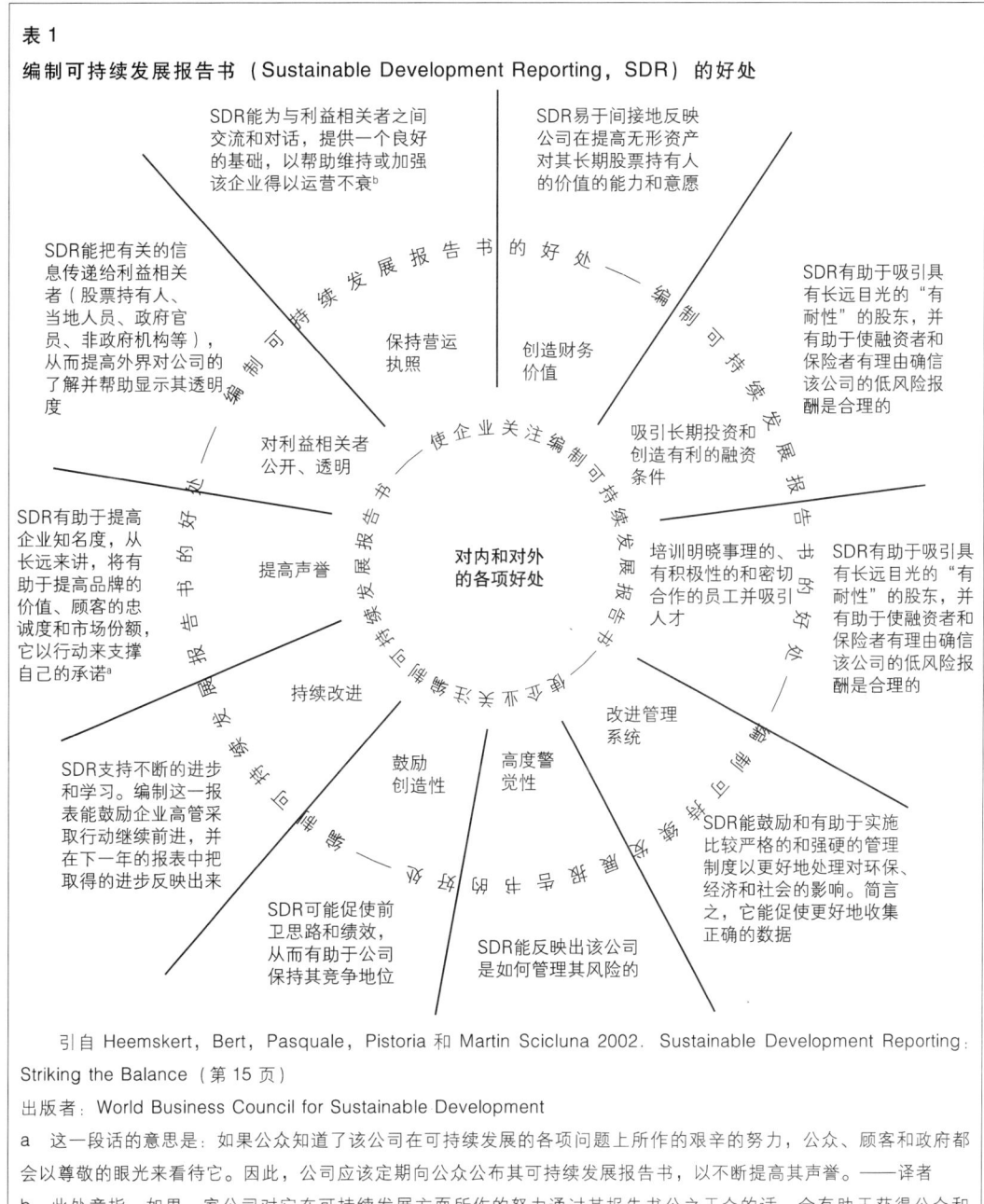

表 1
编制可持续发展报告书（Sustainable Development Reporting，SDR）的好处

引自 Heemskert, Bert, Pasquale, Pistoria 和 Martin Scicluna 2002. Sustainable Development Reporting: Striking the Balance（第 15 页）
出版者：World Business Council for Sustainable Development

a 这一段话的意思是：如果公众知道了该公司在可持续发展的各项问题上所作的艰辛的努力，公众、顾客和政府都会以尊敬的眼光来看待它。因此，公司应该定期向公众公布其可持续发展报告书，以不断提高其声誉。——译者
b 此处意指：如果一家公司对它在可持续发展方面所作的努力通过其报告书公之于众的话，会有助于获得公众和政府的支持，从而使其运营不衰。——译者

---

⑤ http://www.globalreporting.org/AboutGRI/WhatWeDo/OurHistory/——原注

第三稿指导准则中确定了可持续发展报告书的核心内容。编制可持续发展报告书的目的（按第三次指导准则修正稿所述）是"……将企业实现可持续发展目标过程中的业绩进行计量、披露、并向内部与外部的利益相关者报告"（GRI，2006，4）。按披露标准，可持续发展报告书所披露的内容应包括以下内容：

- **战略与概况**：披露企业的战略、概况和治理情况，使可持续发展报告书的使用者能对经营企业的背景情况有一个全面的认识。
- **管理方法**：披露企业是如何处理某一个方面问题的，使可持续发展报告书的使用者对其业绩的背景情况有所了解。
- **业绩指标**：通过披露这些指标，能使企业可以与其他企业在经济、环保和社会三个方面所作努力的结果作对比分析。（GRI，2006，6）

上述前两组披露的内容是不言自明的；业绩指标既有定量指标，也有定性指标，以描述企业的政策、流程和执行效果。例如，人权方面的业绩指标可能包括"歧视案件的发生和采取措施的总数（定量的）和"从企业的运作情况来看，极有可能雇用童工，以及企业所采取的消除童工的措施"（定性的）（G3 指导准则，2006，33）。

GRI 报告称，在 2008 年，全球约有 1 000 家公司自愿采用 G3 指导性准则来编制可持续发展报告书，比 2007 年的企业数增加了 46%（GRI，2009）。这些公司仅占美国标准普尔 500 强企业的 13%，和英国金融时报（Financial Times and Stock Exchange，FTSE）100 家公司中的 22%。按 GRI 的统计结果，2008 年编制可持续发展报告书的全部企业中，欧洲公司占 49%、亚洲公司占 15%、北美公司占 14%、拉丁美洲公司占 12%、大洋洲公司占 6%、非洲公司占 4%。这些数字与毕马威会计师事务所（KPMG）报告的数据相差甚远，KPMG 定期公布其对全球《财富》250 强（Global Fortune 250）和 22 个国家销售收入最高的 100 家公司中编制有关社会责任报表的调查报告。

在 2007 年，瑞典是第一个要求它的国有公司如斯堪的纳维亚航空公司（Scandinavian Airlines，SAS），从 2009 年 3 月起按 GRI 的规定编制可持续发展年度报表的国家。数十年来，最大型的跨国公司编制这一报告书最多的国家是日本和英国的全球性公司，其原因是这些国家对它们施加了压力（KPMG，2008，15）。在日本证券市场上市的公司，必须遵照有关环保和报表编制规定；在英国的公司则经受着来自各区选民的压力，包括政府、媒体、客户和股东，因而必须在各项可持续发展问题上实现透明化。挪威公司被要求编制环保报告书，而法国和德国公司则必须向公众提供社会和环保报告书。由于缺少利益相关者的压力，美国公司在编报公司社会责任报告书上行动要迟缓得多。

从美国证券交易委员会（SEC）最近的行为迹象来看，美国公司缺少编制可持续发展报告书的压力这一情况，不久将成为往事。2009 年 7 月，SEC 组建了投资者咨询委员会（Investor Advisory Committee）。该组织依据对社会责任感兴趣投资团体所获得的信息（如社会投资论坛，Social Investment Forum），"就强制有效编制有关环保、社会与公司治理问题"的内容构成展开研究（Kropp，2009，1）。美国证券交易委员会可能最终要求向它提供报表的公司，除已经明确规定的 10-K[6] 和其他各项财务报表之外,增加一项完整的可持续发展报告书。

如何编制公司的可持续发展报告书

一旦一家公司决定扩展财务报表内容,包含可持续发展报告书时,企业的管理当局就必须确定:应该对哪些经济、社会和环保行为加以量度,在量度中又应采用哪些指标。爱泼斯坦(Epstein,2008)多次论述有关可持续发展报告书的编制和计量问题。最主要的困难问题在于:"实施合适的制度来实现可持续发展,并就可持续发展对财务业绩的影响作出评估,最终必须在两者(企业可持续发展与财务业绩)之间权衡抉择"爱泼斯坦(2008,26)。所做的权衡包括企业利润最大化与企业可持续发展成本相平衡。爱泼斯坦的公司可持续发展模式可用作编制可持续发展报告书的蓝本(见表2)。

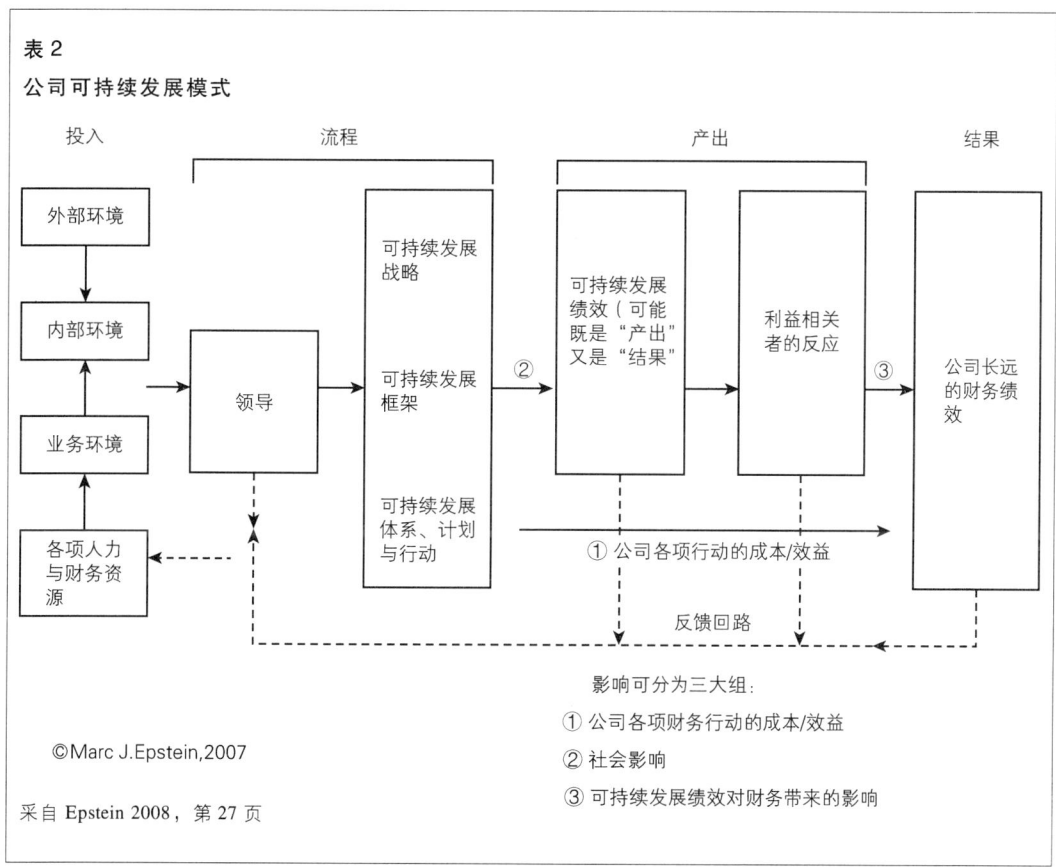

表2
公司可持续发展模式

©Marc J.Epstein,2007

采自 Epstein 2008,第 27 页

为了编制可持续发展报告书,企业的管理层必须确定:哪些业务需要被量度,然后再决定采用哪一种计量指标是最好的。如前所述,GRI 提出了一套完整的编制可持续发展报告书的框架,以及评估公司的经济、社会和环保活动所需要的各项指标,但并没有明确指出公司应该如何对每一项指标进行计量。表3列示了爱泼斯坦的公司可持续发展模式中所包含的各项指标,可

---

[6] Form 10-K,美国 SEC 规定申报的一种表格。——译者

以用这些指标对其动因进行计量。

表3
用于衡量投入、流程、产出和结果的若干可持续发展指标

动因：投入
公司的战略导向可持续发展⑦
营业单位的数目和多样性
生产和销售地域上的多样性
流程、行业和产品对可持续发展的影响
公司财务状况

在行业中的竞争地位
评估管理业绩中属于可持续发展的部分
为达到可持续发展可以取得的资源

动因：流程
访问工厂的次数
公司所作出的承诺和对可持续发展的领导
童工保护
最高管理层参与对可持续发展的管理⑩
董事会处理问题的过程尽善尽美⑪
用于可持续发展的各项资源
采用编码和标准以衡量可持续发展方面取得的发展（包括经认可的设施数目）⑫
专门从事可持续发展工作的职工人数和这些员工所属的层次
员工接受职业道德培训的小时数
获得可持续发展资格认证的供应商数目

动因：产出
工厂关闭的数目
有害废料的数量
包装容器⑧
向少数族裔企业采购的数量
通过慈善事业和善因营销（cause-related marketing）⑨ 捐助的钱
在高层位置上的妇女和少数族裔的百分率和人数
工伤的数字
溢流、事故、喷出的次数
违反人权和劳动法的次数
对职业道德核查的结果
次品率
消费者投诉次数
员工申诉次数
罚款次数
产品召回次数
副产品收入
社会基金（social fund）⑬ 上市公司股票数
获得奖项的次数

动因：结果
得自废料回收的收入
来自推销的收入
因提高声誉而增加的销售额
因减少浪费而降低的材料成本
员工补缺率的减少
收入增加
降低环境清理成本
利润

引自 Epstein 2008，第30页

⑦ 此处指公司提出的经营目标是否与社会和环保方面的目标相兼容、一致。——译者
⑧ 此处指产品的包装尽量少用材料、采用对环境无害的材料，做到环保。——译者
⑨ cause-related marketing 指一家谋利公司和一家非谋利单位为双方各自的利益合作从事的行销业务，包括由非谋利单位在谋利的公司内部为社会或慈善目的推销其产品。但这种业务不属于捐助性质，因而也不能减免税金。——译者引自《维基百科》
⑩ 此处指公司的经理人员未必就是负责可持续发展方面的经理人员，因而负责可持续发展方面的经理人员如果不能取得最高层的支持，就不可能获得令人满意的结果。——译者
⑪ 此处指董事会对各项问题考虑周全，能够做到熟知最终产品的结果并对流程实施控制、减少错失、使顾客和员工有较高的满意度、从而使公司达成其可持续发展方面的各项目标。——译者
⑫ 此处指在某些地区规定必须遵循有关环保和社会方面的法规，公司遵循这些法规的程度由一些独立的机构加以评级。CERES 和联合国机构都制订了可持续发展方面的规定，公司必须援引规定的代号和标准，申明该公司有多少部门达到了这些标准。——译者
⑬ 社会基金（Social Fund）是一个组织，通常存在于发展中国家，旨在向小规模的公众投资提供融资以帮助贫苦大众。——译者引自《维基百科》

爱泼斯坦（2008）模式着眼于企业的各项投入，认为这些投入决定了公司可持续发展进程中需要的预期产出与长期绩效。具体来说，投入包括企业内部投入、外部投入及业务内容投入，同时也包括各项人力物力投入。各项投入是确定需要采用哪些流程来提高可持续发展的基础。管理层采取的各项行动和利益相关者对此的回应，决定了公司长期的财务绩效。该模型包括了这样一套回馈循环[14]，即：通过不间断调节方式评估企业在可持续发展方面所做努力的成本与收益间权衡选择。

在介绍强生公司可持续发展报告书之前，需要对整个制药行业编制可持续发展报告书的情况作一考量。《新闻周刊》近期以企业对环境的影响、企业的"绿色"政策及企业的环保声誉为依据公布了美国最大的500家企业中"绿色"公司的排名次序（McGinn，2009）。可持续资产管理公司（Sustainable Asset Management Inc，SAM）和普华永道会计师事务所（PricewaterhouseCoopers）（2010）近期依据69家全球最大的制药企业对可持续发展绩效调查反馈做出评估，强生公司一向是全球制药行业领军企业之一，见下表所示：

在可持续发展方面领先的单位（2009/2010）		
获得SAM金牌奖的单位：	Roche Holding AG *	瑞典
	AstraZeneca Plc	英国
	Novartis AG	瑞士
	Novo Nordisk A/S	丹麦
获得SAM银牌奖的单位：	Abbott Laboratories	美国
	Johnson & Johnson（强生公司）	美国［于2007/2008获铜牌奖，于2008/2009获银牌奖］
	Sanofi Aventis	法国
获得SAM铜牌奖的单位：	GlaxoSmithKline	英国

* SAM部门领先单位。一家公司必须在经济的、环境的和社会的评价尺度方面总分达到75%，才有资格获得SAM金牌；公司的总分必须达到70%~75%，有资格获得SAM银牌；总分达到65%~70%，才有资格获得铜牌。

引自SAM and PwC，2010（第84页）

http：//www.sam-group.com/htmle/yearbook/? CFID=961207&CFTOKEN=a06ee7afaf158e0c-C0EAEB14-E1BA-B686-402A4B662ED3C9FA

整体来说，制药行业似乎都编制了可持续发展报告书，这可能是因为环保和社会问题密切关系到药品的研究与制造。

强生公司：编制可持续发展报告书的过去与现在

强生公司最初开始制订环保目标是在1990年，随后在1993年断断续续地发布了报告书，于1998年开始有年度报告书。早期的年报主要涉及各项

---

[14] feedback loop，计算机用语。本案例表2"公司可持续发展模式"中用了这个术语，可借以理解它的含义，请参阅。——译者

环保问题,在报表的题目中包含了"环保、健康与安全"字样;但从 2003 年起,强生公司把这一文件简称为"可持续发展报告书(sustainability report)"。表 4 是强生公司从 1993~2007 年之间的 12 份可持续发展报告书的概况。《新闻周刊》(Newsweek)首次美国"最绿色"的大公司作排名时,强生公司位列第三(仅次于惠普和戴尔公司),因为它"对气候变化所作的承诺……已经具有坚强的环保管理……(并且有)全世界最巨大的混合动力车辆(hybrid vehicles)的车队"(McGinn,2009)。

表 4
强生公司可持续发展报告书(1993~2007 年)

	2007	2006	2005	2004	2003	2002
报告书名称	可持续发展报告书	可持续发展报告书	可持续发展报告书	可持续发展报告书	可持续发展报告书	环保、健康和安全可持续发展报告书
醒目的口号	许下承诺的简要说明	热情、实干、前景⑮	让更多的人参与保护我们的地球	把我们的信条付诸实施	健康的人、健康的地球、健康的未来	健康的人、健康的地球
页数	45	36	52	44	50	34
"信条"印在报告书上的位置	封底	p. ii	p. 2	p. 7	封底	封底
	2001	2000	1999	1998	1996	1993
报告书名称	环保、健康和安全可持续发展报告书	环保、健康和安全可持续发展报告书	环保、健康和安全报告书	环保、健康和安全报告书	承担我们对全球环保所作的承诺	一项特殊的责任
醒目的口号	健康的人、健康的地球	健康的人、健康的地球	健康的人、健康的地球	不适用	承担我们对全球环保所作的承诺	一项特殊的责任
页数	34	30	18	39	24	31
"信条"印在报告书上的位置	封底	封底	封底	p. 2	未包括在内	未包括在内

强生公司编制可持续发展报告书所作承诺的中心内容见于它的"信条(Credo)"。在我们与强生公司员工任何一次谈话中,他们在一开始的几分钟内必然会提及这个"信条"(见本案例附录 B)。公司的每一项业务决策,无论是由中层经理或由分管生产的副总裁作出的,都以该"信条"的内容为根据。据公司网站上的解释,"信条"的各项价值,是公司的精髓所在:我们决策的指导思想都已在"我们的信条"中讲清楚了。简言之,"我们的信条"要求我们把所服务的人民的健康放在第一位。

公司的家族成员之一、前任董事长(1932~1963 年)罗伯特·伍德·约翰逊(Robert Wood Johnson)在 1943 年公司成为上市公司的前夕,亲自

---

⑮ "Passion, Performance, Possibilities"是强生公司在 2006 年可持续发展报告书中提出来的口号。"热情"指公司热爱可持续发展;"实干"指公司在这方面做了许多工作,成绩可观,可以从报告书中获悉详情;"前景"指前途光明,会越来越好,更能持续发展。——译者

起草了"我们的信条"。此事远在人们最初听到"公司社会责任"一词之前。"我们的信条"不单纯地只是一个道德指南。我们相信它是经营成功的灵丹妙药。经历了一个多世纪的变革,强生公司是依然旺盛的五六个企业中的一个,这个事实就是明证。

——引自强生公司官方网站,"我们的信条价值",http://www.jnj.com/connect/about-jnj/jnj-credo/?flash = true。

粗略地翻阅强生公司任何一份可持续发展报告书,可以随处看到对"信条"的具体引用,还可以看到强生公司对四类利益相关者所负责任是按下列次序排列的:顾客(包括医生、护士、孩子的父母、消费者、供应商和分销商)、员工、社区(包括当地的和全球范围内的社区)、最后才是公司的股票持有人。强生公司相信,如果它能满足前面三类利益相关者的需求,则它的投资人自然而然地就能获得公道的利润。任何人只要阅读一下来自 http://www.jnj.com/connect/caring/?flash = true 网址的该公司最近(2008年)的可持续发展报告书,就可以看到"信条"的影响显而易见的。

表5
强生公司可持续发展报告书的若干特点(1993~2007年)

	2007	2006	2005	2004	2003	2002
得到公众称许的次数	18	14	16	19	22	21
机构合伙人数目	n/a 不适用	6	13	20	20	20
是否包含了公司的机构图	否	否	否	是	是	是
各表和/图中所列示的指标数						
经济指标	9	9	4	5	5	1
员工健康指标	4	4	4	4	4	4
员工安全指标	4	5	5	5	5	5
环保指标	10	9	12	13	12	17
指标合计数	27	27	25	27	26	27
	2001	2000	1999	1998	1996	1993
得到公众称许的次数	18	14	7	27	4	0
机构合伙人数目	18	17	0	14	10	13
是否包含了公司的机构图	是	是	否	是	是	否
各表和/或图中所列示的指标						
经济指标	1	3	4	4	4	2
员工健康指标	4	0	3	0	0	0
员工安全指标	5	5	5	5	0	0
环保指标	16	12	10	11	7	10
指标合计数	26	20	22	20	11	12

表5概括了强生公司以前编制的12份可持续发展报告书内容的演变进程。该表包括了从1993~2007年间公司的经济、员工健康、员工安全和报告书所列的各项环保指标的数据。在这一期间内,报告书披露信息的数量和

种类有了很大的变化，这反映了强生公司对于应该报告什么、报告的深度与广度以尽到在其"信条"中所确定的责任并满足外部评审组织、机构的要求，在公司内部存在着不同意见。

分管公司全球"环境、健康和安全（Environmental, Health and Safety, EHS）"部的副总裁布赖恩·博伊德（Brian Boyd）对强生公司编制可持续发展报告书一事，提出了深刻见解[16]。博伊德（Boyd）在1990年时最早在强生公司担任环保工程师。他最初致力于一个制造工厂，但是很快地他就参与公司政策方面的工作。1999年他到公司总部，负责编制可持续发展报告书整个流程；到2008年这项工作移往公司通讯部（Corporate Communications）前，他一直是该项工作的领导人。

什么促使强生公司考虑并开始编制可持续发展报告书的？

博伊德：我对此知之不详。可能是因为公司外部的利益相关者对此有兴趣，才促使公司开始考虑的。

强生公司最初考虑发布可持续发展报告书时，有没有什么阻力？

博伊德：有些经理人员向来都不愿意提高透明度，这种情绪现在依然存在。我所负责的环保、健康和安全的小组，处于提出可持续发展报告书内容的第一线，所以直接经受外部的利益相关者对公司的压力，他们需要从公司获得这方面更多、更有用的信息。

他们迫切需要这些信息。有的经理人员并不直接参与编制可持续发展报告书的工作，他们就不支持或不了解增加透明度的必要性。他们认为编制可持续发展报告书，仅仅是一件额外的工作。

站在你的角度看，强生公司编制可持续发展报告书的目的是什么？

博伊德：有两个目的：一是把强生公司在可持续发展方面所做的工作，即强生公司是如何处理与之有关的各项问题的、强生公司的战略如何等，告诉利益相关者。二是利用报告书作为与利益相关者沟通的手段[17]。这是分享信息的途径之一。

你认为编制可持续发展报告书能有哪些有形的/无形的好处？换句话说，强生公司编制可持续发展报告书的目的，除了显然有助于改进公司的公共关系以外，还有什么别的目的？

博伊德：我们知道它能获得许多无形的好处，但具体能获得哪些有形的财务上的好处，却是难以计量的。在开展的各项可持续发展活动与财务成本或节约之间，并不存在直接的连带关系。

在无形的好处方面，可持续发展报告书是为强生公司所有的利益相关者而编制的，从邻近本公司制造工厂的居民到全球本公司投资的社区，都包括在内。在没有信息的情况下，许多人都对一家公司的环保、健康和安全方面

---

[16] 此次访谈发生于2009年5月，本案例中所述访谈的内容是经过了编纂的。——原注

[17] 此处加：公司通过报告书，使各利益相关者对强生公司面临的各项可持续发展方面的问题以及公司如何处理这些问题发生兴趣。他们会提出报告书中缺了什么内容，应该如何改进。因此，通过公布其可持续发展报告书，公司可以获得各利益相关者的反馈意见。——译者

的活动持负面看法——认为公司在这些方面不是毫无作为、便是有负面行为。

通过编制一份综合性的可持续发展报告书,强生公司满足了许多利益相关者(包括评级机构和倡议组织[18])的信息需求。例如某个从事倡议的组织需要知道这些大公司在做些什么;可持续发展报告书的内容就可以"启动[19]"对此问题的讨论。

编制报告书的过程也有助于降低风险。例如,编制可持续发展报告书,能减少应对某一非政府组织[20]发起的一场针对某项问题所作负面宣传活动的可能性。这一类的宣传活动会引起公司销售下降、利润减少。

强生公司使其利益相关者参与到公司编制可持续发展报告书的过程中来,采用的是哪些方法?

博伊德:本公司各利益相关者并没有参与到报表的实际编制过程,但更重要的是,这些利益相关者在公司确定战略和目标[例如 2010 年的"健康的地球(Healthy Planet)战略"]中,都是重要的参与人。公司在确定目标时要和利益相关者开会商讨,但这些利益相关者并不参与编纂报告书。

早期的可持续发展报告书附有一邮资预付的意见反馈卡,可以扯下把对环保、健康和安全方面的意见或建议等写在卡上寄回给公司的环保、健康与安全部门。但实际上收到的反馈意见不多,而增加的开支却比较大,所以几年后就不再这样做了。我们代之以在报告书中写明请各位利益相关者提出反馈意见,并详告电邮地址和/或信邮地址,供对方使用。

强生公司雇有"咨询售货员",向少数指定的利益相关者收集反馈意见。我们也与少数机构[如世界野生动物基金会(World Wildlife Fund)]举行专题会议,收集强生公司在某一个方面应该怎么做的建议和反馈意见。

哪些利益相关团体会收到可持续发展年度报告书?

博伊德:每年,所有的员工都会从网上收到可持续发展报告书;复印文本则寄送各董事会成员、公司的执行委员会和全球各地的最高层经理人员。可持续发展报告书也分送给所有负有社会责任的投资人和兄弟公司。一般的投资人不会收到可持续发展报告书,除非他们专门提出需要一份复印件。当前和以前若干年的可持续发展报告书都经过详细的讨论,并可以从强生公司的网址上查阅或下载。

强生公司是如何决定哪些部分应该复印包括在年度报告中、哪些应该包括在可持续发展报告书中、哪些又都不应包括在这两种报告书中的?是否列入某种报告的标准,是由谁权衡确定的?

博伊德:哪些应属于最重要的方面,这并不全是随意确定的,但也并不那样井然有序(我们希望将来能做到如此)。对于哪一项属于重要问题一

---

[18] advocacy group,姑译作"倡议组织",即游说机构(lobby group),它们在各种方式影响公众舆论,在帮助发展某项政治或社会制度方面(例如碳排放、水污染等问题)起重要作用。——译者

[19] jump-start,借用汽车因电池没了电,不能发动,于是找另外一辆车,把电线接在不能发动的车上,使该车得以发动。例如某个动物保护团体需要知道公司在这方面作了哪些努力,公司的可持续发展报告书如果有这方面的内容,就能与该团体进行对话,也就是赋予这些的对话以"动力"了。——译者

[20] NGO(non-governmental organizations),非政府组织(或民间组织)例如红十字会。——原注

事,尤难处理。对何者属于重大问题的决定,是由一个核心小组来确定的,该核心小组由一组流动性的职能部门领导人(大约10人)组成,并由来自首都华盛顿的外部咨询人员辅助其事。

报告书的实际内容和对该内容最初所作的修改,由各职能部门的领导作出。这些领导人提供与他/她所负责的职能部门有关的数据和问题/内容。报告书的内容,有向社会问题(而非环保、健康和安全问题)倾斜之势,在即将问世的2008年可持续发展报告书中,可以看出这种趋势。

报告书对哪些内容应保守机密,并不附有标准操作程序(Standard Operating Procedure,SOP)。各职能部门领导人进行争论之后,需要判断决定取舍。我总是争辩说,应该有比较高的透明度,但小组中的有些人则认为透明度低一些比较好。我们在发布任何对竞争、法律事务或与业务有关的敏感性数据时,都谨慎从事。

强生公司的可持续发展报告书主要是由哪一个部门管理的?在编制可持续发展报告书的过程中,还有哪些高层人员参与其事?

博伊德:在编制2007年可持续发展报告书的过程中,由公司的全球环保、健康和安全部门主持其事。编制2008年可持续发展的报告书,则移交给公司通讯部负责,该部门是参与编制上一年度的可持续发展报告书的十个职能部门之一。我支持这一权责转移,我认为报告书的内容应该比较均衡,应该更多地报告强生公司对社会的影响,不要局限于有关环保、健康和安全等问题。在强生公司内部,并没有一个专司各项社会问题之责的部门,因而看来可持续发展报告书以转由公司通讯部负责为宜。公司通讯部已经在着手编制年度报告书了。它现在经管这一项目,包括向有关职能部门的领导人收集数据和选定最终包罗在报告书中的细节内容。

各职能部门的领导人仍对他或她在可持续发展报告书中述及的那一部分负责,包括提供有关的数据、确定有关的各项问题,并把这些资料提交给公司通讯部。这一由10人左右组成的小组仍继续碰头,我个人负责编写有关环保、安全和健康等问题的部分。

参与其事的职能部门有哪些?

博伊德:参与其事的职能部门有:公司环保、健康与安全部;企业捐助[21]部;公司通讯部;投资者关系部;人力资源部;采购部;全球经营部;以及其他有关的业务单位的领导人。例如,如果可持续发展报告书中包含了一则强生公司在防治HIV的药物方面进展情况的报导,公司负责这方面工作的部门就会被邀参加这一部分的讨论。

会计/财务部门起着什么作用?

博伊德:在编制报告书的过程中,会计/财务部门并不是主要的参与者。大部分经济或公司财务数据都直接取自年度财务报表。会计/财务部门的人员要遵照SEC和其他有关报表的规定和要求,告诉我们哪些事项应该和不应该包括在可持续发展报告书中。

---

[21] Corporate Contributions,指企业对选举或其他公众事项的献金或捐助。——译者

编制可持续发展报告书的过程中所需要的资料,是由管理会计和/或数据体系中的哪些部分提供和/或传递的?强生公司是不是采用"全球性报表倡议(Global Reporting Initiative,GRI)"所提出的指标一览表所列的内容,作为报告书内容的指导?

博伊德:公司内部没有专门的体系为可持续发展报告书提供数据。各职能部门利用自己内部体系收集并向负责编制报告书的领导人提交有关的数据。

GRI列示的清单,并没能帮助强生公司确定报告书的内容。然而该清单确实有助于协调强生公司报告书的编制工作,使各年的报告书内容前后一致。我们尽力使自己的报告书与GRI协调一致。

强生公司所收集的数据,多半出于公司本身对考核和管理的需要以及利益相关者的需要。强生公司的管理内容,来自它的战略、"信条"和利益相关者。在社会/企业潮流和满足利益相关者对可持续发展报告书的需求方面,强生公司都位居前列[22],因为我们不仅坚持自己的"信条",而且密切注视世界各地向外展示的报告书所包含的内容的趋势,而不只是关注制药业或美国的趋势。例如,在公众开始提倡提供碳排放量的信息之前,我们就已在报告书中列示了这方面的数据。

强生公司现在的可持续发展报告书中的若干项目与最初的内容有所不同。在我们的竞争对手开始在报告书中包含若干GRI指标项目时,虽然这些指标并未给强生公司带来好处,但是,我们也开始把同样一些指标包括在报告书中。道琼斯可持续发展指数在对各公司评级时要求列入某些指标,至今我们仍认为这些指标并无列报的必要。正因为强生公司完全依据哪些对考核和管理企业及对我们的利益相关者的重要性,来选定我们的指标而不依排名次序作为选择的根据,因而在道琼斯可持续发展指数中强生公司的排名落后了。

强生公司的"信条"在发布可持续发展报告书中起到什么作用?"信条"对报告书的内容有哪些影响?

博伊德:在职能部门领导人会议中,并不明显地或全面地提及公司的"信条",但公司的"信条"都始终贯穿于每一项决策或员工的日常行为之中。正因为有了这个"信条",才成就了我们今天的辉煌。"信条"是一个有生命力的文件,强生公司所有的员工都视之为生活和工作的信念,因此它必须贯穿于编制可持续发展报告书的过程之中。

强生公司当前是不是存在第三方核查者[23]?

博伊德:我不太明白你这个问题的意思。强生公司与许多外部的利益相关团体——投资者、学术界、咨询人员、非政府组织和社区机构——接触频

---

[22] 引领潮流(ahead of the curve)意指在别人还没有找到解决某个问题的方法时,某人已领先提出了解决办法。例如对某个问题提出解决方法,总是有先后的,而且总是呈"正态分布"的——先知先觉者是少数,列在该分布曲线的(curve)的前沿,后知后觉者列在后沿,多数人列在中间。引领潮流者,就是在这条曲线中居领先地位者。——译者

[23] third party assurance,即由外部人员对其可持续发展报告书的正确性进行核实和检查。——译者

繁,以了解作为一个对社会和环境负责的公司,我们应该如何行事。我们并不要求这些团体对公司可持续发展报告书的编制过程或最终的报告书进行核查。我们就该问题与利益相关者之间进行沟通,要求他们帮助我们确定公司的战略和目标,使之符合他们的要求。这是公司对利益相关者许下的实际诺言,它对强生公司颇有价值,但不是一种核查。我们不能称之为"第三方的核查",但我们向这些人学到许多东西。他们使强生成为一家更好的公司。

强生公司的可持续发展报告书,当前是否存在保证其质量的正式的第三方核查者?

博伊德:没有。近期内我们也不打算有这样的核查者。要取得这样的核查,价格昂贵、旷日持久,且毫无价值。我们曾经试图对我们的可持续发展报告书取得正式的核查。然而,办成此事并不增加任何价值,因而公司的环保、健康与安全部门在进行到四分之三时,把这件事停了下来。在向核查者详细介绍本公司的情况中,太费时费力。我们并不认为做这样的核查会使利益相关者对报告书的可信度有所提高。

强生公司有没有考虑过编制"三重底线(人民、地球、利润)"的报告书?[24]

博伊德:强生公司已经超越了"三重底线"。我们收集并在报告书中列入了为环保支付的成本,而正式的"三重底线"报告书却并没有为利益相关者增加什么价值。任何一项与可持续发展有关的项目(诸如降低公司的碳排放量)必须通过"投资回报率"门槛和严格的成本/效益分析,才能得以实施。这样,强生公司才能够在降低其碳排放量的同时,为其利益相关者保持高额的回报率。我们并不是对各项可持续发展活动所引起的财务利益视而不见,但就当前可持续性报告书所提供的详细程度而言,我们并不认为正式的"三重底线"报告书在当前有什么价值。此外,从各项可持续发展活动所得的好处,是两方面的——既有其有形的方面,也有其无形的方面。

你还有什么想要补充的吗?

博伊德:强生公司之所以从事可持续发展项目,并不只是为了提高其声誉。公司的"信条"、服务社区、了解利益相关者的期望所在——这一切最终都使顾客们信赖强生公司,自然也就提高了公司的声誉。

公司 EHS 战略与实施部[25]的资深总监伊莉莎白·拉赛勒(Elizabeth Lascelle)对下述各项问题提供了后续资料:

强生公司现在没有对外公布所采用的 GRI 的级别,也没有宣布它遵照 GRI 的纲领办事。强生公司为什么决定如此行事?

拉塞勒:主要原因有二。首先,我们认为作出这些决定的时机没有成熟。其次,我们还需要具备报告更多的社会指标的能力。由于强生公司是个

---

[24] 三重底线(triple bottom line)在本文下面一个章节中详细介绍。——原注

[25] EHS Strategy & Assurance,指负责 EHS(ENVIRONMENT HEALTH & SAFETY)即环保、健康与安全部方面的策略并监督其实施的部门。——译者

实行分权管理制的企业，要这样做仍存在问题。有关员工和其他社会的指标，并不在总管全公司的层次上汇总。当前一个新的全球性人力资源体系正在建立之中，这使我们能够朝着这个方向前进。

强生公司是不是最终会公布它所采用的级别呢？如果是的话，强生公司是不是会1）自己来宣布它将采用的级别，2）把它的可持续发展报告书交由第三方审核，或者3）把它的可持续发展报告书交由 GRI 审核？原因何在？

拉塞勒：是的。我们以后会自己公布所采用的级别。如由第三方作出评估，将使报告书的编制工作增加很多成本，但我们对是否这样做，将继续斟酌再作决定。

会计人员与三重底线（和超越的?）报告书的编制

在本案例前面的一个章节中已对"三重底线"作了简要的叙述。三重底线（triple bottom line，TBL）是用于组织机构业绩考核的工具，它考核的范围比较广泛，不限于经济上的考核。它与平衡记分卡相似之处在于：它建立在利益相关者理论和多指标考核基础之上（Hubbard，2009）。"三重底线（TBL）"一词有时可与"编制可持续发展报告书"互换使用，因为 TBL 在传统的经济指标外，增加了社会和环保业绩指标（有时被称为"人民、地球、利润"）。TBL 这个概念的前提是，利益相关者的定义范围，要比传统的利益相关者所包括的群体——投资者、员工、顾客、供应商——更为广泛，它还包括了受该企业的经济、社会和环保业绩影响的当地社区和政府机构（Hubbard，2009）。

TBL 报告书由经济的、社会的和环保的这三个范畴所构成[26]。GRI 的各项业绩指标，可以很容易地按这三个范畴加以分类。理想的做法是，编制三重底线报告书的企业应确定其各项业绩指标，并在报告书中列示这些指标的完成进度。经济数据可取自年度报表或 10-K 表格，但 TBL 报告书的目的则是更全面地展示该企业的经济影响，以及对经济可持续发展作出的贡献，并且把经济数据与对社会和环保影响的数据整合成为一体。

《联合国、标准普尔和可持续发展报告书》（2006）的作者们认为，可持续发展报告书讨论的是涉及竞争、重要性、价值的内容。TBL 适用于下列价值范畴：

过去主要关注财务底线的公司，进入"三重底线"时代，需要把注意力扩展到对经济的、社会的、环保的和公司治理等各方面的影响。编制该报告书的单位数目正在不断增加，转而关注创造多方面的价值，并与当前和未

---

[26] Xcel Energy Inc. 发布了一份关于三重底线的年度报表。请访查此网址：http://www.xcelenergy.com/SiteCollectionDocuments/docs/2007TBLFull.pdf。——原注

来的经营战略和经营模式联系起来。(31)

上述调查结果表明，在编制 TBL 报告书方面，美国公司落后于欧洲的同行。此外，该研究预见，未来将会依据 GRI G3 指导方针，把 TBL 报告书包括在可持续发展报告书之中。

编制 TBL 报告书，应该被看作为达到目标的一项工具，而不是目标本身。按联合国副秘书长兼联合国环境规划署（UNEP）执行总监阿希姆·斯坦纳（Achim Steiner）的看法：

对于披露非财务方面的信息（尤其是编制可持续发展报告书），有对外和对内两种做法。编制三重底线报告书本身不是目标。它的价值在于使经理人员和员工获得更多的信息，从而促使他们净化和改善环境。它的价值还在于使他们与外部利益相关者之间更好地互通情报，弄清市场和社会对他们有何期望。（UNEP and KPMG 2006，第 3 页）

TBL 并不是强生公司用来达到其可持续发展目标的一项工具。强生公司并不编制 TBL，虽然在 2007 年的报告书中包含了 TBL 中的许多元素，它也并未使用可持续发展报告书这个术语。如前所述，当布赖恩·博伊德在访谈中被问及 TBL 为什么不是编制报表的内容之一时，他回答说"强生公司所做的，已经超越了三重底线的界限"。

就强生公司而言，管理会计师在编制可持续发展报告书中并没有起到重要的作用。管理会计师和其他财务专业人员能否在编制通常的可持续发展报告书或特定的三重底线（TBL）会计报表中起到作用呢？按克劳福德（Crawford，2005）的说法，这些专业人员需要改变他们现有的编制报表方法或者采用一些新的方法，从原先编制单一的财务报表的做法转变为编制多重底线的 TBL 的做法。克劳福德还进一步指明了不同做法适用于哪一种 GRI 业绩考核指标，"以便使缺乏经验的管理和编制可持续发展报告书者，对这项工作也能有所了解"（Crawford，2005，2）。例如，一家公司要求其供应商达到某项社会标准，则其 GRI 业绩指标就要包括一些定量指标，如在约定的期限内付款的合约所占的百分比数；也包括诸如如何处理有关人权方面问题的政策和传统做法的一些定性描述（Crawford，2005，3）。随着 CMA[27] 在劳资关系、国际贸易和对环保工作成绩的评估方法获得更多的教育和培训，他们有可能成为编制强生公司的可持续发展报告书工作中的重要参与者。

本案例的要求

1. 当前还没有对公司提出编制可持续发展报告书的要求，你认为编制这种报告书可能获得的好处和存在的缺点各有哪些？根据本案例所提供的资料、在表 4 和表 5 中所列示的汇总数据，以及强生公司最近的可持续发展报

---

[27] 注册管理会计师（Certified Management Accountant），经过考试合格、由管理会计师协会（IMA）授证的管理会计师。——译者

告书（可从 http://www.jnj.com/connect/caring/?flash=true 取得），在编制可持续发展报告书中，公司重点在哪？理由何在？请从2008年的可持续发展报告书中取得实例，以支持你的论点。

2. 各项管理制度，诸如人力资源管理、成本、资本预算和业绩考核如何与强生公司可持续发展报告书的编制过程结合起来？回答这个问题时，请具体引述该公司2008年的报表资料（网络联结见问题1所示）。请把你所引述的根据与GRI的报表编制程式（见 http://www.globalreporting.org/ReportingFramework/G3Online/）和在表3中所示Epstein的业绩考核指标相比较。

3. 强生公司为可持续发展报告书汇编数据时，并没有要求管理会计干部直接提供资料。那么，管理会计人员在收集和编报可持续发展报告书的数据中，应该起到什么作用呢？如果强生公司编制可持续发展报告书能够从管理会计人员取得数据，是不是有助于这项工作的开展？请说明你的理由（Crawford 2005年的文章，对这个问题提供了背景资料；请从 http://www.managementmag.com/index.cfm/ci_id/2149/la_id/1 取得该文）。

4. 你是否同意强生公司编制可持续发展报告书的做法已经超越了三重底线的说法？理由何在？

5. 强生公司认为确定重要性是件难事，正因为如此，它并没有宣称要按照GRI的指导准则办事。此处"重要性"指的是什么、为什么重要性在社会责任方面的问题上是难以确定的？

参考文献

（略）

附录 A：外部评审机构及其缩写

道琼斯可持续发展北美指数（Dow Jones Sustainable Index North America）

http：//www. sustainability-index. com/djsi _ pdf/publications/Factsheets/SAM_IndexesMonthly_DJSINA. pdf

道琼斯可持续发展北美指数（DJSI North America）包括道琼斯全球指数（Dow Jones Global Index）600 家北美最大公司中在可持续发展方面领先的 20% 的公司。组成这一指数的公司，是根据对公司作有系统的可持续发展的评估，通过评估在 57 个行业中选取在可持续发展方面占领先地位的企业。对此所采用的研究方法是，既依一般的可持续发展趋势、又按具体行业的可持续发展趋势，根据多项评价的尺度（包括气候变化对策、能源消耗、人力资源开发、知识管理[28]、与利益相关人之间的关系和公司治理）对企业作出评估。

金融时报 100 指数（FTSE 100 Index）

http：//www. ftse. com/Indices/FTSE4Good_Index_Series/index. jsp

英国金融时报指数系列（FTSE U. K. Index Series）是用以代表英国公司的业绩情况，向投资者提供一个综合性的和一套互相补充的指数，用以量度英国资本市场所有的金融和工商业部门的绩效。金融时报 100 指数，包含了 100 家高度资本化的蓝筹股公司，大约相当于英国市场的 81%。它被广泛地应用于投资产品（例如衍生工具和交易所交易基金）评估的基础。

社会投资论坛（Social Investment Forum）

http：//www. socialinvest. org/about/

社会投资论坛是美国的一个全国性非营利协会，其成员包括志在促进向社会负责的投资（socially responsible investing，SRI）的实务和增长的专业人士、企业和组织。对负责任的投资实务起决定性作用的，除了对财务状况作良好的分析以外，还要考虑到环保、社会和公司治理方面的条件。论坛的成员通过对投资组合所作的分析、股东请愿[29]和社区的投资，来支持 SRI。社会投资论坛 400 名成员中，包括投资管理和咨询公司、融通基金公司、研究所、财务分析人员和顾问、经纪人、银行、信用社、社区发展机构、非营利协会、养老基金、基金、美洲土著部落和其他各类资产拥有者。

可持续资产管理公司（Sustainable Asset Management Inc. ，SAM）

http：//www. sam-group. com/htmle/main. cfm

SAM 是可持续发展方面领先的资产管理者，它提供可持续发展趋势、战略和投资者感兴趣的各方面广泛的专门知识。

---

[28] 知识管理（Knowledge Management）是一种新的管理思潮和实践，主要是因应当前知识社会、信息爆炸、知识工作者成为员工主流，而被各类组织实施的研究手段和方法。——译者取自《有道词典》

[29] shareholder advocacy，指持有某种主张的股东派人参加公司的股东大会，运用投票权使其主张得以通过的一种做法——译者

附录 B：强生公司的信条

引自 http：//www.jnj.com/connect/about-jnj/jnj-credo/?flash=true

我们的信条

我们深信，我们的首要责任，是向医生、护士和病人负责，
向使用我们的产品和服务的父母们和所有一切人士负责。
为了满足他们的需要，我们所做的一切都必须是高质量的。
我们必须不懈地努力降低成本，保持合理价格。
快速、准确地完成顾客订单。
确保供应商与经销商能够有利可图。

我们对自己的员工——在世界各地和我们一起工作的
男女员工——负责。
每一位员工必须被看作是个独立的个体。
我们必须维护他们的尊严，赞赏他们的优点。
他们在工作中应该有安全感。
给他们的报酬必须是公道和恰当的，工作环境应
清洁、有序和安全。
我们必须时刻想到如何帮助员工实现他们对家庭的责任。
员工们必须感到有提出建议和申诉的自由。
他们必须在按其本身的条件被雇用、给予发展
和被提升方面有平等的机会。
我们的管理层必须能胜任愉快，他们所作所为
必须公正并合乎职业道德。

我们对工作与生活所在的社区以及整个世界
这个大社区负责。
我们必须成为良好的公民——支持好人好事和慈善事业，
并且负担我们应尽的纳税责任。
我们必须鼓励各项公共设施的改善，提供更好的
保健和教育。
我们必须维护使这些设施，使其处于良好的状态，
使我们得以利用、保护环境和各项自然资源。

最后，我们向公司的股东们负责。
业务经营必须能获得合理的利润。
我们必须尝试各项新的倡议。
必须进行研究、对新的有创造性的建议必须进行
探索、教训必须汲取。
必须购置新的设备、提供新的设施、并推出新的产品。
必须积谷备荒。
如果我们能够遵照这些原则来经营，股东们就
应能得到公道的回报。

Johnson & Johnson

Johnson & Johnson: A Case Study on Sustainability Reporting

Susan Borkowski
La Salle University

Mary Jeanne Welsh
La Salle University

Kristin Wentzel
La Salle University

> *Imagine a future where reporting on environmental and social performance is as routine as reporting on financial performance.*
> — (Gilbert 2002, 26)

INTRODUCTION

The phrase "sustainable business" can be associated with a wide range of corporate initiatives related to issues such as a company's impact on the environment, programs to help employees live healthier lives, community development programs, customer safety programs, and fair trade practices. In turn, information about these initiatives is of interest to multiple stakeholders, including investors who are interested in socially responsible investing, consumers who want to buy "green" products, and community groups concerned about the environmental impact of neighboring businesses. Clikeman (2004, 24) provides this working definition of sustainability: "a philosophy that weighs the current economic benefits of activities against the effects of those activities on future generations." In other words, socially responsible companies assess not only the short-and long-term economic implications of their current activities, but also the long-term environmental and societal effects of their current actions, leading to the triple bottom line approach of reporting environmental, social, and economic performance.

With exceptions in some countries (e.g., Japan, Sweden, Norway), companies are not required to provide separate reports on corporate social responsibility. Demand for information from stakeholders and a growing recognition that traditional accounting reports are not well-suited to providing this type of information, however, has led an increasing number of companies to issue separate sustainability reports. How does a company decide which of a myriad of sustainability initiatives to pursue? How is information about a company's socially responsible activities gathered, assessed, and disseminated? To provide some insight into these questions, Johnson & Johnson and its relatively long history of providing sustainability reports serves as the focus of this case study. The company first began setting environmental goals in 1990, with intermittent public reports following in 1993, and annual sustainability reports beginning in 1998.

THE EMERGING IMPORTANCE OF SUSTAINABILITY ACCOUNTING

While there is no formal regulation requiring that all publicly-traded companies provide a stand-alone report detailing information on sustainability initiatives, more companies worldwide voluntarily disclose detailed data about their triple bottom lines of environmental, social, and economic performance. Clikeman (2004) argues that when a company practices, documents, and discloses its sustainable development activities to its stakeholders, the company will reap many benefits not usually associated with releasing data in an annual financial report. These benefits are summarized by Clikeman from a more detailed list developed by the World Council for Sustainable Development (see Table 1) and include:

- Provides a sound basis for dialogue and discussion with stakeholders;
- Channels pertinent information to targeted stakeholders and thus enhances corporate visibility and helps demonstrate transparency;
- Helps build reputation, which, over the long term, will contribute to increased brand value, customer loyalty, and market share;
- Encourages and facilitates implementation of rigorous management systems to better monitor environmental and social risks;
- Assists the company in demonstrating its business values and principles about environmental and social issues;
- Helps attract "patient" shareholders who have a long-term horizon and helps justify lower-risk premiums from investors and creditors (Clikeman 2004, 24).

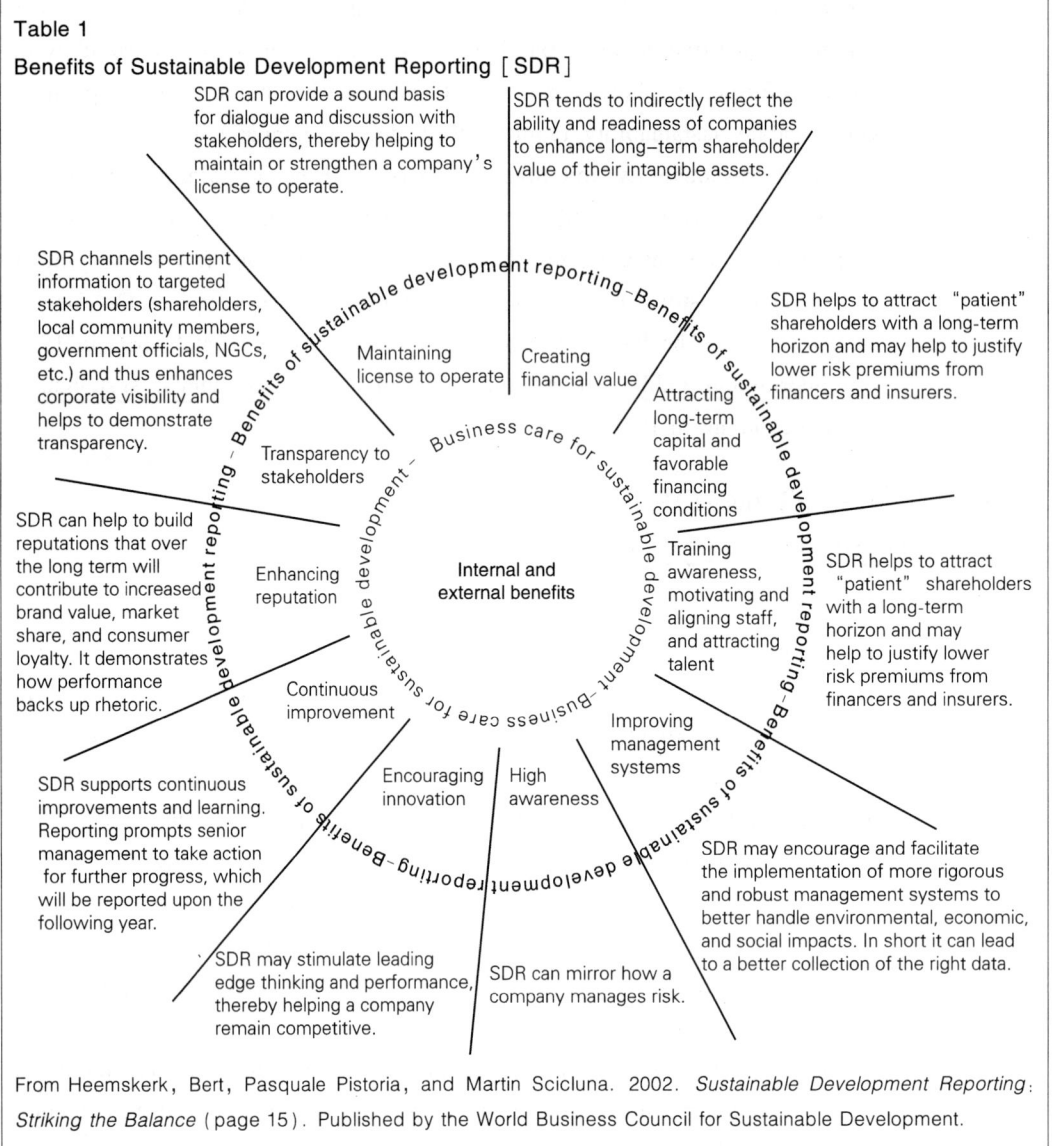

Along with the absence of consistent regulations requiring corporate sustainability reporting, there is also a lack of reporting standards analogous to generally accepted accounting principles. Since 1997, however, there has been an ongoing effort to establish standards for sustainability reporting. In 1997, the Boston-based nonprofit CERES (Coalition for Environmentally Responsible Economies) started a Global Reporting Initiative (GRI). The United Nations Environment Programme joined as a partner in 1999, the same year that an exposure draft of GRI Sustainability Reporting Guidelines was released. In 2002, CERES set up the GRI as an independent body.[①] The GRI's mission is to "integrate and unify the many standards in the marketplace into a single,

---

① http://www.globalreporting.org/AboutGRI/WhatWeDo/OurHistory/

generally accepted sustainability reporting framework, encompassing environmental, social, and economic performance" (Gilbert 2002, p. 21). The GRI released its first sustainability reporting framework and guidelines in 2000, its G2 revision in 2002, and its current G3 iteration in 2006 (GRI 2006).

The G3 guidelines set out the core content for a sustainability report. The purpose of sustainability reporting, as defined in the G3 guidelines, "... is the practice of measuring, disclosing, and being accountable to internal and external stakeholders for organizational performance towards the goal of sustainable development." (GRI 2006, 4) The standard disclosures to be included in any sustainability report should address:

• **Strategy and Profile**: Disclosures that set the overall context for understanding organizational performance such as its strategy, profile, and governance.

• **Management Approach**: Disclosures that cover how an organization addresses a given set of topics in order to provide context for understanding performance in a specific area.

• **Performance Indicators**: Indicators that elicit comparable information on the economic, environmental, and social performance of the organization. (GRI 2006, 6)

While the first two sets of disclosures are self-explanatory, performance indicators are both quantitative and qualitative, requiring descriptions of corporate policies, processes, and effects. For example, human rights performance indicators could include "Total number of incidents of discrimination and actions taken" (quantitative) and "Operations identified as having significant risk for incidents of child labor, and measures taken to contribute to the elimination of child labor" (qualitative) (G3 Guidelines, 2006, 33).

The GRI reports that more than 1 000 companies worldwide voluntarily adopted G3 guidelines for their sustainability reports in 2008, an increase of 46% over 2007 (GRI 2009). These companies represent only 13% of the companies listed on the Standard & Poor's 500 in the U.S., and only 22% of the companies listed on the FTSE 100[2] in the U.K. The GRI results indicate that European companies account for 49% of the 2008 reports, Asian companies 15%, North American companies 14%, Latin American companies 12%, Oceania 6%, and Africa 4%. These results vary significantly from those of KPMG, which periodically publishes a survey on social responsibility reporting by the Global Fortune 250 and the 100 largest companies by revenue in 22 countries.

In 2007, Sweden was the first country to require its state-owned companies, such as Scandinavian Airlines (SAS), to prepare annual GRI-based sustainability

---

[2] Please see Appendix A for an explanation of external validating organizations and abbreviations used in this case.

reports as of March 2009. For decades, the rates of reporting among the largest multinational companies have been highest among Japanese and U. K. global companies due to country-specific pressures (KPMG 2008, 15). Companies that list on the Japanese stock exchange must comply with environmental performance and reporting regulations, while companies in the U. K. face pressure from various constituencies, including the government, media, consumers, and shareholders, to be transparent on key sustainability issues. Norwegian companies are required to produce environmental reports, while French and German companies must provide both social and environmental reports to the public. U. S. companies have been much slower to report on corporate social responsibility, given the lack of pressure from their stakeholders.

The lack of U. S. companies reporting on their sustainability activities may soon be a thing of the past, if recent actions by the U. S. Securities and Exchange Commission (SEC) are any indication. In July 2009, the SEC formed an Investor Advisory Committee. This group is studying input from groups interested in socially responsible investing (such as the Social Investment Forum) on what constitutes "effective mandatory corporate reporting on environmental, social and governance issues" (Kropp 2009, 1). The SEC could eventually require complete sustainability reports from its filing companies in addition to the already mandatory 10K and other financially-specific reports.

HOW TO IMPLEMENT CORPORATE SUSTAINABILITY REPORTING

Once a company decides to expand from financial reporting to include sustainability reporting, management must decide which economic, social, and environmental activities should be measured, and what metrics to use to obtain those measurements. Epstein (2008) discusses many implementation and measurement issues related to corporate sustainability reporting. The overriding issue centers on the difficulty in "implement(ing) the proper systems to pursue sustainability and to evaluate the impacts of sustainability on financial performance and the tradeoffs that ultimately must be made" (Epstein 2008, 26). These trade-offs include maximizing the corporate bottom line while balancing the costs associated with managing corporate sustainability. Epstein's corporate sustainability model provides an effective blueprint for implementing sustainability reporting (Table 2).

Commitment to sustainability reporting requires management to decide what activities need to be measured, and then to identify the best metric for measurement. As previously mentioned, the GRI provides a complete sustainability reporting framework and the required indicators to assess a company's economic, social, and environmental activities, but does not dictate how a company should measure each indicator. A sample of possible metrics to measure the drivers in Epstein's corporate sustainability model is presented in Table 3.

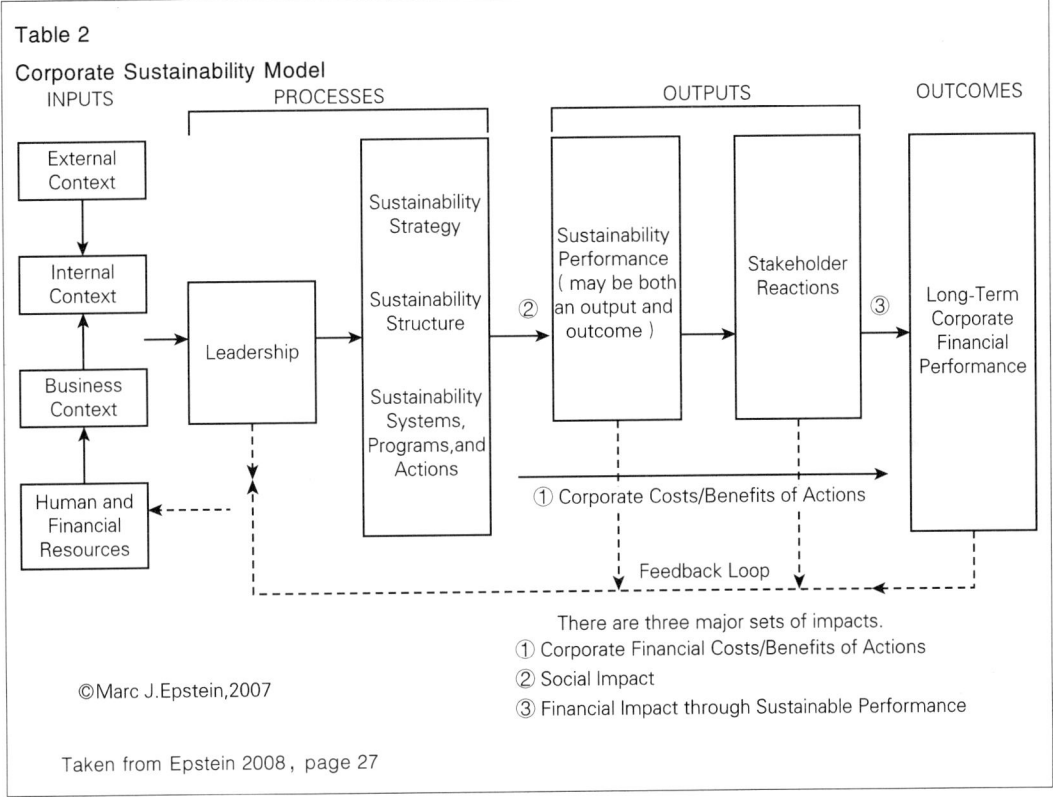

Epstein's (2008) model looks at an organization's inputs to determine the sustainability processes needed to produce the desired outputs and long-term outcomes. Specifically, inputs include internal, external, and business content, along with the human and financial resources of the corporation. Inputs provide the foundation for determining what processes are needed to improve sustainability. Managerial actions and stakeholder reactions determine long-term corporate financial performance. The model includes feedback loops for evaluating the cost and benefit trade-offs of an organization's sustainability efforts so that adjustments can be made along the way.

Table 3

Some Sustainability Metrics to Measure Inputs, Processes, Outputs and Outcomes

DRIVER: Inputs
Alignment of corporate strategy to sustainability
Number and diversity of business units
Geographic diversity of production and sales
Sustainability impact of processes, industry, and product
Corporate financial position
Industry competitive position
Sustainability component in managerial performance evaluation
Resources available for sustainability

DRIVER: Processes
Number of plant visits
Commitment of corporate and sustainability leadership
Child labor protection
Access of sustainability management to top management
Excellence in board processes
Resources devoted to sustainability
Adoption of codes and standards for sustainability improvement (including number of facilities certified)
Number and level of staff devoted to sustainability
Hours of ethics training per employee
Number of suppliers certified for sustainability

DRIVER: Outputs
Number of plant closing
Volume of hazardous waste
Packaging volume
Amount of minority business purchases
Money contributed through philanthropy and cause-related marketing
Percent and number of women and minorities in senior positions
Number of injuries
Number of spills, accidents, discharges
Numbers of human rights and labor violations
Results of ethics audit
Rate of defective products
Number of consumer protests
Number of employee grievances
Number of fines
Number of product recalls
By-product revenue
Number of social funds listing company stock
Number of awards received

DRIVER: Outcomes
Revenue from recycled waste materials
Revenue from cause-related marketing
Increased sales from improved reputation
Reduced cost of materials due to reduced waste
Employee turnover reduction
Revenue growth
Reduced cost of environmental cleanup
ROI
Profits

Taken from Epstein 2008, page 30.

  Before looking at Johnson & Johnson's sustainability reports, consider the bigger picture of sustainability reporting in the pharmaceutical industry. Newsweek recently issued its first rankings of the greenest companies in America, assessing the environmental impact, green policies, and environmental reputation of the largest 500 companies in the U.S. (McGinn 2009). The most recent assessment of sustainability performance by Sustainable Asset Management Inc. [SAM] and PricewaterhouseCoopers (2010) is based on the responses of 37 of the 69 largest pharmaceutical firms worldwide. Johnson & Johnson consistently ranks as one of the world's industry leaders as shown in the table below:

SUSTAINABILITY LEADERS 2009/2010		
SAM Gold Class:	Roche Holding AG*	Switzerland
	AstraZeneca Plc	United Kingdom
	Novartis AG	Switzerland
	Novo Nordisk A/S	Denmark
SAM Silver Class:	Abbott Laboratories	United States
	Johnson & Johnson	United States [Bronze Class in 2007/2008, Silver Class in 2008/2009]
	Sanofi Aventis	France
SAM Bronze Class	GlaxoSmithKline	United Kingdom

* SAM Sector Leader. To qualify for the SAM Gold Class, a company must achieve a minimum total score of 75% across economic, environmental, and social criteria. To qualify for the Silver Class, a company must achieve a total score in the range of 70-75%. To qualify for the Bronze Class, a company must achieve a total score in the range of 65-70%.

Taken from SAM and PwC, 2010 (page 84)

http://www.sam-group.com/htmle/yearbook/? CFID = 961207&CFTOKEN = a06ee7afaf158e0c-C0EAEB14-E1BA-B686-402A4B662ED3C9FA

———The pharmaceutical industry as a whole appears to embrace sustainability reporting, probably because of the environmental and societal implications associated with researching and manufacturing pharmaceutical products.

JOHNSON & JOHNSON: SUSTAINABILITY REPORTING, THEN AND NOW

Johnson & Johnson first began setting environmental goals in 1990, with intermittent public reports following in 1993, and annual reports beginning in 1998. The early annual reports focused primarily on environmental issues and included "Environmental, Health and Safety" in the title, but by 2003, Johnson & Johnson described the document simply as a sustainability report. Table 4 presents a summary of Johnson & Johnson's 12 sustainability reports published from 1993 to 2007. In Newsweek's first ranking of the greenest big companies in America, Johnson & Johnson ranked third (behind only Hewlett-Packard and Dell) because of its "commitment to climate change... strong environmental management in place... (and the) largest fleet of hybrid vehicles in the world" (McGinn 2009).

The heart of Johnson & Johnson's commitment to sustainability reporting appears to be its Credo. In any conversation with a Johnson & Johnson employee about the company, the Credo (included as Appendix B) will be mentioned within the first few minutes. Every business decision, whether made by the mid-level manager or the vice president of production, is Credo-driven. As explained on the corporate website, it is the Credo values that are at the core of the company:

The values that guide our decision making are spelled out in Our Credo. Put simply, Our Credo challenges us to put the needs and well-being of the people we serve *first*.

Robert Wood Johnson, former chairman from 1932 to 1963 and a member of the Company's founding family, crafted Our Credo himself in 1943, just before Johnson & Johnson became a publicly traded company. This was long before anyone ever heard the term "corporate social responsibility." Our Credo is more than just a moral compass. We believe it's a recipe for business success. The fact that Johnson & Johnson is one of only a handful of companies that have flourished through more than a century of change is proof of that.

—From the Johnson & Johnson corporate website, *Our Credo Values*, http://www.jnj.com/connect/about-jnj/jnj-credo/? flash = true

TABLE 4
JOHNSON & JOHNSON'S SUSTAINABILITY REPORTS 1993 – 2007

	2007	2006	2005	2004	2003	2002
Name of Report	Sustainability Report	Sustainability Report	Sustainability Report	Sustainability Report	Sustainability Report	Environmental, Health & Safety Sustainability Report
Catchphrase	Profiles in commitment	Passion, performance, Possibilities	Engaging more people, preserving the planet	Living our credo	Healthy people, healthy planet, healthy futures	Healthy people, healthy planet
Number of pages	45	36	52	44	50	34
Location of Credo	Back cover	p. ii	p. 2	p. 7	Back cover	Back cover
	2001	2000	1999	1998	1996	1993
Name of Report	Environmental, Health and Safety Sustainability Report	Environmental, Health and Safety Sustainability Report	Environmental, Health and Safety Report	Environmental, Health and Safety Report	Sustaining Our Worldwide Environmental Commitment	A Special Responsibility
Catchphrase	Healthy people, healthy planet	Healthy people, healthy planet	Healthy people, healthy planet	n/a	Sustaining Our Worldwide Environmental Commitment	A Special Responsibility
Number of pages	34	30	18	39	24	31
Location of Credo	Back cover	Back cover	Back cover	p. 2	Not included	Not included

Even a casual reading of any of Johnson & Johnson's sustainability reports reveals constant specific references to the Credo and Johnson & Johnson's responsibilities to its four groups of stakeholders in this order: customers (including doctors, nurses, patients, mothers, fathers, consumers, suppliers, and distributors), employees, the community (both local and global), and finally, the shareholders. Johnson & Johnson believes that if it meets the needs of the first three groups of stakeholders, then a fair profit should automatically accrue to its investors. The impact of the Credo becomes evident as one reads the most recent (2008) sustainability report, available at http://www.jnj.com/

connect/caring/? flash = true.

An evolution of the content of Johnson & Johnson's 12 sustainability reports is summarized in Table 5, including the economic, employee health, employee safety, and environmental indicators reported from 1993 through 2007. The amount and type of information that is reported changed significantly during this reporting period, reflecting Johnson & Johnson's own internal struggle to determine what should be reported, and in what quantity and depth, to satisfy its responsibilities as defined by its Credo and by external validating organizations and agencies.

TABLE 5

SOME CHARACTERISTICS OF JOHNSON &JOHNSON'S SUSTAINABILITY REPORTS 1993–2007

	2007	2006	2005	2004	2003	2002
Number of recognitions	18	14	16	19	22	21
Number of organizational partners	n/a	6	13	20	20	20
Organizational chart included	No	No	No	Yes	Yes	Yes
Indicators presented in tables and/or graphs						
Economic indicators	9	9	4	5	5	1
Employee health indicators	4	4	4	4	4	4
Employee safety indicators	4	5	5	5	5	5
Environmental indicators	10	9	12	13	12	17
Total indicators	27	27	25	27	26	27
	2001	2000	1999	1998	1996	1993
Number of recognitions	18	14	7	27	4	0
Number of organizational partners	18	17	0	14	10	13
Organizational chart included	Yes	Yes	No	Yes	Yes	No
Indicators presented in tables and/or graphs						
Economic indicators	1	3	4	4	4	2
Employee health indicators	4	0	3	0	0	0
Employee safety indicators	5	5	5	5	0	0
Environmental indicators	16	12	10	11	7	10
Total indicators	26	20	22	20	11	12

Brian Boyd, Worldwide Vice-President for Environmental, Health and Safety (EHS), provided insights on Johnson & Johnson sustainability reporting in an interview. ③Boyd started as an environmental engineer at Johnson & Johnson in 1990. He initially focused on one manufacturing plant, but he quickly became involved in corporate policy. In 1999 he came to corporate with responsibility for the sustainability reporting process, which he headed until 2008 when the responsibility was moved to Corporate Communications.

What prompted Johnson & Johnson to consider and then start sustainability reporting?

Boyd: I don't really know. We might have started because of increased

---

③ The interview took place May 7, 2009. Interview responses have been edited.

interest by external stakeholders.

When J&J first considered issuing sustainability reports, was there any resistance to issuing sustainability reports?

Boyd: There has always been and continues to be reluctance to increase transparency on the part of some managers. My Environmental, Health and Safety group is on the front line of the sustainability report content, so we see the pull from external stakeholders for more and better information.

There's a genuine desire for information. Some managers who are not directly involved in sustainability reporting issues do not support or understand the need for increased transparency. Sustainability reporting just becomes one more thing to do.

What is the purpose of sustainability reporting at Johnson & Johnson from your perspective?

Boyd: Two purposes:

To share with stakeholders what Johnson & Johnson is doing on sustainability, how Johnson & Johnson is dealing with various relevant issues, what Johnson & Johnson's strategies are, etc.

And to serve as a tool of engagement with stakeholders. It's a way to share information.

What are the tangible/intangible benefits you see from sustainability reporting? In other words, why does Johnson & Johnson produce the sustainability report beyond the obvious purpose of corporate public relations?

Boyd: We see a lot of intangible benefits, but tangible financial benefits are difficult to measure. There's no straight line connecting sustainability activities and any financial costs or savings.

As an intangible benefit, the sustainability reports are produced for the full range of Johnson & Johnson's stakeholders, from the neighbor living near a manufacturing plant to the global investment community. In the absence of information, many people assume the negative about a company's environmental, health, and safety activities—that the company is either doing nothing or doing bad things.

By producing one comprehensive sustainability report, Johnson & Johnson is able to satisfy the information needs of many stakeholders, including ratings companies, advocacy groups, etc. For example, the advocacy community wants to know what large companies are doing; the sustainability reports can jump-start the conversation.

The reporting process also helps to mitigate risk. For example, the sustainability report reduces the possibility of dealing with a negative advertising campaign by an NGO[④] on an issue, which could cascade into reduced sales and decreased profits.

In what ways does Johnson & Johnson engage its stakeholders in its sustainability reporting process?

Boyd: Stakeholders are not engaged in the actual reporting process, but, more importantly, they're valued participants in defining strategies and goal-setting (such as the Healthy Planet 2010 strategy). Meetings are set up with stakeholders to identify goals, but stakeholders aren't used in putting together the report.

The early sustainability reports included postage-paid feedback cards that could be detached and sent back to Environmental, Health and Safety with comments, suggestions, etc. That was an expensive addition to the sustainability report and we didn't get much feedback, so we stopped after several years. We've replaced the card with a statement inviting feedback from stakeholders and providing the e-mail and/or mailing addresses to which any feedback should be directed.

Johnson & Johnson uses consultants to get feedback from smaller directed groups of stakeholders. We also set up focused meetings with smaller groups, such as the World Wildlife Fund, to gather suggestions and feedback about what Johnson & Johnson should be doing in a given area.

Which stakeholder groups receive the annual sustainability report?

Boyd: Every year, the sustainability report is sent electronically to all employees, with hard copies going to the board of directors, the executive committee, and top senior managers worldwide. The sustainability report is also sent to all socially responsible investors and peer companies. Regular investors do not receive the sustainability report unless they specifically request a hard copy. The current and several prior years of the sustainability reports are prominently discussed and are available for download or printing on the Johnson & Johnson website.

How does J&J decide what goes into print (in its annual report versus its sustainability report) and what is not reported in either venue? Who sets the thresholds and weights the issues?

Boyd: The decision on what the most important areas are is not totally ad hoc, but it's also not made as methodically as it might in the future. The materiality issue is especially hard to deal with. A fluid group of function leaders (about 10) form the core group to make materiality decisions, with the help of an external consultant from Washington, D. C.

The actual content and initial editing of that content is left to each function

---

④ NGO refers to non-governmental organizations such as the Red Cross.

leader, who provides the data and the issues/topics that are relevant to his/her functional area. There has been a move to more reporting on social issues rather than on environmental, health, and safety issues, which should be evident in the upcoming 2008 sustainability report.

There is no SOP on what should be kept confidential. It's a judgment call that follows debate among the function heads. I always argue for greater transparency and some in the group want less. We're careful not to release any data that is sensitive in any competitive, legal, or other business context.

In what division is Johnson & Johnson's sustainability reporting primarily managed? What other offices are considered important participants in the sustainability reporting process?

Boyd: Through the production of the 2007 report, the Worldwide Environmental, Health and Safety group was in charge of the sustainability report. The 2008 sustainability reporting responsibility was moved to Corporate Communications, which was one of the 10 function leaders involved in the production of Johnson & Johnson's previous sustainability reports. I supported the shift because I think the report needs to be more balanced, with more about Johnson & Johnson's social impact and less about the narrower environmental, health, and safety issues. No one group in Johnson & Johnson has the responsibility for social issues, and Corporate Communications seemed a good place to move the sustainability report. Corporate Communication already does the annual report. It now administers the project, including collecting data from the relevant function heads and choosing what stories eventually will be published.

Each function head is still responsible for his or her own piece of the sustainability report, including providing the data and identifying the relevant issues, and submitting these to Corporate Communication. The group of 10 or so will continue to meet and I'll edit environmental, safety, and health issues.

What are the functional groups that participate?

Boyd: The functional groups that participate are Corporate Environmental, Health, and Safety; Corporate Contributions; Corporate Communications; Investor Relations; Human Resources; Procurement; Worldwide Operations; and relevant business unit leaders. For example, if the sustainability report contains a story of Johnson & Johnson's HIV pharmaceutical advances, that business unit leader is brought in for that part of the discussion.

What is the role of accounting/finance?

Boyd: Accounting/finance is not a primary participant in the process. Much of the economic or corporate financial data come directly from the annual report. The accounting/finance people are used to answer questions about what can and cannot be included according to SEC and other reporting regulations and requirements.

What sorts of management accounting and/or data systems provide input and/or feed data into the sustainability reporting process? Does Johnson & Johnson use the Global Reporting Initiative [GRI] indicator list as a guide for content?

Boyd: No specific systems provide data for the sustainability reports. Each functional group uses its own internal systems to collect and report the relevant data to the project leader.

The GRI list didn't help Johnson & Johnson decide what to report. The list did help in coordinating what Johnson & Johnson was reporting, and provided consistency in what was reported from year to year. We try to align our report with the GRI as best as we can.

The data Johnson & Johnson tends to collect is driven by what the company itself wants to measure and manage, and by what its stakeholders need. What Johnson & Johnson wants to manage comes from its strategy, Credo, and stakeholders. Johnson & Johnson is ahead of both the societal/business curve and what stakeholders want in its sustainability reporting because we stay true to the Credo and because we closely monitor global trends in what data are reported worldwide, not just in pharma or in the U.S. Here's an example: We were reporting on carbon emissions before there was much public push for the information.

There are some line items reported now in the sustainability reports that weren't originally reported by Johnson & Johnson. When competitors started reporting some GRI index line items, Johnson & Johnson started to include the same metrics, even though they provide us no use or benefit. The Dow Jones Sustainability Index requires certain metrics when ranking companies that even now we feel are not worth reporting, so Johnson & Johnson receives a lower ranking on the Dow Jones Sustainability Index strictly due to our choice to measure and manage what is important to the company and to our stakeholders, rather than what is important to rating agencies.

What role does Johnson & Johnson's Credo play in the decision to issue sustainability reports? How does the Credo influence the content?

Boyd: The Credo is not discussed explicitly or overtly in any of the function head meetings, but it informs every decision or action taken by an employee on a daily basis. We are who we are because of the Credo. The Credo is a living document that all Johnson & Johnson employees live and work by, so it necessarily underlies the whole sustainability reporting process.

Does Johnson & Johnson currently have any informal third party assurance?

Boyd: I'm not sure I understand your question. Johnson & Johnson has frequent contact with many external stakeholder groups—investors, academics, consultants, NGOs, and community organizations—to understand what we need to do to be a socially and environmentally responsible company. We don't ask these groups to provide any assurance of the final sustainability reports or of the reporting process itself. The interaction with stakeholders is to help us define our strategy and goals to meet the needs of our stakeholders. This is real engagement with stakeholders and provides significant value to Johnson & Johnson, but it is not assurance. We don't call it third party assurance, but we learn a lot from these people. They make Johnson & Johnson a better company.

Does Johnson & Johnson currently have any formal third party assurance of its Sustainability Reports?

Boyd: No and we don't plan to in the near future. The process is very expensive and time-consuming, with no value added. In the past we tried to get formal assurance for a sustainability report. The process was so nonvalue-added that Environmental, Health and Safety stopped the process three-fourths of the way through. There was too much time and effort spent educating the firm about the business. We didn't think the report would result in any increase in the level of confidence stakeholders would have in the report.

Has Johnson & Johnson considered reporting a triple bottom line (people, planet, profit)?⑤

Boyd: Johnson & Johnson is beyond triple bottom line. We already collect and report the costs of being environmentally responsible, but formal triple bottom line doesn't add any value to the stakeholders. Every sustainability project (such as those to reduce the corporate carbon footprint) must pass a hurdle ROI rate and rigorous cost/benefit analysis in order to be implemented. So, Johnson & Johnson is able to both reduce its carbon footprint while maintaining consistently high returns to its stakeholders. We don't ignore the financial benefits of sustainability activities, but we don't see any value to a formal triple bottom line type of reporting, given the depth of detail currently in the sustainability reports. Besides, the benefits are both tangible and intangible.

Anything you'd like to add?

Boyd: Johnson & Johnson does not undertake sustainability projects and actions just for its reputation. Having values driven by the Credo, engaging with the community, understanding stakeholder expectations—these all create the ultimate trust from Johnson & Johnson's customers, and from that, Johnson & Johnson's corporate reputation automatically improves.

---

⑤ Triple bottom line is described more fully in the next section of the paper.

Elizabeth Lascelle, Senior Director, EHS Strategy & Assurance, provided follow-up information on the following questions.

Johnson & Johnson currently does not report its GRI guidelines application level and does not declare itself "in accordance" with GRI guidelines. Why has J&J made this decision?

Lascelle: There are two main reasons. First, we don't feel our process for determination of materiality is robust enough yet. Second, we need to be able to report more social metrics. This has been problematic due to the decentralization of Johnson & Johnson. Employee and other social metrics are not rolled up at the enterprise level. A new global HR system is being implemented right now that will move us in this direction.

Is Johnson & Johnson planning to eventually declare a level? If yes, will J&J most likely 1) self-declare a level, 2) have its sustainability report third-party-checked, or 3) have its sustainability report GRI-checked? Why?

Lascelle: Yes. We expect to self-declare. Third-party evaluation adds significant cost and time to the process of report generation, but we continue to re-evaluate options for doing so.

ACCOUNTANTS AND TRIPLE BOTTOM LINE REPORTING (AND BEYOND?)

Brief mention was made to triple bottom line in the preceding section of the case. The triple bottom line (TBL) has emerged as one tool for measuring organizational performance in a broader sense than just economic performance. It is similar to the balanced scorecard in that it is based on stakeholder theory and multiple measurements (Hubbard, 2009). The term is sometimes used interchangeably with sustainability reporting because TBL adds measures of social and environmental performance to traditional economic measures (sometimes referred to as "people, planet, profit"). Underlying TBL is the premise that corporate stakeholders are more widely defined than traditional stakeholder groups—investors, employees, customers, suppliers—to include local communities and governments that are affected by a firm's economic, social, and environmental performance (Hubbard, 2009).

A TBL report is organized by the three categories: economic, social, and environmental. ⑥ GRI performance indicators are easily grouped into the three categories and, ideally, a firm reporting its triple bottom line will set performance indicator goals and report progress toward meeting those goals.

---

⑥ Xcel Energy Inc. publishes an annual triple bottom line report. http://www.xcelenergy.com/SiteCollectionDocuments/docs/2007TBLFull.pdf

Economic data may come from an annual report or 10-K, but the intent of a TBL report is to provide a broader picture of a firm's economic impact and contribution to a sustainable economy and to integrate economic data with social and environmental impact data.

The authors of the UNEP, Standard & Poor's and SustainAbility report (2006), argue that sustainability reports are about competition, materiality, and value. TBL fits in the value category:

Where companies once focused mainly on their financial bottom line, the triple bottom line era opened out the focus to take in wider economic, social, environmental and governance impacts, and a growing number of reporters are refocusing on multi-dimensional value creation and the links to their current and future business strategies and business models. (31)

According to this survey, U. S. -based companies lag behind their European-based counterparts in TBL reporting. Furthermore, the survey predicts that the future of sustainability reports will include TBL reporting within the context of the GRI G3 guidelines.

TBL reporting should be viewed as a tool to achieve a goal, not a goal in itself. According to Achim Steiner, United Nations Under Secretary General and Executive Director, United Nations Environment Programme:

There is both a public and a business case for non-financial disclosure and sustainability reporting in particular. Triple bottom line reporting is not a goal in itself. Its value lies in mobilising better informed managers and employees in cleaning up and improving. Its value also lies in supporting better communication between them and external stakeholders about what markets and society expect. (UNEP and KPMG 2006, p. 3)

TBL is not a tool that Johnson & Johnson uses to meet its sustainability goals. Johnson & Johnson does not prepare a TBL and does not use such terminology in its sustainability report, although the 2007 report contains many elements that would be found in a TBL report. As previously noted, when Brian Boyd was asked in the interview why TBL is not a part of the reporting process, he stated "Johnson & Johnson is beyond triple bottom line."

Management accountants do not play a significant role in the sustainability reporting process at Johnson & Johnson. Can management accountants and other financial professionals play a role in the implementation of sustainability reporting in general, and triple bottom line (TBL) accounting specifically? According to Crawford (2005), these professionals will need either to adapt existing skills or develop some new skills in order to change from the single dimension of a financial reporting model to the multidimensional TBL model. Crawford further matches each skill set with the relevant GRI performance indicators "to provide some perspective for those who have limited exposure to managing and reporting sustainability" (Crawford 2005, 2). For example, if a company requires suppliers to meet certain social criteria, GRI performance indicators include quantitative measures such as percentage of contracts paid in accordance with the terms and qualitative descriptions of policies and procedures to deal with all aspects of human rights (Crawford 2005, 3). As CMAs acquire the additional education and training in areas such as labor relations, international trade, and environmental assessment processes, they could become valued participants in Johnson & Johnson's sustainability reporting.

CASE REQUIREMENTS

1. Given that sustainability reporting is not currently required of companies, what do you see as the possible benefits and disadvantages of sustainability reporting? Using the information in the case, the summary data reported in Tables 4 and 5, and Johnson & Johnson's most recent sustainability report (available at http://www.jnj.com/connect/caring/?flash = true), what aspects of sustainability reporting seem to be a priority for the company, and why? Provide examples from the 2008 sustainability report to support your answers.

2. How are various management systems such as human resource management, costs, capital budgeting, and performance measurement incorporated into Johnson & Johnson's sustainability reporting process? Support your answer with specific references from the 2008 report (link provided in question 1). Compare your sources with those in the GRI's reporting framework (http://www.globalreporting.org/ReportingFramework/G3Online/), and the performance measures with Epstein's metrics presented in Table 3.

3. When compiling data for its sustainability reports, Johnson & Johnson does not request direct input from its managerial accounting staff. What should be the role of management accountants in collecting and reporting sustainability data? Could Johnson & Johnson's sustainability reporting be improved with input from managerial accountants? Why or why not? (The Crawford 2005 article at http://www.managementmag.com/index.cfm/ci_id/2149/la_id/1 provides additional background material.)

4. Do you agree with the statement that Johnson & Johnson's approach to sustainability reporting is beyond triple bottom line? Why or why not?

5. Johnson & Johnson cites concerns with determining materiality as one reason it does not declare itself in accordance with GRI guidelines. What is meant by materiality and why is materiality difficult to determine for social responsibility issues?

REFERENCES

Clikeman, Paul. 2004. "Return of the Socially Conscious Corporation." *Strategic Finance*. April. http://www.imanet.org/pdf/2281.pdf

Crawford, David. 2005. "Managing and Reporting Sustainability." *CMA Management for Strategic Business Ideas*. February 7. http://www.managementmag.com/index.cfm/ci_id/2149/la_id/1

Epstein, Marc. 2008. "Implementing Corporate Sustainability: Measuring and Managing Social and Environmental Impacts." *Strategic Finance*. January. http://www.imanet.org/pdf/01-08-epstein.pdf

Gilbert, Sean. 2002. "The Transparency Evolution." *The Environmental Forum*., November/December: 18-26. http://www.globalreporting.org/Learning/JournalArticles/

GRI. 2006. "Number of companies worldwide reporting on their sustainability performance reaches record high, yet still a minority." July 15. http://www.globalreporting.org/NewsEventsPress/PressResources/PressRelease_14_July_2006_1000GRIReports.htm

GRI. 2009. *GRI Online Reporting Framework*. http://www.globalreporting.org/ReportingFramework/G3Online/

Heemskerk, Bert, Pasquale Pistoria, and Martin Scicluna. 2002. "Sustainable Development Reporting: Striking the Balance." World Business Council for Sustainable Development, Switzerland. December. http://www.wbcsd.org/web/publications/striking_the_balance.pdf

Hubbard, Graham. 2009. "Measuring Organizational Performance: Beyond the Triple Bottom Line." *Business Strategy and the Environment* 19 (December): 177-191. http://www.environmental-manager.org/wp-content/uploads/2009/03/beyond_tbl.pdf

ICAEW. 2004. *Sustainability: The Role of Accountants*. London: October. http://www.icaew.com/index.cfm/route/117162/icaew_ga/pdf

Johnson & Johnson. 2009. *Sustainability Report* 2008. http://www.jnj.com/connect/caring/?flash=true

KPMG. *International Survey of Corporate Social Responsibility Reporting* 2008. http://www.kpmg.com/Global/IssuesAndInsights/ArticlesAndPublications/Pages/Sustainability-corporate-responsibility-reporting-2008.aspx

Kropp, Robert. 2009. "Socially responsible investors welcome signs that the SEC is considering mandatory ESG reporting. *SocialFunds.com*, July 31. http://www.socialfunds.com/news/article.cgi/article2747.html

McGinn, Daniel. 2009. "The Greenest Big Companies in America."

Newsweek. September 28. http://www.newsweek.com/id/215577

SAM and PwC. 2010. *The 2010 Sustainability Yearbook: Sustainability Investing, The Paradigm for Institutional Investors.* Sustainable Asset Management Inc. and PricewaterhouseCoopers. http://www.sam-group.com/htmle/yearbook/?CFID=961207&CFTOKEN=a06ee7afaf158e0c-C0EAEB14-E1BA-B686-402A4B662ED3C9FA

UNEP and KPMG. 2006. Carrots and Sticks for Starters: Current Trends and Approaches in Voluntary Standards for Sustainability Reporting. http://www.unep.fr/scp/publications/details.asp?id=WEB/0120/PA

UNEP, Standard & Poor's and SustainAbility. 2006. Tomorrow's Value: The Global Reporters 2006 Survey of Corporate Sustainability Reporting. http://www.sustainability.com/aboutsustainability/article_previous.asp?id=865

APPENDIX A: EXTERNAL VALIDATING ORGANIZATIONS AND ABBREVIATIONS

DOW JONES SUSTAINABLE INDEX NORTH AMERICA

http: //www. sustainability-index. com/djsi _ pdf/publications/Factsheets/SAM_IndexesMonthly_DJSINA. pdf

The Dow Jones Sustainability North America Index (DJSI North America) captures the leading 20% in terms of sustainability out of the largest 600 North American companies of the Dow Jones Global Index. The components are selected according to a systematic corporate sustainability assessment that identifies the leading sustainability-driven companies in each of the 57 industry sectors. The underlying research methodology accounts for general as well as industry-specific sustainability trends and evaluates corporations based on a variety of criteria, including climate change strategies, energy consumption, human resources development, knowledge management, stakeholder relations, and corporate governance.

FTSE 100 INDEX

http: //www. ftse. com/Indices/FTSE4Good_Index_Series/index. jsp

The FTSE U. K. Index Series is designed to represent the performance of U. K. companies, providing investors with a comprehensive and complementary set of indices that measure the performance of all capital and industry segments of the U. K. equity market. The FTSE 100 comprises the 100 most highly capitalized blue chip companies, representing approximately 81% of the U. K. market. It is used extensively as a basis for investment products, such as derivatives and exchange-traded funds.

SOCIAL INVESTMENT FORUM

http: //www. socialinvest. org/about/

The Social Investment Forum is the U. S. national nonprofit membership association for professionals, firms, and organizations dedicated to advancing the practice and growth of socially responsible investing (SRI). Critical to responsible investment practice is the consideration of environmental, social, and corporate governance criteria in addition to standard financial analysis. Forum members support SRI through portfolio selection analysis, shareholder advocacy, and community investing. The 400 members of the Social Investment Forum include investment management and advisory firms, mutual fund companies, research firms, financial planners and advisors, broker-dealers, banks, credit unions, community development organizations, nonprofit associations, and pension funds, foundations, Native American tribes, and other asset owners.

SUSTAINABLE ASSET MANAGEMENT INC. (SAM)

http://www.sam-group.com/htmle/main.cfm

SAM is a leading asset manager in the field of sustainability, providing extended know-how and expertise on sustainability trends, strategies, and interest of investors.

APPENDIX B: THE JOHNSON & JOHNSON CREDO

From http://www.jnj.com/connect/about-jnj/jnj-credo/?flash=true

Our Credo

We believe our first responsibility it to the doctors, nurses and patients,
to mothers and fathers and all others who use our products and service
In meeting their needs everything we do must be of high quality.
We must constantly strive to reduce our costs
in order to maintain reasonable prices.
Customers' orders must be serviced promptly and accurately.
Our suppliers and distributors must have an opportunity
to make a fair profit.

We are responsible to our employees.
the men and women who work with us throughout the world.
Everyone must be considered as an individual.
We must respect their dignity and recognize their merit.
They must have a sense of security in their jobs.
Compensation must be fair and adequate,
and working conditions clean, orderly and safe.
We must be mindful of ways to help our employess fulfill
their family reponsibilities.
Employees must feel free to make suggestions and complaints.
There must be equal opportunity for employment, development
and advancement for those qualified.
We must provide competent management,
and their actions must be just and ethical.

We are responsible to the communities in which we live and work
and to the world community as well.
We must be good citizens-support good works and charities
and bear our fair share of taxes.
We must encourage civic improvements and better health and educatic.
We must maintain in good order
the property we are privileged to use,
protecting the environment and natural resources.

Our final responsibility is to our stockholders.
Business must make a sound profift.
We must experiment with new Ideas.
Research must be carried on, innovative programs developed
and mistakes paid for.
New equipment must be purchased, new facilities provided
and new products launched.
Reserves must be created to provide for adverse times.
When we operate according to these principles,
the stockholders should realize a fair return.

Johnson & Johnson